TITANIC

The unfolding
STORY

© Haynes Publishing, 2011

The right of Carol King and Richard Havers to be identified as the authors of this Work has been asserted by them in accordance with the Copyright, Designs & Patents Act 1988.

First published in 2011

A catalogue record for this book is available from the British Library

ISBN: 978-0-857331-67-0

Published by Haynes Publishing, Sparkford, Yeovil,
Somerset BA22 7JJ, UK
Tel: 01963 442030 Fax: 01963 440001
Int. tel: +44 1963 442030 Int. fax: +44 1963 440001
E-mail: sales@haynes.co.uk
Website: www.haynes.co.uk

Haynes North America Inc., 861 Lawrence Drive,
Newbury Park, California 91320, USA

Images © Mirrorpix

Creative Director: Kevin Gardner
Designed for Haynes by BrainWave

Printed and bound in the US

TITANIC

The unfolding
STORY

Carol King and Richard Havers

Introduction

ti·tan·ic adj.

1. Of or relating to the Titans.

2. a. Having great stature or enormous strength; huge or colossal.
   b. Of enormous scope, power, or influence.

◀ The Titanic prepares to leave Southampton.

Has any ship in history been better named? When she was built in 1912 the Titanic was the largest ship in the world. Equipped with two four-cylinder, triple-expansion steam engines and one low-pressure turbine, each driving a propeller, she had a top speed of 23 knots (26 mph or 43 km/h).

Her 159 coal burning furnaces and 29 boilers made it possible to carry a total of 3,547 passengers and crew. Of the Titanic's four 62-foot (19 m) funnels only three were functional; the fourth provided ventilation that helped to make her the most luxurious ship afloat. In those far-off days before air travel helped shrink the globe – and seven years before man even flew across the Atlantic – the Titanic was the way to travel. The ship was a magnet for the rich, famous and powerful, who were keen to travel on her maiden voyage from Southampton via Cherbourg to New York City. First-class passengers availed themselves of luxuries found in top hotels: a swimming pool, gymnasium, squash court, Turkish bath, and rooms with ornate wood panelling and expensive furniture where they could mingle before and after eating dinner in the finest of restaurants. It was a fabulous way to cross the Atlantic. So much so that the first-class passenger list for her maiden voyage reads like a "who's who" of the post-Edwardian world. Built for the White Star Line at Harland & Wolff's shipyard in Belfast, the Titanic was designed to rival the Mauretania and the Lusitania owned by Cunard Lines. It was corporate one-upmanship at a time when sea travel and control of the sea was what helped to make nations important.

When the Titanic set sail for New York City on 10 April 1912 with 2,224 passengers on board there was immense pride at the White Star Line and in Britain there were few who did not feel a sense of awe. Among her passengers were millionaire John Jacob Astor IV and his wife; industrialist Benjamin Guggenheim; the owner of New York store, Macy's, Isidor Straus and his wife; prominent landowner Sir Cosmo Duff-Gordon and his wife, the couturier Lucy; and influential journalist William Thomas Stead. There were businessmen, politicians, film stars, theatrical producers and socialites, as well as J. Bruce Ismay, the managing director of White Star Line, and the ship's builder, Thomas Andrews.

On the night of Sunday 14 April the Titanic was proceeding to New York on a somewhat more southerly course than had been anticipated because of an iceberg warning. At 11.40 p.m., the look-outs, Fred Fleet and Reginald Lee, spotted a large iceberg directly ahead of the ship. They sounded the ship's bell three times and Fleet telephoned the bridge shouting "Iceberg, right ahead!" Thirty-seven seconds later the Titanic hit the mountain of floating ice. The pages of *The Daily Mirror* reveal the unfolding story of the Titanic from her construction to the realisation of the enormity of the disaster that befell her and its consequences. We, literally, read history as it happened. In those days, before radio and rolling television formats, newspaper reports were the quickest way news could be disseminated; but such was the confusion at the time and lack of on-the-spot communications, sometimes events were reported incorrectly. This unique exploration of one of the modern world's most appalling disasters is captivating. Reading the prose, sometimes in language that is of its time, helps us to immerse ourselves in a world that seems immediate and alive rather than dusty history.

The skill of the newspaper journalists in getting to the heart of the story and its impact on so many is there in black and white for all to read. The stories that came to light in the days, weeks and months following the sinking of the Titanic may well have passed some of us by in the intervening 100 years. Movies in particular have retold the story in ways that best suited the box-office, rather than opting for historical accuracy. Indeed, the real facts provide a more fascinating insight into the tragedy and surpass any fictionalised accounts created for the big screen in thrilling accounts of bravery and courage, human error and the failings of those in power.

The journalists, who were almost always nameless, and who used their pens to create pictures in a world where the written word was still the most immediate way to bring people the news, have left behind a record of an event that captured the sympathy and imagination of the world. So, while this book is a testament to the people that lost their lives on the Titanic, it is also a tribute to great journalism.

Carol King & Richard Havers

The Titanic being built in the Harland & Wolff shipyard, Belfast.

The Birth of the Big Ships

September **1908** – August **1911**

The excitement of the competition between Cunard and the White Star Line to build the fastest, the biggest and the best liner for crossing the North Atlantic reached fever pitch as the first decade of the twentieth century came to a close.

◀ Built by Swan, Hunter and Wigham Richardson at Wallsend, the Mauretania was the largest and fastest liner to have been built at the time. Her revolutionary steam turbines propelled the 31,938-ton liner at 24 knots carrying 2,165 passengers and over 800 crew. She is seen here leaving the River Tyne for her first trials at sea on 7 April 1907; the Mauretania stayed in service with Cunard until 1934.

16 September **1908**

It was announced yesterday that the names of the 60,000-ton White Star liners ordered from Messrs. Harland and Wolff, of Belfast, will be the Olympic and the Titanic. It is understood they will cost between £3,000,000 and £4,000,000.

11 February **1909**

The White Star Company state that their new 45,000-ton liners, Olympic and Titanic, will probably be equipped with combination, reciprocating, and turbine engines.

25 May **1910**

50,000-TON LINER

Proposed New Sister Ship to Mauretania on the Atlantic Service.

It is stated in Liverpool shipping circles that the Cunard directors have decided on building an entirely new type of liner of a tonnage of something like 50,000 for their Atlantic service.

The new liner is intended for the Liverpool and New York service, along with the Lusitania and Mauretania. She will approximate, if she does not exceed, in size the Olympic and Titanic, now building at Belfast for the White Star Line.

A rate of speed of not less than 22 knots is understood to have been decided upon.

1 September **1910**

The rush of Americans homeward is now at its height, and during August no fewer than 7,100 cabin passengers left these shores for the States by White Star steamers. Of these 3,500 passengers travelled first class.

19 September **1910**

SOUTHAMPTON'S NEW TIDAL DOCK

Preparing to Accommodate Four of the Largest Liners Afloat.

Good progress is being made with the new sixteen-acre wet dock at Southampton, which, when completed in about a year's time, will accommodate four of the largest liners afloat, and will be one of the largest docks in the world.

The dock has now become a tidal dock, the last obstacle to the

outside waters entering the basin, having been removed. It will have a depth of forty feet at low water, and will be 1,700 feet long and 400 feet wide.

There will be ample accommodation for the vessels of 40,000 tons now being built by the White Star Line for their new Southampton and New York service.

20 October **1910**

MAN AND THE ELEMENTS

Man in his ceaseless war against the elements has had to give best to the air in his latest attack upon it. Tossed and buffeted by angry winds, Mr. Wellman and his gallant companions have been forced to abandon their aerial craft and take refuge in one which man has had greater experience in perfecting.

Man and the sea are old, old enemies; man and the air have only recently begun to come to grips.

What mastery he holds over the sea is shown in the mammoth vessel that is to enter the water to-day at Belfast. She is so vast that over 5,000 human beings may find in her a home. So scornful of the sea and its power has man become that when he goes out to face it he takes a ballroom with him, a gymnasium, all the luxuries of hotel life that dry land civilisation can give him. In fact, he ceases to consider the sea, and builds merely a huge and immensely powerful floating island that he can drive along at a swift pace, and on it builds a town.

For his pleasure he builds a verandah café to his island, fifty feet above the waves; for his sport he makes a fish pond; for his games a racquet court, "What I can enjoy on land I can enjoy on sea," he says, and so he shows his contempt for his old enemy by bringing to it every luxury he can conceive.

And yet it was not so very long ago that man had to respect the sea. In his dealings with it then there was no place for luxury. The sea was so far master of the situation that it was able to resent even the most modest of land-like comforts.

Even in the first days of steamships it allowed no licence. The saloon table could risk no luxuries. It was a long and surly thing, oilcloth covered, from which the passenger would eat only those preserved and artificial foods that the sea admitted. The saloon itself was liable to sudden invasion from the waters without. The sea made its own timetable; no man dared dictate to it how many days and hours it should allot to the passing ship from port to port. That their ships should eventually reach port in safety was all men asked, dependent as they were on the mood of the waves. Then men asked the sea's permission. Now, in the security of inland offices they lay down laws and work out schedules that are followed with monotonous regularity with or without the waves' permission.

But the sea can still make a fight, though its ways are different now. Alone in its violent moods it can but break a little of the floating islands that men now force upon it, as a petulant child may tear at the clothing of an athlete; so it takes its revenges in ways which in former days men found harmless. It works by stealth, by the blinding force of the fog, or waiting for its enemies' craft to approach the shore, grows angry and beats it to death on the rocks, hurting it as it cannot do alone with its own mere force.

But man has yet to conquer the air. Like the sea, seventy years ago, the air allows no liberties. Man may occasionally think he has triumphed, but let him become audacious, and the air asserts its strength. The airship goes where the air wishes yet the time will come, not perhaps in our day, but our children may see it, when aerial Olympics will be launched and man has learned to regard the winds with as little concern as he now regards the waves.

But there will be a hard fight and a heavy toll of lives taken before that day.

20 October **1910**

TO-DAY'S DINNER TABLE TOPICS: LUXURY

The Olympic launched to-day. Recount some of her wonders. Ocean travel strangely different nowadays from what it was. Perhaps you regret the change – the romance has gone. Yes, but comfort replaces it. Which is the more desirable?

Travel altogether is wonderfully luxurious. Years ago all our luxury was in our homes, now it is out of them. Are we really more indulgent in luxury than our predecessors; was not their luxury as great in proportion to the standard of comfort of the age as is ours?

21 October **1910**

THE WORLD'S LARGEST SHIP LAUNCHED AT BELFAST YESTERDAY

Yesterday the White Star liner Olympic, the world's largest ship, was launched at Belfast in the presence of thousands of sightseers. There are no fewer than two million and a half rivets in this giant ship, which will carry 2,960 people. She is 882ft. 6in. long over all and a

walk three times round her deck is a mile. The photograph gives an idea of her immense height.

MAMMOTH LINER – WORLD'S LARGEST SHIP
New White Star Giant Olympic Launched in 62 Seconds.

The world's largest ship – the 45,000-ton steamer Olympic, for the White Star Line – was launched yesterday from Messrs. Harland and Wolff's yard at Belfast.

As the great leviathan shot into the water, enthusiastic cheers from the thousands of spectators lining the quays rent the air. Lord Pirrie, head of the firm, superintended the arrangements, which did not include a naming ceremony. Those present included the Lord-Lieutenant and the Countess of Aberdeen, and Miss Asquith.

The launch, which was accomplished without the least hitch, occupied exactly 62s., and the maximum speed was 12½ knots.

The Olympic, which follows a long line of predecessors, each marking an advance on the other, is the largest and strongest ever built. Some idea of her size may be gathered from the following dimensions:–

Length over all, 882ft. 6in.; breadth over all, 92ft. 6in; breadth over boat deck, 94ft.; distance from top of funnel to keel, 175ft.; number of steel decks, 11; number of watertight bulkheads, 15.

SUMPTUOUS FEATURES

The Olympic has a displacement of 60,000 tons and a walk three times round her deck will be a mile.

She will have accommodation for about 2,500 passengers besides a crew of 860. Some idea of the extent of the accommodation may be gathered, from the fact that there will be over 2,000 sidelights and windows in the ship and 2,500,000 rivets.

Among the novel features provided on board are a floral café, with vines and trellis-work, ballroom and skating rink, Turkish bath, racquet court and roof garden, besides gymnasium, swimming bath, and nursery.

She has taken nearly two years to build, and her cost, when complete, will be between £1,500,000 and £2,000,000.

11 November 1910

WORLD'S LARGEST SHIP IN MINIATURE

A model of the new White Star liner Olympic, which may now be seen at the Piccadilly Hotel. The Olympic is the largest ship in the world, and has no fewer than 2,500,000 rivets.

18 November 1910

FLOATING THEATRE

Hotel Luxuries on World's Largest Liner Which Will Cost Two Million.

Tenders for the largest passenger vessel in the world, which will cost some £2,000,000, have been invited by the Cunard Line from Messrs. John Brown, Limited, of Clydebank, and Messrs. Swan, Hunter, Wigham and Richardson, of Wallsend-on-Tyne.

The plans, which have been approved by Lloyd's, provide for such luxuries on board as a Turkish bath, a theatre and a swimming pond.

The new Cunarder is to be built for the Liverpool-New York route, and will accommodate 3,790 passengers. She will have a total displacement of 50,000 tons; thus exceeding the White Star liner Olympic by 5,000 tons. She will be 885ft. long by 95ft. broad, will have a speed of twenty-three knots, and be propelled by turbines, but will also carry oil fuel.

The Clyde Trust has decided to apply for parliamentary powers to construct the largest tidal and graving dock in Great Britain, at a cost of £1,000,000.

10 December 1910

MAURETANIA'S RACE AGAINST TIME

350 Firemen Engaged for Dash Across Atlantic and Back.

TWELVE DAYS TRIP

Elaborate preparations have been made for the Mauretania's attempt at a record dash across the Atlantic and back in twelve days.

The giant liner leaves the Mersey to-day, and the Cunard officials hope that she will he back within twelve days, and so be able to land her passengers from America in time to spend Christmas in Europe.

For this trip over 350 firemen have been signed on. They will work by shifts at top pressure. Nearly 7,000 tons of coal have been taken on board.

Eighty thousand pieces of linen sufficient for the double journey have been placed on board in Liverpool to prevent delay in New York.

Still, within forty-eight hours at that port 12,000 tons of coal, provisions, water, baggage, and mails will have to be handled – 3,000 people will be engaged in the work – making the cost of this quick turn-round upwards of 50 per cent higher than the usual preparations.

Every possible preparation has been made to ensure success, and the shipping experts believe that the Cunard Company's boat will accomplish the feat without a hitch.

It is hoped that the Mauretania will average twenty-six knots all the way, which would itself be a record.

10 December **1910**

50,000-TON LINER

The announcement that the Cunard Company have placed an order for the construction of a liner of 50,000 tons with Messrs. John Brown and Co., of Clydebank, was officially confirmed yesterday by that firm.

The latest Cunarder, which will be the largest ship in the world, will, it is understood, be the first of two ships of a similar type to be employed exclusively on the New York-Liverpool mail service.

She will have a displacement of 5,000 tons more than the new giant White Star liners Olympic and Titanic, and 18,000 tons more than the Cunard Company's Mauretania and Lusitania.

Her average speed will be twenty-three knots, two knots less than her sister ships, but two knots in excess of the most recent White Star boats.

The following table shows the great size of the huge ship:

	Length ft.	Breadth ft.	Tonnage
New Cunarder	885	85½	50,000
Olympic	882	92	45,000
Mauretania	790	88	32,000

The cost of the new liner will be about £2,000,000, and it is estimated that she will take two years to build.

Including the members of the crew, the liner will be able to carry nearly 5,000 souls.

Luxurious accommodation will be provided, and in addition to elegant suites and flats there will be a theatre and a swimming bath.

The building of the new liner was decided upon as a result of the Hamburg-America Line beginning to construct a mammoth liner of 50,000 tons.

30 December **1910**

NEW WIRELESS RECORD

Atlantic Liner Cedric in Touch with Europe or America Throughout Voyage.

The White Star liner Cedric, which left Liverpool on Saturday last for New York, has accomplished a new record in wireless communication. Refitted with powerful apparatus, she has kept in communication with the English and French coasts at 1,250 miles distance; also with Flores Island on three successive days.

A wireless message received last night says:– "We have been in communication with, the European and American coast every day of the passage, and are now 1,140 miles from New York. Via Marconi Wireless Telegraph Company." No transatlantic vessel has ever before been in direct touch with land on every day of the voyage.

26 January **1911**

NEW YORK'S PROBLEM OF THE PIERS

Discussion Whether They Should Be Lengthened for New Giant Liners.

New York, Wednesday. Before the Board of Army Engineers the question was to-day discussed of granting permission for an extension of the White Star and Cunard piers by 100ft. to accommodate the Olympic and other big liners now building.

Engineers contend that it would be dangerous to navigation to extend the piers at the narrowest part of the river, and say that there is room for longer piers above and below the present piers.

Numerous commercial concerns, underwriters and railroads recommend the granting of the extension.

2 March **1911**

NEW YORK'S PIER PROBLEM

No Room to Dock New Liner Olympic on Arrival in June.

New York, Wednesday. It is reported from Washington to-day that the War Department will refuse the permission applied for to extend the White Star piers by 100ft. to berth the largest liners.

This refusal means that there will be no room to dock the new monster liner, the Olympic, when she arrives here at the end of her first journey on June 21.

7 March **1911**

NEW YORK PIER PROBLEM SOLVED

Extension Necessary to Dock Giant Liner Olympic Sanctioned by War Secretary.

Washington, Monday. Mr. Dickinson, Secretary for War, has given permission for the extension of the two Chelsea piers at New York 100 feet, further out into the North River, so as to admit of the docking of the latest and longest steamships.

It was at first reported that the War Department had refused to sanction the extension, without which there would have been no room to dock the monster liner Olympic on her arrival at New York on her first visit on June 21.

8 March 1911

Messrs. Harland and Wolff at Belfast yesterday announced the date of the launch of the new White Star mammoth liner Titanic as May 31.

3 April 1911

THE WORLD'S LARGEST VESSEL IN THE WORLD'S LARGEST GRAVING DOCK

The caisson gate which closes the entrance to the dock. The photograph gives an idea of the height of the Olympic.

◗ The Olympic in the new dock, which has a total available length of 886ft. 6in. With collateral works it has cost £350,000.

◗ Thousands of people stood on both banks of the river to watch the White Star liner Olympic, the world's largest vessel, creep slowly into the world's largest gracing dock, which was formally opened at Belfast on Saturday. The dock is emptied by the means of pumps and engines which can do this work in the space of 100 minutes, the amount of water dealt with being about twenty-three million gallons.

2 May 1911

BIGGEST ANCHOR EVER CAST

Weighing sixteen tons, the biggest anchor ever cast was yesterday dispatched from Dudley, where it was made, for the White Star liner Titanic. Twenty horses were needed to draw it to the station.

The new White Star steamer Olympic will be open for public inspection at a charge of 2s. 6d. per visitor, at Belfast, Liverpool and Southampton in aid of charities at the respective ports prior to the first sailing from Southampton on Wednesday, June 14.

18 May 1911

PROFITS OF WHITE STAR LINE

A profit of £1,058,519 on the year's working is recorded in the report of the Oceanic Steam Navigation Company, Liverpool (the White Star Line), for the year ending December last. The total at the credit of profit and loss account, after making deductions, is £571,387, while dividends amounting to £225,000 have been paid to shareholders during the year.

LARGEST LINER AFLOAT

Speed Trials of Olympic Are To Be Begun Off Belfast To-Day.

The "Blue Peter" flag was hoisted yesterday at Belfast on the White Star liner Olympic, of 45,000 tons, the largest vessel ever built.

To-day the Olympic's compasses will be adjusted and her speed and machinery trials begun.

The public were admitted on Saturday to make a tour of inspection over the huge vessel. So many were the visitors that a sum of about £2,000 received in entrance fees will be handed over to Belfast hospitals.

MAMMOTH LINER'S TEST TRIP

Crowds Watch the Olympic Leave Belfast for Her Trial.

The White Star liner Olympic, the largest ship afloat, which was launched on October 20, left Belfast yesterday for her steam trials outside Belfast Lough.

The mammoth liner was towed down the Channel by five tugs, both sides of the river being crowded with sightseers.

The Olympic will proceed to the Mersey on Wednesday, after the launch of the Titanic, and will have on board Lord and Lady Pirrie, Mr. Bruce Ismay and Mr. Pierpont Morgan.

TYNE SHIPBUILDING BOOM

Mammoth New Floating Dock for Medway Building for the Admiralty.

There is a remarkable boom in the shipbuilding trade at Newcastle and on the Tyne generally. The new Medway floating dock, 700ft. long by 165ft. beam, is capable of lifting 32,000 tons. It covers two and a half acres, will be the biggest Admiralty dock built, and will have to be launched in two sections and bolted together in the river afterwards. Altogether there are three docks under construction for the Government. Two liners are being built for German firms, and various orders are waiting their turn, so that the present prosperity will more than last the year out.

LUXURIES FOR OCEAN TRAVELLERS ON BOARD THE OLYMPIC, THE NEW MAMMOTH WHITE STAR LINER

A private view of the Olympic, which with her twin sister, the Titanic, holds the distinction of being the largest vessel afloat, was given at Southampton yesterday.

➤ (1.) The swimming bath. (2.) The Turkish bath. (3.) Looking down on the vessel's deck. The photograph was taken from the top of one of the funnels. The portraits are of Lord Pirrie (wearing dark cap), the chairman of Messrs. Harland and Wolff, the builders, and Captain Smith in command.

A huge iceberg adrift in the Atlantic was sighted during her voyage from New York by the White Star liner Baltic, which arrived yesterday at Queenstown with 1,807 passengers on board.

14 June 1911

ROCKET AS STRIKE SIGNAL

Seamen's Officials Say That Men Will Leave Work To-day.

The firing of a rocket at seven o'clock to-night will, it was stated at South Shields last night, be the signal to begin the seamen's strike on the Tyne.

In London, Liverpool, Glasgow, Southampton and other ports last night it was announced that the international strike will begin to-day. Every English port, the men's leaders declared, would be useless, and Holland, France, Belgium, Germany and Denmark would be involved. Mr. Havelock Wilson, addressing a meeting at Southampton, said he expected 10,000 men would refuse to sign on unless the minimum rate of wages of £5 10s. a month, were conceded.

The secretary of the Southampton branch of the International Seamen's Union yesterday urged all union seamen not to sign on except at the union's rates. It was further stated that the Cunard, White Star, Allan, and Canadian Pacific passenger lines would be involved.

Mr. Joseph Cotter, general secretary of the Union of Ships' Stewards, Cooks, Butchers and Bakers, also made a pronouncement yesterday at Liverpool. It was that they hoped by next week to hold up all the ships in the port of Liverpool, including the Lusitania and Mauretania.

The dispute, which has been going on for so long, is between the officials of the seamen's union and the shipowners. The union demands, amongst other things, the establishment of a conciliation board. The owners refuse to recognise the union. Inquiring at the offices of the International Shipping Federation yesterday, *The Daily Mirror* was informed that the threatened strike caused small concern, and that an international movement was impossible.

15 June 1911

LONDON: SEAMEN JOIN THE GREAT SHIPPING STRIKE

"War Is Declared" at a Dockside Meeting.

ROCKET SIGNALS
Big Liners Without Crews at Liverpool and Southampton.

OWNERS FIRM
Chinese Crews Sign on Under Police Protection at Barry.

With the firing of three rockets at the docks and the unfurling of a banner bearing the inscription, "War is now declared," the London seamen last night proclaimed their adherence to the "International Seamen's Strike."

How many of the London men, who, afloat and ashore, number over 100,000, will adhere to the movement remains to be seen. At the meeting at the docks last night some 2,000 were present.

Before this, the strike had been officially declared at a number of provincial ports, and at some of them with immediate effect.

Thus at Liverpool yesterday 350 men refused to sign on for the Teutonic, and 300 for the Empress of Ireland, and during the day pickets were established at the docks.

At several ports, however, the declaration of the strike was accorded a lukewarm reception.

A "carnival camp" for strikers near South Shields, where the strike was declared yesterday, was so poorly attended that local reporters were asked to assist in making up the teams for a tug-of-war.

At Hull the rocket fired as a signal only rose a few feet and then fell among a large crowd, several people narrowly escaping injury.

The Shipping Federation's general manager told *The Daily Mirror* that plenty of men were willing to work at the London rate of £4 10s. per month for Seamen and £5 for firemen, and that the shipowners were not greatly perturbed.

At Barry Docks last night two Chinese crews signed on under police protection. Several leading Liverpool shipping companies have agreed to receive deputations of their men, and the men's leaders decided last night not to declare a strike against the Cunard and Booth lines pending a conference respecting their grievances.

LONDON MOVES

War was declared by the seamen and firemen of London last night.

A crowd, numbering about 2,000 men, assembled outside the Maritime Hall at the West India Dock gates last night. Headed by bands playing the Marsellaise, three processions marched to the meeting place from Leman-street, Canning Town and the Victoria Dock district.

Mr. J. Havelock Wilson addressed the meeting, urging the men to strike.

"Never in twenty-one years," he said, "have the men had such an opportunity as now. You don't know how I have punished my body in order to lead you to victory. If you are not men, I can't make you men."

He then called upon those willing to fight to hold up their hands. Most of the audience did so.

THREE ROCKETS FIRED

At that moment three rockets were fired from a balcony overhead, and a banner was unfurled, bearing the words:

Seamen's International Movement, 1911.

WAR IS NOW DECLARED

Strike Home. Strike Hard for Liberty.

The crowd shortly afterwards dispersed and Mr. Havelock Wilson told *The Daily Mirror* that the strike had commenced from that moment, "They said that I couldn't get 200 men to follow me," he said, "Look at the crowd to-night! When I asked those men, who were not members of the union, whether they would follow me, you heard how they cheered."

A sailor in the crowd said: "I don't like the rockets; that's the sailor's distress signal."

PROVINCIAL PORTS AFFECTED

Although no dislocation was to be noticed in the Port of London yesterday, several provincial ports were affected by the declaration of the strike. Here are reports received yesterday from various places including Southampton. Olympic sailed, sailors' demands being conceded. General strike of seafaring men has begun. Union Castle and Royal Mail crews demanding increased wages.

Not one man signed on for the Union Castle liner Briton which is due to sail on Saturday. L. and S.W. steamers' crews

demand 35s. a week minimum. Ships' cooks and stewards decide to join general strike.

SHIPOWNERS' VIEW

"There may be local disorders, but I do not think there will be any serious interruption of trade," said the general manager of the Shipping Federation, the paramount shipowners' organisation, to *The Daily Mirror* yesterday afternoon.

"English seamen are not going to strike for the benefit of foreign seamen, which settles the question of an international strike. There is no common ground, for seamen in British ships are better paid and cared for than the men in most foreign ships.

"No good man with a good discharge to show ever need remain long without a ship. The wages paid are generally the rate of the port – in London now it is £4 10s. a month for seamen and £5s. for firemen. If some men won't sign at these rates, others will.

"We cannot agree to a Conciliation Board till there is some organisation to deal with, Mr. Havelock Wilson is president of the, Sailors and Firemen's Union, but that is an unregistered union, publishing no lists of members, and we do not regard it as representative. This federation controls 13,000,000 tons of shipping. The Atlantic Combine stands out from it, with the exception of the Atlantic Transport Line, which has always belonged to the federation.

"The Olympic is a White Star vessel, belonging to the Combine, and is, therefore, not in the federation. If they choose to concede £6 to their firemen to get the ship away punctually, that is their business."

SEAMEN'S CASE

Mr. Havelock Wilson told *The Daily Mirror* before the meeting last night that he was not going to speak too confidently, but he believed the shipowners were going to be surprised.

"The Olympic people gave way this morning," he said, "and paid their firemen £6 a month. Before I left the town 250 sailors and firemen had come into the Southampton branch of the union since last night, Amsterdam and Rotterdam are held up already, and it will be the same directly we give the signal at all the British ports, including, of course, London. For London will be the headquarters."

Another official of the union said: "We do not disclose our total

The Daily Mirror

THE MORNING JOURNAL WITH THE SECOND LARGEST NET SALE

No. 2,384.   Registered at the G.P.O. as a Newspaper.   **FRIDAY, JUNE 16, 1911**   One Halfpenny.

SEAMEN GAIN THE FIRST SUCCESSES IN THE WAR THEY HAVE DECLARED AGAINST THE EMPLOYERS.

From Liverpool, where the lead was given for the seamen's strike, comes the news that the men have gained the first successes. It was announced last night that the White Star Line and the Canadian Pacific Line had come to terms with their men and had conceded an all-round advance of 10s. a month. (1) The Canadian steamer the Empress of Ireland, due to sail to-day. She was crewless yesterday, and is seen above lying in dock. (2) Firing a rocket at Sunderland, as a signal that the strike had begun. (3) Mr. Tom Mann addressing a meeting near the Liverpool docks. He is telling the men to strike for liberty.

membership, but I can assure you we shall be twice as strong in a week as we are to-day.

"Some sailors' and firemen's grievances seem trivial, perhaps, but taken together they mean a great deal. And the wages question must be dealt with. Cost of living has gone up and wages in most trades with it, but not the seaman's wages. His wife and family have to live. Road-workers in London used to get 16s. a week; now they get 30s. a week. Why should the seaman and fireman be imposed upon?"

Maritime Hall is scarcely visible for posters and pamphlets. Mme. Sorgue, the French Socialist leader, has a poster of her own in gloomy, black type, signed "Sorgue, French," and running:

"Beware! Beware! Beware! Do not play into the hands of your enemies by allowing them to rush you into premature action."

UNION POETS

The Transport Workers' Federation and the Sailors' and Firemen's Union are both strong in poets. Here is a sample verse:

Seamen, firemen of all nations, you who plough the mighty deep,
Are you, men or are you cattle, wide awake or deep in sleep?
Whilst the workers all around you fight the fight for liberty
Won't you up and join the conflict, fighting with them to be free?

Here are briefly the men's demands:

Minimum wage, £5 10s. for sailors and firemen on cargo vessels. Passenger boats 10s. extra.

Overtime 9d. an hour until midnight; 1s. per hour between midnight and 6 a.m.

Lowest rate for men sailing by the week to be 35s. Overtime rate as above.

"Be men and demand these rates," ends the manifesto that fixes them.

16 June 1911

SUCCESSES FOR MEN IN SHIPPING WAR

White Star and Other Big Lines Give Increases.

LONDON PICKETS

Men Refuse to Sign On Except on Union Terms.

TROOPS FOR NEWPORT

The first successes in the shipping war have been won by the men.

It was announced last night that the White Star Line, whose liners, Teutonic and Baltic, were crewless at Liverpool, and whose mammoth liner Olympic was only got away from Southampton by conceding her crew's demands, had come to terms with the men, and conceded a 10s. a month all-round advance.

The Lamport and Holt Line made a similar arrangement with their men. At Middlesbrough Messrs. Alfred Holt and Co. conceded a 10 shilling advance before signing a crew for their steamer Ajax.

The manager of the Canadian Pacific Railway has also granted the 10s. concession, so far as the Empress of Ireland, which leaves Liverpool for Canada to-day, is concerned.

The Shipping Federation, controlling thirteen million tons, holds out, however, and states that its members are confident that the strike cannot last.

In Newport there was considerable excitement owing to the arrival of 250 men of the Devon Regiment.

At Cardiff yesterday nine vessels obtained crews, mainly composed of coloured men.

In London the crews of a number of large liners refused to sign on, and pickets are established at the docks.

"STRIKE DOOMED TO FAILURE"

That the seamen's strike is doomed to failure, was the opinion expressed yesterday by Mr. Cuthbert Laws, the general manager of the Shipping Federation.

Although the White Star Line has effected a settlement, he said, the Federation was nevertheless determinedly opposed to the creation of a Conciliatory Board.

Mr. A. Hunt, the Southampton manager of the Union Castle Line, said last night that the mail boat Briton was due to sail on Saturday, but up to the present the crew had not signed on.

If a full crew should not sign on the managers had decided to withdraw the sailing, and there would be no outward-bound mail boat for the Cape on Saturday.

17 June 1911

PROGRESS OF SHIPPING WAR

Both Owners and Seamen Confident of Success.

LONDON DISORDER

Both sides in the shipping war profess satisfaction with the position of affairs as reported up to last evening.

Owners belonging to the Shipping Federation say that they have been caused no inconvenience by the strike of sailors and firemen, while the men's representatives declare that all is well with their cause, "There are now fourteen steamers in London which cannot get crews," said Mr. Havelock Wilson, secretary of the Seamen's and Firemen's Union to *The Daily Mirror* yesterday. They include large ships like the Minnewaska, Dunottar Castle, and Lake Erie.

"I do not say that these ships have actually been detained, because their sailing day has not arrived, but they have all tried to sign on crews and have failed."

DOCKERS JOIN IN

"And now dockers are joining the seamen and firemen. Four gangs of dockers struck work at the Albert Dock this morning in sympathy with the sailors, and dockers at Glasgow, Southampton and Goole have also come out."

Optimism is deep-rooted at the offices of the Shipping Federation. Mr. Cuthbert Laws, the general manager, told *The Daily Mirror* that in no case had any firm of owners belonging to the federation conceded the men's demands, although, as a matter of fact, members of the federation were free to pay whatever rate of wages they liked. The only owners who had given way were the White Star, Cunard and Booth Lines, all of whom were outside the federation.

There was some disorder at the Albert and Victoria Docks yesterday morning. The Nelson boat Highland Rover attempted to sign oil. A crew, but only one man actually signed the articles, and he was severely handled by the strikers.

In a telegram to the President of the Board of Trade yesterday the men's leaders protested against the Board of Trade offices at South Shields being used to advertise for men for Southampton, and called attention to the large number of Chinese being signed on.

21 June 1911

NO LINERS FOR NAVAL REVIEW

Seamen's Strike Holds Up Vessel Chartered by Admiralty.

The seamen's strike, although a settlement has been reached in the Atlantic lines, has attained such dimensions at Southampton that the big liners are at a standstill. One effect will be that several big liners chartered for the Coronation Naval Review will not sail.

Messrs, Donald Currie and Co. give notice that owing to the refusal of the men on strike to accept the permanent increase of 10s. per month offered, the sailings of the steamers Armadale Castle, Carisbrooke Castle, Dunvegan Castle and Norman, intended for the Coronation Naval Review, are unavoidably cancelled.

The Royal Mail Steam Packet Company have been obliged to cancel the sailing of their steamers Asturias, Ortona, Oruba and Danube to the Naval Review.

At Hull the crew of the Wilson liner Eskimo, which has been chartered by the Admiralty for the Naval Review, have withdrawn from their contracts.

More satisfactory reports came from Liverpool, where first the Cunard and then in turn the White Star, Allan, Dominion, American and Booth lines conceded terms which the men agreed to.

The terms, roughly, were that the Cunard and Booth line men were to receive an advance of 10s. a month all round. The men's committee asked for 15s., but recommended the men to accept 10s. As a result men were last evening eagerly signing on.

LONDON'S RIVERS OF RADIANCE

Buildings Transformed Into Fairy Palaces by Myriad Lights

BANK'S BRILLIANCE

London robbed the heavens of their stars last night, and became a jewelled fairyland.

All the day decorations were as nothing to the brilliance that burst out when night fell. Each street became a living river of radiance.

Two places, however, were conspicuous lakes of light to which many rivers led – the Bank and Pall Mall.

The neighbourhood of the Bank was most vivid of all. Thousands upon thousands of lamps had transformed the buildings into fairy palaces, almost too dazzling in their brilliance.

JEWELS OF LIGHT

Three thousand lamps and more shone from the front of the corner building of Lombard-street; a similar number from the offices of the Scottish Provident Company opposite; the Bank of England itself was a glittering palace of 5,000 lights, and from the premises of the Union of London and Smiths Bank no fewer than 7,000 fairy lamps defied the dark.

The Royal Exchange, the Mansion House, and other buildings, contributed to the vast effect. A magician had been at work, and transformed everything.

Round the pillars of the Bank and along the facade were white lights, pink-shaded, with magnificent designs and many coloured crowns. On the roof were torches innumerable.

The Royal Exchange had sloughed its workaday skin and become a many faceted jewel, and the Mansion House – outlined in blue and white – cascaded light.

Lombard-street was festooned all along with red and green and white and gold, and spanned with radiant arches. Cornhill showed terraces of green and red and gold.

BRIDGE ILLUMINATED

London Bridge became when night fell a gossamer bridge to which clung glow-worms innumerable, and beneath the dark bosom of the river reflected dancing gleams.

Serenely beautiful were Pall Mall and Cockspur-street – not so blazing with light as the Bank – more subdued, but more refined.

Roses, shamrocks and thistles shone in Cockspur-street. Anchors and stars gleamed, and there one saw a model of the Olympic, with all lights aglow, as the giant liner may well appear at sea.

White lights in Pall Mall displayed tapestries hung on the walls of the clubs. Especially fine was the Royal Automobile Club. The building was nearly covered with dark red cloth fringed with starry white lights, and high above shone a great crown.

Piccadilly was a stream of light. Golden globes hung from masts all along the road in endless lines of fairy fires, and behind them on the left the trees of the Green Park gleamed darkly.

All through the evening London's people flocked into the streets, and wandered wondering down avenues of light and fancied themselves in fairyland.

STRIKE RIOTS AT HULL

Child Among Injured After a Police Baton Charge.

LINERS DESERTED

A sudden extension of the seamen's strike to the dockers caused a complete stoppage of work at Liverpool yesterday and every Atlantic liner in the port was paralysed, while at Hull serious rioting broke out, the police charged the strikers, and further trouble was only averted, by the arrangement of a truce.

The position, at every important port is critical, and many

industries are threatened. Coal shipments have practically ceased in the North, and in the Midlands prices of butter and similar commodities have gone up. The position became serious at Hull early in the day, when the lightermen and millers, as well as the men from the fish docks joined the strike.

31 July 1911

Atlantic liners are experiencing a rush of returning Coronation visitors, the Lusitania and the White Star boat Canada having specially big passenger lists.

16 August 1911

LIVERPOOL CITIZENS ARMING TO DEFEND THEMSELVES AND THEIR PROPERTY FROM STRIKE VIOLENCE

TROOPS CLEAR LIVERPOOL STREETS WITH BAYONETS
Labour War Spreads All Over Country.

FIRST SHOTS FIRED
100,000 Strikers Establish Reign of Terror – Citizens Arm.

LONDON TROUBLED
30,000 Hands Idle at Manchester and Bread Famine Feared.

PASSENGERS HELD UP
The labour situation through the country grows every day more grave.

Yesterday, it assumed a new aspect. It is no longer only the commerce of the country that is being harassed.

From almost every centre comes news of a railway strike growing with lightning rapidity, and bringing even passenger traffic to a standstill so abruptly that holiday-makers in the Northern Midlands were held up in: thousands. In Liverpool the condition of affairs goes steadily from bad to worse. Early yesterday morning troops were in conflict with mobs in the streets and shots – whether volleys or not – were undoubtedly fired for the first time in this calamitous period.

The Cunarder Caronia, the Ellerman boat City of Corinth, and

the White Star boat Zeeland cannot possibly sail to-day.

26 August 1911

ROUND WORLD IN 39 DAYS
French Non-Stop Traveller Breaks Record After Race Against Time.

Page 6   THE DA

THE LIVERPOOL DOCKS IN

Once more ships can freely load and unload in the Liverpool docks, where work had been suspended since June 28 last. After the strikes had been settled elsewhere the Liverpool men still remained out because of the refusal to reinstate

Paris, August 25 – The Paris journalist, M. Jager-Schmidt, on the staff of the illustrated daily, *Excelsior*, who has been making a dash round the world, will complete his long journey to-morrow in record time.

He set out from the office of the *Excelsior* in Paris on July 17 at 1.19 p.m. It was expected that he would be able to go round the world in forty days, but, according to his present progress, he should complete the journey in thirty-nine days seventeen hours. His object was to beat the round-the-world record of sixty-three days held by M. Stiegler, of the *Matin*.

M. Jager-Schmidt is now on the White Star liner Olympic, which should reach Cherbourg at eleven o'clock to-night.

A powerful motor-car awaits the journalist at Cherbourg, and will take him full speed to Paris, where he is due between six and seven o'clock tomorrow morning.

M. Jager-Schmidt arrived at Plymouth on the Olympic yesterday evening, and left in good time for Cherbourg.

MIRROR   August 26, 1911

L WORKING ORDER AGAIN.

wo hundred and fifty tramwaymen, but that refusal was rescinded, whereupon the strike ceased. The photograph shows how the docks, deserted a few hours before, ave awakened again to full activity.

FRENCHMAN CIRCLES THE WORLD IN THIRTY-NINE DAYS.

M. André Jager-Schmidt, a journalist on the staff of the Paris newspaper *Excelsior*, arrives in Paris early to-day, having circled the world in thirty-nine days, a day under the time stipulated. (1) Leaving Paris. (2) The route he took.

The World's Largest Liner

September **1911** – December **1911**

The liner, Olympic had its maiden voyage to New York on 14 June 1911. Unlike other ships of the day Olympic was a much sleeker design, partly made possible by its dummy fourth funnel which acted as an air vent for the engines. Three months after its first transatlantic crossing it was involved in a serious incident with a Royal Navy ship shortly after leaving Southampton.

CRUISER IN COLLISION WITH WORLD'S LARGEST LINER

H.M.S. Hawke Crashes Into Olympic Off Cowes.

BOTH SHIPS DAMAGED
Not a Single Person Injured on Either of the Vessels.

OLYMPIC BADLY HOLED
Warship Saved from Sinking by Watertight Bulkheads.

SPECTATORS ON SHORE
The giant Atlantic liner Olympic, the largest vessel afloat, was seriously damaged in collision with the first-class cruiser Hawke in Cowes Roads yesterday.

The White Star liner had left Southampton with passengers and mails for New York at 11.25 yesterday morning, and was proceeding through Cowes Roads when the accident occurred.

Not a soul was injured on either vessel, thanks to the efficacy of the watertight compartments.

Both vessels were heading eastward, the liner for the open Channel, the cruiser for Portsmouth at a greater speed.

Coming up from round the Needles the Hawke was overtaking the Olympic, and from the Isle of Wight side it appeared that the cruiser was abeam of the liner and apparently about to cross her bows.

Then, however, the Hawke slackened speed, apparently with the object of crossing from the island side of the strait to the mainland side astern of the liner. It was at this moment that the accident inexplicably occurred, the warship seeming to drive head-on into the other vessel's stern.

Whether the way which the cruiser still retained or the current or the wash of the 45,000 tons passenger ship or a combination of all three factors caused the accident is not evident, but the crash of warship ramming liner was the next thing seen and heard by the crowds at Cowes a mile and a half distant.

CONVERSE OF GLADIATOR DISASTER
It was the converse of the disaster of three years ago, when an American liner – the St. Paul – ran down the cruiser Gladiator a mile or two away in the Solent.

The Olympic was struck on the starboard quarter and badly holed. Indeed, according to a Lloyd's message dispatched during the afternoon, while the Olympic was still lying at anchor in Cowes Roadstead, the damaged liner was drawing 39ft. of water aft and 31½ft. forward. There was considerable water, too, in the after hold.

It is estimated roughly that nearly 40ft. of the Olympic's plating was torn and rent, the damage extending both above and below the water-line.

The Hawke, which was undergoing steam trials after extensive repairs at Portsmouth, was seriously damaged, her bows being crumpled and the plates torn to the water's edge, but she left for Portsmouth under her own steam.

The tugs Grappler and Volcano were sent to assist the cruiser on her way back to Portsmouth, but their services were not required.

The watertight bulkheads were closed at once, and stood the strain admirably.

Arriving at Portsmouth Dockyard about four o'clock in the afternoon under her own steam, H.M.S., Hawke was dipping slightly, having taken in water in her fore compartments and damaged her bow. She made her appearance steaming astern.

The Olympic was carrying 782 first-class passengers, which is claimed to be a record for any ship crossing the Atlantic.

The outgoing passengers include a number of well-known American millionaires. All told, the Olympic had nearly 3,000 souls on board.

COLLISION SEEN BY CROWDS
Cowes (I.W.) Sept. 20 – The world's largest liner, the Olympic, belonging to the White Star Line, outward bound from Southampton for New York, was ran into by the cruiser Hawke off Cowes shortly before one o'clock this afternoon.

The accident caused the greatest excitement at Cowes, where many people had gathered along the sea front and were watching the progress of the stately liner as she steamed slowly and gracefully, eastwards towards Spithead.

The cruiser Hawke entered the Solent by the Needles Passage, and was steaming in the same direction as the Olympic, being bound for Portsmouth.

LARGE HOLE TORN IN LINER
When she overtook the liner off Cowes the Hawke was going at a fairly fast speed, and was apparently about to pass the Olympic on the starboard side, but unexpectedly drew to port, and crashed stem on into the Olympic's starboard quarter.

The collision occurred near the Prince Consort buoy, about a mile and a half from Cowes, and although it was raining at the time the light was good.

The Olympic was unable to proceed on her voyage, and

The Daily Mirror

THE MORNING JOURNAL WITH THE SECOND LARGEST NET SALE

No. 2,467.   Registered at the G.P.O. as a Newspaper.   THURSDAY, SEPTEMBER 21, 1911   One Halfpenny.

A HOLE THAT THREATENED 3,000 LIVES: THE GASH ON THE OLYMPIC'S QUARTER CAUSED BY A COLLISION WITH H.M.S. HAWKE YESTERDAY.

The scene of yesterday's collision, and also the spot where H.M.S. Gladiator met disaster under similar circumstances in April, 1908.

The map above shows the scene of yesterday's collision, and also the spot where H.M.S. Gladiator met disaster under similar circumstances in April, 1908.

But for the water-tight compartments into which a modern steamer is divided, the collision which occurred in the Cowes Roads yesterday afternoon, between the Olympic, the largest liner afloat, and the cruiser Hawke, might have ended in a terrible disaster. The moment the accident occurred the order was given for the Olympic's water-tight bulkheads to be closed, so that, although she made a good deal of water, it was confined to the damaged compartment. All told, the great liner was carrying 3,000 persons, including 732 first-class passengers, the wealth on board representing at a rough estimate the enormous sum of £100,000,000. The photograph, taken immediately after the accident, shows one of the holes in the Olympic. The men standing inside give an idea of its size. The main damage, however, was a hole, thirty feet in length, below the water-line, through which the water rushed into the third class saloon.—(Kirk and Sons, Cowes.)

after some time she came about and steamed slowly towards Southampton. But she had to cast anchor in Cowes Roads and await the arrival of tugs.

At about half-past three tugs arrived and the great liner was towed slowly back to Southampton.

A large hole was rent in the liner's quarter about 20ft. from her stern.

Much excitement prevailed among passengers on the Olympic, but there was no sign of anything like a panic.

The order was at once given for the watertight compartments to be closed.

The Hawke went astern, and when the vessels parted the gap in the Olympic's quarter could be distinctly seen, whilst the Hawke's bow was badly buckled.

Although both vessels made a good deal of water, there was no immediate danger.

Two Cowes tugs promptly put off to the scene of the collision, but their services were not needed.

HEARD FROM THE SHORE

The crash of the impact was distinctly heard at Cowes, and there were many eye-witnesses of the collision.

A well-known Solent yachtsman who was watching the progress of both vessels as they passed out to eastward, said the Olympic was following the usual course, passing out through Cowes Roads for Spithead, "The Hawke came up from westward," he said, "travelling at a good speed and going in the same direction as the Olympic. She quickly overtook the liner and appeared to go straight at her and hit her stern.

"I cannot understand how the collision could have happened, unless something went wrong with the Hawke's steering gear."

Another eye-witness said: "The Hawke appeared to be about to pass the Olympic on the starboard side, and suddenly drew to port and crashed into the Olympic's stern."

"DRAWN BY SUCTION"

His theory was that the cruiser was drawn into the Olympic by suction.

A bag containing clothing and other articles, marked "Dr. Downton," was washed out of the rent in the Olympic's side, which is about twenty feet across, going down some distance under the water-line.

As a motorboat passed the damaged liner it was observed that some of the passengers made signals as though they desired to leave the vessel.

"So far as I could make out," said a gentleman who saw the accident from Cowes Pier, "the Olympic was steering a course past Spithead at the time with the cruiser following closely behind."

For a time the two vessels ran practically parallel, and suddenly the liner seemed to swing out and the Hawke crashed into her just behind her rear funnel.

PALATIAL HOTEL AT SEA

A veritable floating hotel – "the highest pitch of skill and perfection yet reached in naval architecture" – such is the Olympic, the vessel that made her maiden voyage in June this year.

On board are all the amenities of the finest hotel, with many additions. In the matter of comfort, decoration and magnificence, it is almost impossible to expect anything finer.

The 350 first-class rooms are the last word in luxury. One hundred of them are for single occupants only.

The suites ate decorated in Empire, Louis XV., Louis XVI., Georgian, Queen Anne, modern and old Dutch styles, and have private bathrooms. Each room has a cot bed in brass, mahogany and oak.

The immense dining-room is decorated in the style of early Jacobean times, differing from most great halls of that period, however, in that it is painted white instead of being in sombre oak.

Forming a fitting background for many a brilliant gathering on board is the reception-room, with its exquisitely proportioned white panelling in Jacobean style.

The reading and writing rooms are no less luxurious, while for those who wish to lunch or dine à la carte there is a magnificent restaurant in the style of the Louis XVI. period.

Perhaps the most remarkable feature of all the magnificence on board is the fine oak staircase, which leads, from deck to deck, and, as a piece of workmanship, has no equal on shipboard.

For such of the first-class passengers, as are, athletically inclined there are a swimming bath, a gymnasium, and a squash racket court, to say nothing of Turkish and electric baths to ease wearied muscles.

ELECTRIC LIFTS

Second-class passengers, too, have not been overlooked. For them there is a dining saloon capable, of holding 394 people, and extending the full breadth of the vessel, while the state-rooms are so arranged as to ensure natural light to each.

As for the third-class accommodation, ocean travellers of a few years back would have deemed it luxurious.

On board will be found numerous palm houses; there is also a

verandah café while sheltered promenades and electric lifts seem commonplace comforts in the midst of the floating palace.

DAMAGE TO THE HAWKE

The damaged cruiser Hawke is lying off Portsmouth alongside the boathouse jetty, where she presents a pitiable spectacle.

Some twelve feet of her upper deck is twisted, her stem appears to be completely gone, and all her plating is ripped open.

Her foremost torpedo-tube is exposed and her fore compartments are full of water while the bows, from the force of the slantwise impact, are twisted completely round to starboard.

H.M.S. Hawke, which is a twin-screw protected first-class cruiser of 7,350 tons, is attached to the Portsmouth command of the Home Fleet.

Her commander is W. F. Blunt. Her speed is twenty knots, her complement of men 540, and she carries fourteen guns (including two Maxims).

Her length is 360ft., and beam 60ft., as compared with the mammoth liner's length of 840ft. and beam of 98ft.

Captain Blunt, who was in command of the Hawke, has had an exceptionally distinguished career, and has been regarded in the Navy as one of the coming men.

He got his step to commander in 1904, and is very high up in the list due for promotion.

LARGEST SHIPS IN THE WORLD

The accident to the Olympic temporarily removes from the service the largest ship in the world.

There is one larger ship – the Hamburg-American liner Imperator, which is now being built at Hamburg, and will not go on her maiden voyage until next year.

The comparative dimensions of the Olympic, the Imperator, and the British-built ship Mauretania, are as follow:

	Length	Breadth	Tons	H.P.	Speed
Mauretania	790ft.	88 ft.	32,000	75,000	25½ knots
Olympic	882ft.	92½ft.	45,000	45,000	21 knots
Imperator	810ft.	95ft.	50,000	75,000	22 knots

THE DELAYED MAILS

In consequence of the accident to the Olympic, the packet appointed to convey the mid-week mails to America, the mails for Canada intended for dispatch by that packet will be sent by the Empress of Britain, sailing from Liverpool to-morrow, and those for the United States by the Mauretania, sailing from Liverpool on Saturday.

MEN WHO SAW THE CRASH COMING
Passenger Who Felt the Collision Under Him.

"HARDLY ANY SHOCK"
(FROM OUR SPECIAL CORRESPONDENT)

Southampton, Sept. 20 – As soon as the news of the accident reached Southampton, Captain Berton, of the Iolanda, the largest steam yacht in the world, set off for the liner in a fast motor-launch.

On the Olympic was Mr. Hugo R. Johnstone, a friend of the Iolanda's owner, who was in an especial hurry to get back to New York.

Special permission was accorded him to leave the liner and board the launch so that he might reach England in time to catch the earliest outgoing boat from Liverpool. He was the only passenger to leave the ship before she reached Southampton.

By the courtesy of Captain Berton I was enabled to interview Mr. Johnstone on the Iolanda.

"I was standing on the starboard quarter," he said, "watching the cruiser gradually overtake the liner, which was steaming slowly just off Cowes, on her way to Cherbourg.

"As I watched the battleship gradually overhauled the boat, steaming very close to her on her starboard quarter."

TWO SECONDS TOO LATE

"Then all of a sudden the cruiser went hard to port, with the idea evidently of turning under the stern of the Olympic.

"The helmsman apparently misjudged the enormous length of the Olympic, and instead of clearing her she struck her forward of the stern post, making a huge hole in her.

"The pilot in charge of the Olympic, seeing the accident was likely to occur, telephoned 'Full steam ahead' to get out of the warship's way, but it was just a couple of seconds too late to clear.

"The collision occurred, and the impetus of the liner going forward nearly turned the battleship over.

"Where the cruiser struck the Olympic was in the third-class quarters.

"Luckily, just before the collision the third-class passengers had all gone on deck to hand in their tickets; otherwise a great number would undoubtedly have been killed, because the bow of the battleship smashed right through their third-class quarters.

"The Olympic's band had a very narrow escape, as they were in the next compartment.

"Two of the watertight compartments of the Olympic are flooded right out, and the hole below the water-line, I was told, is bigger than the one above."

ONLY DOCK LARGE ENOUGH

Mr. Johnstone said he was standing on the upper deck on the starboard quarter of the boat, talking to a friend, and the collision took place just under his feet.

Just before the collision he remarked to his friend that he was

perfectly certain that the cruiser could not clear the Olympic, but that there would be a collision – and then it happened.

The Olympic is going to Southampton on the morning tide to-day, where she will be patched up and sent to Belfast, which is the only dry dock in the world large enough to take her.

The accident will prove a very serious matter for the White Star Line, for, apart from the cost of repairing – possibly £1,000,000 – nearly every vacant berth on the Olympic up to December had been booked. Her repair may take something like four months.

Soon after eight o'clock this evening passengers were taken off the Olympic, lying at anchor off Calshot Castle, by the tender Duchess of York.

Commander Blunt.

A special train left for Waterloo at 9.30 with about 100 passengers on board, reluctantly returning to London, to which many of them had only just said "good-bye."

I have talked to a number of the passengers and there is a remarkable uniformity of opinion as to the cause of the collision.

NOT A PLATE DISLODGED

"I saw the whole affair," said Mr. Thomas Hastings, of New York. "The Hawke had been coming up behind us for fully ten minutes. We were going about twelve knots and she about fourteen, I should think. When the Hawke was almost abreast of us she suddenly made as if to pass under our stern.

" 'She has not got much room for it,' I immediately remarked to a friend who was standing with me. Before he could answer she had crashed into us. Her steering seemed to have gone wrong.

"There was hardly any perceptible shock on the Olympic and no sort of panic."

Mrs. W. H. Truesdale, another New York passenger, told me she was having lunch in the Olympic's restaurant when the collision occurred. "Not a plate on the table was dislodged and not a drop of water was spilled at any table so far as I could see."

(1) Stern view of the Olympic, with the Hawke at her bows.

(2) The hole in the Olympic's starboard quarter. The Olympic was struck abaft the fourth funnel, and the damage is thus confined to the stern. The great liner was on her way to Cherbourg to pick up some of her passengers from the Continent and the Hawke was undergoing steam trials after being extensively repaired.

The bows of the Hawke, showing how they were crumpled by the collision. She was also damaged below the water-line.

OLYMPIC'S TWENTY MILLIONAIRES

Wealth Represented On Board Estimated At £100,000,000.

RECORD PASSENGER LIST

In many ways the Olympic created history yesterday.

She was carrying 732 first-class passengers – said to be a record. Amongst them were more than twenty well-known millionaires, while on board there were altogether 3,000 souls.

At a rough estimate the wealth represented on board reached the enormous sum of £100,000,000. The Olympic had on board:

First-class passengers	732
Second-class passengers	501
Third-class passengers	860
Total passengers	2,093

The total passenger accommodation of the gigantic liner is something like 2,400, apportioned as follows: 750 first class, 550 second class, and 1,100 third class.

MANY FAMOUS NAMES

Among the Olympic's 732 first-class passengers was Mr. Waldorf Astor, M.P. The Conservative M.P. for Plymouth and a son of Mr. W. W. Astor, the multi-millionaire ground landlord of New York, who is a naturalised Englishman.

▶ Liners were the only method of transatlantic travel until shortly before World War 2. Charlie Chaplin (far right) on board the Olympic in 1921.

22 September 1911

HUSTLERS RACE TO CATCH LINER

Olympic Millionaire Boards Adriatic at Last Moment After Special Train Ride to Liverpool.

The damaged Olympic, attended by a retinue of tugs, came painfully home to harbour in Southampton yesterday and landed her passengers and luggage.

The most remarkable feature about the accident seems to have been the absence of excitement, alarm, or anxiety amongst the passengers when the collision occurred.

Those who did display any feeling in the matter were those who were in a great hurry to reach New York, and their feelings were those of annoyance at this interruption of their plans.

How two hustling millionaires strove to circumvent the delay

caused by the accident is told below.

The third-class passengers are to remain at Southampton and will be transferred to the St. Louis, sailing to-morrow, and the Majestic, on Wednesday next.

Four hundred of the third-class passengers are Scandinavian emigrants, and they will be accommodated at local hotels.

MILLIONAIRE'S "SPECIAL HUSTLE."
(FROM OUR OWN CORRESPONDENT)

Liverpool, Sept. 21 – Mr. E. W. Sheldon, counsel for the United States Trust Company, New York, and one of the American millionaires driven back to England by the Olympic collision, left here to-night after a remarkable "hustle" across the country.

After a whirlwind rush north to Liverpool by special train, he caught the White Star liner Adriatic last night by three lucky minutes.

He learnt at 11.30 a.m. at Southampton yesterday that if he could get to Liverpool by six o'clock last night he could have a berth on the Adriatic. The ordinary train services were useless, so he engaged a special train and settled down to the wild rush north from Southampton.

Prior to this he had inquired the price of a private special to London. "Twenty-seven pounds," was the answer.

So he decided to go to Liverpool direct, paying £78 plus first-class fare for the special train, which consisted of an engine, a first-class coach, and the guard's van.

A guarantee was given him that the 260 miles' journey would be done in six hours. This would bring him to Liverpool three minutes after the Adriatic left. But he risked it, and won.

The time-table of his journey over 260 miles of Midland and South-Western and North-Western railways was as follows:

	p.m.
Southampton (dep.)	12.33
Birmingham, New-street (arr.)	4.16

Transferred from M.R. line to L.N.W.R. Engines changed.

Birmingham (dep.)	4.20
Liverpool, Edge Hill (dep.)	6.22
Liverpool Dockside (arr.)	6.39
Left for New York	6.42

Over the last two miles and a half from station to quay, the train crawled behind an incredible signalman, who walked with a red flag.

Urgent business demanded Mr. Sheldon's presence in New York at the earliest possible moment. Here is the story of his special hustle to catch the Adriatic, which is due at New York on Friday of next week.

He started his journey north seated in solitary state in the middle compartment of an otherwise empty coach, with another empty coach between him and the engine and a luggage and guard's van at the rear. "Sheldon's special" went whizzing past express trains, and ordinary trains were all side-tracked to let him pass.

It was 6.22 when he reached Edge Hill Station at Liverpool, two miles from Riverside, where the Adriatic lay, with steam up, ready to leave for New York at 6.30 – eight minutes for the last two miles.

Then came the millionaire's ordeal, which left him a nervous wreck at the journey's end; that rush through the length of England at top speed settled down to a slow snail-like agonising crawl.

Rail traffic on this section must not go faster than four miles an hour, and must be preceded by a signalman walking ahead on the track carrying a red flag.

The special took seventeen minutes to cover the last two miles!

It was 6.39 when the train puffed into the quayside station, its solitary passenger standing at the window clutching the handle of the door. "Am I in time," he gasped. "You're all right," said the White Star official, who was waiting. "Come right aboard. We'll see to the baggage." Sheldon, quivering with excitement, stepped rapidly across to the landing-stage and up the gangway, refusing a word to anybody.

He was led to his room, which he promptly entered and locked in the face of the White Star official, whom he evidently mistook for a persistent Pressman.

Two minutes later the gangways were drawn ashore and the Adriatic's booming whistle of departure rang hoarsely over the river.

The great hustle had proved O.K.

OLYMPIC'S SAD HOMECOMING
(FROM OUR SPECIAL CORRESPONDENT)

Southampton, Sept. 21 – The Olympic came back to Southampton this morning, being berthed at Quay 44 shortly after half-past ten.

She left her anchorage off Cowes at a quarter to nine, and fully two hours before she got into Southampton I saw her in the distance. She was staggering slowly back, her four big funnels standing out distinct in a cloud of sunlit smoke.

Although she was proceeding under her own steam, five tugs attended her, like hospital nurses supporting an injured queen, two towing, two guarding her damaged starboard side, and one at the

stern, helping her to get her head round when she turned to come into Southampton Water.

There was the atmosphere of a funeral about the quay when they brought back the wounded giantess with that great gaping, ugly gash in her side, moving so slowly that she hardly seemed to be moving at all, and her decks lined with a seemingly vanquished army of silent, disappointed people.

But few were allowed on the quayside to see the great ship's homecoming. The first thing that they looked for was the wound in her side.

The rent is, close by the stern, about seventy feet from the rudder, and extending quite 25ft. above the water-line. How far below the water the cut goes it is impossible to say until the divers have made their report.

At its widest part, near the top, the gash is, perhaps, 15ft. across. But it is the lower and hidden damage which matters most.

"It is not what you can see now, but what divers will probably find out that counts most," said a famous shipping expert to me.

As soon as the liner was properly berthed the luggage was got off, and then the passengers left the ship and made their way through the big wooden shed on the quay to the special train.

Before the special started I talked with a number of the passengers about their experiences.

A well-known English businessman told me how he lost his Turkish bath.

"I was in the Turkish bath at the time of the collision," he said, "and I immediately rushed on deck, I saw the Hawke backing away from us. I tried to find the Turkish bath later on, but although I made several efforts to do so I never succeeded!"

SUCKED OUT OF HER COURSE
(FROM OUR OWN CORRESPONDENT)

Portsmouth, Sept. 21 – The theory of the accident, which finds most favour with the experts at Portsmouth is the suction theory.

A navigating officer remarked to me to-day that he was given to understand that the vortex created by the speed of the liner's immense bulk rendered the Hawke absolutely helpless.

Interviews with naval men who were aboard the Hawke at the time of the collision with the Olympic throw very little light upon the cause of the mishap. The utmost coolness and perfect discipline prevailed on board, and every order was promptly carried out.

The first intimation of the accident was the telegraph signal to the engines to stop and reverse, and this was carried out within thirty seconds. The check to the cruiser's momentum was insufficient to prevent the collision.

Every man below was shaken off his feet, but each stuck to his post, and though no one knew whether the Hawke was doomed every instruction was carried out with absolute coolness.

THROWN OFF THEIR FEET

"The force of the impact," said a bluejacket of the Hawke, "threw us all off our feet, and the Hawke heeled so much that we thought she was going over.

"This was, I believe, due to the upper part of the bow locking itself in the hole in the liner's side, and as the Olympic continued, on her way she dragged the cruiser's bow with her."

The pumps of the damaged cruiser were working all night to relieve the pressure on the bulkheads.

It was not until the Hawke was in dock at Portsmouth and pumped out late in the afternoon that the real extent of the damage was laid bare.

Below the water-line the cruiser has sustained even more injury than above. The formidable ram which projected some 12ft. from the stem has been bent round to starboard in an extraordinary manner.

Scarcely a rivet is left intact, and the huge structure of steel is little better than a disordered mass of twisted plates.

It is estimated that at least twenty feet of the bow will have to be cut away and replaced.

A court of inquiry into the collision will be held at Portsmouth, but the date has not yet been fixed.

RACE TO BUY NEW BERTHS

"I would have swum ashore rather than wait for the crowd."

It was this spirit which resulted in Mr. Magee, a San Francisco estate agent, being the first passenger to leave the Olympic after the collision, and the first to secure another berth in the Adriatic that sailed from Liverpool last night.

Mr. Magee, abounding in the desire to "get home quick," left – in more senses than one – the rest of his "hustling" compatriots almost before they realised they were stranded.

Seeing a small boy in a small boat near the Olympic, he shouted: "I'll give you £2 to get me ashore!" The boy agreed, and Mr. Magee slid down a rope from the Olympic's side, only to find himself dangling tip to the waist in water. He had been too quick even for the boy to get the boat alongside.

Scrambling aboard, Mr. Magee landed at Cowes, caught the excursion steamer to Southampton, telephoned to the White Star office, and booked four berths on the Adriatic – two for himself and wife, two for Mr. and Mrs. Gibson, his friends, left on the Olympic.

Having got his berth Mr. Magee raced back to the Olympic and in an interview yesterday said: "The whole lot only cost me £50, and the fun was cheap at the price, considering that I shall be on my way home within, thirty hours of the smash."

◆ This photograph was taken within one minute of the vessels clearing each other after the collision in Cowes Roads, and shows the cruiser Hawke at the stern of the Olympic, which it will be seen is still under way.

23 September 1911

OLYMPIC LUGGAGE
Rammed Liner's Disconsolate Passengers Sit Amid Piles of Sodden Goods.

Divers were still working on the Olympic yesterday at Southampton, and it is hoped she may be able to proceed to Belfast for repairs within a week.

Her crew have refused to accept three days' pay, and yesterday decided to issue summonses to secure a larger amount of wages.

Disconsolate passengers sat among sodden heaps of luggage on the quayside yesterday. Many of their effects have been totally ruined.

Now that all the millionaire and first-class passengers of the rammed liner Olympic have been successfully "accounted for," people are wondering what has become of the second and third-class passengers.

There were 500 second-class passengers on the Olympic.

These were people who would travel first class on smaller boats – professional and business men. But the second-class passengers could not afford to take special ferry boats and special trains.

The White Star Line are therefore accommodating such of the 500 as intend to return to the United States – and this is nearly all of them – on the White Star liners Arabic and Cedric, which leave Liverpool on September 26 and 28 respectively, and on the St. Louis, which leaves Southampton to-day.

In all cases the berths will be second class, and the difference in the cost of the berths on those ships and the Olympic will be made up in cash.

The cost of second-class accommodation on the ships concerned is:

Olympic, from £14.
Arabic, from £11.
Cedric, from £12.
St. Louis, from £11 10s.

Third-class passengers are being cared for in the same manner. Only in their case the cost of their enforced stay in England is being defrayed by the White Star Company.

Many Americans have also been stranded in Paris, most of those who went to Cherbourg to catch the Olympic having gone to Paris.

➤ The giant liner passing down the Solent one minute before the collision occurred.

NAVAL INQUIRY

Captain Grant, of the Portsmouth Navigation School, presided yesterday over the court inquiry on the cruiser Hawke into her collision with the S.S. Olympic.

25 September 1911

PATCHING THE OLYMPIC

Giant Liner To Go to Belfast This Week After Temporary Repairs.

Satisfactory progress is being made at Southampton with the work of temporarily patching the hull of the White Star liner Olympic, which was damaged in collision with the cruiser Hawke.

The divers who examined the giant liner are understood to have found a gaping hole below the water-line of similar dimensions to the rent on the starboard side.

The Olympic is drawing over thirty-five feet of water, and will have to be considerably lightened to enable her to enter Belfast Harbour, whither she is expected to proceed this week.

5 October 1911

OLYMPIC GOES TO BELFAST

Temporary repairs having been completed, the giant White Star liner Olympic left Southampton yesterday for Belfast, where she will be permanently repaired and overhauled after her collision with H.M.S. Hawke.

9 October 1911

The damaged White Star liner Olympic was towed into Belfast Harbour on Saturday by six tugs, and berthed at the fitting-out jetty near the new graving dock.

➤ Divers preparing to go down at Southampton. Note the great rent in the vessel's starboard quarter.

11 October 1911

The world's largest ship, the new White Star liner Titanic (45,000 tons), sister-ship to the Olympic, will, it was announced yesterday, leave Southampton and Cherbourg on her first voyage to New York on April 10 1912.

17 November 1911

OLYMPIC v. HAWKE IN THE LAW COURTS

Captain and Pilot Describe Solent Collision.

CASE FOR THE LINER
Theory of Suction Discounted by Passenger Vessel's Skipper.

Light was thrown yesterday in the Admiralty Court upon the collision on September 20 between the mammoth liner Olympic and the first-class cruiser Hawke. Two cases were down for hearing before Sir Samuel Evans, assisted by the Trinity Masters, viz:

(1) The owners of the Olympic (the White Star Line), v. Commander W. F. Blunt, of H.M.S. cruiser Hawke.

(2) The Commissioners for Executing the Office of Lord High Admiral of the United Kingdom v. the owners of the Olympic.

The White Star Line was represented by Mr. Laing, K.C., Mr. Stephens and Mr. Dumas.

It will be remembered that the Olympic, laden with American millionaires, and the Hawke came into collision off Cowes when the liner was on her way from Southampton to New York. No lives were lost, but considerable damage was done and great inconvenience was caused.

CHARGES AND COUNTERCHARGES
On behalf of the Hawke it was pleaded that shortly before 12.45 p.m., while carrying out a steam trial, she was proceeding up the Solent. The weather was clear and the wind a fresh W.S.W. breeze. The cruiser was making fifteen knots, and a good look-out was being kept. The Olympic was seen about three miles distant and about two points on the port bow.

The Hawke continued her course and speed along her starboard side of the Channel, rounding Egypt Point under port helm. The Olympic, after emitting two puffs of steam from her whistle when she was between Thorn Knoll and West Bramble Buoys, drew over close to the port side of the Hawke.

The helm of the Hawke was ported a little and kept aport, but owing to the close proximity and high speed of the Olympic the bows of the Hawke were, it was alleged, caused to swerve to port towards the Olympic.

A series of rapid orders was then given, but, notwithstanding, the Olympic with her starboard quarter struck the port side of the Hawke's stem a heavy blow, doing considerable damage.

Allegations of negligence were made against those on board the Olympic in:

Not keeping a good look-out.

Coming too close to the Hawke.

Going at a speed which in the circumstances was excessive and improper.

Entering the Solent main channel at an improper time or in an improper manner.

Taking too wide a sweep round the West Bramble Buoy.

Not starboarding sufficiently or in due time.

Proceeding at an excessive speed.

And not easing, stopping or reversing the engines in due time or at all.

The case for the Olympic was that the collision was caused solely by the negligent navigation of the Hawke.

The liner was in charge of a duly licensed Trinity House pilot while on a voyage from Southampton to New York, with passengers and mails.

The Hawke was first observed three to four miles distant, and the Olympic proceeded on following the deep-water channel and under a starboard helm, assisted by her engines, rounded the West Bramble Buoy, her whistle sounding two short blasts when she starboarded.

HAWKE COMING UP ASTERN

The Olympic having straightened for the eastern channel, her port engine, which had been working full speed astern to assist her starboard helm, was put full speed ahead.

Her turbine, which had been stopped while rounding the buoy, was again started, and she proceeded on a course to pass south of the Ryde Middle in about mid-channel.

At this time the Hawke was distant about a quarter of a mile, and coming up astern on the starboard quarter of the Olympic.

The Hawke as she came on overhauled the Olympic until she was about abeam of the Olympic on her starboard side and between one or two cables distant, and was then on a parallel course.

The Olympic kept her course with her engines working full speed ahead, but the Hawke suddenly altered her course towards the Olympic, as if acting under a starboard helm, causing imminent danger of collision.

Although the helm of the Olympic was put hard aport to throw her quarter clear, the Hawke with her stem struck the starboard quarter of the Olympic a heavy blow, causing her serious damage.

The Oceanic (White Star) Company charged the Hawke with:
Improperly starboarding.
Not easing or stopping her engines in due time.
Improperly attempting to pass to the southward of the Olympic.

CAPTAIN SMITH'S ACCOUNT

The case for the Olympic was, by arrangement, proceeded with first. Captain Edward John Smith, her commander, was called, and, replying to Mr. Laing, said he was formerly commander of the White Star liner Adriatic.

He took charge of the Olympic on her first voyage in June last.

On the occasion in question he was on the bridge with the pilot. The fourth officer was at the telegraph and the fifth officer in the conning tower. The Olympic steered very well.

A short time after they were on their course he saw the Hawke drawing up on their starboard beam, going faster than they were.

For an appreciable time they seemed to run at even speed. Then the Olympic, commenced to draw ahead, or the Hawke dropped astern.

Immediately afterwards the cruiser's bow came to port, as if she had starboarded. She turned very quickly and struck the Olympic on the quarter almost a right-angle blow.

He had before this called out to the pilot: "He is starboarding, and he is going to hit us."

The pilot then gave the order for the Olympic to port, and that was carried out.

The Olympic was knocked round a good deal. At the time of the

collision both engines of the Olympic had been stopped. That order was given by the pilot.

ON HER FOURTH VOYAGE

Sir Rufus Isaacs (cross-examining): How many voyages had this vessel made? – Three voyages. We were on our fourth.

Their maximum speed, said Captain Smith, was about 22½ knots. They got steadied on their course about 12.43, and he then saw the Hawke 2½ points on their starboard quarter, about half a mile away roughly.

The collision happened three minutes after they got steadied on their course.

Sir Rufus: That gave the Hawke a great deal to do in three minutes, to overhaul the Olympic. Do you think she could do it? – I don't know how fast she was going. We were not going so fast at that time.

Had you reached your full speed at the time of the collision? – No, I think about sixteen knots.

Did it occur to you that there was any danger of her being sucked into your quarter? – No, there was nothing in the conditions up to the moment she started to fall into us that led me to think she was in any danger at all.

But did the possibility of force operating to draw her into your quarter ever occur to you? – No.

Captain Smith said, further, that he would take that into account if a vessel was sufficiently close to him.

PILOT'S EVIDENCE

Mr. George William Bowyer, the pilot of the Olympic, said he let the Hawke know by signal that he was on a starboard helm and making for the eastern passage.

He went half-speed astern on the port engine, and proceeded for a few yards and then went full speed astern on the port engine to make the turn round the West Bramble Buoy.

He put the helm hard astarboard. These manoeuvres were to round the West Bramble Buoy, and they were usual to get out of the eastern channel.

When he steadied on his course he was going eleven to twelve knots. He thought the Hawke was to pass on his port.

"When," continued witness, "I saw the Hawke swinging I wondered what she was up to, and thought it rather tricky. Captain Smith said: 'I don't think she will go under our stern' as she came towards us, and within a few seconds of her striking us I was standing amidships with the man at the wheel, and I could not see her.

"I told Captain Smith, who was standing on the starboard side of the bridge: 'If she is going to strike, let me know in time to put the helm hard aport.'

"He did not do so for a few seconds, and then I sang out: 'Is she going to strike?' He said: ' Yes, she is to strike us on the stern.'

"I then said: 'Hard aport!' We had just got the wheel over and stopped when we felt the jar."

What was the effect of the blow on the Olympic?
– It made us sheer to starboard.

The hearing was adjourned until to-day.

18 November 1911

SEA SUCTION PROBLEM

Judges and Experts in Hawke-Olympic Cases to See Tank Experiments.

Experiments in a tank at Teddington were mentioned yesterday when the hearing of the lawsuits arising out of the collision off Cowes last September between the liner Olympic and the cruiser Hawke was resumed before the President of the Admiralty Division and Trinity Masters.

Each vessel makes charges against the other of negligent navigation and each claims damages.

The Attorney-General, appearing for the Admiralty and Captain Blunt, of the Hawke, said that certain witnesses for the Admiralty would refer to the Teddington experiments, and that experts on the Olympic's side should have the opportunity of seeing them. It was decided that the experts, as well as the President and Trinity Masters should visit Teddington to-day.

These experiments have, it is understood, to do with the suggestion put forward by the Attorney-General, in cross-examination, that the Hawke might have been drawn by suction or some other force into the quarter of the Olympic.

Maritime amenities just before the collision were described by Mr. D. W. Alexander, the Olympic's fourth officer, who was at the bridge-telegraph at the time.

He said that when the Hawke seemed about to pass he rang an order to dip the ensign, and saw the Hawke dip hers in reply.

Then he saw the Hawke fall astern, and heard the captain tell the pilot she was coming into them.

It was not possible that the Hawke should have been sucked into the Olympic from that distance.

Mr. Wilde, the Olympic's chief officer, said that he could not understand why the Hawke starboarded her helm "unless it was curiosity on the part of the cruiser." There was no need for her to have done so.

The hearing was adjourned after other evidence had been given.

OLYMPIC LEAVES DOCK

After undergoing repairs costing £100,000, as a result of the damage she sustained in collision with H.M.S. Hawke, the White Star liner Olympic left dock at Belfast yesterday, and will proceed to Southampton to-day.

Owing to the division of opinion of experts in the Olympic-Hawke lawsuit, suction power experiments were, carried out on Saturday in the National Physical Laboratory at Teddington, wax models of the two ships being drawn through the water at various speeds.

CRUISER'S TACTICS

Witness Says He Thought Hawke Was "Making Narrow Shave" with Olympic.

That the Hawke "was making a very narrow shave of it" was the impression related to the Court yesterday of Colonel Saxton White, manager of Armstrong, Whitworth and Co., a passenger on the Olympic, of the collision between the two vessels which forms the subject of counter actions for damages in the Admiralty Court.

He said that the Hawke changed her course after being parallel with the Olympic, and pointed straight at the Olympic. He thought that the Hawke intended to "cross our stern," and was running it fine.

Until the Hawke was within a few yards of the Olympic he thought she would pass astern. Then he crossed the deck to see the Hawke come under the stern, and his daughter, who was with him, cried "She has struck us."

The blow was a right-angled one. He returned to the side and saw the Hawke recovering from a heavy roll. Her bow seemed to be twisted forward in the Olympic's direction.

Mr. Lashmar, master of the yacht Belinda, said he saw the collision from the yacht. The Hawke suddenly turned into the Olympic. Until she did he did not think there was danger of a collision. Captain Pritchard, formerly captain of the Mauretania, said, that he had passed close to other vessels with big ships, but had never come across a case of one being sucked into the other. (The Admiralty have foreshadowed this defence in cross-examination, and experiments have been made with models at Teddington in a tank.)

Mr. Lewis, a first-class Liverpool pilot, said he had never experienced anything like suction, or difficulty in steering under

the circumstances. Evidence as to the damage to the vessels having been given, the hearing was adjourned.

The Olympic, having completed her repairs, left Belfast for Southampton yesterday, exactly two months to a day since her collision.

TURNED ROUND LIKE TOP

Hawkes Commander Describes Effect on Cruiser of Collision with Olympic.

The Hawke's case in the counter-actions arising from the collision between that warship and the giant liner Olympic was presented to the President of the Admiralty Division and the Trinity Masters yesterday, when the hearing of the actions was resumed.

Commander William Blunt, of the Hawke, was the Admiralty's first witness, and he told at how at the time of the collision his vessel was carrying out "power trials."

When he came to the bridge after lunch he saw the Olympic about one and a quarter miles away on the port bow. He saw her alter her course and take the eastern channel, and he altered his own ship's course to give her more room, being careful to put the Hawke on his own side of the channel. When the Olympic was abeam she was coming unpleasantly close, and he gave the order: "Port five and steer for the right-hand fort." The vessels were almost "bridge to bridge" then, and only three-quarters of a cable apart.

"I had one eye on the Olympic and one eye on my course," said the commander, "because of the unpleasant proximity of the vessels. It was not dangerous. I am not going to say it was, as I have been closer in the fleet; but it was precious uncomfortable."

Later the ship swerved to port, and he called out: "What are you doing? Port! Hard a-port!" After that the report came, "Helm jammed!" and he ordered: "Stop port! Full astern starboard!" and, jumping down, put his own hand on the lever, pressing it down to "Full astern!"

Then the Hawke struck the Olympic's starboard quarter and listed quite 15deg. to starboard, being "turned round like a top." The Olympic was going at a greater speed, and the Hawke's engines were reversed before the impact, and her speed, fifteen knots, had been reduced to about eight at the time of impact.

Great care was taken with the steering-gear, and before the collision the ship had answered her helm. The cause of the jamming was that the quarter-master put the wheel over faster than the steering engine was designed to run.

"Suction pure and simple," caused the Hawke's head to come to port, and the helm was never starboarded by his orders or to his

knowledge. It could not have been done without. The jamming of the helm had had nothing to do with the collision. He was thinking of suction in the sense of "instability of equilibrium in steering" when the vessels came in unpleasant proximity.

Answering one question in cross-examination, Captain Blunt made an explanation. Mr. Laing (for the Olympic) quietly remarked, "Much obliged," and the commander retorted with a smile, "Oh! delighted."

The Olympic should have given the Hawke more room, said the commander. The "swerve" came when the vessels were 300ft. apart, before the collision his vessel had no heel.

After other evidence the case was adjourned.

22 November 1911

COMMANDER OF THE HAWKE AS WITNESS

Commander William Frederick Blunt, R.N., captain of H.M.S. Hawke, gave evidence for the Admiralty yesterday in the actions arising out of the collision between his cruiser and the White Star liner Olympic.

23 November 1911

OFFICER'S LOST NOTES

Hawke's Navigator Cross-Examined About Book Lost in Olympic Collision.

Whether H.M.S. Hawke or the liner Olympic was responsible for the collision between the two was the subject of further inquiry yesterday in the Admiralty Court.

Lieutenant Aylin, the Hawke's navigating lieutenant, was cross-examined by Mr. Laing, K.C., about the notebook, jerked from his hand overboard in the collision, mentioned on the previous day. It contained, said the witness, entries with regard to points, times, and speeds.

The President asked whether it had occurred to the witness or to his commander to try to reproduce at once the notes while the facts were fresh in their memories. He replied that it did not.

Geoffrey Bashford, first lieutenant of the Hawke, then gave evidence. He attributed the collision to suction. The hearing was adjourned.

The White Star liner Olympic arrived at Southampton yesterday afternoon and will resume her transatlantic sailings on Wednesday next.

20 December 1911

OLYMPIC PILOT BLAMED

Judge Accepts the Suction Theory of the Hawke Collision.

Sir Samuel Evans, gave his judgment yesterday in the cases arising out of the collision in the Solent on September 20 between H.M.S. Hawke and the White Star liner Olympic. He found that –

The collision was solely due to the faulty navigation of the Olympic's pilot.

There must be judgment, with costs, for Commander Blunt in the action against him, and as to the other action judgment must be entered for the Olympic on the defence of compulsory pilotage, each side to pay their own costs.

The Olympic's owners, the Oceanic Steamship Company, had brought an action against Commander W. F. Blunt, of the Hawke, and the Admiralty, while there was a cross-action by the Admiralty against the owners of the Olympic, against whom negligence was alleged.

The Judge said that the evidence established

Captain Bowyer, the pilot of the Olympic.

the fact that the vessels were never on parallel courses. He thought the Olympic, having the Hawke on her starboard side, ought to have got out of the Hawke's way.

He accepted the suction theory advanced by the Hawke, and was satisfied that she did not starboard, as alleged. The cause of the collision was that the Olympic came too close to the Hawke.

It is stated that the case has put the Admiralty to a charge exceeding £10,000, and it is estimated that the costs on both sides will amount to not less than £20,000.

Challenges for the White Star Line

January **1912** – 3 April **1912**

The coal strike affected everyone, but it was the shipping industry that was particularly vulnerable because of the prodigious amounts of fuel needed to power liners like the Olympic and Titanic. The late winter weather turned out to be awful, which delayed the sea trials of the Titanic from April 1 until the following day, a little over a week before her maiden voyage.

Winston Churchill, First Lord of the Admiralty at the launch of H.M.S. Iron Duke in October 1912.

FOOTBALL GROUND FOR MR. CHURCHILL

First Lord to Speak in Belfast's Nationalist Quarter.

AFTERNOON MEETING

The problem of the venue of Mr. Winston Churchill's Home Rule demonstration in Belfast is settled at last.

It was announced last night that the scene of the demonstration will be the Celtic Park football ground at Belfast.

This ground is in the heart of the Nationalist quarter of the city and the stands alone are capable of accommodating nearly 15,000 persons.

The announcement came from London, Captain Guest, M.P., having returned to confer with the Chief Whip on the subject.

Earlier in the day the standing committee of the Ulster Liberal Association had conferred at Belfast, and the decision was issued in the evening by the secretary of the Ulster Liberal Association.

The hour of the meeting has been fixed for one o'clock on February 8.

The Celtic grounds belong to the Nationalists, and are controlled by a board of directors who are Roman Catholics.

Great satisfaction has been caused in Belfast, our correspondent telegraphed last night, and it is confidently believed that a peaceful way has been found out of a very serious situation.

The fact that the meeting, as it is now understood, will be held in the afternoon is also regarded as making for peace.

IMPORTING CONSTABLES
(FROM OUR OWN CORRESPONDENT)

Belfast, Jan 29 – Unionist preparations to resist Home Rule go on apace side by side with the arrangements made by the authorities to minimise trouble on the occasion of the Churchill demonstration.

Orangemen are undergoing drill and instruction, and a telegram from Bangor states that that town alone could provide 500 drilled men at short notice.

About 100 members of the Unionist Club there have volunteered to be drilled, and they will commence to-night.

Moreover, the use of Lady Clanmorris' estate at Bangor Castle has been applied for with a view to open-air manoeuvres.

Twelve hundred specially-picked volunteers, who have been detailed to hold Ulster Hall on February 7 and 8, will each be provided with a baton for those days.

Since their selection from the ranks of Orangemen and Unionist clubs they have been nightly drilling in dozens of halls, builders' yards and other large suitable buildings loaned for the purpose.

Some excitement was caused in Belfast to-day by a party of constabulary fully accoutered and with their carbines slung over their shoulders, who marched through Royal-avenue along the footpath.

They were evidently from the country districts, as the local police have their metal numbers worn conspicuously on their tunic collars.

MEETING ON LINER SUGGESTED

During the past few days considerable bodies of constabulary have arrived at Lisburn, seven miles from here, and marched to several barracks just outside Belfasts southern municipal boundaries.

Seen after to-day's committee meeting of the Ulster Unionist Council, one of the honorary secretaries of the Belfast Conservative Association stated that business consisted chiefly of discussing details of the Unionist plan of campaign.

Mr. David Foy, district master of the Sandy Row Orangemen, on leaving the meeting, said:

"One thing is absolutely certain. Mr. Churchill's meeting will not take place in any public building or space in any one of the three Unionist parliamentary divisions of Belfast.

"Lord Pirrie," he added, "may lend the Titanic for the purpose."

The Duke of Abercorn, in a letter to the council to-day, says he is in full accord with the decision arrived at regarding Mr. Churchill's visit.

12 February 1912

DOCK THE FIRST LORD DID NOT SEE

Why the Admiralty Must Spend £60,000 at Belfast.

TASK OFF DREDGING
(FROM OUR OWN CORRESPONDENT)

Belfast, Feb. 11 – Mr. Churchill's visit to Glasgow, where he

In an effort to find new and faster ways of travelling between continents the Airship was seen as offering great potential. Their susceptibility to catastrophe made them it a difficult proposition. This Naval airship was wrecked by a sudden squall in late 1911.

inspected the site of what is to be the largest graving dock in the world, was not only of supreme importance to the nation, but of special interest to Belfast.

"Build your great dock," said Mr. Churchill, "Build it long and build it deep, and, above all, build it wide."

It happens that Belfast is at present the proud possessor of the largest dock in the world. There is no other dock so long, so deep, and so wide.

It was this dock that would have been the centre of Mr. Churchill's attention had the circumstances of his stay in Belfast enabled the Harbour Commissioners to receive him and show him over the docks and harbour.

Stepping into the vacant shoes of the First Lord of the Admiralty, I was given permission at the Belfast Commissioner's office to see the docks.

Mr. W. Redfern Kelly, the engineer-in-chief, who would have been Mr. Churchill's guide, was also my guide, and thus I saw what Mr. Churchill would have seen and heard what he would have heard.

THE ADMIRALTY WILL PAY

The Admiralty is desirous of using Belfast for docking Dreadnought battleships and cruisers, as the world's largest dock would be of enormous strategic value in case of a naval war in the north.

But there is one slight difficulty. The 300ft. wide Victoria Channel, which gives access to Belfast Docks, has a depth of 32ft. only at high water.

The Admiralty require that depth at all states of the tide, and the question is, who should bear the necessary cost of dredging?

The Harbour Commissioners are willing to undertake the dredging and permanently maintain the channel, which runs as straight as a dart out to sea, in a navigable condition for the largest warships at all tides providing the Admiralty pay the first cost, £60,000.

It was to decide this question that Mr. Winston Churchill wished to see the docks himself.

Having taken his place I may perhaps presume so far as to give the answer: The Admiralty will and must pay the £60,000.

Mr. Redfern Kelly spent much time in showing me round the magnificent docks and explaining things just as he would have explained them to the First Lord of the Admiralty.

£350,000 DRY DOCK

We first went to the largest dry dock in the world. It is 850ft. long and 126ft. wide and 50 ft. deep. It cost £350,000, and the twenty-three million gallons of water it holds when flooded can be pumped out in a hundred minutes.

At present the dock is occupied by the world's largest liner, the Titanic, which begins her Atlantic sailings next month.

We walked round the dock, and gazed admiringly upwards and downwards on the monster bulk it contains, but the ship is so large that one cannot see its real size.

Then we went down steep stone steps to the base of the dock, walking under the enormous flat bottom of the vessel from one side to the other, made a tour of the power and pumping stations, surveyed the channel and the picturesque surroundings from the dock caisson and well, then took the liberty of answering the question just as Mr. Winston Churchill would have answered it, and as the Admiralty must answer it sooner or later.

LINER AND SUPER-LINER

Undoubtedly the Government must pay the cost of dredging the channel, and thus secure first claim on the world's largest dock when war is declared.

Perhaps Mr. Churchill will kindly accept my decision on this vitally important subject and save himself another journey to Belfast.

By the courtesy of Lord Pirrie I was also able to visit Messrs. Harland and Wolff's yard in company with Mr. Redfern Kelly.

We saw the model of the first steed ship built by the firm in 1863.

"We could put two vessels of that size in one of the Titanic's funnels," said one of the firm's engineers.

A ship even larger than the Titanic is now being built. It is to be called the Gigantic, and I walked under the keel, so that I could boast of having in one day walked under the largest completed ship in the world and under the bare keel of one still larger.

23 February **1912**

PREMIER AND COLLEAGUES TRY TO AVERT COAL WAR

In shipping circles an optimistic feeling prevailed yesterday that the coal strike would be averted.

None of the big ocean going companies seemed seriously alarmed, for the White Star and the American lines can coal at New York or Cherbourg and the cape boats at Madeira and Las Palmas should occasion arise. The Olympic takes 6,000 tons of coal for the round-trip; Southampton to New York.

28 February **1912**

WORLD'S LARGEST LINER DAMAGED

The largest vessel in the world, the White Star liner Olympic, reported yesterday by wireless that she has met with a mishap in mid-Atlantic, having thrown a blade of her port propeller, while homeward bound.

The liner is due at Southampton this afternoon. She will proceed afterwards to Belfast for repairs and will sail from Southampton for New York on Thursday of next week instead of Wednesday.

The Olympic, which cost £1,500,000 made her maiden voyage last June and was in collision in September with the cruiser Hawke.

5 March **1912**

After leaving Belfast, where a new blade had been fitted to her propeller, the White Star liner Olympic had to put back owing to stormy weather, and was rebirthed in the dry dock.

22 March **1912**

Nearly 100,000 tons of shipping are lying idle at Southampton. Amongst the ships in dock are the White Star liners Oceanic and Majestic, the American liners St. Paul, New York and Philadelphia and half a dozen of the London and south-western cross channel steamers.

3 April **1912**

The White Star liner Titanic left Belfast yesterday morning, and after undergoing speed trials proceeded to Southampton.

◗ This floatplane was the pinnacle of aviation achievement in 1912, little wonder that liners and travel by ship were so important.

48

Maiden Voyage

When the news was received via the wonder of wireless telegraphy that the Titanic had hit an iceberg there was at first incredulity that such a thing could have happened. At first all seemed well as reports appeared to indicate that everyone was accounted for and safe. All too quickly the full horror of the disaster began to unfold.

◀ The second-class deck of the Titanic.

51

EVERY ONE ON BOARD WORLD'S GREATEST LINER SAFE AFTER COLLISION WITH ICEBERG IN ATLANTIC OCEAN

TITANIC'S WIRELESS SIGNAL BRINGS VESSEL TO SCENE

46,000-ton Ship, with 2,300 Aboard in Peril.

EYERYONE SAFE

Morning of Suspense Ends in Message of Relief.

PASSENGERS TAKEN OFF

Helpless Giant Being Towed to Port by Allan Liner.

The White Star liner Titanic, the greatest ship the world has ever known, has met with disaster on her maiden voyage.

She left Southampton on Wednesday last and carried about 2,300 passengers and crew on board, with 3,400 sacks of mails.

On Sunday she came into collision with an iceberg, and immediately flashed out wireless messages for help.

Many steamers rushed to her aid, but her fate and that of the thousands on board remained in doubt on both sides of the Atlantic for many hours.

It was at length known that every soul was safe, and that the vessel itself was proceeding to Halifax (Nova Scotia), towed by the Allan liner Virginian.

All her passengers had by that time been taken aboard two of the liners that hurried to the scene in reply to the wireless message.

DRAMATIC TELEGRAMS OF DISASTER

So many and so conflicting were the reports that reached London yesterday concerning the fate of the Titanic that until detailed and definite tidings come to hand it is difficult to establish much more than the one all-important and outstanding fact that:

Every man, woman and child on the great liner is safe.

It would appear that once again the value to humanity of wireless telegraphy has been established, for at least five vessels are known to have hastened to the aid of the world's greatest ship when she flashed forth her appeal for help.

Three at least arrived in time to be of the greatest service, as is evident from the following series of dramatic Reuter messages which reached London yesterday at the times named (NB – New York time is five hours behind London):

6.15 a.m. (New York) – A telegram received here from Montreal says:

"The liner Virginian reports in a wireless communication that the liner Titanic, which is reported to have been in collision with an iceberg, has requested assistance. The Virginian is hastening to her aid."

8.40 a.m. (New York) – A telegram from Cape Race says:

"The wireless telegraph operator on board the Titanic reported the weather calm and clear, the position of the liner being then 41.46 north, 50.14 west.

"The Virginian at midnight was 170 miles west of the Titanic, and is expected to reach her at ten o'clock this morning.

"The Olympic at midnight was in 40.32 north latitude, 61.18 west longitude. She is also in direct communication with the Titanic, and is hastening to her."

BLURRED MESSAGES

8.45 a.m. (New York) – The liner Baltic has also reported herself within 200 miles of the Titanic, and says she is speeding to her help.

The last signals from the Titanic came at 12.27 this morning. The Virginian's operator says that these were blurred and ended abruptly. – Reuter.

9.50 a.m. (New York) – A telegram from Cape Race says: "At 10.25 on Sunday evening the Titanic reported she had struck an iceberg. The steamer said that immediate assistance was required.

"Half an hour afterwards another message was received saying that the Titanic was sinking by the head, and that the women were being taken off in lifeboats." – Reuter.

1.50 p.m. (New York) – Up to this hour the officials of the White Star Line have not received a word regarding the reported accident to the Titanic. The company have issued the following statement:

"Twelve hours have passed since the collision of the Titanic is reported to have taken place. We have heard nothing of an accident.

"It is very strange that the Titanic's sister ship Olympic, which has a wireless installation of sufficient strength to send a message across the Atlantic, should have sent us nothing. The Olympic should be alongside the Titanic at two this afternoon."

2.58 p.m. (New York) – A dispatch from Halifax states that all the passengers of the Titanic had left the ship by 3.30 this morning.

3.50 p.m. (New York) – The Montreal Star reports from Halifax that the Titanic is still afloat and is making her way slowly to Halifax.

The Daily Mirror

THE MORNING JOURNAL WITH THE SECOND LARGEST NET SALE.

No. 2,645. | Registered at the G.P.O. as a Newspaper. | TUESDAY, APRIL 16, 1912 | One Halfpenny.

DISASTER TO THE TITANIC: WORLD'S LARGEST SHIP COLLIDES WITH AN ICEBERG IN THE ATLANTIC DURING HER MAIDEN VOYAGE.

Disaster, it was reported yesterday, has overtaken the great steamer Titanic, the largest and most luxuriously appointed vessel afloat. The liner, which is the latest addition to the White Star fleet, left Southampton last Wednesday on her maiden voyage to New York, and was in the vicinity of the Newfoundland banks, to the south of Cape Race, when she struck an iceberg, an ever-present peril in those latitudes at this time of the year. "Wireless" has again demonstrated its immense value, assistance being summoned by this means. The photograph shows the mighty vessel leaving Southampton on Wednesday.—(Daily Mirror photograph.)

4.50 p.m. (New York) – A message from Montreal timed 8.30 a.m. says:

"The Titanic is still afloat and heading towards Halifax.

"The women and children have not been taken off, though the lifeboats are ready in case of emergency. It is thought that the bulkheads will prevent her sinking."

A later message, says: "Wireless telegraphy brings the word that two vessels are standing by the Titanic, and that all the passengers have been taken off."

5.20 p.m. (New York) – "The transfer of the passengers from the Titanic is now being carried out. Twenty boat loads have already been taken on board the Cunarder Carpathia."

This last report was sent by wireless telegraphy to Mr. Franklin, vice president of the White Star Company in New York, by Captain Haddock, of the Olympic, which is nearing the Titanic.

The dispatch adds that the Parisian and Carpathia are in attendance on the Titanic, and that the Baltic is nearing the ship.

Unofficial telegrams state that the Virginian has taken the Titanic in tow.

7.40 p.m. (New York) – Mr. Franklin at one o'clock this afternoon gave out the following message received from the Boston office of the White Star Line:

"Allan line, Montreal, confirms report Virginian, Parisian and Carpathia in attendance, standing, by Titanic."

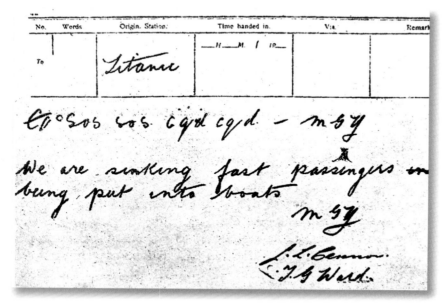
← The last message received from the Titanic.

PASSENGERS TRANSHIPPED
Montreal, April 15 – It is now confirmed here that the passengers of the Titanic have been safely transhipped to the Allan liner Parisian and the Cunarder Carpathia.

The Virginian is still towing the Titanic towards Halifax. – Exchange Telegraph.

NO LIVES IN DANGER
New York, April 15 – The White Star officials here state that the Virginian is standing by the Titanic and that there is no danger of loss of life.

A wireless telegraph message to Halifax states that all the passengers were safely taken off the Titanic at 3.30.

Mr. Franklin, vice-president of the White Star Company, states that the Titanic is unsinkable. The fact that she was reported to have sunk several feet by the head was, he said, unimportant. She could go down many feet at the head as the result of water filling the forward compartments and yet remain afloat indefinitely. – Exchange Telegraph.

STRUGGLING TOWARDS PORT
New York, April 15 – A wireless message received at Boston from St. John's, Newfoundland, states that the Titanic is slowly struggling towards Cape Race.

An unsigned wireless message, timed 8.30, has been received at Montreal, stating that the Titanic is still afloat, and is slowly steaming towards Halifax, Nova Scotia. The forward compartments are full of water, but if the vessel is able to withstand the strain it is hoped to make port.

News has now reached here that at 11.10 a.m. (Canadian, time) the local agents of the White Star Line at Montreal received another wireless message confirming the earlier reports that the Titanic was not only afloat but that the liner's engines were also working.

At this time the local agents were not aware whether the Virginian was with the Titanic, but they believed that she was standing by, and that possibly the women and children might have already been transferred. – Exchange Telegraph.

LLOYD'S MESSAGE
According to a Lloyd's telegram, the signal station at Cape Race cabled yesterday as follows:

"10.25 p.m. yesterday (Sunday) the Titanic reports by wireless that she has struck an iceberg, and calls for immediate assistance. At 11 p.m. she was reported sinking by head. Women being put off in boats. Gave her position as 41.46 N., 50.14 W.

"Steamers Baltic, Olympic, and Virginian are all making towards the scene of the disaster. The latter was the last to hear the Titanic's signals. At 12.27 a.m. to-day (Monday) she reported them, then blurred and ending abruptly. It is believed that the Virginian will be the first ship to reach the Titanic."

WONDER OF WIRELESS
Thanks to the wonderful modern invention of wireless telegraphy, which ten years ago was unknown, the Titanic was able to flash messages over the ocean asking for aid.

The wireless signal for "assistance wanted" is now "S.O.S.," the more familiar letters, "C.Q.D.," having been abandoned because they led to confusion with other code signals.

As a result of these "S.O.S." messages, five ships went to the assistance of the Titanic – the Baltic and the Olympic, of the White Star Line; the Virginian and the Parisian, of the Allan Line, and the Cunarder, Carpathia. The two last named took off boat-loads of passengers.

Thus the passengers of the Titanic owe their safety to the invention of wireless, to the wondrous discovery of which it is due that every large liner is now in communication with any liner or battleship within hundreds of miles.

On the high seas in these days one has only, as it were, to touch a button to give the alarm and immediately there is a general rush to aid. The ocean, it may almost be said, is as well guarded as London by her fire brigade.

Every wireless operator on every ship has his ear glued eternally to the receiver, waiting for messages from the vasty deep. Suddenly taps out . . ., – – –, . . . , S.O.S.. It spells out HELP. He is all alert to locate the sender of the message, and then the rush across the ocean on the errand of deliverance.

A marvellous picture this of man's battle with the weapons of science against the cruel forces of elemental nature.

ANXIOUS WIVES OF THE CREW

The majority of the 900 men forming the Titanic's crew are either natives of Southampton or are domiciled at that port.

The first half-pay notes given to the wives or dependents of the members of the Titanic's crew became payable yesterday, and after receiving their money women gathered in small groups at the Southampton dock gates, many of them with babies in their arms, and anxiously discussed the latest news respecting the liner.

AT LEAST £150,000 LOSS

A rate of fifty guineas per cent, was quoted by underwriters yesterday for business in reference to the Titanic.

One prominent City underwriter said that even if the vessel made port her owners would have to face a loss of at least £150,000.

In the event of total loss it would be a very serious matter for the owners. For insurance purposes her hull was valued at a million.

LINERS IN PERIL

New York, April 15 – From reports received from various sources it is certain that a great ice-field with many bergs has been obstructing the west-bound transatlantic sea lane off the Newfoundland Grand Bank for the past week.

Ships captains estimate its length at seventeen miles, with a breadth of some thirty-five.

The Cunard liner Carmania arrived, here yesterday from Adriatic and Mediterranean ports, and reports having run through the pack on Thursday afternoon. She sustained no actual damage, although she was in grave danger for a time.

The passengers say that they sighted twenty-five icebergs, one cluster; indeed, no farther than 100 feet away. The liner had to feel her way through an ice lane for hours.

The French liner Niagara did not escape unscathed. She was holed twice beneath the water-line, and had some of her plates buckled.

At a given moment a wireless telegram was sent from her to the Carmania for assistance, but later the captain decided that he was able to navigate his ship to port without help, having temporarily repaired the damage to the Niagara's hull.

The steamers Kura, Lord Cromer and Armenian, which arrived here during the last few days, also report having had dangerous experiences and baring sustained more or less damage by the ice.

It is known also that at least one full-rigged ship and one fishing smack are imprisoned in the floes. – Reuter's Special Service.

PHENOMENAL QUANTITY OF ICE
(FROM OUR OWN CORRESPONDENT)

Liverpool, April 15 – The Canadian Pacific liner Empress of Britain, which arrived at Liverpool from Halifax yesterday, reports the presence of an immense quantity of ice in the Atlantic.

Last Tuesday, when three days out from Halifax, she encountered an ice field 100 miles in extent, with enormous bergs, and steered a wide course, which delayed the vessel.

The Empress of Britain had previously received a wireless message from the Allan liner Virginian warning her of the presence of ice. The extent of the ice was regarded as phenomenal.

"On our way home," said Captain Murray, of the Empress of Britain, to me, "we met a very large piece of ice, which was interspersed with huge bergs. It was a solid piece of ice, and we had to run about seventy miles south to get clear of it. We were north of the position where the Titanic struck the iceberg.

"The current which ran along the coast to Newfoundland carried the ice south, and it is probably a part of this field of ice I met with that has carried on to the New York track."

In fact, the ice pack or berg which the Titanic has run into is thought to be that met and left behind by the Empress of Britain.

ANOTHER LEVIATHAN BUILDING

The accident to the Titanic calls attention to another great ship for the White Star Line, the keel of which was laid during the past week in Messrs. Harland and Wolff's Belfast yards.

This vessel, which will be named the Gigantic, will be 924ft. long, 94ft. broad, and of nearly 54,000 tons gross register, and will thus be considerably larger than any other vessel.

MENACE TO NAVIGATION

Of all the perils of the deep the peril of the iceberg is one of the must dreaded.

Just at present, when the ice is beginning to break up in the Arctic and come South, the icebergs are a great menace to navigation in the North Atlantic.

Bringing with them their own Arctic temperature and meeting

the warm air and water of the Gulf Stream, they tend to produce dense fogs in their vicinity. Thus a ship may blunder unsuspectingly upon them. They are frequently of vast size – veritable islands – on which a ship, even of such enormous proportions as the Titanic, would crumple like paper.

Only one-eighth of the berg is above water; the rest is submerged. And when it is remembered that bergs miles in length and with peaks many hundred feet above water have been seen, the terrible danger of these floating, unsuspected islands becomes very real.

In 1903 twenty steamers met with bad accidents near the Banks, and two were totally lost.

16 April **1912**

LINER THAT COST £1,500,000
Titanic's Two Miles of Walks and Beds of Roses on Board.

MAPS FOR PASSENGERS
To be a passenger on the Titanic is to be a resident in a luxurious town of over 3,000 inhabitants.

Life on board is life timed and arranged always with a view to comfort. Indeed, the passenger is almost safer when caressing the Atlantic than in crossing a busy London thoroughfare. Built by Messrs. Harland and Wolff, the Titanic was launched at Belfast on May 31 last year. She cost £1,500,000. It was only on Wednesday last that she left Southampton on her maiden voyage to New York. The departure of the Titanic was perhaps somewhat ill-omened.

HAWSERS SNAPPED
When leaving Southampton Water the suction from the big liner caused the hawsers holding the liner New York to the quayside to snap.

Immediately, the stern of the New York began to drift towards the Titanic and a collision seemed inevitable.

The Titanic's engines were stopped and her three tugs cast off and went to the assistance of the New York. Fortunately they were able to secure her to the quay again, but at one time only fifteen feet separated the two vessels.

With a cross tonnage of 46,382 tons, the Titanic is over 1,000 tons more than her sister ship the Olympic. She is over 882ft. long, 92ft. 6in. broad, and 73ft. from the keel to the top of the deck bridge.

◗ The Titanic and New York almost collide.

TWO-MILE WALK ON BOARD
There are ten decks, and so complicated are the numerous passages, saloons and stairways that the passengers are provided with special guide maps in their staterooms to show them the way about.

One can go for a two-mile walk on the Titanic without going over the same point twice. Before sailing all the stewards of the liner had to be instructed in the geography of the giant ship, in order to learn the shortest route to various parts of the ship.

Like a smart seaside resort, the Titanic – infinitely more commodious than a hotel – provides every luxury a wealthy pleasure-loving public can wish. A fully-equipped Turkish bath, squash racquet court, swimming bath, gymnasium, ballroom, and skating-rink are some of these. Glass enclosed "sun parlours" are one of the most delightful innovations on the Titanic. Those who wish to take their meals on deck may visit the verandah café, made to represent those on the Riviera.

SHIP'S MENU
The lighting of one of the first-class dining saloons is so arranged that the room appears to be bathed in sunshine, a warm sunset light shining through the windows.

With accommodation for 2,500 passengers and crew, the catering of the Titanic is a colossal business.

Some of the stores which the Titanic took on board at Southampton were:

Fresh meat	73,000lb.
Fresh fish	11,000lb.
Fresh butter	5,000lb.
Sausages	2,500lb.
Eggs	40,000.
Sugar	10,000lb.
Potatoes	40 tons.

21,000 DISHES AND PLATES

There are, for instance, 21,000 dishes and plates, while the silver and cutlery run into several tons in weight.

Over 600 passengers can be accommodated

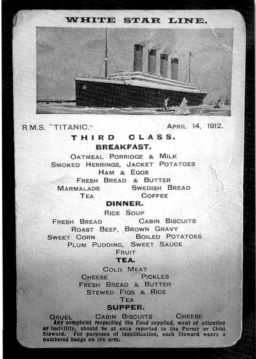

WHITE STAR LINE.

R.M.S. "TITANIC." APRIL 14, 1912.

THIRD CLASS.

BREAKFAST.
Oatmeal Porridge & Milk
Smoked Herrings, Jacket Potatoes
Ham & Eggs
Fresh Bread & Butter
Marmalade   Swedish Bread
Tea   Coffee

DINNER.
Rice Soup
Fresh Bread   Cabin Biscuits
Roast Beef, Brown Gravy
Sweet Corn   Boiled Potatoes
Plum Pudding, Sweet Sauce
Fruit

TEA.
Cold Meat
Cheese   Pickles
Fresh Bread & Butter
Stewed Figs & Rice
Tea

SUPPER.
Gruel   Cabin Biscuits   Cheese

Any complaint respecting the Food supplied, want of attention or incivility, should be at once reported to the Purser or Chief Steward. For purposes of Identification, each Steward wears a numbered badge on the arm.

at a time in the first-class dining saloon.

The Titanic is propelled by three screws driven by two sets of reciprocating engines of 30,000 horse power and a low-pressure turbine engine of 16,000 horse power.

Steam power is provided, by twenty-nine boilers, which are fed by 159 furnaces. The boilers are over 15ft. in diameter. Each engine crank-shaft weighs 118 tons.

Each of the four funnels if placed horizontally would hold a dinner party of fifty people. The height of the funnels above the boat-deck is 81ft. 6in.

STAIRCASE INSIDE FUNNEL

From the top of funnel to the keel is 175ft. – almost as high as the Monument. One of the funnels, which is not at present used, may be climbed from the inside by an iron staircase which runs to the top of the structure.

These four elliptical funnels are each wide enough to allow two "Tube" trains to pass through and still leave room to spare. The most expensive passage that can be booked on the Titanic costs £870 in the height of the season. For this two bedrooms, wardrobe-rooms, sitting-room, private bathroom, servant's room and a private promenade deck can be obtained.

The lowest booking for a first-class passage is £25 without meats, while the cheapest passage on the Titanic is £7 15s. – the third-class fare which includes meals.

Expert gardeners have even been engaged to plant out beds of roses and carnations in some parts of the vessel.

UNLUCKY CAPTAIN

Titanic's Commander in Command of Olympic at time of Collision.

In command of the Titanic on her disastrous maiden voyage is Captain Edward John Smith, who has been a commander on the White Star Line for five-and-twenty years. It is an unhappy coincidence that Captain Smith was in command of the Olympic last September on the occasion of her collision in the Solent with the cruiser Hawke.

In his evidence before the Admiralty Court he stated that he took charge of the Olympic on her first voyage last June, having formerly commanded the same company's liner the Adriatic.

At the time of the collision the Olympic was in charge of a duly-licensed Trinity House pilot, and the judgment of the Court was that the collision was due to the Olympic's pilot. Captain Smith, a Staffordshire man, born sixty years ago, is one of the best known and most popular shipmasters on the North Atlantic route.

TWO GREATEST LINERS' PERIL

Twice within eight months the two most colossal vessels that the world has ever seen have met with disaster. It is as though Nature grudged man his triumph over the nation-sundering ocean and revenged herself upon his puny presumption.

Last year it was the Olympic whose mass of 45,000 tons collided with a warship that clave a hole in her side.

Yesterday it was the Titanic, mightier still in weight, yet for all her mammoth proportions a mere tub in the face of the overwhelming ice-mountain of the Atlantic. So disaster crashed upon her, threatening 3,000 lives and the destruction in one blow of a floating township valued in gold at over 2¼ millions.

But the inventions of man proved mightier than the brute force of the inanimate elements. The unsinkable ship built by all the resources of centuries of science withstood the shock, messages carried by the harnessed waves of the air brought speedy help, and every life, it seems, was saved, and the ship herself proceeded unaided to port.

IRISH PRIDE IN THE TITANIC
(FROM OUR OWN CORRESPONDENT)

Belfast, April 15 – Nowhere has the news of the disaster to the Titanic been received with greater regret than in Belfast, the birthplace of the world's mightiest ship.

Every stage of her construction, as in the case of her predecessor, the Olympic, was followed with the keenest interest and local pride.

Her launching was the occasion of a general holiday, and, while undergoing her final preparations for sea, she was daily inspected by hundreds, and on Sundays by thousands, of admiring visitors.

The Titanic sailed from Belfast for Southampton on Tuesday, April 2, her departure, which had been fixed for the previous day, having been delayed by the violence of the weather. This incident at the outset of her career was regarded by many as being ominous, especially having in memory the adventurous experiences of the sister ship Olympic.

However, Tuesday, morning, was fine, and in brilliant sunshine the great liner cast off her moorings at the new deep water wharf, and she steamed away a stately and resplendent maritime figure after the half-dozen tugs which brought her down Belfast Lough had performed their task.

Having had her compasses adjusted and gone through a series of trials to the completest satisfaction of the officials concerned, the giant vessel left the Lough at 9 p.m. on Tuesday night and safely berthed in Southampton at 11 p.m. on the following night, having made a splendid run, which augured well for her maiden voyage.

So far as can be traced by inquiries amongst Belfast shipping agents there have been only two direct bookings from Belfast by the Titanic, the passengers being a visitor from America, named Mr. Wyckoff Vanderholt and a young Belfast electrical engineer, named Ervine.

To no one will the news come with a greater shock than to Lord Pirrie, slowly recovering from a severe operation. When the Titanic was launched he remarked that she would be his last and supreme effort in marine architecture.

SHIP THAT IS "UNSINKABLE"

Though she smashed into an iceberg, a collision that would have meant the foundering of any liner a few years ago, the Titanic still

Mr. Benj. Guggenheim.   Miss Gladys Cherry.   Major A. Peuchen.   Miss Esther Bowen.   Mr. W. T. Stead.

floats. She is indeed practically unsinkable.

The increase in a modern liner's size is accompanied by greater steadiness, better behaviour and greater safety. All the beams, girders, and stanchions in the Titanic's framework were specially forged and constructed, the deck and shell-plating were of the heaviest calibre, so as to make the hull a monument of strength.

The Titanic's transverse bulkheads number fifteen, extending from the double bottom to the upper deck at the forward end, and to the saloon deck at the after end, in both instances far above the load water-line. The builders state that any two of these compartments might be flooded without in any way involving the safety of the ship.

INSURED FOR £1,000,000

The Titanic is insured at Lloyd's for £1,000,000, which of course does not include any valuables or specifics that she may have been carrying at the time of the accident.

1,455 PASSENGERS ON BOARD

A Few of Those on the Titanic Worth £50,000,000.

SOME WELL-KNOWN NAMES

The number of passengers on board the Titanic when she left Queenstown on her voyage, including the Cherbourg passengers, was, says Reuter:–

First class	350
Second class	305
Steerage	800
Crew	903
Total	2,358

The total mail on board was 3,418 sacks. At Cherbourg 142 first-class, thirty second-class and about eighty third-class passengers were embarked.

Among the passengers on board were Colonel and Mrs. J. J. Astor, Major A. W. Butt, President Taft's aide-de-camp; Mr. B. Guggenheim, of the well-known banking firm; Mr. C. M. Hays, president of the Grand Trunk Railway; Mrs. Hays and Miss Hays, Mr. J. Bruce Ismay, chairman of the White Star Line; Countess of Rothes, Mr. W. T. Stead, Mr. Clarence Moore, Mr. Isidor Straus, Mr. George D. Widener and Mr. W. Roebling.

A list sent out by a London news agency includes Lord Ashburton, his Excellency Manuel de Lizardi, the Hon. and Mrs. L. Grove Johnson, Mr. Gustave Scholle, secretary of the United States Legation, and Mr. W. K. Vanderbilt, jun.

The Countess of Rothes was on her way to America to meet the Earl of Rothes.

Many of the first-class passengers were well-known American multi-millionaires, who were returning to the States after a holiday stay in this country.

REPRESENT £50,000,000

"At a moderate estimate," a prominent American resident in London told *The Daily Mirror* yesterday, "the passengers represent a wealth of at least £50,000,000. Two of them alone are worth £20,000,000!"

Forthwith this gentleman compiled the following table showing the wealth of a few of the passengers:–

Colonel J. J. Astor	£10,000,000
Mr. G. D. Widener	£10,000,000
Mr. Isidor Straus	£4,000,000
Mr. Benjamin Guggenheim	£2,000,000

Mr Isidor Straus.   Mrs Cavendish.   Mr. Clarence Moore.   Major A. W. Butt.   Mr. Charles M. Hays.

Mr. Charles M. Hays	£1,500,000
Mr. William Dulles	£1,000,000
Mr. Elmer Taylor	£1,000,000
Mr. Frederick M. Hoyt	£1,000,000
Mr. Clarence Moore	£1,000,000

In addition to these nine passengers representing between them over £30,000,060, there are several others who, if not actually millionaires, are extremely wealthy, and would easily approximate another £20,000,000.

There was also a vast quantity of precious jewellery and art treasures belonging to the passengers stored in the strong room of the ship.

When a wealthy American and his wife visit Europe they always return with magnificent gems bought in Paris or London, and the total value of these would certainly run into seven figures.

MEMORABLE WEDDING

Mr. G. D. Widener, who is the son of the millionaire who purchased the famous Rembrandt picture "The Mill," from Lord Lansdowne for £100,000 last May, had a large number of works of art on board, including a superb a piece of Sevres china which he had purchased in London for a considerable sum.

Colonel Astor figured in a divorce suit brought by his first wife in New York two and a half years ago.

Last year he married again, his bride being Miss Madeleine Talmage Force, a beautiful young girl. The wedding created a furore of anger, resentment and indignation. One of the chief objections being that the bridegroom was forty-seven and the bride not twenty years old.

Mr. Isidor Straus, who is a member of Congress, is partner in the great firm of R. H. May, of New York, while Mr. Guggenheim belongs to an American banking house.

Of the other millionaires Mr. Clarence Moore is a famous owner of steeplechase horses, of Washington; Mr. William Dulles is a private gentleman of Philadelphia. Mr. Taussig is a New York business magnate; and Mr. Frederick M. Hoyt is of the "New York Four Hundred."

One of the wealthy English passengers is Mr. J. Bruce Ismay, head of the White Star Line, and one of the best known shipowners in the country.

He has a beautiful estate and mansion in Dorsetshire, which is valued at £150,000.

MR. STEAD'S MISSION

Mr. W. T. Stead, the editor of the "Review of Reviews", was on his

Colonel J. J. and Mrs. Astor.

The Countess of Rothes.

Mr. Bruce Ismay.

Lord Ashburton.

way to attend the convention which to close the "Man and Religion Forward Movement," which has been operating in America for some months with the object, of inducing business men to take an active part in religious movements.

Of the other passengers, Lord Ashburton is a member of the family of Baring. He married, a few years ago, Miss Frances Donelly, an American actress.

Mr. J. B. Thayer is president of the Pennsylvania Railroad,

Mr. Washington Roebling is the millionaire president and director of John A. Roebling's Sons Co., iron and steel wire and wire-rope manufacturers. He it was who directed the construction of Brooklyn Bridge.

16 April 1912

ONE TOUCH OF NATURE

Draughtsmen, expert in floating architecture, sat in their drawing offices and prepared designs for the new great palace of the seas, that was to carry restless comfort-loving people from one world to another. An exquisite little model of the palace was made in wood, with the innumerable plates and rivets marked thereon, from which model, again, a score of detailed plans were made showing each section enlarged. All this employed the well-paid work of scores of clever people: but all this was but a prelude to the real thing.

The real thing, after this relatively abstract preparation, was the concrete battle with resistant matter. Work of the disciplined hand was to follow labour of directing mind.

At once, with formidable din of ringing blow, you may imagine the workshops in the shipyard beginning to hammer upon the hints provided. An army of workmen, a colony of workshops, a population supported upon this! Frames and plates for the gigantic vessel's sides, plates for the keel which must be "sighted" till its evenness is perfect, riveting of steel-frame ribs, staying by cross-girders, a slow building up of the sides of the sea-monster. You see, then, a mighty scaffolding erected by regiments of carefully divided men, each section of them mastering each piece, as the unearthly forest of pine poles rears itself along the length of the building berth. Meanwhile, more men labouring with trained minds and obedient bodies, hour by hour, week by week, proceed with the making of the bulkhead divisions, the deck plates, the deck structures, each in its careful order and situation. Huge hydraulic gantries with electric power assist in the riveting and flattening. Thousands of pounds of electric power, thousands of pounds for the men employed (between three and four thousand of these), thousands of pounds in valuable matter expended, two years or so of unceasing toil in the slow creation of a vessel of many thousand tons – it all amounts at the end to something like a million and a half in money; if, for the moment, you consider money as representative of worth.

And then the launching – the huge building slips, the floating crane, with its enormous pillars, the sense of wonder and triumph on that breezy day with a high tide when the Leviathan leaves workshop to receive her final touches – the bowels of her Vulcanic heat, followed by the dry dock finishings. Next – the inauguration, the proud display of her perfection. Now all is ready and the combined skill, the converging effort of an army o f human beings, has resulted at last in this comfortable sea-home for those who buy their passages in it. A permanent population is appointed to live here, with the changing passengers ready to begin the voyage….

There is much in that warning of the philosophers about the grain of sand mightily influential as obstacle in the way of mechanism; or in their thoughts of human endeavour wrecked, by some little kink in the brain, some mote in the eye, some stone falling by chance, so that the very philosopher himself, who was to

The Daily Mirror

THE MORNING JOURNAL WITH THE SECOND LARGEST NET SALE.

No. 2,646.   Registered at the G.P.O. as a Newspaper.   April 17, 1912   One Halfpenny.

PASSENGERS BOARDING THE TITANIC AT QUEENSTOWN AND SOME OF THE VICTIMS AND SURVIVORS OF HISTORY'S MOST TERRIBLE SHIPWRECK.

Chief Purser McElroy (clean-shaven) and Dr. W. F. N. O'Loughlin, the chief ship's surgeon. Both are missing.   Mr. K. H. Behr, the famous tennis player, saved.   Sir Cosmo Duff-Gordon, Bart., and his wife, who is better known as "Lucile." Both of them are reported saved.

Embarking on the Titanic at Queenstown last Thursday. This was the last port at which the ill-starred vessel called.

Mr. Daniel Marvin, reported missing, and his bride, who is saved. They were on a wedding trip.   Mr. Head (missing), a prominent member of Lloyd's.   Colonel J. J. and Mrs. Astor, returning from their honeymoon. She is saved, but his body has been picked up dead.

Queenstown was the last port at which the ill-fated Titanic called. She sailed on Thursday with the good wishes of everyone, only to founder less than a week afterwards. Two young brides, Mrs. J. J. Astor, the wife of the millionaire, and Mrs.   Daniel Marvin, who had been spending their honeymoon in Europe, have been widowed by the disaster. Mr. Christopher Head was formerly Mayor of Chelsea.—(Daily Mirror, Dover-street Studios, and Russell.)

shatter worlds by his speculation, now lies ashes and nothingness. For Nature, in her careless manner, steps in and makes, the time and the labour, the constant effort of the many intelligences, void and helpless before a piece of herself, a futile iceberg, left floating in the monster's way. In one second, by a mere touch of this Nature, our stepmother, the striving of an army of men is turned to mockery. The Titanic has met an iceberg on her maiden voyage overseas.

17 April 1912

ONLY 868 ALIVE OF 2,200 ON SUNKEN LINER TITANIC

Greatest Ship Ever Built Lies in Two Miles of Ocean.

DEATH TOLL OF 1,300
No Hope Left of Any Boatloads Being Picked Up.

WIDOWS AND ORPHANS

Further news of the appalling disaster to the Titanic, the greatest ship that man has ever built, only adds fresh horrors.

It appears to be now established that 1,300 souls went to their deaths in mid-Atlantic with the sinking of the liner.

The Cunard steamer Carpathia is steaming through fields of ice to New York, with 868 survivors on board a tragic freight of widowed wives and fatherless children.

All hope is now abandoned that any other of the Titanic's 2,200 still lives. The Virginian and Parisian now report that they have picked up no one, and icy cold weather must have been fatal long since.

The mightiest of all craft that man, aided by all the resources of centuries of human knowledge, launched forth but a week since on her maiden voyage now lies irrecoverable, in two miles of all-devouring ocean, having met a mountain of ice in her passage from land to land.

Nothing now remains of that proud triumph of marine architecture save masses of wreckage adrift among swirling ice floes.

It is good to know that the women and children were first to leave the doomed vessel. The best traditions of the sea were observed, as the Prime Minister feelingly observed in the House of Commons yesterday.

SHIP OF SURVIVORS

The latest and most direct news of the survivors of the terrible disaster comes from the captain at the Cunarder Carpathia, via New York. It runs as follows:–

Captain Rostron, of the Carpathia, in a wireless message to the Cunard Company here, sent from 41.45 N. by 52.20 W. says:–

I am proceeding to New York, unless otherwise ordered, with about 800 survivors.

After having consulted Mr. Bruce Ismay (chairman of the White Star Line) considering the circumstances and with so much ice about I considered New York the best port to make for.

There is a large number of icebergs and near us a twenty miles field with bergs amongst it.

More definite figures are contained in an official statement from New York by Reuter saying:–

The White Star Line announce officially that they have received positive news that the number of survivors from the Titanic is 868.

The dispatch was transmitted by the Olympic.

ALL HOPE ABANDONED

St. John's (Newfoundland), April 16. The latest available advices from Cape Rice indicate that only the people on board the Carpathia were saved from the Titanic.

The messages say that all the boats launched are accounted for, and that they were mostly filled with women and children… From this it is inferred that most of the men on board the ship went down with her.

All hope of any passengers or members of the crew of the Titanic other than those on board the Carpathia being alive has now been abandoned.

This afternoon all the steamers which had been cruising in the vicinity of the disaster continued their voyages. – Reuter.

Montreal, April 16, 11 a.m. – The weather station on the Gulf of St. Lawrence reports that heavy fogs are lying off Nova Scotia.

A heavy thunderstorm broke in the neighbourhood last night and is travelling eastward.

Such conditions, it is pointed out, leave little hope of the rescue of any Titanic survivors who may still by adrift on rafts and in boats. – Reuter.

⬧ Survivors approaching the Carpathia.

IN OPEN BOATS AMID ICE FLOES

New York, April 16 – The Carpathia is now making for New York with the 868 survivors, who alone can tell the tale of the midnight plunge into the angry whirlpool of ice, wreckage and drowning men with which the great ship went to her burial.

They alone can relate the bitter experiences of the wintry night spent in open boats on a lonely sea, of the waiting for morning and of the hope of rescue.

The wireless messages have told how in the darkness their crews had to guide the boats with the greatest caution to prevent their being jammed in the ice or overturned by the swirling floes, so that the heavily laden craft became widely separated from each other.

There followed hours of heart-breaking anguish before daylight came – and the Carpathia.

The Carpathia proceeded cautiously, sounding her fog-whistle almost continuously, until one after another she picked up the scattered lifeboats.

The White Star agents learned to-day from the Oceanic that all the Titanic's boats have been accounted for.

This, together with the abandonment of the long-cherished idea that the Virginian or Parisian might have picked up some additional survivors, has dispelled most of the hopes that the number of those saved may be increased beyond the pitiful 868. – Reuter's Special.

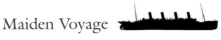

WHITE MAN'S LAW

"Women and children. First." The eternal rule of chivalry, the White Man's law, was in force upon the doomed Titanic – this fact stands out already in the meagre news that has reached land concerning the happenings of that awful night.

It is the one touch of light that relieves the black tragedy that carried 1,300 men to their death.

The list of the saved (says Reuter) is mainly composed of women, though several men's names appear upon it.

A Marconi message received from the Olympic at the White Star Line's offices reports that of the passengers saved nearly all were women and children.

Another report gives the following figures concerning 315 survivors on board the Carpathia:–

	Women	Children	Men
Saloon	132	6	63
Second class	88	10	16

This shows a proportion of three women and children to every man – an indication that order and discipline prevailed on the ship of death to the last.

Of the remaining 500 odd survivors it is evident that the great majority were women and children.

Mr. Parton, the White Star Line's London manager, said: "What discipline must have been maintained! The fact that nearly all saved were women and children shows that."

DUE NEW YORK TO-MORROW

New York, April 16 – According to a wireless message received by the Customs, the Carpathia will arrive on Thursday afternoon.

The Treasury officials at Washington have directed that the Customs regulations shall be waived in order to facilitate the landing of everybody. – Reuter.

Another telegram states that the Carpathia is not due at New York until to-morrow evening or Friday morning.

The scene of the collision was in round figures 1,000 miles due east from New York and 680 miles south-east from Halifax (Nova Scotia).

Washington, April 16 – At the direction of President Taft the Secretary for the Navy has ordered the fast scout cruiser Salem to proceed to sea immediately from Hampton Roads to meet the Carpathia.

The Salem is equipped with the best wireless apparatus with a range of 1,000 miles, and will obtain a complete list of survivors and send the names by wireless telegraphy to the Government here. – Reuter.

NO SURVIVORS ON PARISIAN

Halifax, April 16 – Captain Haines, of the Allan liner Parisian, sent a wireless report to-night stating that no survivors of the Titanic were on board, and that he had no information as to the fate of the missing passengers. – Exchange Telegraph.

A telegram from Montreal states that the Allan Line has issued the following communication:

We are in receipt of a Marconigram, via Cape Race, from Captain Gambell, of the Virginian, stating that he arrived on the scene of the disaster too late to be of service, and is proceeding on his voyage to Liverpool.

No mention is made of the rescue of any of the Titanic's passengers. – Reuter.

TWO MILES UNDER THE SEA

The company's officials in New York hold out no hope that any passengers have been saved other than those on board the Carpathia.

All along the coast the wireless instruments were attuned, and the operators sat at their instruments throughout the night, endeavouring to catch the flash of the rescue ship.

The Halifax Government expert states that the Titanic lies in two miles of water between Sable Island and Cape Race. – Reuter's Special.

POWER OF AN ICEBERG
(FROM OUR OWN CORRESPONDENT)

New York, April 16. Only one thing is talked about here wherever one goes the disaster to the Titanic has overwhelmed everybody.

Theories as to the precise cause of the final crash are freely canvassed. Mr. Lewis Nixon, the eminent naval architect, gives it as his opinion that the liner struck a "growler" or submerged iceberg.

"It would be as hard as rock," he explained, "and something had to give way. As the iceberg did not, the great ship had to crumble.

"It is conceivable that the impact had such tremendous force as to buckle the longitudinal plates from end to end, shearing off or starting rivets, and thus opening the watertight compartments throughout the length of the vessel."

Another theory, generally scouted, is that the bulkheads for some inexplicable reason failed to act.

Shaken and dazed by the immensity of the disaster, Mr. Franklin, the vice-president of the International Mercantile Marine, answered questions throughout the day.

Yesterday he repeatedly asserted his conviction that the Titanic was unsinkable. To-day he is abused and accused. He denies most strenuously that the White Star officials kept the news of the unparalleled loss of life secret for many hours.

Mr. Franklin says that 202 of the 325 first-class passengers of the Titanic and 114 out of the 285 second-class passengers have been accounted for.

THE KING'S MESSAGE

The King has telegraphed to the White Star Line as follows:–

The Queen and I are horrified at the appalling disaster which has happened to the Titanic and at the terrible loss of life.

We deeply sympathise with the bereaved relatives, and feel for them in their great sorrow with all our hearts. GEORGE R. I.

Queen Alexandra telegraphed:–

It is with feelings of the deepest sorrow that I hear of the terrible disaster to the Titanic, and of the awful loss of life.

My heart is full of grief and sympathy for the bereaved families who have perished.

Messages of sympathy have been received by the White Star Line from the German Emperor, Prince Henry of Prussia, the President of the Board of Trade, the Postmaster-General and Lord Derby.

◗ King George V and Queen Mary.

FRENCH LINER'S S.O.S. CALL

New York, April 16 – The French liner Niagara, on arriving here to-day, reported that on Wednesday night she was approximately in the vicinity where the Titanic sank.

She ran into a field of ice and was so badly bumped that her commander sent out the wireless call, S.O.S.

A thick mist prevailed at the time. The ship was running at reduced speed, and had been brushing against small ice floes for some time when there came a severe shock.

Those sitting at dinner at the time were thrown from their seats to the floor, dishes and glassware were scattered over the saloons and stewards were thrown down.

The scared passengers rushed on to the decks in swarms.

The captain made an inspection, and subsequently sent out a second wireless message saying he could proceed to New York under his own power. – Reuter.

ICE ABNORMALLY FAR SOUTH

Halifax (N.S.), April 16 – Captain Farquhar, a veteran navigator, who has, just returned from Northern seal fishery, thinks that the present season has been an exceptional one.

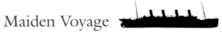

Not only were there immense quantities of heavy ice, but the ice had been unusually continuous, and heavy gales had driven the ice many miles south and beyond the ordinary ice limit.

The most experienced men in navigation had been completely thrown off their guard, not expecting to meet ice so far south, during this season of the year. – Exchange Telegraph.

The liner Canada, from Portland (Maine) arrived at Liverpool yesterday, and reported that on April 10 she passed ten miles of heavy, broken and an open field of ice, and also several large bergs in the region of the sinking of the Titanic.

WARNED THE TITANIC OF ICE DANGER
(FROM OUR OWN CORRESPONDENT)

Paris, April 16 *La Presse* publishes a telegram from Havre stating that the liner Touraine, which has arrived at that port, entered an ice field last Wednesday night just after midnight.

In order to lessen the shock from the ice the Touraine's speed was reduced to a little over twelve knots. The ice was lying very low in the water. The same day two icebergs were observed.

The Touraine was in communication with the Titanic from the afternoon of Friday, April 12, until about nine o'clock in the evening, and her captain warned the Titanic of the position of the iceberg.

Captain Smith replied by wireless, thanking the captain of the Touraine for the information.

RESCUED ON BOARD THE CARPATHIA

Cunarder Steaming to New York Through Field of Ice.

NAMES OF SURVIVORS

Of the 2,100 to 2,200 souls on board the Titanic it seems only too terribly certain that but 868 have been saved.

This at any rate, according to Reuter, is the number of survivors given officially by the White Star Company in New York, and received by them in a wireless message from the Olympic.

These survivors are, so far as it is possible to ascertain aboard the Carpathia, for the White Star officials in New York hold out no hope that any passengers have been saved other than those on this vessel.

The list of missing or unaccounted for contains some notable names. Amongst them are those of Colonel J. J. Astor, the millionaire, who has only just returned from touring Egypt with his young bride; Mr. Guggenheim, another millionaire, and Mr. W. T. Stead, the famous journalist.

Anything like a correct estimate of the number originally on board is impossible at present. So far as it is possible to give actual numbers, the Titanic carried 325 first-class passengers, 285 second-class, and 710 third-class. The crew, in addition, numbered about 900.

The Cunard Company in New York, says Reuter, state that the Carpathia, with the survivors on board, is slowly steaming through the field of ice to New York. She is outside the wireless radius from land, and the Olympic has been relaying messages.

17 April **1912**

NOTABLE NAMES AMONG THE MISSING

Millionaires Who Perished When the Titanic Sank.

NO NEWS OF MR. STEAD

Daughter Fears That Her Father Is Not Among the Survivors.

ANXIOUS RELATIVES

CAPTAIN'S FATE

New York, April 16 – It is reported here that Captain Smith, who commanded the Titanic, is among those drowned. – Exchange.

DISTINGUISHED MEN MISSING

Halifax (N.S.), April 16 – Among the notable passengers still unaccounted for here are Colonel John Jacob Astor, Mr. Benjamin Guggenheim, Mr. Isidor Straus, Mr. George D. Widener, the son of the railway magnate; Mr. H. Markland Molsom, the Montreal banker; and Mr. W. T. Stead.

It is feared that all these passengers have been lost, and no mention is made of Mr. W. T. Stead in any list of survivors.

In spite of the definite reports of the loss of Colonel Astor, the members of his family apparently still have hope of his safety.

This afternoon the Canadian Pacific Railway were instructed to send a special train to Halifax in order to be in readiness to convey Colonel and Mrs. Astor to New York. However, the information received here leaves practically no doubt that Colonel Astor has perished. – Exchange.

In the course of an interview with a Press representative yesterday, Mr. Stead's daughter stated that no news whatever had been received of her father. She was afraid that he was not among the survivors reported to be on the Carpathia.

WHO'S WHO AMONG THE MISSING

The following are some biographical details of well-known passengers reported lost or missing:–

COLONEL J. J. ASTOR

Colonel John Jacob Astor, who is believed to have perished, was born on July 13, 1864, and he was the great-grandson of John Jacob Astor, who laid the foundation of the family fortune.

He travelled a great deal, and afterwards managed the family estates, for nearly all his vast fortune was invested in real estate, and he owned miles of houses and shops in New York. He built the Astoria Hotel, New York, adjoining that of his cousin, the Waldorf Hotel, which now form one building under the name of the Waldorf-Astoria Hotel, the Hotel St. Regis and the Knickerbocker Hotels.

His fortune is estimated at £30,000,000, and his residences in town and country are fitted with every conceivable luxury.

In September last he married Miss Madeleine Force, a beautiful eighteen-year-old girl, an alliance which created a great amount of interest and adverse criticism in America.

MAJOR ARCHIBALD W. BUTT

Aide-de-camp to President Taft. He had recently been in Italy, and had paid a visit to the Pope.

MR. JACQUES FUTRELLE

Well-known author and short story writer, has also had experience in American journalism and theatrical management.

MR. BENJAMIN GUGGENHEIM

A member of the famous Guggenheim family of capitalists, associates of Mr. Pierpont Morgan, and world famous in connection with Alaskan development and copper production.

MR. WASHINGTON AUGUSTUS ROEBLING

Head of the great wire cable firm of John A. Roebling's, Sons and Co., Trenton (N.J.). The entire construction of Brooklyn Bridge was left to him owing to the death of his father.

MR. W. T. STEAD

The well-known journalist and editor of the "Review of Reviews." Only a day before he sailed Mr. Stead wrote to *The Daily Mirror* about his daughter's performance in a play she was touring.

"It is her first venture of the kind," he said, "and naturally I want it to be a success."

MR. C. CLARENCE JONES

New York stockbroker, had been visiting European capitals in connection with the purchase of American Embassy sites.

MR. FRANK D. MILLET

An American painter, who resided for a long time in London.

MR. ISIDOR STRAUS

Was a member of the United States Congress from 1893-5; a partner in the firm of L. Straus and Sons, importers of pottery and glassware, New York.

MR. GEORGE D. WIDENER

The son of Mr. Peter A. Widener, a Philadelphia millionaire, who recently bought the famous picture, "The Mill," from the Marquis of Lansdowne.

MR. D. W. MARVIN

Mr. D. W. Marvin, who is missing, was the son of the head of one of the biggest cinematograph firms in the United States. He was returning with his bride after a three weeks' honeymoon in this country. When the couple left England they were so obviously happy that their friends described them as "a pair of children." Mrs. Marvin is among the saved.

Among the victims, it is feared, is Mr. Christopher Head, a prominent member of Lloyd's, who had himself undertaken a large share of the Titanic's insurance. He was a member of the firm of Henry Tread and Co.

OPERATOR'S COOLNESS

The parents of Mr. John George Phillips, the wireless operator on the Titanic, were bowed down yesterday with anxiety for their son's fate.

It now appears that the following telegram received by Mr. G. A. Phillips, of Godalming – "Titanic making slowly for Halifax. Practically unsinkable. Don't worry." – was not from his son.

Mr. Phillips states that he has now learnt that the telegram came from his brother in London, who had sent it to reassure him.

Mr. J. G. Phillips, whose age was twenty-five, was regarded by his superiors as one of the most efficient operators in the Marconi service.

He had control of the most powerful wireless set ever used at sea, and messages show that he remained nobly at his post and sent out messages with coolness and dispatch.

Mr. Harold Bride, the junior wireless operator of the Titanic, was only a little more than twenty-one years of age.

He lived with his parents at Shortlands, Kent, and so keen was he to become an expert operator that some two years ago he created a private wireless receiving station in his father's garden.

The House of Representatives at Washington yesterday unanimously passed a resolution extending its sympathy to the relatives of those who met their deaths in the Titanic disaster.

LORD PIRRIE NOT TOLD

Great Shipbuilder Too Weak To Be Informed of the Disaster.

Not even in the romantic history of Lord Pirrie, who once a poor orphan lad, became the greatest shipbuilder in the world, is there anything so extraordinary as the fact that if he is told the Titanic has sunk he may die.

As chief of the firm of Harland and Wolff, who built the Titanic, he is mainly responsible for its construction, if only for the reason that it was his brain more than anything that made the building of the Titanic possible.

The Titanic was the realisation of his ideal of shipbuilding, and now that the giant vessel has sunk his relatives are afraid of telling him of the catastrophe, because a recent operation performed at his mansion near Godalming has left him so weak that they are afraid the shock of the news would kill him.

He is lying in a room into which no newspaper is allowed to enter. But for the fact that an operation was found necessary he would have been one of the passengers on board the Titanic, for it was his invariable custom to take a personal triumph in the maiden voyages of the mammoth vessels which his shipyards at Belfast turned out.

The Titanic was his joy and his pride; it has sunk on its first voyage, while the great shipbuilder is on a sick-bed.

PREMIER'S SYMPATHY

The great tragedy of the sea cast a heavy shadow over the Commons yesterday.

A touching tribute to the "willing sacrifices" made for the women and children and to the loss sustained by the "nearest and dearest in their desolated homes" was made by the Prime Minister.

"I am afraid we must brace ourselves to confront one of those terrible events in the order of Providence which baffle foresight, which appal the imagination, and which make us feel the inadequacy of words to do justice to what we feel," said the Prime Minister, in a voice broken with emotion.

"We cannot do more at the moment than give a necessarily imperfect expression to our sense of admiration that the best traditions of the sea seem to have been observed in the willing sacrifices which were offered to give the first chance of safety to those who were least able to help themselves, and to the warm and heartfelt sympathy of the whole nation with those who find themselves suddenly bereft of their nearest and dearest in their desolated homes."

A long, low murmur of sympathy went up from both sides.

NO DEFINITE REASON

Mr. Norman Craig, K.C., M.P. for the Isle of Thanet, was perhaps the luckiest passenger who actually booked to travel by the Titanic. At the very last moment he decided, for no definite reason, not to make the journey.

When the first lists of those who were on board were published after the disaster the name of Mr. Craig was given as one of the victims.

But the famous K.C. was sale and sound, playing golf, and in entire ignorance of the anxiety he was causing his friends or of the terrible fate of the Titanic.

"I certainly booked my passage on the Titanic," Mr. Craig told *The Daily Mirror* yesterday, "and up to the day before I fully intended sailing. My intention was just to make the trip out on her for a blow of fresh air, and to return as quickly as possible on the Mauretania.

STILL LONGING FOR THE TRIP

"At the last moment I suddenly decided not to sail. I cannot tell you why; there was simply no reason for it. No; I had no mysterious premonitions, or visions of any kind. Nor did I dream of any disaster. But I do know that at practically the last moment I did not want to go.

"I was not absolutely decided about it then, for I found myself still hankering after the trip.

"Having finally decided, I cleared off into the country away from all news. It was not until I returned home on Monday evening that I heard anything of what had happened.

"I certainly did congratulate myself, but at the same time it was a shock to me, for I had arranged to go with friends – a husband and wife. They sailed, and I am afraid he is amongst the missing."

AMBASSADOR'S GOOD FORTUNE
(FROM OUR OWN CORRESPONDENT)

Paris, April 16 – Mr. Robert Bacon, the departing United States Ambassador, said to-day that he had intended to leave Cherbourg on the Titanic, but owing to the postponement of his final audience with the President of the Republic until to-day was obliged to change his plans.

"My wife, my daughters and myself," said the Ambassador, "have had a very happy escape, and to-day we received a large number of telegrams of congratulation on our good fortune."

DISASTER ANTICIPATED

An extraordinary story of a passenger's presentiment of the coming disaster to the Titanic was related yesterday to *The Daily Mirror* by a well-known solicitor.

"Barely a day before the Titanic, sailed," he said, "a wealthy business man came to me, and considerably surprised me by asking if I would consent to be a guardian to his two little boys. I naturally asked him what he meant, and he replied: –

"'To-morrow, I and my wife are sailing on the Titanic. I cannot tell you why, but I feel that something is going to happen, and that we shall never see our children again.

"'It is impossible to shake off this feeling. In these circumstances, it will afford me considerable relief if you will consent to act as guardian.

"'I haven't any doubt that all this sounds very absurd, and even my wife laughs at me, but I do not like sailing feeling that my boys are not left in anyone's care, supposing that something should happen.'

"Up to the present," concluded the solicitor, "neither his name, nor that of his wife, appear among the saved."

Two other apparently well authenticated cases of premonition of the disaster are related.

One man who sailed from Southampton, said to be a fireman named Coffey, having grave, indefinable misgivings, left the boat at Queenstown.

Another, a steward, is stated to have told his wife before his departure that he wished he had not signed on.

PASSENGERS' FEAR OF WRECK

The sinking of the Titanic, it is anticipated, will affect the booking of passages for some time to come.

"I should not be surprised if many people avoid travelling across the Atlantic at this time of year," said a representative of a well-known shipping agent's to *The Daily Mirror* yesterday.

"Although we have not slackened much in our Atlantic bookings to-day," said another agent, "probably we shall notice a big drop towards the end of the week. Only to-day someone who had booked a second-class passage previous to the wreck of the Titanic wanted it changed to a first-class booking, 'Because,' he said, 'if there is a wreck the first-class passengers will be taken off first.'"

17 April **1912**

THE TRUE ROMANCES

People who read many novels – hardened reviewers, for example, who spend much time in grappling with the eccentric excitement of "blood-curdling" romance are often heard to complain of the improbability, or the impossibility, of the events described in them. The book you have in your hand is "sensational." For many the epithet is synonymous with untrue. In face of such a calamity as this of the Titanic, one may well ask why Truth should not be sensational. For when Nature, or when real men and women, provide us with "sensations" they have a lugubrious manner of outdoing the romance-writers at their own game.

From comic to tragic, all along the scale, the extraordinary, the "impossible," the unreal quality in the life outside books rivals and outruns the carefully prepared surprises within them. Take a year's news, haphazard, from any year and see.

Suppose a girl without remarkable attractions were the heroine of a book. Imagine it in what Mr. Anstey called a "highly stimulating cover" with frontispiece in crude colours. The heroine is unattractive. Yet by a certain self-confidence the author asks us to assume she deceives clever men into lending her money, keeps creditors away, plots and plans for a life of comfort on nothing a year, finally gives it out that she has disappeared dead perhaps? – with all her liabilities. An impossible story? So unlike life? No, the story is true, the heroine was a real woman, the author was no human being. Who does not remember Miss Charlesworth?

Who does not remember Mme. Humbert's safe? The murder stories, secret, improbable, told in the newspapers every year – are they "like life"? Or must we blame the author of Nature for not keeping close enough to her ?

And now, tragically, in silence of two world's listening, bit by bit, leaks out the horror of a sea-disaster no novelist would dare to dream of. It would be too sensational, too unreal, for a book. Dare we make our protagonist a Captain hardened in sea-service, who suffers a great disaster with his ship, and then is given a second ship – the biggest on earth. And then, with half his floating population, all the wealth, all the hopes, all the calculations of business and provisions faithfully made in case of damage that can be repaired or even of grave disaster, with all these and what other sorrows and joys we shall never know of sinks sheer into the abyss with absolutely nothing to ripple the calm surface where a mountainous monster was! No, no, these novelists are absurd. Such romances as these pass all bounds of likelihood. These things don't happen. "People don't do these things." Shut up the silly book and throw it away.

Shut up your novel. Take up your paper. There is the news full in your face – ugly, unavoidable. With all its dream-like unreality, it is yet real. It is true. This unreal thing has happened! Fate and the Furies wrote the story you held incredible, which yet we must believe, against our hopes, as day by day brings terrible confirmation of it.

THIS MORNING'S GOSSIP

Social preoccupations are, for the moment, entirely in abeyance in view of the news that seems every hour more terrible from the scene of the Titanic disaster. Hundreds of people here in London had friends on board, and many of the Americans whose deaths are feared or reported were popular and well known in London society.

To the mass of English people, of course, the best known name on board is that of Mr. W. T. Stead. The famous journalist, much-hated and much-loved, himself a good friend and a good enemy, has hundreds of friends on both sides of the Atlantic. He was on his way to New York to attend one of the semi-religious, semi-moral conferences in which he was always deeply interested. News of Mr. Stead will be eagerly looked for hour by hour.

Mr. Stead's controversial vigour and outspokenness were always the delight of his admirers, and in America he had thousands of these. His appearance as critic, especially in any new sphere, has always been greeted with a storm of controversy, as there has never been any mincing of matters in the expression of his opinions. We may take his appearance, quite lately, as dramatic critic for an example.

It was only late in life that he entered a theatre, The subdued sarcasm, the gentle rebuke, of the hardened dramatic critic who cannot and must not say all that he thinks, were unknown to him. One of the first plays he saw was a light and airy musical play, not presumably taken too seriously by anyone else. It was Mr. Stead's way to take all things seriously. He at once boldly printed his opinion of the play in question. To him it was "a pestilent and pestiferous farrago of filth." That, one may easily see, caused more excitement than thirty of the ordinary milder criticisms, and that gives the measure of Mr. Stead's attitude towards the world.

Mr. P. A. Widener, of Philadelphia, another of the passengers on the Titanic, is known in London chiefly as the purchaser of "The Mill" Rembrandt's picture about which there was so much talk a little time ago. Mr. Widener has for long been a great traveller. His interest in art, though recent, was as enthusiastic as that of many another American millionaire. Already his collection of fine pictures is well known to the connoisseurs. It may be remembered that, some time ago, he purchased from Genoa certain celebrated Van

Dycks in defiance of the Italian law aimed against the exportation of such things.

These pictures belonged to a certain noble, but decaying, Genoese family, and it was considered quite probable by the authorities that they might be tempted to get rid of them. It was, therefore not altogether easy to do so, and the sale of the pictures was only effected at last by having them rolled off their frames and carried in harmless-looking bundles across the Italian frontier in a motor-car to Paris.

NO TIME FOR JOY BELLS

As I passed St. Paul's Cathedral this morning full of anxiety for the Titanic and the probable appalling loss of life, my ears were offended by a joyous peal of bells from one of the western towers.

Church bells have long been a nuisance. Surely in this instance they were something worse! – A Reader.

17 April **1912**

TEAR-STAINED WOMEN'S WAIT FOR GOOD TIDINGS

Harrowing Scenes at All the White Star Line Offices.

FRIENDS ON TITANIC

Pitiful Plight of Seven Southampton Children Left Parentless.

LONDON AND NEW YORK

Rejoicings in American City Stilled by News of Disaster.

Anxiety, poignant and almost unrelieved, held two continents in grip all yesterday waiting for tidings of the great ship which the sea had swallowed up.

At three great capitals–London, New York and Paris – agonised relatives of those on board the Titanic thronged the offices of the White Star Company for news from those they feared lost.

Southampton, whence hail most of the 800 or 900 members of the crew, was a town of mourning and desolation, and in Liverpool and Belfast, too, keenest anxiety was felt on behalf of sons or husbands or fathers who went out on the great ship.

OFFICE OF TRAGIC INQUIRY

In London the saddest places of all were the offices of the White Star Line Cockspur-street and Leadenhall-street.

Guarded by special constables, the offices were besieged all day by anxious relatives – sobbing women dressed in black seeking to learn the fate of their husbands, sons and loved ones.

It was a tragic scene, and as the heart-broken inquirers groped their way out of the doors the golden spring sunshine which flooded Trafalgar square only emphasised the contrast of life and death.

And it was the women who waited. For the only news of those saved was that stating that the majority are women and children. There was no news of the men – only silence.

All the shipping offices at Charing Cross and Cockspur-street had their flags flying at half-mast.

From an early hour people began to arrive in taxi cabs to seek the latest news.

"HOW CAN I WAIT?"

Patiently the officials searched the lists again and again, but too often their reply was: "His name is not here."

One athletic girl in a Harris tweed costume was a pathetic figure. The news dashed her hopes, but she was told there might be better news if she came back in an hour or an hour and a half:

"How can I wait all that time?" she asked in pitiful tones. "It's an eternity!" Nevertheless, she returned two hours later, and when the name which meant so much to her was not on the lists again her composure gave way and she left the office sobbing.

Many of the women could not make themselves leave the office. They stood at the desk thinking in a kind of stupefaction.

One elderly woman leant against the staircase for support, and as tears coursed down her cheeks repeated: "He was a passenger; he was a passenger."

It was harrowing to see these people, who had fathers, mothers, sisters, wives and brothers aboard the Titanic. Inside the offices there was an atmosphere of strained, dreadful calm; people avoided each other's eyes and spoke in whispers.

Trembling fingers ran down the lists, followed by a gasp of relief or a sigh of pain at the presence or absence of names so eagerly sought.

On the sea of faces around the board could be detected joy, hope, anxiety and despair.

STUPEFIED WITH GRIEF

One woman arrived with a handkerchief to her eyes. She was sobbing pitifully and could hardly control herself to speak to a sympathetic official.

Sitting on the seats were two young women waiting for news. They sat rigidly calm, holding each other's hands for mutual comfort. They seemed stupefied with grief and anxiety.

When the first list of names was published there was a stir of excitement amongst those who waited. None, however, appeared to recognise the names of their relatives and friends in the list.

A little later came a glad incident which relieved the terrible strain of the morning.

A middle-aged woman, with a white, drawn face, hurried into the Cockspur-street offices. A few minutes later she came out – a different woman.

She had had unmistakable good news. Her face was wreathed in joy. Her eyes shone with relief and pleasure.

A MOTHER'S RELIEF

A journalist sat near a lady who was wearing out her heart waiting patiently for information. He inquired if she had any relative on board.

"Yes," was the reply. "My three children were going out to join their dad, and I was following next week."

On being informed that the name was "Davis," the journalist scanned the list, and among the survivors found the names of Miss Agnes Davis, Miss Mary Davis and Master John Davis. He drew the lady's attention to the fact, she almost collapsed with joy, as she exclaimed: "Thank God, thank God!"

A foreigner and his wife, a plump woman of about thirty or thirty-five, both of them evidently in poor circumstances, entered the office with timid footsteps, and, in broken English, inquired after a relative who had travelled steerage on the Titanic.

It was impossible to allay their fears, and they retraced their steps to the door, the woman trying hard to keep back her tears as she muttered in broken English: "It is terrible."

At the Leadenhall-street office's of the White Star Line there was a constant stream of men and women inquiring for the fate of their relatives and friends.

The vagueness and uncertainty of the published reports only added to the anxiety of the callers.

"If I could only know one way or the other!" was the cry made by most of the distracted relatives.

"I shall never see my son again," cried a mother whose twenty-year-old son was aboard the Titanic.

By night the situation in the White Star Line's offices grew more and more tragic.

All day long many had waited, scanning each succeeding list of survivors with feverish hope, a few to go out into the world again aglow with new joy, but more destined to sink back in heavy despair until the next list fanned the smouldering hopes afresh.

Late in the evening an elderly woman who had lingered on quietly and calmly for hours suddenly found the beloved name, incredibly, on the list of the saved.

Her eyes swam mistily, and all the pent-up feelings of the day found vent as she realised the abounding joy of the moment.

And around her sat on the others, those who waited still, interminably, for the next list or the next, prepared to abide, sleepless, hollow eyed, till morning, so they might, banish the agonising, corroding uncertainty…

ORPHANED FAMILY OF SEVEN
(FROM OUR OWN CORRESPONDENT)

Southampton, April 16 – Southampton is a town of grief to-day.

It went to bed last night secure in the belief that those of its sons who were in the Titanic – the bulk of her crew – were safe, humanly speaking. It awoke this morning to learn that most of them had gone down with their ship.

In the first moments of its grief the fact that most of the saved were women and children was a matter only for listless comment. Only later did the heroism of their menfolk become apparent to the widows of Southampton and – ever so little – lightened their grief.

There were agonising scenes at this, the Titanic's home port, when the full force of their loss fell upon the families of the crew.

There is scarcely a street in Northam, which is on the riverside, that has not been stricken by the blow. Nearly one half of the Titanic's crew, apart from the restaurant staff, resided in the town.

Most of these people, the wives and families of firemen, greasers and trimmers, have been suffering severely during the coal strike, and the sailing of the Titanic seemed the dawn of better times.

Crowds of relatives gathered round the White Star Line offices near the docks yesterday morning in quest of news concerning relatives on board the ill-fated vessel.

One member of the crew whose fate is still in doubt left seven children at home, including a recent new arrival.

Since sailing day the mother has died, and now their other parent has been taken from them.

LOOKED FORWARD TO WEDDING

In another instance preparations have been in progress for a wedding of a member of the crew on the Titanic's return, and there are countless other cases too painful for utterance.

Four members of one family – father, cousin and two sons were firemen on the liner.

One hears little of them, indeed, save in outline, for the bereaved are silent with their woe.

In the riverside district there are women in the shops and in the streets, with tears in their eyes, discussing their common fate of widowhood, but silent to the stranger.

Every one from the docks is bombarded with questions, but the authentic news yesterday was all too meagre.

Many mothers are prostrate with grief, and an intense gloom prevails throughout the town.

All the offices of other shipping companies bear flags at half-mast and similar tokens are displayed at the public offices.

As night drew on, after a day of suspense and uncertainty, the sad scenes were intensified, and it was with mingled fading of relief and dread it was learned that Mr. P. A. Curry, manager of the White Star Line here, had specially cabled to the New York office for news of the crew of the Titanic.

POSTING THE LIST

The information, it was announced would be published immediately on its arrival, and if necessary the offices of the superintendents, in Trafalgar-chambers as well as the general office, would be kept open all night, so that relatives of members of the crew might have the latest tidings.

At 8 p.m. outside the general office was posted a large poster lit with oil lamps, to the effect that the moment the names of the crew, saved or dead, came in they would be posted up at the west gate of the docks.

In less than a quarter of an hour an immense silent crowd were waiting patiently in the dark for tidings of their loved ones.

When the list was posted later nearly one name in two was a Southampton one, and there were agonising scenes as each name was recognised and often read aloud.

An endless list of names – mere names meaning nothing to the general public, meaning so much, so terribly much, each one of them, to just the few nearest to them.

Beginning with the names of Captain Smith and Mr. Lightoller, the second mate, the list contained the names of:–

A master-at-arms	48 trimmers
3 quartermasters	4 stewardesses
1 look-out man	95 stewards
3 engineers	12 cooks
13 A.B.'s	8 scullions
1 writer	7 bakers
3 storekeepers	3 butchers
101 firemen	1 barber
2 electricians	1 controller
22 greasers	11 substitutes

The list shows in all 342 names of men (and four stewardesses) hailing from Southampton and the neighbourhood.

The Mayor of Southampton, Mr. Henry Bowyer, has sent the following message to the Lord Mayor of London:–

I propose opening a relief fund for distressed dependents of the crew of the Titanic, the majority of whom reside in Southampton. May I appeal for your cordial co-operation?

Anxious throngs still surround the White Star offices at midnight.

NEW YORK HUSHED TO AWE

New York, April 16 – "Eighteen hundred men, women and children went down with the Titanic." That was the incredible news whispered along Broadway last night and for once New York's light laughter was stilled.

The word was passed from lip to lip and sent buzzing over the busy wires. Men stopped and looked at each other. It was so hard to realise.

Diners in Fifth-avenue mansions paused from their jests, and when men came out from the opera or play they learned what had happened hours before in mid-Atlantic.

They carried the news back to the playhouse, but many did not dare to tell their women folk.

There were fathers and mothers, husbands and wives on the Titanic.

Along Broadway, where the lights flash by night and where no one is ever outwardly sad, the news swept down like some great grey smothering hand.

Before every bulletin board great crowds jammed and struggled to get news.

The crowd jostled and pushed, but there were no hasty words. Men were too stunned to grow angry at trampled feet or elbowed ribs. Police reserves were called, but even they lost something of their sternness in the face of a city's mourning.

A cabaret song was stopped in one of the great dining places. A girl started to sing – it was the kind of song one sometimes hears at cabaret shows – but a low murmur of disapproval swept down the room, and the song was stopped.

At one long bar was a party of gay young men. The gayest of them had just ordered a round of drinks, and was just raising his glass with a cheery "Here's how," when the barman turned from a telephone and said,

"Gentlemen, the Titanic has sunk with 1,300 people." The gay young man put down his glass untouched, went out, his friends following.

The bowling-green in front of the White Star Company's offices was filled with a dense mass of anxious friends and relatives.

Now a woman shrieked and fell in a crumpled heap on the pavement, now a man cursed or mumbled a prayer. But still they waited here or at the doors of the newspaper offices.

PRESIDENT TAFT'S ANXIETY

New York, April 16 – Throughout, this morning millionaires mingled with an immense crowd of poorer people hovering outside the White Star offices here.

Relatives of Mr. Daniel Guggenheim, Mr. Isidor Straus, and the son of Colonel John Jacob Astor, owner of one of the four or five biggest fortunes in the States, continually made anxious inquiries.

Mr. Vincent Astor was in a state of great agitation. He had been walking up and down the corridor of the White Star offices all night, constantly imploring the officials for news.

At Carnegie Hall, prayers were offered for the safety of Mr. W. T. Stead, who was on his way here to speak on behalf of the men's forward religious movement.

Among the most frequent inquirers was President Taft, who is mourning the loss of Major Butt, one of his most intimate friends and his aide-de-camp. Major Butt was returning from a special mission to Rome, where he had been to consult the Pope regarding the precedence at public functions of the new American Cardinals.

PASSENGER'S PEARL NECKLACES

The value of the Titanic for insurance purposes was given as £1,000,000, although her cost was £1,500,000.

The reason for this reduction was that the resources of her owners were sufficient to meet the balance. Even then an undertaking was given that the owners would pay the first £250,000 of any loss or damage that occurred. Anything over that is to be met by the underwriters.

Mrs. Widener, the wife of the millionaire, who was on board, has a jewellery policy of £180,000, which includes three pearl necklaces valued at £50,000 each. She wore at least one of these necklaces constantly, and even, it is stated, when in bed at night.

The groups of underwriters concerned are awaiting news of those necklaces as anxiously as they awaited news of the owner's rescue.

CONSTERNATION IN PARIS

Paris, April 16 – The consternation and grief in the American colony of Paris at the Titanic disaster passes description.

The offices of the company are besieged by weeping inquirers. There is hardly a leading hotel without visitors having relatives and friends on board.

An Unprecedented Disaster

18 April **1912** – 1 May **1912**

Without television or radio news the unfolding story in the aftermath of the tragedy was revealed by the day's newspapers. Individual tragedy jostled with the overwhelming sense of national grief as everyone attempted to come to terms with what had happened.

◁ A crowd gathers at Southampton for news of the Titanic.

DEATH-TOLL INCREASED BY 165

Only 705 Survivors of Titanic On Board Carpathia.

A WORLD WAITING

Cable Steamer Leaves Halifax on Funeral Mission.

SON'S TRAGIC CURSE

Pathetically slowly, the Cunard liner Carpathia is nearing New York with her tragic load of widowed wives and orphaned children.

The eyes of the whole civilised world are following her as she ploughs her way all too draggingly along through the ocean and the ice fields that cumber the track.

For on board she carries all that are left of the 3,200 souls who set sail with such high hope last week for the maiden voyage of the Titanic, the greatest ship the world has ever known, man's supreme challenge to the powers of nature.

Now that ship has been shattered, and all that remains is sunk in 12,000ft. of Atlantic Ocean. Of her human freight two in every three have perished, fathers, husbands, bread-winners.

And the world waits upon the Carpathia – waits to hear the appalling truth of that midnight crash when the 46,000-ton steamship met the mountain of ice.

CARPATHIA WITH 705 SURVIVORS

The following cablegram was received by the White Star Line last evening from their New York office:–

"Carpathia now in communication with Siasconsett reports 705 survivors aboard."

These figures would seem to be the final official number of survivors and increase the death-toll by 163 to nearly 1,500.

The first news that came to hand concerning the terrible death-toll of the Titanic put the figures of the survivors on board the Carpathia at 675.

TRAGEDY IN FIGURES

Then came what purported to be official figures – 868. Last evening from many sources came telegrams estimating the survivors at only 700 or 705.

Mere figures, these, yet of tragic significance to those left behind. To you who read 700 or 701 means little enough. To the orphaned child or widowed bride of that one left to fend for themselves, with the tragic memory of a dear one who is no more, that is everything in the world worth having.

CABLESHIP'S GRIM ERRAND

Halifax, April 17 – The cableship Mackay-Bennett has been chartered by the White Star Company to go to the scene of the Titanic disaster.

In the hope that some bodies may be picked up coffins are being taken, and several undertakers and embalmers will be on the ship.

The Mackay-Bennett sailed at two o'clock. In addition to the undertakers, she carries a Church of England clergyman, who will perform the last rites over any bodies that may be found.

SON'S TRAGIC MISSION

Halifax (N.S.), April 17 – Colonel Jacob Astor's son arrived here this morning, and he is chartering a steamer for the purpose of going in search of his father's body.

RELIEF FUNDS OPENED

The King and Queen Send Nearly £1,000 to Mansion House.

The King and Queen have once more shown their practical sympathy with their distressed and suffering subjects by subscribing handsomely to a fund which the Lord Mayor of London opened yesterday on behalf of those who have suffered by the Titanic disaster.

At the Easter banquet at the Mansion House last night the Lord Mayor announced that he had received the following telegrams:–

York Cottage, Sandringham

I am commanded to inform your Lordship that the King subscribes five hundred guineas and the Queen two hundred and fifty guineas to the Mansion House Fund your Lordship is so kindly raising for the relief of those who are in need through the awful shipwreck of the Titanic. – William Carrington.

Sandringham

Queen Alexandra will give £200 towards the fund which your Lordship is raising for the relief of the relatives of those who have lost their lives in the terrible disaster to the Titanic. – Colonel Streatfield.

By last night, the Lord Mayor, to use his own words, had "within a few hours, a considerable sum, amounting to thousands of pounds, in hand, a tribute to the generosity of the British public."

The appeal was instituted largely at the request of the Mayor of Southampton, where the distress is especially acute, but the fund will not only be for relatives of the crew, but for all those left in distress by deaths in the disaster.

NOT ENOUGH LIFEBOATS
Titanic's Builder Blames Government for Inadequate Regulations.

One of the most important questions which has been raised in consequence of the disaster is whether there were a sufficient number of lifeboats on the Titanic.

The Right Hon. A. M. Carlisle, who, formerly general manager to Messrs. Harland and Wolff, built the Titanic and partly designed her, said, when interviewed yesterday by *The Daily Mail*, that he did not consider the lifeboat accommodation required by the Board of Trade regulations was sufficient.

"I do not think it is sufficient for big ships," he said, "and I never did. As ships grew bigger I was always in favour of increasing the lifeboat accommodation. Yet it remains the same for a ship of 50,000 tons us for one of 10,000.

"When working out the designs of the Olympic and the Titanic I put my ideas before the davit constructors, and got them to design me davits which would allow me to place, if necessary, four lifeboats on each pair of davits, which would have meant a total of over forty boats.

"Those davits were fitted in both ships. But, though the Board of Trade did not require anything more than the sixteen lifeboats, twenty boats were supplied.

"The White Star Company did, of course, supply boats of very much greater capacity than those required by the Board of Trade. I think I am correct in saying that the provision, in cubic capacity, was practically double that which was required.

"At the same time, it was nothing like sufficient, in case of accident, to take off the majority of the passengers and crew.

"I have no doubt that the Government of this country, and the Governments of other countries, will now look more seriously into the matter."

SAFETY WANTED, NOT LUXURY
Mr. Walter Winans, the millionaire sportsman, expresses himself sensibly on the disaster.

"Does it not seem strange, charging a passenger £870 for the best stateroom on the Titanic," he writes to *The Daily Mirror*, "and not giving him a private lifeboat? I am sure it would pay better than giving him a lot of useless decoration.

"By the way, the Titans defied the gods and were thrown into the sea, so it was a bad-omened name to give a ship."

"SINKING!" – TITANIC'S CRY
Have been in collision with iceberg – We are in a sinking condition and require urgent assistance.

This was the message flashed from the Titanic to the Cunard liner Caronia in Mid-Atlantic.

But the Caronia was 700 miles away – too far to be of any assistance, as her master Captain Barr, sadly explained last night when the vessel arrived at Queenstown.

Captain Barr said it was on Monday morning at half-past four in lat. 43.45N., long. 42.20W., that he received the wireless appeal from the Titanic, which further stated that she had been in collision with an iceberg.

Not near enough to render assistance himself, Captain Barr sent wireless messages out indicating to steamers nearer the Titanic than he was the nature of the accident to that vessel.

The intelligence created a painful sensation on board, and Captain Barr's officers and crew deeply regretted that they were precluded from being of service on the sinking liner.

TITANIC'S LAST "GOOD-BYE"
The best known message from the Titanic before the disaster was received by the Tunisian, which yesterday reported on arrival at Liverpool, speaking to the Titanic by wireless on Saturday midnight, and sending a message, "Good luck." To this the Titanic replied, "Many thanks. Good-bye."

WAITING, WAITING…
Another day of waiting – endless waiting and aching suspense, hope grimly fighting with despair, with but the barest scraps of news to ease the strain on brain and heart.

All through the long night and on into yesterday a tired out little band of women and men kept an anxious vigil in the White Star Company's London head offices in Cockspur-street.

They waited for a name – just the word or two that meant to them the whole world of difference between life and death.

There were fourteen or fifteen of them there yesterday morning lying back in chairs or on the leather-covered seats, some soundly sleeping, some reluctantly waking to a day that brought yet no new hope.

All night long the office remained open, the staff replying to an almost incessant stream of callers and telephone calls.

In one corner an elderly woman lay huddled up in a chair, her head thrown back. She had been there since six o'clock on Tuesday evening. She was still there at six o'clock last evening.

The stream of inquiries was not so constant as on Tuesday, but yesterday more questions were asked about the safety of members of the crew of the lost liner than previously. One extremely touching incident occurred early in the afternoon.

THE CREW AND THE SWELLS

For some minutes a poorly-dressed middle-aged woman stood among the crowd outside, gazing silently at the office. With an effort she at last forced herself to enter.

"Have you any news of the crew yet?" she asked, in a strained voice, of a clerk.

"None yet," she had to be told.

"Will – will they bother about the names of the crew as much as about the others – the swells?" she managed to control her voice to ask.

She was assured that every name of those saved would be sent in as soon as possible and published.

Biting her lips to keep back her tears and keeping her eyes averted, she murmured, "Thank you," and, turning swiftly, made for the door.

But there, her gathered strength deserted her. Swaying slightly, she staggered against a pillar and, burying her face in her handkerchief, gave way to piteous heaving sobs and tears.

A few minutes later a man and a woman – a fashionable, well-dressed pair – entered and asked if a friend had really joined the ship at Cherbourg. Obviously they hoped to be told "No," but there was no getting away from the passenger list; there was the name of the friend whom they had tried to hope was not on board – and the name was not among those of the saved.

WIDOWED SOUTHAMPTON
(FROM OUR OWN CORRESPONDENT)

Southampton, April 17 – The gloom which settled over Southampton when confirmation of the Titanic's loss was received is deepening, and to-night, the wives and other relatives of the crew still keep anxious vigil at the White Star offices.

Here, where are the homes of most of the crew, their kinsfolk have hoped and watched all day for news of survivors of fathers, husbands, brothers, sons. They have waited silently, anxiously, and for most the tidings came not.

To-night many of them have been waiting almost continuously for twenty-four hours for tidings of the breadwinners of many humble homes. The suspense is agonising, and heartrending scenes have been common.

"Will the list never come?" one poor woman exclaimed, as her fainting form was borne away.

Nothing approaching this appalling blow has ever fallen upon the port, though disasters to the local seafaring community have been by no means rare, and memories of the Stella and Hilda disasters are still recalled.

WIDOWS IN EVERY STREET

Here there are widows in nearly every street in certain parts, and already two deaths of bereaved people have taken place.

One case was recorded yesterday, another almost as pathetic comes to light to-day.

A wife recently confined has died since the news was broken to her, and the child has died also.

In two neighbouring streets in the Shirley district are two young widows, married only a few weeks since, the voyage in one case being the husband's first.

In yet another street there are three widowed women living side by side.

Crowds remained practically all last night outside the White Star

The Daily Mirror

THE MORNING JOURNAL WITH THE SECOND LARGEST NET SALE.

No. 2,648.   Registered at the G.P.O. as a Newspaper.   April 19, 1912   One Halfpenny.

WHY WERE THERE ONLY TWENTY LIFEBOATS FOR 2,207 PEOPLE ON BOARD THE ILL-FATED TITANIC?

Something must be done by the Board of Trade to insist upon a larger number of lifeboats being provided for giant liners. Only twenty lifeboats were supplied by Messrs. Harland and Wolff for the Titanic, and even twenty, according to the Right Hon. A. M. Carlisle, the man who, as general manager to the company, was responsible for the building, was four in excess of the number required to comply with the Board of Trade regulations. "As ships grew bigger I was always in favour of increasing the lifeboat accommodation," said Mr. Carlisle, "yet it remains the same for a ship of 50,000 tons as for one of 10,000." The photograph shows the lifeboats on board the Titanic. It was taken while the giant liner was in Queenstown Harbour on Thursday of last week, in sight of land for the last time. Two boats, or even three if necessary, may be swung as easily as one on this type of davit. It will be seen that there is only one in the photograph.

Company's offices, and increased greatly in number from daybreak onwards.

The company's officials granted all possible information to the bereaved inquirers, the names of the saved being posted on a notice board as soon as received.

There were pathetic scenes outside the offices as the wives learnt the worst.

Hopeless misery has cast its wing over the town, causing the wholesale cancellation of social engagements and public meetings.

19 April 1912

CAPTAIN SMITH SHOOTS HIMSELF ON BRIDGE

Commander's Suicide after Grim Struggle with Revolver in Library.

"NOT ENOUGH OFFICERS, NOT ENOUGH BOATS."

Survivors' Appalling Indictment of the Equipment of the "World's Largest Liner."

DEATH-TOLL NOW TOUCHES NEARLY 1,600

Heartrending Scenes at Arrival of Carpathia with Her Tragic Freight at New York.

TITANIC PASSENGERS' STATEMENT OF THE TRUTH

Three Italians Shot Dead in Panic-Stricken Rush for the Lifeboats.

The Carpathia has brought back its terrible freight of living and dead.

Dead men can tell no tales – but the living have written an indictment of mismanagement at sea that will thrill the world.

A committee of the Titanic's survivors met on board and wrote down the truth as they saw it – how the Titanic went down, and why; how so few people were saved, and why; and how, in the hour of his agony Captain Smith, commander of the world's largest and most luxurious liner, shot himself dead on the bridge of his sinking ship.

Two continents wept when the Titanic went down. But the sinking, terrible as it was and horrifying, is as nothing to the charge which those responsible must face.

The world will know why nearly 1,600 people died – the world will find out who is to blame.

SURVIVORS' DESCRIPTION OF THE CATASTROPHE

New York, April 18 (10.10 p.m.) – The following statement, issued by a committee of the surviving passengers, has been given to the Press:–

We, the undersigned surviving passengers of the Titanic, in order to forestall any sensational and exaggerated statements, deem it our duty to give to the Press a statement of the facts which have come to our knowledge, and which we believe to be true:–

On Sunday, April 14, at about 11.40, on a cold, starlit night, the ship struck an iceberg, which had been reported to the bridge by the look-out, but not early enough to avoid collision.

Steps were taken to ascertain the damage and save the passengers and the ship.

Orders were given to put on lifebelts, the boats were lowered, and the usual distress signals were sent out by wireless telegraphy and rockets were fired at intervals.

Fortunately, a wireless message was received by the Carpathia about midnight. She arrived on the scene of the disaster about 4 a.m. on Monday.

The officers and crew of the Carpathia had been preparing all night for the rescue work and for the comfort of the survivors. These were received on board with the most touching care and kindness, every attention being given to all, irrespective of class.

Passengers, officers and crew gladly gave up their state-rooms, clothing and comforts for our benefit. All honour to them.

The English Board of Trade passengers' certificate on board the Titanic allowed for a total of approximately 3,500. The same certificate called for lifeboat accommodation for approximately 950 in the following boats:– Fourteen large lifeboats, two smaller boats, four collapsible boats. Life preservers were accessible in apparently sufficient number for all on board. The number saved was about 80 per cent of the maximum capacity of the lifeboats.

The boats at all times to be properly equipped with provisions, water, lamps, compasses, lights, etc. Life-saving boat drills should be made frequent and thoroughly carried out and officers should be armed at boat drill.

A greater reduction in speed in fog and ice, as the damage if a collision actually occurs is liable to be less.

We feel it our duty to call the attention of the public to what we consider the inadequate supply of life-saving appliances provided for modern passenger steamships and recommend that immediate steps be taken to compel passenger steamers to carry sufficient boats to accommodate the maximum number of people carried on board.

The following facts were observed and should be considered in this connection:– In addition to the insufficiency of lifeboats, rafts, etc., there was a lack of trained seamen to man the same; stokers, stewards, etc., are not efficient boat handlers.

There were not enough officers to carry out the emergency orders on the bridge and to superintend the launching and control of the lifeboats and an absence of searchlights.

The Board of Trade rules allow for entirely too many people in each boat to permit the same to be properly handled.

On the Titanic the boat deck was about 75ft. above water, and consequently the passengers were required to embark before lowering of the boats, thus endangering the operation and preventing the taking of the maximum number the boats would hold.

In conclusion we suggest that an international conference should be called, and we recommend the passage of identical laws providing for the safety of all at sea.

We urge the U.S. Government to take the initiative as soon as possible. – Reuter.

The statement is signed by Mr. Samuel Goldenberg chairman of the Passengers' Committee, and twenty-five others. – Reuter.

HEART-BROKEN MESSAGE TO BEREAVED FROM THE WIDOW OF THE CAPTAIN

The following message was posted outside the White Star offices at Southampton yesterday afternoon. It is signed by Mrs. Smith, the widow of Captain E. J. Smith, R.N.R., of the Titanic:–

CAPTAIN SMITH'S SUICIDE

New York, April 18 – The survivors state that the captain of the Titanic shot himself on the bridge.

New York, April 18 (11 p.m.). – It is asserted by one passenger of the Carpathia that Captain Smith committed suicide on the bridge of the Titanic before she went down and that the chief engineer also committed suicide.

The same passenger states that three Italians were shot dead in the struggle for the lifeboats. According to this circumstantial account of the captain's end the revolver was wrested from his hands in the library, but he broke away to the bridge and shot himself through the mouth. – Reuter.

LANDING 13 LIFEBOATS

New York, April 18 (10 p.m.). – The first survivors began to leave the ship at 9.35.

The delay in docking was due to the necessity of taking off the Titanic's thirteen lifeboats. – Reuter.

WOMEN GO MAD IN THE BOATS

"Indescribable Sufferings" After the Liner Went Down.

"NEARER MY GOD TO THEE"

New York, April 18 – Miss Andrews, an elderly lady, interviewed by the Exchange representative, said that the crash occurred at 11.35 p.m. on Sunday night. The women and children got off in the lifeboats at 12.45 a.m. The Titanic sank at 2 a.m. and the Carpathia picked up the boats at 8.30 a.m.

"Many women are insane," she added. "Mrs. Astor is aboard. We didn't know until daybreak whether we would be rescued. We were in open boats eight hours and the suffering of all was indescribable."

ROUSED FROM SLEEP BY COLLISION

New York, April 18 – Miss Bonnell, of Youngstown, Ohio, said the Titanic was ploughing through ice fields when the collision occurred. A large proportion of the passengers were asleep.

The bottom bow drove into the iceberg, and the lower plates were torn asunder.

Large volumes of water rushed in with irresistible force, and the liner began to sink rapidly by the bow. The Titanic seemed to slide across the top of the berg. The passengers hurriedly seized their clothing, and immediately the lifeboats were made ready.

As the liner continued to gradually recede into the trough of the sea the passengers marched towards the stem.

HYMN AS SHIP WENT DOWN

The orchestra belonging to the first cabin assembled on deck as the liner was going down and played "Nearer My God to Thee."

In some of the boats women were shrieking for their husbands, others were weeping, but many bravely took a turn with the oars. – Exchange Telegraph.

"By that time most of the lifeboats were some distance away, and only a faint sound of the strains of the hymn could be heard. As we pulled away from the ship we noticed that she was 'hogbacked,' showing that she was already breaking, in two.

"She was not telescoped, the force of the impact being sustained on the keel more than the bows.

"We were in the small boats for more than four hours before we were rescued by the Carpathia."

KILLED BY BLOCKS OF ICE

New York, April 18 – Mr. C. H. Stengel, a first-class passenger, said that when the Titanic struck the iceberg the impact was terrific, and great blocks of ice were thrown on the deck, killing a number of people. The stern of the vessel rose in the air, and people ran shrieking from their berths below.

Women and children, some of the former hysterical, having been rapidly separated from husbands, brothers and fathers, were quickly placed in boats by the sailors, who, like their officers, were heard to threaten men that they would shoot if male passengers attempted to get into boats ahead of the women.

Indeed, it was said that shots were actually heard.

Mr. Stengel added that a number of men threw themselves into the sea when they saw that there was no chance of their reaching the boats. "How they died," he observed, "I do not know."

THEY DIED TOGETHER

New York, April 18 – Mr. and Mrs. Isidor Straus were drowned together, Mrs. Straus refusing to leave her husband's side.

According to the descriptions given by fellow passengers, the noted New York millionaire and his wife went to their deaths together, standing arm in arm on the first cabin deck of the Titanic, Mr. Straus quietly and tenderly reassuring his wife so far as he could.

As the lifeboats were receding from the scene of the disaster the couple were observed standing still calmly awaiting their inevitable fate.

CARPATHIA ARRIVES IN A STORM

New York, Thursday – It is a wild night outside the harbour and there is a heavy fog over the bay.

Rain is falling and there is lightning at intervals.

Despite heavy weather, the Carpathia maintained a limited speed of thirteen knots per hour.

When she passed the quarantine station doctors went aboard. – Exchange Telegraph.

Later – Darkness and heavy rain delayed the warping into the dock of the Carpathia, which was accomplished very slowly.

TRAGEDY OF ABSENT NAMES

"John Smith, Carpenter," and What It Means.

MORE SURVIVORS LISTS

Two further lists of survivors of the Titanic were made public last night – one a short list unclassified issued in New York by the Cunard Company and the other a list of some 130 odd names of third-class passengers or crew sent by wireless from New York to the offices of the White Star Line. The list of steerage passengers is yet far from complete, but at best the death-toll in the third class can hardly be less than 450 names missing from the list.

The grim record is all the sadder and more moving because of the circumstances in which the majority of them went out.

They were emigrants, and on such a boat as the Titanic, the best class of emigrants. They had left the old life behind with all its troubles and impossibilities and dragging-down hopelessness; they had cast this slough off, and were going forth, full of hope once more, to a new existence where everything would be begun all over again.

And then to be caught like rats in a trap! And no way out. On the horizon, life and high hopes; facing them, the agony of a long-drawn-out and horrible death.

"John Smith, carpenter," among the names of missing does not convey much in glancing down the list. But "John Smith missing" means a whole world of tragedy somewhere.

Somehow or other, things had gone wrong in England; somehow he was not the success he felt he ought to have been.

So for the sum of £8 1s. – the price of a third-class cabin on the Titanic – John Smith purchased the chance of another start in life.

Then one night, when almost in touch with the promised land, John Smith found himself in the middle of a huddled group of distraught fellow-creatures, faced with a death which was certain, but which was not swift.

WOMEN'S VIGIL FOR NEWS OF DEAR ONES

Waiting All Night at the White Star Offices for Names of Titanic's Saved.

Still they waited yesterday – the wives, mothers, sisters, daughters of the men who went down with the Titanic.

It was the fourth day of burdensome suspense to anguished hearts. To those who waited and watched for the remaining names of the saved it was the most dreadful day of all. For the news might arrive at any minute.

Just before 10 p.m. a further list was posted up, and there was an almost frantic rush on the part of the sad crowd inside, to gather the latest tidings.

One woman who had several relations on board the Titanic was completely overcome with emotion when she discovered that the names of loved ones were missing from the list.

Since the first sinister news of the disaster to the Titanic shocked the world on Monday morning, hundreds and thousands of men, women and children have waited, half in hope, half in fear, for a name, for the word or two making all the difference between life and death to them.

Day after day they have crowded the offices of the White Star Line, anxiously scanning the typed lists on the notice boards, questioning the quiet-spoken officials.

Yesterday the inquiries and visitors were not quite so numerous as previously, but all day long there was a steady stream of grave-faced men and sad-eyed women seeking for news.

Some of the men and women had been up all night in London, snatching what sleep they could in the offices in Cockspur-street.

WOMAN'S TWO-DAYS' WAIT

One woman had not left the building, except for a few short intervals to snatch some food, for two whole days. But yesterday morning, assured that no news could be expected for some hours and that she would be instantly informed by telegraph when any did come, she left the office and went sadly home.

Another, young to know such tragedy, was a youth sixteen or so, whose father was engaged on the liner. He has haunted the building since Monday, and could no longer keep his feelings and fears to himself.

"Tell me," he said, to a clerk, "tell me all you know. If my father is dead, don't hide it from me. I can bear the news; I know he is drowned. You can't shock me any more than I have been shocked."

In a corner, sitting silently with a friend, was a woman, dressed in deep mourning, whose eyes had such deep, black hollows, under them that at first sight it almost looked as if they had been bruised.

ALWAYS IN TEARS

Once an elderly lady groped her way from the notice board, where she had not found the name she was yearning to read. She went to the counter and began to ask if there was any news of her son.

But before she could properly frame her question great gulping tears choked her, and she turned away, her question unasked – but answered for all that.

And so, for hour after hour, things went on, the same familiar, grief-stricken figures coming in again and again, scanning the typed lists of passengers saved, and departing.

Always there was no fresh news.

Resignation – a sort of deadened bowing to a cruel fate – was the keynote of the scene. The waiting ones had become hardened; they had passed through the first anguish of fierce despair, and the ache in their souls was perhaps less poignantly wrenching.

Some – the more hopeful ones – still expressed the sort of half-hearted conviction that some of the Titanic's passengers "must have been picked up by other vessels" than the Carpathia.

WAITING FOR–?
(FROM OUR OWN CORRESPONDENT)

Southampton, April 18 – There were farther heartrending scenes here to-night, when, shortly before midnight, the mayor appealed to the waiting crowd of wives and other relatives of the Titanic's crew who had been anxiously scanning the lists of survivors – first posted at 7 p.m. – to go home and rest.

There was little likelihood, continued the mayor, of further news for some hours, owing to atmospherical difficulties in the western ocean.

Slowly and sadly the crowd then dispersed, and many women were led away sobbing bitterly.

It was exactly 7 p.m. when the first large sheet of names of survivors on the Carpathia was affixed to the board outside the White Star offices here.

There were about 400 persons present then, but soon a huge crowd had gathered.

The names were written just as received, without any explanation whether they were third-class passengers or crew. Most of the thirty names in the first list were foreign and were not recognised by anyone in the crowd.

Mr. Currie, the Southampton manager of the White Star, said the names were also being sent straight to the London offices for distribution.

"We are getting the names very slowly," he said, "for the atmospheric conditions are bad, and it will be hours before we get them all.

"As each name is received we have to send a telegram to the passenger's home in Italy, Scandinavia, France, or wherever it may be."

CROWD WATCHES IN SILENCE

Police formed a cordon in front of the board to keep back the crowd, which rapidly grew to an enormous size as the news that the names were being announced spread through the town. The dead silence of the waiting throng was most impressive.

One little private message by wireless was posted after the first

list: "Jimmy, – Please call at 93, Millbrook-road for information about Patsy."

In Southampton the home of many of the Titanic's crew, the tragedy is too deep for tears.

One widow, Mrs. Preston, of 42, Millbank-street, told me that her son, Thomas Charles Preston, aged twenty-two, who was a coal trimmer on the Titanic, was the main support of herself and her four younger children. She has no means of livelihood, for she can no longer work at the washtub, and her second son is an errand boy, earning only a few shillings a week.

JUST A CHANCE

"There is just a chance that Tom may be in a boat," she said, "for when the men are given boat stations they generally have one of each class in a boat."

Mrs. May, of 75, York-street, told me she had both her husband and eldest son on the Titanic as firemen.

"I have seven other younger children," she said, "besides my son Arthur. His wife and little son, two months old, also live with us, so there are ten of us here. God help us!"

The White Star Line announce that they are prepared to relieve temporary needs of relatives of the crew at Southampton and settle legal payments as soon as possible.

All announcements as received are posted in black ink on sheets of white paper a yard square and in letters three inches deep, so that names can easily be read.

HUMAN SACRIFICE TO RED TAPE
Recommendations for Life-Saving Hung Up Since Last July.

FULL INQUIRY TO BE MADE

"There must be a full inquiry into the loss of the Titanic. The disaster creates a new situation which will need to be most carefully considered."

So said Mr. Buxton, President of the Board of Trade, in the House of Commons yesterday afternoon, in the course of a lengthy statement on the regulations governing passenger ships. Board of Trade regulations required on a ship of 10,000 tons and upwards accommodation for 960. The life-saving appliances on the Titanic were as follows:–

	Accommodating
16 boats on davits	990
Additional boats and rafts	178
48 life-buoys, and 3,560 life-belts.	

Thus there was accommodation for 1,168 persons in boats and rafts, with 3,608 floating appliances. The certified maximum of passengers and crew was 3,500, and the actual number when the vessel left, 2,208.

Mr. Buxton explained that the rules now in force were originally drawn up in 1890 and revised in 1894. The highest provision was for vessels of 10,000 tons and upwards. (N.B. – There are nearly fifty British liners of over 10,000 tons up to the now building Gigantic of 54,000 tons.)

Mr. Buxton went on to say that in view of the increased size of modern vessels the Board of Trade only last year suggested a revision of these rules, and referred to the Advisory Committee on merchant shipping the question of the revision of the rules and any particular provision to be made in the case of steamers of large size.

After considering this report, together with the views of the expert adviser the Board of Trade were not satisfied that the increased provision recommended by the Committee was adequate, and referred the matter back to the Committee for further examination.

"Only last year," are the Minister's words. Only a few months wasted while thousands of lives are hazarded every day! And now, apparently, 1,500 lives sacrificed to Governmental RED TAPE.

RACING ACROSS ATLANTIC

"I wish the House to understand quite clearly," said Mr. Buxton "that up to the present it has never been the intention of the Board of Trade regulations, and so far as I know it has not been supported by any responsible expert authority, that every vessel, however large and well equipped as regards watertight compartments, should necessarily carry lifeboats adequate to accommodate all on board."

It had always been considered by expert authorities that the subdivision into watertight compartments should be taken into account in considering the minimum number of boats required.

Racing across the Atlantic for a time record he could do nothing to discourage.

"TOO DEPRESSING"?

"I am not going to read any more about it for a day or two: it is all too depressing!"

We heard that remark yesterday, not without a certain sense of the truth in it. Indeed, the papers have made dramatic but depressing reading since 1912 displaced its predecessor in history: it will live, this year, as memorable mainly for its threats of war and civil strife, for its catastrophes and misfortunes. You may be a very calm Londoner, going about your business as Londoners invariably do, when they can, in wars, in strikes, and in plagues. (And what, indeed are men who work for a living to do except go about their business?) But your calm gradually becomes a calm of depression as the human, news contrasts each day with the news of Nature outside the newspapers – as the sun and the sky suggest thoughts of joy, at variance with the thoughts of pity and death amongst men.

So, for a moment, there comes to many people the thought of an escape, into the forgetful spring, from all these haunting thoughts of life lost for some and hope gone for others, who must suffer from the dreadful silence of those they left, only a few days ago, prosperously started on their journey. Has not the thought of death in spring, indeed, always a certain bitterness? Thus it happens that we think with envy of those remote people who "never hear what is going on," but remain apart from loud news of disasters and distress, like Virgil's husbandman, cultivating their garden in peace of mind.

Happy people! – yet people, perhaps, mistaken, and removed not so much from distress of mind, as from the finer tradition of human sympathy and fellowship. For this news we read every day, this "depressing" intelligence of death and suffering, helps, we cannot help thinking, to form a common consciousness of everlasting oneness amongst myriads of men. A thing that without our daily, and hourly knowledge of it might pass ineffectively as mere rumour in local insignificance does indeed establish, by being brought vividly home to those who think and feel, everywhere, a universal current of world-sympathy, more powerful than the sympathy of any individuals. Loss and sorrow unite men who pass over a hilly dangerous way together. This world-consciousness hears to-day the appeal made to it, not only to devise whatever practical precautions there may be against such calamities as this of the Titanic in future, but also to help and console those saved, to unite with them in mourning for their lost, and to feel intimately, through it all, that sense before alluded to of the comradeship of all men. This may not be the world's most cheerful task at present. But it is the world's duty, and duty, when it is done faithfully, is never so "depressing" as a flight from the things it best behoves us to think about, even into the loveliest of gardens under the warmest of April skies.

THIS MORNING'S GOSSIP

Mr. Bruce Ismay, who is amongst the survivors of the Titanic, is very well known in society. His daughter, it may be remembered, was only married two or three weeks ago.

It was at first said that Miss Ismay was with her husband on the voyage, but this now appears to be untrue.

There is no doubt that the Lord Mayor's appeal for the widows and orphans of those on board the Titanic is causing the very liveliest satisfaction, and an enormous sum of money will be raised. Already people of the social world are taking the matter up, and one hears people at dinner asking one another whether they have sent to the various funds.

Women are taking the matter up quite as eagerly as men, and it will be noted with satisfaction how well women are responding to the call. Never in one's remembrance has a tragedy called forth such very genuine and heartfelt sympathy. Wherever one goes the awful disaster is talked about, and almost everybody one meets seems to have known someone on board the ill-fated ship.

Naturally, at this time of year, there are comparatively few well-known English people going to America. A couple of months ago it would have been a very different matter, for English visitors to the States have been very numerous indeed this winter. A great many of those who were on board the Titanic came from Paris, and comparatively few are known to any great extent in the social world here.

WHAT MILLIONS COULD NOT BUY

Mr. John Jacob Astor Among the Missing Passengers.
➤ Colonel John Jacob Astor.

MAN OF MANY PARTS

Death levels all. Not even £80,000,000 could save John Jacob Astor! He has gone to his death just as though he were the poorest steerage passenger on board the Titanic.

Money is a good deal, but it could not save the millionaire's life.

The following message received yesterday would seem to signify that the last hope of Mr. Astor's safety has vanished:–

New York, April 18 – Early this morning a message was received at Siasconsett from the Carpathia saying that Mr. John Jacob Astor was not on board the vessel. – Reuter.

Mr. Astor's last public act before he died was to marry, in the face of a storm of indignant protest. Miss Madeleine Force, a young and pretty girl of eighteen. He was on his way back to the States with his young bride when the disaster happened.

Mr. Astor had just previously been divorced, and by the decree of the Court, he was forbidden to remarry. This decree only, applied to the State of New York, but owing to the indignation the match aroused throughout America, no fee, however large, would tempt any clergyman, with the exception of one, to perform the marriage service.

BALL WHICH COST £6,000

On the evening that his divorce was made absolute, Mr. Astor gave a big reception, dinner and ball to celebrate the event. There were 180 guests, who dined at nine elaborately decorated tables.

To each of the ladies French parasols were presented. These were followed by briar pipes, with gold fittings and amber mouthpieces, and gold match-boxes to the men.

In the succeeding dances, Pompadour ribbon scarves and sashes, fringed with gold and silver, were given to every couple, while ivory fans were given to each of the ladies as they departed. The ball cost over £6,000.

When Mrs. Caroline Astor, the mother of Mr. Astor, died, she left the leadership of New York society vacant, and no one had since been thought to possess the necessary qualities to take the place of that wonderful woman, who with a word, could admit to or banish from New York's "upper ten." The question which was agitating New York was whether, with the Titanic's return, the young schoolgirl debutante would wield the sceptre.

MILLIONAIRE'S FATAL DECISION

If the Lusitania had sailed as was intended on April 6 Mr. Benjamin Guggenheim, the well-known American "copper" millionaire, would not have taken a passage on the Titanic, and so would probably have been alive to-day.

According to a business friend of his, who yesterday gave the story of the events ending so tragically to *The Daily Mirror*, Mr. Guggenheim had booked his passage on the Lusitania.

"But it so happened that the Lusitania's sailing had to be cancelled on account of her being under repair. The Carmania, another Cunard liner, was put on in her place, but Mr. Guggenheim did not care about crossing on her and decided to go by the next fast boat.

"This happened to be the Titanic, sailing on the 10th. Mr. Guggenheim took his passage on the Titanic, went over to Paris on business for a few days, and picked her up at Cherbourg."

Mr. Guggenheim was a member of a famous family of capitalists, associates of Mr. Pierpont Morgan, and was world-famous in connection with Alaskan development and copper production.

MRS. ISMAY'S GRIEF

Wife of White Star Director Rendered Speechless at Telephone.

Many strange stories of foreboding that some disaster would overtake the Titanic on her maiden voyage continue to come to hand.

COLLAPSED AT TELEPHONE

It was after motoring from Devonshire to Fishguard on Monday evening that Mrs. Bruce Ismay received the telegram informing her of the Titanic disaster.

With an effort she reached the telephone office, but was so overcome with emotion that utterance became impossible, and for an hour following she remained in a state of collapse, till the news of her husband's safety came in a telegram.

MISHAP TO MR. STEAD FORETOLD

Mr. R. Penny, of Bristol, who, says the *Western Daily Press*, Bristol, for many years has known Mr. W. T. Stead personally, received the following letter from Mr. Stead, dated April 9 last:–

Dear Penny, – Thank you very much for your kind letter, which reaches me just as I am starting for America. I sincerely hope that none of the misfortune which you seem to think may happen to myself or my wife will happen, but I will keep your letter and will write to you when I come back. – I am, yours truly, (Signed) W. T. STEAD.

Asked as to the subject of the letter sent to Mr. Stead before his voyage Mr. Penny said it referred to certain mishaps which it seemed probable to the writer might occur in the near future.

DIED LIKE A SOLDIER

Washington, April 18 – President Taft, discussing the Titanic tragedy to-day with a few personal friends at the White House, and referring with emotion to the loss of his military aide-de-camp, Major Butt, said: "As soon as I heard that 1,200 persons had gone down I knew that he had gone down, too. He was a soldier, and remained on deck where he belonged." – Reuter.

WHEN THE TITANIC RETURNED!

When Mr. Frost, one of Messrs. Harland and Wolff's most experienced employees, joined the Titanic it was with the definite promise that on his return he would be appointed departmental manager.

UNABLE TO SLEEP

Among the restaurant staff of the Titanic there were, it was stated yesterday, ten cousins of the manager, Mr. I. Gatti, whose name is among the missing, and who lived with his wife and child at

Southampton. On Sunday night, at about the hour of the disaster, Mrs. Gatti had a strong presentiment of danger. Throughout the night she was unable to sleep, and next morning she came to London to make inquiries at the White Star Line offices.

"WILL DAD BE DROWNED?"

Mr. Walter Harris, of Enfield Highway, a second-class Titanic passenger, it was related yesterday, was having tea with friends just before leaving home, when one of the party, who practises palmistry, looked at his hand and said she "did not like it."

"Is daddy going to be drowned? "asked Harris' little son.

Mr. Harris' name is among the missing.

NO NEWS OF OUR HUSBANDS

Mrs. Thayer, wife of the vice-president of the Pennsylvania Railroad, says Reuter, has telegraphed from the Carpathia, "No news of Mr. Thayer." Mrs. Hays, the wife of the president of the Grand Trunk Railway, sends a similar wireless message.

£10,000 FILM LOST

Mr. Oscar Hammerstein related yesterday how a few days before the Titanic sailed he had a visit from Mr. Harris, who was taking back with him the moving picture films of "The Miracle," which he had secured for £10,600 and a royalty, "These have all been lost now," added Mr. Hammerstein.

FATHER'S SAD HOMECOMING

On his arrival at St. John's (Nova Scotia) yesterday by the steamer Corsican, the Rev. A. C. Crosfield, of Hartford Vicarage, Huntingdon, learned for the first time of the disaster to the Titanic, on which was his adopted son, whom, says the Exchange Telegraph Company, he was to meet at Detroit preparatory to a holiday trip in Canada, and, realising there was very little hope that his son had survived, he determined to return to England by the first steamer.

ON A SICK BED

Lord Pirrie, Father of Titanic, Is Told Sad News at Last.

"BECAUSE HE WORRIED."

Lord Pirrie knows the worst.

Lying on his bed of sickness at Witley Park near Godalming, the father of the Titanic, the man whose great comprehensive brain made it possible to build the greatest ship the world has ever known, has had to be told the dreadful news of what has befallen her on her first trip.

As was pointed out in *The Daily Mirror* of Tuesday last, the tragic tidings were being kept from him as long as it was humanly possible to do so. To tell him might have killed him.

But no man of Lord Pirrie's stamp is content to lose touch with the doings of the world for long; even on a bed of sickness, even against his doctor's orders, at vital risk to himself, he must know what is going on.

So long as he is in the world he must be of the world.

WHY HE HAD TO BE TOLD

And so Lord Pirrie has learned the awful truth; the chairman of the great shipbuilding firm of Harland and Wolff knows that the wonder ship which he conceived and his company carried out is lying, a broken, battered mass of iron, steel and wood, full two miles under the grim Atlantic.

The news could not be kept from him any longer, *The Daily Mirror* was last night told by a member of Lord Pirrie's household.

He wanted to know how the Titanic was progressing; and somehow – one knows how bad news has a way of coming instinctively to those mainly concerned in it – he began to get an inkling that all was not well with her.

And so, because he worried, the truth had to be broken gently to him. Not the whole, dreadful truth – for the newspapers are still kept away as much as possible from him – but the salient points of it.

Lord Pirrie knows that the Titanic has sunk, and that many of the human beings who entrusted themselves to her keeping have been lost.

"Some of the newspapers had to be shown to him," said *The Daily Mirror's* informant. "We kept the news from him as long as we could, but it could not be kept from him for ever.

MIGHT HAVE BEEN A PASSENGER

"How it has affected him it is not easy to say at present. To-night he is not perhaps quite so well as he has been recently.

"I believe that he has not said a great deal on the subject yet, but that he has expressed a great-hearted sympathy concerning the dreadful loss of life and the many poor people who have been affected by the loss of the Titanic.

"What Lord Pirrie is told rests mainly with Lady Pirrie. Messages are continually coming for him, but they all go to Lady Pirrie first."

But for the fact that he had to undergo an operation Lord Pirrie might have been a passenger on the Titanic.

Hitherto it has been his invariable habit to take his personal share in the triumphs of the first voyages of the great ships which his brain has enabled his firm to turn out at Belfast.

The Daily Mirror
THE MORNING JOURNAL WITH THE SECOND LARGEST NET SALE.

No. 2,649.   Registered at the G.P.O. as a Newspaper.   SATURDAY, APRIL 20, 1912   One Halfpenny.

BANDSMEN HEROES ON THE SINKING TITANIC PLAY "NEARER, MY GOD, TO THEE!" AS THE LINER GOES DOWN TO HER DOOM.

20 April **1912**

THE FINAL SCENES OF TRAGIC HORROR ON THE SINKING TITANIC

Survivors' Accounts of the Most Terrible Experiences in the World.

CRIES FROM THE SEA
Englishman Tells How Men Played Cards Ignorant of Their Doom.

MR. W. T. STEAD'S END
Explosion of Boilers that Broke the Vessel in Two.

The humble truth of the catastrophe that overwhelmed the Titanic and carried 1,600 souls to their deaths is revealed in the vivid and awful accounts given by the survivors.

Their narratives differ in many points of detail – they saw what happened from different points of view – but in the main points there is for the most part agreement. How no one on board realised what had happened after the collision, how a party of card-players resumed their play after a moment's interruption, how the men died like heroes, how the ship was blown in two by the explosion of the boilers and sank bows first – all this is told, together with stories of unspeakable horrors and sufferings and marvellous escapes and the heartrending sundering of brides from husbands...

The first reports that stated that Captain Smith shot himself dead on the bridge after a struggle with his brother-officers in the library is now discredited, and believed to have emanated from the hysterical imaginings of survivors overwhelmed by the horrors of the situation.

ENGLISHMAN'S FULL STORY
The following account of the disaster by an Englishman, Mr. Beesley, formerly science master at Dulwich College, is given in a Reuter's Special Service message from New York:–

The temperature was very cold, particularly on the last day. In fact, after dinner on the Sunday evening it was almost too cold to be on the deck at all.

I had been in my berth about ten minutes, when at about 10.15 I felt a slight jar. Soon afterwards there was a second shock, but not sufficiently large to cause any anxiety to anyone. The engines, however, stopped immediately afterwards. I went up on deck in my dressing-gown, and I found only a few people there who had come up in the same way to inquire why we had stopped but there was no

It is a curious and sad coincidence that a brother of Mr. Bruce Ismay, the chairman of the White Star Line, is at present lying ill and forbidden to know the fate which has come upon the great ship which a week ago sailed forth in all the splendour and pride of her new life.

LINERS AVOIDING THE ICE
Further changes are being made in the routes of Atlantic liners in view of the ice peril that sank the Titanic.

The Cunard Line and other lines announce another amendment in the west-bound track, which will come into force right away.

All the steamers at present on their way to America will now take a course which will place them quite clear of ice.

As far as homeward steamers are concerned their track is much to the south of the outward track, and does not take them anywhere near the ice regions.

sort of anxiety in the mind of anyone.

We saw through the smoking-room window that a game of cards was going on, and I went in to ask if they knew anything. They had noticed the jar a little more, and, looking through the window, had seen a huge iceberg go by close to the side of the boat.

GAME OF CARDS RESUMED

They thought that we had just grazed it with a slanting blow, and had been to see if any damage had been done.

The game of cards was resumed, and without any thought of disaster I retired to my cabin to read until we started again. I never saw any of the players or the onlookers again.

A little later, hearing people going upstairs, I went out again, and found that everybody wanted to know why the engines had stopped.

Going up on the deck again, I saw that there was an unmistakable list downwards from the stern to the bows.

Again I went down to my cabin where I put on some warmer clothing. As I dressed I heard the order shouted, "All the passengers on deck with lifebelts on."

We all walked up slowly with the lifebelts tied on over our clothing, but even then we presumed that this was merely a wise precaution the captain was taking.

There was a total absence of any panic or expression of alarm. I suppose this must be accounted for by the exceeding calmness of the night and the absence of any signs of an accident.

The ship was absolutely still, and except for the gentle, almost unnoticeable, tilt downwards, there were no visible signs of the approaching disaster.

But, in a few moments, we saw the covers being lifted from the boats and the crews allotted to them standing by and uncoiling the ropes which were to lower them. We then began to realise that it was a more serious matter than we had at first supposed.

Presently we heard the order: "All men stand back away from the boats. All ladies retire to the nest deck below," which was the smoking-room or "B" deck.

The men all stood away and waited in absolute silence, some leaning against the end railings of the deck, others pacing slowly up and down.

The boats were then swung out and lowered from "A" deck. When they were level with "B" deck, where all the women were collected, the women got in quietly, with the exception of some, who refused to leave their husbands.

In some cases they were torn from their husbands and pushed into the boats, but in many instances they were allowed to remain, since there was no one to insist that they should go.

Looking over the side one saw the boats from aft already in the water slipping quietly away into the darkness.

Presently the boats near me were lowered with much creaking, as the new ropes slipped through the pulleys and blocks down the 90ft. which separated them from the water.

An officer in uniform came up as one boat went down, and shouted out, "When you're afloat row round to the companion ladder and stand by with other boats for orders."

"Aye, aye, sir," came up the reply, but I don't think any boat was able to obey the order, for when they were afloat and had their oars at work the condition of the rapidly settling liner was much more apparent.

All this time there was no trace of any disorder, no panic or rush to the boats, no scenes of women sobbing hysterically, such as one generally pictures happening at such times.

Everyone seemed to realise so slowly that there was imminent danger that when realisation came it was extraordinary how calm everyone was, how completely self-controlled we were as the boats filled with women and children were lowered and rowed away into the night.

Presently word went round that men were to be put in boats on the starboard side, I was on the port side. Most of the men walked across the deck to see if this was true.

I remained where I was, and shortly afterwards I heard the call, "Any more ladies?" Looking over the side of the ship, I saw boat No. 13 swinging level with B deck, half-full of women. Again the call was repeated, "Any more ladies?" I saw none coming.

Then one of the crew looked up and said, "Any ladies on your deck, sir?" "No," I replied. "Then you'd better jump," said he.

I dropped and fell into the bottom of the boat as they cried "Lower away!"

BABY RESCUED JUST IN TIME

As the boat began to descend, two ladies were pushed hurriedly through the crowd on B deck, and a baby, ten months old, was passed down after them. Then down we went, the crew shouting out directions to those lowering us until we were some 10ft. from the water.

Here occurred the only anxious moment we had during the whole of our experience from the time of our leaving the deck to our reaching the Carpathia.

Immediately below our boat was the exhaust of the condensers, and a huge stream of water was pouring all the time from the ship's side just above the water-line.

It was plain that we ought to be smart away from it if we were to escape swamping when we touched the water.

We had no officers on board, and no petty officers or member of

the crew to take charge.

So one of the stokers shouted, "Some one find the pin which releases the boat from the ropes and pull it up!"

We felt as well as we could on the floor and along the sides, but found nothing. It was difficult to move among so many people. We had sixty or seventy on board.

Down we went, and presently, what with the stream of water from the exhaust and the swell of the sea, we were carried directly under boat No. 14, which had filled rapidly with men, and was coming down on us.

ESCAPE BY SECONDS

"Stop lowering fourteen!" our crew shouted, and the crew of No. 14, now only 20ft. above, cried out the same.

But those above could not have heard, for down she came – 15ft., 10ft., 5ft., and a stoker and I reached up and touched the bottom of the swinging boat above our heads.

The next drop would have brought her on our heads, but just before she dropped another stoker sprang to the ropes with his knife open in his hand.

"One," I heard him say, and then "Two," as the knife cut through the pulley rope. The next moment the exhaust stream carried us clear, while boat No. 14 dropped into the water. Our gunwales were almost touching.

Our crew seemed to me to be mostly cooks. They sat in their white jackets, two to an oar, with a stoker at the tiller.

After some shouting and discussion we elected as captain the stoker who was steering, and all agreed to obey his orders. He set to work at once to get into touch with the other boats.

It was now one o'clock in the morning. The starlit night was beautiful, but, as there was no moon, it was not very light. The sea was as calm as a pond.

LAST FLASH OF LINER'S LIGHTS

In the distance the Titanic looked enormous. Her length and her great bulk were outlined in black against the starry sky.

Every porthole and saloon was blazing with light. It was impossible to think that anything could be wrong with such a leviathan were it not for that ominous tilt downward in the bows.

At about 2 o'clock we observed her settling very rapidly, with the bows and the bridge completely under water.

She slowly tilted straight on end, with the stern vertically upwards, and as she did so the lights in the cabin and saloons died out, flashed once more, and than went out altogether.

At the same time the machinery roared down through the vessel with a groaning rattle that could have been heard for miles. It was the weirdest sound surely that could have been heard in the middle of the ocean.

It was not yet quite the end. To our amazement, she remained in that upright position for a time which I estimate as five minutes. It was certainly for some minutes that we watched at least 150ft. of the Titanic lowering up above the level of the sea, looming black against the sky. Then with a quiet slanting dive she disappeared beneath the waters.

Then there fell on our ears the most appalling noise that human beings ever heard – the cries of hundreds of our fellow-beings struggling in the icy water, crying; for help with a cry that we knew could not be answered.

We longed to return to pick up some of those who were swimming, but this would have meant the swamping of our boat and the loss of all of us.

KISSED LOVED ONES' KNEES

New York, April 19 – The scenes in dock as the survivors landed were full of suppressed excitement.

Men were in hysterics, women fainting, children almost crushed in the arms of those welcoming them.

Men fell down to kiss the knees of their beloved ones, women shrieked and wept and collapsed in the arms of their brothers and husbands.

The number of badly injured was not nearly so large as had been imagined. The cases requiring hospital attention were few, but the strain of the trial of their lives had left unmistakable signs in their faces of the arrivals.

Some could barely talk, others could not refrain from shouting. What was a joyous occasion to some killed the last rays of hope in the breasts of others. Many were the affecting scenes both of joy and sorrow.

Among the most affecting scenes at the landing was the sight of the women steerage survivors as they came down from the deck, thinly clad and shivering, their eyes red with constant weeping.

In their faces was the drawn, tense look or a desperate haunting fear. They were taken care of at once by members of the numerous charitable organisations who were at hand.

It was learned from the survivors that five – some said six – of the rescued died on board the Carpathia and were buried at sea. Three of these were sailors, the other two or three were passengers.

OFFICIAL FIGURES OF SAVED

New York, April 19 – According to official figures which have been issued by the officers of the Cunard Line, 705 of the persons aboard the Titanic at the time of the collision were saved.

Of this number 202 were first-class passengers,
115 second-class,
178 third.

The remaining 210 saved were members of the crew.

Many survivors were picked up from the water. In the statement the officials make no mention of the number missing.

SHOT WHILE TRYING TO RUSH A BOAT

Lady Duff Gordon's Grim Story of Her Own Escape.

The following stories were given by survivors to Reuter's representatives at New York:–

New York, April 19 – Lady Duff Gordon, who left in one of the last boats, said that panic had begun to seize some of the remaining passengers by the time her boat was lowered.

Everyone seemed to be rushing for that boat. A few men who crowded in were turned back at the point of Captain Smith's revolver, and several of them were felled before order was restored.

"I recall being pushed towards one of the boats and being helped in," she said. "Just as we were about to clear the ship a man made a rush to get aboard our lifeboat.

"He was shot and apparently killed instantly. His body fell in the boat at our feet. No one made any effort to move him, and his body remained in the boat until we were picked up.

"I saw bodies in the water in all directions. The poor souls could not live long in the terribly cold water."

FIFTH OFFICER'S COURAGE

A young Englishwoman, who requested that her name might be omitted, told a thrilling story of her experience in one of the collapsible boats, which was manned by eight of the crew and commanded by the fifth officer, Mr. Lowe, whose action she described as saving the lives of many.

Before the boat was launched he passed along the deck of the Titanic commanding the people not to jump into the boats, and otherwise restraining them from swamping the craft.

When the collapsible boat was launched he succeeded in putting up a mast and sail. He collected other boats, and in some cases, where the boats were short of adequate crew, he did an exchange whereby each was properly manned.

Mr. Lowe threw lines to connect boats two by two, so that all

moved together. Later he went back to the wreck.

One boat succeeded in picking up some of those who had jumped overboard and were swimming about.

BOAT ONE-THIRD FILLED

On his way back to the Carpathia he passed one of the collapsible boats which was on the point of sinking with thirty persons on board, most of them in scant night clothing. They were rescued in the nick of time.

The relator of this account said that some of these people died on the way to the Carpathia.

One of the Carpathia's stewards gave an interesting account of how the first boatload of passengers was rescued, he said:–

"Just as it was about half-day we came upon a boat with eighteen men in it, but no women. It was not more than a third filled. All the men were able to climb up a Jacob's ladder which we threw over the port side. Every one of them was given a glass of brandy, or as much coffee as he wanted.

"Between 8.15 and 8.30," continued the steward, "we got the last two boats, crowded to the gunwale, almost all the occupants of which were women. After we had got the last load on board the Californian came alongside.

"The captains arranged that we should make straight for New York, while the Californian looked around for more boats. We circled round and round and saw all kinds of wreckage."

"THEN BEDLAM CAME."

"While we were pulling in the boatloads the women were quiet enough, but, when it seemed sure that we should not find any more persons alive, then bedlam came. I hope never to go through it again.

"The way those women took on for the folk they had lost was awful. We could not do anything to quiet them until they cried themselves out."

Major Arthur Penchen, of Toronto, an experienced yachtsman, after assisting members of the crew to fill the first five boats, was assigned by the second mate to take charge of boat 6. Just as he entered the boat Mr. Hays, president of the Grand Trunk Railway, who went down with the ship, came to wish him God-speed.

None of the passengers thought the ship would sink so soon. Mr. Hays predicted that she would keep afloat for at least eight hours, during which time help was sure to arrive, according to Major Penchen.

REFUSED TO ENTER A LIFEBOAT

Mr. Jacques Futrelle, the novelist, says a Reuter's special message, was one of those who parted from his wife and steadfastly refused

to accept a chance to enter a lifeboat when he knew that the Titanic was sinking under him.

How he went to his death is told by Mrs. Futrelle, who said:–

"Jacques is dead, but he died like a hero, that I know. Three or four times after the crash I rushed up to him and clasped him in my arms, begging him to get into one of the lifeboats.

"'For God's sake, go!' he fairly screamed, and tried to push me towards the lifeboat, I could see how he suffered. 'It's your last chance; go,' he pleaded.

"Then one of the ship's officers forced me into a lifeboat, and I gave up all hope that he could be saved."

NIGHT ON A RAFT

Of all the recitals of personal adventure in the Titanic disaster, that of Colonel Gracie, of the United States Army, who jumped from the topmost desk of the Titanic when she sank and was sucked down with her, is (says Reuter) the most extraordinary.

Colonel Gracie on reaching the surface again swam until he found a cork raft, and then helped to rescue others. He gives the exact time of the sinking of the Titanic as 2.22 a.m., which was the hour at which his watch was stopped by his leap into the sea.

"After sinking with the ship," he said, "it appeared to me as if I was propelled by some great force through the water.

"This might have been occasioned by explosions under the water, and I remembered fearful stories of people being boiled to death. The second officer has told me that he has had a similar experience."

PRAYED FOR DELIVERANCE

"Innumerable thoughts of a personal nature having relation to mental telepathy flashed through my brain, I thought of those at home as if my spirit might go to them to say 'Good-bye' for ever. Again and again I prayed for deliverance, although I felt sure that the end had come.

"I had the greatest difficulty in holding my breath until I came to the surface. I knew that once I inhaled the water would suffocate me.

"When I got under water I struck out with all my strength for the surface. I got to air again after a time, which seemed to me to be unending.

"There was nothing in sight save the ocean, dotted with ice and strewn with large masses of wreckage. Dying men and women all about me were groaning and crying piteously.

"The second officer and Mr. J. B. Thayer, jun., who were swimming near me, told me that just before my head appeared above the water one of the Titanic's funnels separated and fell apart near me, scattering the bodies in the water. I saw wreckage

everywhere and all that came within reach I clung to."

Colonel Gracie relates how, by moving from one piece of wreckage to another, he at last reached the raft.

"Soon," he continued, "the raft became so full that it seemed as if she would sink if more came on board her. The crew for self-preservation had therefore to refuse to permit any others to climb on board."

"GOOD LUCK – GOD BLESS YOU!"

"This was the most pathetic and horrible scene of all. The piteous cries of those around us still ring in my ears, and I will remember them to my dying day.

"'Hold on to what you have, old boy!' we shouted to each man who tried to get on board. 'One more of you would sink us all!'

"Many of those whom we refused answered as they went to their death: 'Good luck – God bless you!'

"So we passed the night, with the waves washing over and burying the raft deep in water. We prayed through all the weary night, and there never was a moment when our prayers did not rise above the waves.

"Men who seemed long ago to have forgotten how to address their Creator recalled the prayers of their childhood and murmured them over and over again. Together we said the Lord's Prayer again and again."

EXHAUSTED WIRELESS OPERATORS

New York, April 19 – The refusal of the operators on board the Carpathia to answer questions concerning the disaster is now explained. It was due to the physical exhaustion of both the men.

They sent a large number of personal messages from survivors to friends ashore, and received replies from the latter.

Mr. Harold Cottam, the Marconi operator on the Carpathia, did not go to bed at his usual time on Sunday night, and as a result he caught the first message of the Titanic. This was responsible for saving hundreds of lives.

FATHER'S PRIDE IN HIS SON

The proudest father in London sat in a City office yesterday afternoon.

He was Mr. J. A. Bride, the father of Mr. Harold Bride, the junior Marconi operator of the Titanic, who after a thrilling rescue and with injured feet, calmly took over the Marconi operator's work on the Carpathia.

Mr. Bride, who is a shipping agent in City Road, was even more affected than when, last Tuesday, he heard of the disaster and concluded that his son must have been drowned.

"Am I proud?" said Mr. Bride to *The Daily Mirror*. "I cannot express how glad I am – not so much at my son being safe and sound as the fact that he seems to have done the right thing.

"He acted I believe, as an Englishman should. I know my boy – he takes things pretty quietly and never makes a fuss about anything."

▸ Harold Bride.

"YOU GO. I WILL STAY."

Heartbreaking Partings Between Husbands and Wives – Two of the Heroes.

New York, April 19 – On landing from the Carpathia Mrs. J. J. Astor told the members of her family what she could recall of the disaster. She had no very definite idea as to how her husband, Colonel Astor, met his death. She recalled that in the confusion, as she was about to be put into one of the boats Colonel Astor was standing at her side.

From other narratives it appears that the conduct of Colonel Astor was deserving of the highest praise. He devoted all his energies to saving his young bride, who was in delicate health.

He helped to get her into the boat and as she took her place he requested the permission of the second officer to go with her for her own protection. "No, sir," replied the officer, "no men shall go in the boat until the women are all off."

Colonel Astor then inquired the number of the boat and turned to work clearing the other boats and reassuring frightened and nervous women.

Mrs. Churchill Candee, of Washington, was taken from the Carpathia with both her legs broken. She received her injuries while getting into the lifeboat. "Major Archibald Butt and Colonel Astor died like heroes," she said.

WOMEN AT THE OARS

Mrs. Edgar T. Meyer, of New York, said that after the first shock she and Mr. Meyer ran to the lifeboats. She pleaded with her husband to be allowed to remain with him. He finally threw her into the lifeboat, reminding her of their nine-year-old child at home.

Mrs. Meyer, with an English girl, rowed in her boat for four and a half hours. "We were well away from the steamer when it sank," she said. "There were about seventy of us widows on board the Carpathia."

Mrs. W. D. Marvin, of New York, who was on her honeymoon trip, was almost prostrated when she learned on reaching the dock that her husband had not been picked up.

"As I was put into the boat he cried to me," she said, "'It's all right, little girl. You go. I will stay.' As our boat shoved off he threw me a kiss, and that was the last I saw of him."

George Rheims, of New York, who was on the Titanic with his brother-in-law, Mr. Joseph Holland, a London resident, said that many of the passengers stood round for hours with their lifebelts on. When all the boats had gone he shook hands with his brother-in-law, who would not jump, and leaped over the side of the boat.

He swam for a quarter of an hour, and reached a lifeboat. It had eighteen occupants, and was half under water. The people were in the water up to their knees. Seven of them died during the night. Only those who stood all the time remained alive. – Reuter's Special Service.

OUT TO SMASH RECORD?

New York, April 19 – Various statements are being put forward regarding the speed at which the Titanic was travelling when she struck. One which purports to be that of a petty officer of the liner says that there were general orders to smash the record, and the ship was making twenty-one knots when the collision occurred. – Reuter.

Several survivors assert, says Reuter, that the Titanic was going at the rate of twenty-three knots an hour when she struck the iceberg.

SLEPT THROUGH COLLISION

New York, April 19 – Mr. Hugh Woolner, of London, the son of the late Mr. Thomas Woolner, the sculptor, said that after the collision he saw what seemed to be a continent of ice.

"It was not thought at first," he said, "that the liner had been dealt a dangerous blow. Some of the men were in the gymnasium taking exercise, and for some minutes they remained there, not knowing what was going on above their heads.

"After a while there was an explosion, then a moment later a second explosion. It was the second which did most damage. It blew away the funnels, and tore a big hole in the steamer's side.

"The ship rocked like a rowing boat, and then careened over on one side to such an extent that the passengers making for the boats slid into the water. The ship filled rapidly."

There is abundance of evidence that the shock of the collision with the iceberg was scarcely noticeable. Many people seem to have slept through it. – Reuter.

SLOWLY KILLED HOPES

Man Faints and Women Break Down After Waiting in Vain for Names.

Once again, for the fifth dreadful day, the London offices of the White Star Line were thronged yesterday with hundreds of sad-faced, silent men and women, waiting and watching for the name, the word or two which meant the difference between life and death.

It was perhaps the most dreadful day of all. Previously there had been the chance – a slender chance, it is true, of some wonderful unexpected news being flashed across the wires. There had been just the hope that other ships than the Carpathia might have picked up survivors from the Titanic.

But yesterday that hope was dead. It was known that only comparatively few fresh names of saved ones could be expected.

Every hour that passed uneventfully hammered its growing message of despair firmer and firmer into many already torn, aching hearts.

One man, probably a father or a brother, was so affected by the fact that the name he sought never came that he at last lost control of himself, and, staggering from the office, fell insensible on the steps. A policeman rendered first aid, and succeeded in restoring the poor fellow to consciousness.

And then the awful, gaunt-eyed tragedy of it all would be thrown out into relief by the one thrice fortunate watcher who found that eagerly-sought name.

The clerks knew her well. They had seen her come each day, garbed in mourning clothes, to sit there, weary and listless, ever since that awful morning – how many ages ago! – when the news came through.

They posted a list again yesterday, and there was a flutter of hopeless hope in the hearts of those who waited.

The lady in black reached the list and scanned the names, and suddenly:–

"Saved, my God, saved!" she cried, half-hysterically, and ran towards the door.

A poor woman, a relative of one of the crew from her appearance, completely broke down in the early afternoon.

Sitting alone, hope ebbing from her soul as the cruel, silent minutes sped on, her tears suddenly began to fall fast. With a great effort she managed to control her emotion for a moment and, rising, passed swiftly from the building out into the sun-flooded streets – anywhere.

GIRL'S JOY AT LOVER'S RESCUE
(FROM OUR OWN CORRESPONDENT)

Southampton, April 19 – Hundreds of people were this afternoon wearing mourning for those for whom all hope has been abandoned.

I have visited several homes which are plunged in the deepest grief. One poor woman lost her first husband in the wreck of the Stella, and now her second in the Titanic.

Three young girls, who reluctantly left the White Star office at 2 a.m., when it was announced that no further names could be received till 6 a.m., returned at 2.30 a.m., and stood shivering in the street till, for sheer pity, they were asked to come inside and sit by the manager's office fire.

One of them was in a hysterical state of fear for the life of her sweetheart, a young fellow named Johnstone, and the other two girls were faithful friends who would not leave her. Her sobs were heartrending till her lover's name appeared in the list of survivors, and then she swooned with joy.

A White Star official informed me that he thinks they can identify from the passenger and crew lists in the office all except about fifty of the 728 names received. The approximate figures and the analysis so far as it goes shows roughly 350 men and 378 women and children saved. These figures include 190 men of the crew and fifteen women employed as stewardesses or in the ship's laundry.

"I cannot understand that awful wicked lie from America about Captain Smith shooting himself," he said afterwards. "Nobody who knew him as I did could possibly believe he would do such a thing. He was one of the best men God ever made, and one of the bravest and truest."

It has been heartbreaking to witness the agony of the women at the White Star office since 7.15 this morning, when the first list of the crew survivors was put up. They stuffed handkerchiefs and gloves in their mouths to deaden the sound of the sobs they could not withhold. A little invalid girl in a perambulator hugged her mother's arm as the poor woman bent over her, wailing amid her sobs. She stretched up her face to kiss, with the words in a baby lisp: "Let me love you, mumma. Daddy will come back soon." The mother could not speak.

FACED DEATH ALONE

Sublime in its supreme unselfishness, the death of Captain E. J. Smith was the death of an English captain – he perished with his ship.

Face to face with certain disaster, he was calm and self-possessed, thinking only of the lives of those in his charge. He ignored his own peril.

And then, when all that human foresight could do and had been done unavailingly to save the Titanic, he still remembered his quiet little band of hardworking officers, and released them from duty.

"It's every man for himself at such a time as this," he said. "I release you. Look out for yourselves."

But for Captain Smith there was no one to give the word of release. His place was with his riven vessel to the end.

Standing on the deck of his ship, alone, a solitary and heroic figure, Captain Smith faced death in the swirling, ice-cold sea with all the calm, death-defying heroism that is the tradition of the men of the British Navy.

Poignantly sad in its realism is the word picture of the passing of the Titanic's captain given by Mr. George A. Braden, of California.

He states:-

"I saw Captain Smith while I was in the water. He was standing on the deck all alone.

"Once he was swept down by a wave, but managed to get to his feet again. Then, as the boat sank, he was again knocked down by a wave and then disappeared from view."

Extraordinary rumours cabled from America were to the effect that Captain Smith shot himself as the Titanic was sinking, but this picturesque version was generally discredited yesterday.

Captain E. J. Smith, R.N.R., of the Titanic, had been in the service of the White Star Company for thirty-eight years, and was sixty years of age.

Until last year, at the time of the Olympic collision, when he was in command of the liner, he had met with no serious accident.

He was a native of Staffordshire, and served his apprenticeship to the sea with Gibson and Co., of Liverpool.

During the South African war he twice carried troops to the Cape in the Majestic, and was decorated by the Government for his work as a transport officer.

He held an extra master's certificate, and was honorary commander of the R.N.R. He leaves a wife and a thirteen-year-old daughter.

Not the least of the heroes of the catastrophe were the Titanic's bandsmen.

BANDSMEN'S LAST HYMN

In the whole history of the sea there is little equal to the wonderful behaviour of these humble players. In the last moments of the great ship's doom, when all was plainly lost, when presumably braver and hardier men might almost have been excused for doing practically anything to save themselves, they stood responsive to their conductor's baton and played a hymn, "Nearer, My God, to Thee."

There were two bands on board the Titanic, one, a saloon orchestra, comprising five men the other, a deck hand, numbering three, so Mr. Black, of the Liverpool firm which controlled the band, yesterday told *The Daily Mirror*.

"Probably," he said, "they all massed together under their leader, Mr. Wallace Hartley, as the ship sank. Five of the eight, Mr. Hartley, P. C. Taylor, J. W. Woodward, F. Clark and W. T. Brailey, were Englishmen; one J. Hume, was a Scotsman, and the remaining two, Bricoux and Krins, were French and German respectively."

Mr. Wallace Hartley, the man who got his men together and played the tune which must have given blessed consolation to hundreds in their last moments of life, was a young Yorkshireman.

Only thirty-four, he was well known and popular in Bridlington, Harrogate and Leeds' musical circles. He was to have been married shortly, his fiancée being a Boston girl, whose bereavement is double, for she only lost her father a few weeks ago.

It is a coincidence revealed yesterday that Mr. W. T. Stead, when issuing a special book of hymns, was the first to reveal the fact that "Nearer, My God, to Thee" was a favourite hymn with King Edward.

THE LIFEBOAT QUESTION

Some striking opinions were obtained from prominent public men by *The Daily Mirror* yesterday on the question of the Titanic's boat accommodation for her passengers and crew.

Mr. T. Gibson Bowles, the well-known politician, who is the author of "Sea Law and Sea Power," said that he was too horrified to express his feelings adequately.

"For years I have been attacking the Board of Trade, not particularly on the question of boat accommodation of liners, but on shipping matters generally," he said.

"By the Board of Trade regulations still in force the number of boats for life-saving purposes is decided by the tonnage of the vessel, and not by the number of human souls on board.

"As a consequence we have small vessels which are forced to carry far more boats than they need while vessels like the Titanic are allowed to sail with an insufficiency of boats."

"THIS TERRIBLE LOSS OF LIFE."

"Is not such a system a scandal to the country? I say that a Board of Trade which allows such regulations to go into force should be abolished.

"The indignation of the whole country should be aroused by this terrible loss of life, which might have been prevented had the regulations been sound and adequate."

Sir Clement Kinloch-Cooke, M.P., said:–

"I think there ought to be a sufficient number of boats on every ship to save the lives of every person aboard.

"I shall be ready to add my support to any movement which may be started to investigate this serious matter."

"TO GET AT THE TRUTH."

New York, April 19 – After summoning Mr. Bruce Ismay to appear before the Special Committee appointed by the Senate to inquire into the Circumstances of the Titanic disaster, Mr. Smith, the chairman of the committee, said:–

"We will not fail to give the public all the facts of the case. We are going to get at the truth." – Exchange Telegraph.

Mr. Smith, who had a conference with Mr. Ismay and Mr. Franklin during the night, afterwards said that Mr. Ismay made a very frank statement, but he preferred that the public should hear his story from his own lips, when he appears before the committee.

Mr. Franklin said that the White Star Line welcomed the Government inquiry, and that the investigation could not be conducted on too broad lines to suit the company. – Reuter.

◆ Bruce Ismay.

MR. ISMAY'S GRIEF

New York, April 19 – Mr. Bruce Ismay, of the White Star Line, gave out the following prepared statement on the pier:–

In the presence and under the shadow of this catastrophe of the sea, which overwhelms my feelings too deeply for expression in words, I can only say that the White Star officers and employees will do everything humanly possible to alleviate the sufferings and sorrow of relations and friends of those who perished.

The Titanic was the last word in shipbuilding. Every regulation prescribed by the British Board of Trade had been strictly complied with. The master, officers and crew were the most experienced and skilful in the British service.

I heartily welcome a most complete and exhaustive inquiry, and any aid which I and my associates and our builders and navigators can render is at the service of the public and the Government, both in the United States and Great Britain. Under these circumstances I must deter making any further statement.

Mr. Ismay also stated informally: "I do not know the speed at which the Titanic was going. She hit the iceberg a glancing blow." – Reuter.

WHY MR. ISMAY WAS ON TITANIC

It was due to his personal interest in the welfare of his great business that Mr. J. Bruce Ismay, the managing director of the White Star Line, was on board the Titanic.

He is one of the most prominent figures in the shipping world, and takes a keenly justifiable pride in the great steamship line which he controls.

A man of strong personality, with a remarkable grasp of the detail of his vast business, Mr. Ismay has always made it his invariable custom to travel on all new White Star liners on their maiden voyages.

Thus he was able to deal immediately with any alterations or emergencies that might arise on a new ship.

The destruction, under such terrible conditions, of a ship, upon the building of which he had spent so many months, has been a deeply personal blow,

Mr. Ismay is the eldest of three sons and two daughters of the late Mr. T. H. Ismay, founder of the White Star Line.

His brother, Mr. J. Bower Ismay, is the owner of Bloodstone, which ran second in the Grand National. Mr. James Ismay and Mr. Bower Ismay have now both retired from the firm.

Mr. Bruce Ismay served a portion of his apprenticeship in Liverpool and America, and before succeeding his father he was mostly in America. He and his brother, Mr. Bower Ismay married two sisters of a well-known American family.

Mr. Bruce Ismay is president of the Transatlantic Combine, and conducted all the negotiations with Mr. J. Pierpont Morgan, the representative of the American stockholders.

TITANIC'S DESIGNER FAINTS

There was a poignantly dramatic incident during the memorial service held at St. Paul's Cathedral yesterday for those who perished in the Titanic disaster.

Among the large congregation that included Mr. Sydney Buxton and Mr. John Burns and many foreign Ambassadors was the Hon. Alexander Carlisle, the designer of the Titanic, who occupied a reserved seat in the choir.

Obviously deeply moved, Mr. Carlisle was very pale when he entered the Cathedral. After taking his place he appeared deeply

affected by the playing of the Dead March, and suddenly, while the sad, solemn strains of the Liturgy of St. Chrysostom were being sung, he fell back in a faint.

Help was quickly at hand. Mr. Carlisle was taken from the Cathedral, and after being attended by police ambulance men recovered sufficiently to be driven home.

Seldom was there a scene of more tragic mourning in the Cathedral. It was a congregation truly representative of the grief of a nation, and, indeed, of many nations whose citizens are among the toll of missing.

Nearly all the foreign embassies in London were represented, great ambassadors coming to offer the tribute of great empires to the noble dead.

Interest was also great outside the Cathedral, where a great crowd collected and waited in silence.

THIS MORNING'S GOSSIP

Already many well-known ladies, in London and New York, are, it is reported, offering to adopt, or to be responsible for the education of any fatherless and motherless children who may turn out to be rescued from the Titanic. This suggestion shows how enormously the hearts of people have been touched. It is at least some small consolation to think that those who survive will in some slight measure be consoled for the loss of friends they hold dear who perished.

22 April **1912**

STRONG FEELING AGAINST MR. ISMAY
White Star Chairman Resents "Brutal Unfairness" of Inquiry.

ORDERED TO STAY
Thrilling Evidence of Titanic's Junior Wireless Operator.

SECOND OFFICER'S ESCAPE
Sucked Down and Blown to Surface by Boiler Explosion.

New York, April 20 – The seriousness of the Senatorial investigation into the loss of the Titanic was disclosed yesterday evening, when Senator Smith at first flatly refused to permit any of the officers or crew of the Titanic to sail on the Red Star liner Lapland despite the protests of Mr. Burlingham, counsel for the White Star Line.

Later, as the result of a conference, it was decided to permit all but twelve of the crew and the four rescued officers – Messrs. Lightoller, Pittman, Boxhall and Lowe – to depart, but not to allow Mr. Bruce Ismay to leave.

Although Mr. Ismay urged that he should be allowed to go for the present, pleading that he was on the verge of a collapse, his request was not granted.

Mr. Ismay, discussing the work of the investigating committee

The Daily Mirror

THE MORNING JOURNAL WITH THE SECOND LARGEST NET SALE.

No. 2,650.   April 22, 1912.   One Halfpenny.

MRS. ELEANOR SMITH, WIFE OF THE TITANIC'S COMMANDER, WHOSE HUSBAND WENT DOWN WITH HIS VESSEL SHOUTING "BE BRITISH."

"To My Poor Fellow-Sufferers. "My heart overflows with grief for you all, and is laden with sorrow that you are weighed down with this terrible burden that has been thrust upon us. "May God be with us and comfort us all. "April 18, 1912."

"Yours in deep sympathy, (Signed) "ELEANOR SMITH."

The sympathy of the whole world goes out to Mrs. Smith, the widow of Captain E. J. Smith, the heroic commander of the Titanic. Though no woman could have lost her husband in more tragic circumstances, she has borne her overwhelming grief with a bravery which compels admiration. In the midst of her distress her thoughts have been as much for others as for herself. This is proved by the heartbroken message which she sent to her fellow-sufferers. The message, which is reproduced above, was posted outside the White Star offices in Southampton. The above photograph is said to be the only one in existence of Mrs. Smith. It was taken ten years ago, and shows her with her daughter Melville, now fourteen years of age.

with interviewers to-day, described it as "brutally unfair." He said:–

"I cannot understand this inquiry. They're going at it in a manner that seems unjust, and the injustice lies the heaviest upon me.

"Why, I cannot even protect myself by having my counsel to ask questions. Don't misunderstand me by thinking I mean questions calculated to upset witnesses – on the contrary, questions intended simply to evolve meanings.

"MY CONSCIENCE IS CLEAR."

"I have searched my mind with the deepest care. I am sure I did nothing I should not have done. My conscience is clear.

"I took a chance of escape when it came to me. I did not seek it. Every woman and child had been cared for before I left the boat, and more, all the men within reach had been cared for before I took my turn.

"It is true, I'm president of the company, but I didn't consider myself any different from the rest of the passengers. I took no other man's place."

During the debate in the Senate at Washington to-day on the resolution concerning the regulation of ocean traffic, Mr. McCumber took occasion to register a protest against "the trial, conviction, sentencing and execution of one who is connected with the Titanic on the floor of the Senate yesterday without fair, honest and full consideration."

Mr. McCumber was evidently referring to the speech of Mr. Raynor, in which he made a violent attack on Mr. Bruce Ismay. – Reuter.

SENATOR SMITH AND MR. ISMAY

New York, April 20 – Senator William Alden Smith, of Michigan, chairman of the Senate Committee which is investigating the loss of the Titanic, said to-day:–

"Mr. Bruce Ismay sent a wireless message to Mr. Franklin, the general manager, in which he urged that the outward bound liner Cedric should be stopped to take himself and the survivors of the crew of the Titanic aboard and back to England.

"This message, however, was picked up by the wireless apparatus on a United States Government boat.

"Washington was at once communicated with. That is why the Senate Committee was so prompt in arriving in New York.

"I was on the pier when the Carpathia put in. Not only was Mr. Ismay eager to return to England on the Cedric, but he has been eager to get away on the Lapland since his arrival in New York.

"We require Mr. Ismay to remain here, however, as I have not concluded his examination." – Exchange Telegraph.

MR. HAROLD BRIDE'S STORY

New York, April 20 – The investigation here concluded to-day, and Mr. Bruce Ismay and other White Star officials have been subpoenaed by the Senate Committee to appear in Washington on Monday.

Mr. Cottam, the wireless operator of the Carpathia, who appeared before the committee yesterday, was further examined.

He stated that after picking up the Titanic's boats the Carpathia at first made towards Halifax, but afterwards changed her course for New York.

He denied having sent any message stating that all the passengers were safe, or that the Titanic was in tow.

Owing to the constant dispatch of messages he had had less than ten hours' sleep in three days.

He gave full details of the disaster to the Baltic, which was then steaming toward the scene of the wreck. This was about half-past ten on Monday morning.

Mr. Bride, the assistant wireless operator of the Titanic, who was wheeled in a chair, both feet having been injured in the course of his escape, was also called.

Perhaps the most interesting part of his evidence related to the steamer Frankfurt. He said that twenty minutes after Phillips, the chief operator, had sent out the C. Q. D. signal, the Frankfurt operator interrupted to ask what was the matter.

By that time the Carpathia was on her way to the rescue, and although, judging by the strength of the signals, the Frankfurt was the nearer of the two vessels, Phillips, remarking that the man was a fool, replied telling him to keep out.

Bride explained that Phillips' idea was that he preferred to trust to the Carpathia than to send out a message accepting the help of a vessel which had been so much slower in responding, and thus, perhaps, lead the Carpathia to think she was not wanted. "He preferred to hang on to the certainty."

Mr. Bride, in concluding his evidence, said that he saw the captain, who had not donned a life preserver, on the bridge until just before the Titanic went down.

The water had reached the bridge and the captain jumped into the sea.

CAPTAIN SMITH'S LAST ORDER

In his evidence Mr. Lightoller, second officer (says a Reuter's special message), said he was in the sea with a lifebelt an hour and a half.

When the Titanic sank he was in the officers' quarters. All but one of the lifeboats were gone. Mr. Murdoch (the first officer) was trying to launch it.

Did you see Mr. Ismay then? – No.

When did you see him? – When he was uncovering the boats. He was standing on the boat-deck.

When you saw Mr. Ismay twenty minutes after the collision were other passengers near him? – I did not see anyone in particular, but there might have been.

"Although ice had been reported," he added, "I was not anxious about it."

You did not post an additional look-out? – No.

Mr. Murdoch relieved him at ten o'clock. The weather was calm and clear, and stars on the horizon were observable.

After the crash he found Mr. Murdoch and Captain Smith on the bridge. He last saw Captain Smith walking the bridge.

What was the last order of Captain Smith? – "Put the women and children into the boats and lower away."

What did you do? – I obeyed the order.

How were the passengers selected to fill the boats? – By sex.

Who determined who should go? – I did. Whenever I saw a woman I put her in, except the stewardesses. I turned those back.

He explained (proceeds Reuter) that when the first boat was lowered the deck was 70ft. above the level of the water. By the time it came to the last boat, however, the deck was but a few feet above, and the steamer was sinking rapidly.

He maintained throughout his remarks that the boats were well filled, the preference always being given to women.

SUCKED UNDER AND BLOWN UPWARDS

In accounting for the saving of so many of the crew, Mr. Lightoller declared that he had especially inquired and had ascertained that out of every six persons picked up from the water five were either firemen or stewards.

Further, he explained how some of the lifeboats went back after the Titanic had sunk and rescued men from the sea.

He said no demonstration had occurred on board, and there was not even any lamentation among those who were left behind.

In describing his own escape, the officer recounted how he stood in the officers' quarters and dived as the ship sank. He was sucked under and held fast against a blower.

Then came a terrific gust up through the blower, due probably to a boiler explosion. He was blown clear, and came to the surface near a boat.

MRS. STRAUS, HEROINE

Mr. Crawford, the bedroom steward on the Titanic, told of the late Mr. and Mrs. Straus. He said that Mrs. Straus put her maid into a boat and started herself to enter.

Then she walked up to her husband and said, "We have been living a number of years together. We are not going to separate now."

"Did you see any struggle on deck for lifeboats?" – "No; everybody was orderly."

Witness said he saw Mr. Ismay on the boat deck assisting Mr. Murdoch to put women into a lifeboat, Mr. Ismay afterwards helped Mr. Murdoch to lower the boat. – Reuter's Special Service.

SEAMEN KEPT UNDER GUARD

New York, April 20 – Fortunate were the members of the Titanic's surviving crew on board the Lapland, who sailed this morning.

Generous merchants and others had fitted them out with clothes, hats, brushes, razors and numerous other things for use, together with sums of money for their immediate needs. Other sums will be sent later by the relief committee.

The stories of the American survivors of the Titanic will be told before the Senate Committee at its sittings in Washington.

Subpoenas are being sent out to-day.

A number were served in the hotel where the New York hearings are being held. A score of seamen are confined to a room in the hotel under the guard of the committee's detectives.

This afternoon's session was very brief. After one or two questions had been put to the Titanic's third officer, the hearing was adjourned till Monday in Washington. – Reuter.

TAPPED WIRELESS
Virginian's Captain Tells Story of Attempt at Rescue.

160 MILES DETOUR
Olympic Passengers Contribute £1,400 to Relief Fund.

Flags were half-mast high on the Olympic when she arrived at Plymouth on Saturday from New York, and general gloom prevailed on board, most of the crew having lost near friends, if not relatives.

It was just before eleven o'clock last Sunday, in fact, within twenty minutes of the iceberg being struck, that the Olympic heard her wounded sister's cry for help.

It did not reach Captain Haddock direct, as his ship was 500 miles distant. It came to him through the Celtic, and then in response a desperate effort was made. At a speed of between twenty-three and twenty-four knots, the Olympic rushed towards the Titanic for twelve or thirteen hours.

All this while there was no serious alarm felt, the ship being thought to be unsinkable, and then came the startling news from the Carpathia that she had arrived too late, that the Titanic had foundered, and that the survivors were on board the Carpathia.

The intelligence created a consternation, and as soon as possible on the Monday afternoon Captain Haddock dispatched a wireless message conveying the distressing news to New York.

OLYMPIC'S RACE TO HELP TITANIC
CAPTAIN HADDOCK EXPLAINS
(FROM OUR OWN CORRESPONDENT)
Southampton, April 21 – Captain Haddock this afternoon, in the presence of Mr. Curry, of the White Star Line, made the following very important statement to me:–

"On the passage from Cherbourg to Southampton I received a letter from two newspaper correspondents requesting me to explain this message that had been published:–

All Titanic passengers safe. Titanic proceeding slowly to Halifax under her own steam, which telegram caused a drop of twenty to sixty guineas in reinsurances at Lloyd's on Monday afternoon.

"It was supposed that this message emanated from the ship,

because it came through Reuter, they said.

"The correspondents asked me whether the message emanated from this ship, and, if so, how it came to be sent if it was not true.

"What I told them I now tell you. A message came to the Olympic from one of our oldest passengers, a lady, from New York, reading:–

"Are all Titanic passengers safe?

"That message was received on board at 10.27 New York mean time (about 3.25 Greenwich time).

"At another period of the day – I think it was earlier – we were in communication with another ship, the Asian, from which I tried to get information about the Titanic.

"She could give me very little indeed, but amongst the words used were these:–

"Towing oil tank steamer to Halifax.

"I have written to my owners:–

I have denied, in the presence of our Marconi operators, that such a message as 'All Titanic passengers safe' was either received or sent from the Olympic.

The only solution that I can offer for the Reuter message is the enclosed Marconigram, which may have been tapped in transmission, and word 'are' missed out, which would make it read: 'All Titanic passengers safe.'

The remaining words, 'Titanic making slowly for Halifax under her own steam,' might be suggested by the Asian message, the copy of which is already in your possession.

The message I received, probably from a constant White Star traveller, and I, on receipt of the message, made the same mistake, and left out the word 'are,' and telephoned the inquiry office to put up a notice reading, 'All Titanic passengers safe,' nothing more was added.

We have been most carefully through every message from the ship. No copy of my error, plain or coded, or of the remainder of the message sent through Reuter was sent from the Olympic – H. J. Haddock, master.

"That is my explanation. When we picked up the Titanic message asking for assistance we were 505 miles away from the Titanic.

"We steamed hard towards her for fourteen hours before we picked up the Carpathia signals, and knew there was nothing more we could do.

"A week before the disaster," continued Captain Haddock, "the Olympic steamed near the spot where the Titanic sank. We passed, in fact, over it, or a few miles north.

"We never saw a single particle of ice of any description, and the observations in the locality were so perfect that from the bridge of the Olympic we could see twenty miles on either side.

"There was no sign of ice. The field ice must have travelled south very rapidly, indeed. I have never known an ice field travel south so fast."

Captain Haddock looks extremely ill, worried and fagged. His pale cheeks and dark side whiskers make him, though a short, spare man, a conspicuous figure.

"Captain Smith had never had an accident with a ship till the Hawke collided with the Olympic when he was in command," said another officer to me.

"He was the calmest man I have ever known, and if we had heard the story of his shooting himself – which he didn't – we should never have believed it for a moment."

Standing on the lofty top deck of the Olympic and looking down seventy-five feet at the water, it was possible to-day to realise the terrible condition of things on her sister ship last Sunday at midnight.

The St. Louis and Majestic beside her in the dock looked like tugboats, and one could understand how in the immense saloons people sat unperturbed after the shock of the collision with the iceberg, which was hardly felt amidships.

ARRIVAL OF THE VIRGINIAN

The Allan liner Virginian, which was at first erroneously reported to have been towing the ill-fated Titanic to Halifax, arrived at Liverpool yesterday morning.

Captain Gambell, the commander of the vessel, relates how he got a message from Cape Race that the Titanic wanted assistance.

He turned back, and got into wireless communication with other vessels, which were also proceeding to the scene of the disaster.

It was only when he received a wireless intimation from the Carpathia that she had the Titanic's survivors on board, and advising him to return to his usual track, that Captain Gambell resumed the voyage to Liverpool, which had been lengthened 169 miles.

He Marconied the Olympic, denying that he had picked up any survivors. He was at an utter loss to explain from what source the statement that he was towing the Titanic emanated.

SAILORS' LIFEBOAT DRILL

The full details of the terrible end of the Titanic were not communicated to the passengers, but everyone knew that she had gone down, and that many lives had been lost.

When it seemed the Virginian might be needed the sailors of H.M.S. Algerine, who were returning from the China station on board the liner, had orders to stand by the lifeboats.

Beds and cots, too, were prepared for the reception of any survivors who might be picked up in boats.

A ship's officer added that when the Virginian was first called upon by the Titanic the stokers worked like demons to get her to the scene of the disaster as soon as possible.

The next thing was a message from the Carpathia saying that all the Titanic's boats had been picked up. The same officer stated that they encountered an ice field which was at least fifty miles long. They were four hours in passing it. It was the biggest field seen for years.

NINE HOURS' RACE TO TITANIC

The White Star liner Baltic, which has arrived at Liverpool, reports having received a message from the Titanic appealing for assistance. The message broke off abruptly.

The Baltic steamed towards the scene of the disaster for nine hours, when a Marconigram was received from the Carpathia to the effect that all boats had been picked up and that further assistance was not required. Thereupon the Baltic resumed her voyage.

SAVED BY CHANCE

Already the terrible lessons of the Titanic disaster are being learned.

More boats, more wireless operators, searchlights and regulation

of passenger-carrying ships – these are the demands to which the grim death toll gives emphasis.

Mr. Ismay has announced (says a Reuter message from New York) that he has given instructions to all lines under the control of the International Mercantile Marine Company to equip all steamers with sufficient lifeboats and rafts to carry all the passengers and crew without regard to the regulations prescribed by the Government of any nation.

The White Star liner Olympic arrived at Southampton on Saturday, and work was at once begun on the task of fitting her with more boats and rafts.

SAVED BY TEN MINUTES

If the Titanic had received the fatal blow from the iceberg at 10.50 p.m. instead of 10.40 not a single soul would have been saved!

Ten minutes more and the wireless operator on board the Carpathia would have been in bed, the Titanic's call for help would not have been heard, and the 705 passengers who went away in lifeboats would have perished.

It was solely because the Carpathia's wireless operator happened

by chance to have delayed for ten minutes turning in on the fateful Sunday night that he was at his post and received the Titanic's urgent signal for help.

"Had he gone to rest as usual," said Dr. Kemp, the Carpathia's physician, "there would have been no survivors."

Most people will be amazed to learn that on many ships only one wireless operator is carried, and consequently during several hours of each day there is no one in charge of the apparatus to receive messages.

"It is nothing less than a public scandal," a Marconi expert said to *The Daily Mirror* yesterday.

"Wireless telegraphy is installed in a ship primarily for the purpose of saving life, but, as a matter of fact, the apparatus is regarded as more of a luxury for passengers.

◀ Milbank-street, Southampton, is a street of tragedy, as at house after house may be found some grief-stricken woman who is mourning the loss of one or more relatives. The photographic diagram, shows some of the houses over which hangs the shadow of death.

WHEN SHIPS CANNOT HEAR

"Only on the long-distance boats – the boats fitted with the most powerful apparatus – are two operators employed.

"They take turns at the apparatus in four-hour watches, so that there is always one man on duty to send or receive messages.

"But on short-distance boats – those fitted with apparatus carrying up to 200 miles – there is only one operator, and therefore when he retires to rest there is no one to take his place. The ship might be within ten miles of a sinking vessel and yet the distress signal would not be heard.

"Clearly this is a matter sufficiently grave to call for the strictest investigation.

"Every vessel fitted with wireless ought to be compelled by the Board of Trade regulations to carry two operators, so that there should always be somebody on duty in case of emergency.

"You must understand that no blame whatever attaches to the Marconi Company. The responsibility rests solely with the shipping companies, who, presumably from motives of economy, have except in a few instances, engaged only one operator instead of two."

22 April **1912**

JOY TURNED TO GRIEF

Southampton, April 21 – The agony of suspense in hundreds of homes here has been prolonged by the tragic discovery that the lists of survivors telegraphed from New York are inaccurate.

Not only have names and initials been sent over in confusion, but it is now found that scores of names sent as those of survivors are the names of missing.

Further than this, many persons whose names were not in the lists of survivors are alive.

All lists were withdrawn last evening from the boards here, because they were known to be inaccurate.

DIED TRYING TO SAVE THE MAIL

Washington, April 20 – Of the five postal clerks employed on the Titanic two were Englishmen, named respectively E. D. Williamson and Jago Smith. The other three were Americans.

According to official advices received by the Postmaster-General here, all five completely disregarded their own safety when the vessel struck, and began to carry the 200 sacks of the registered mail to the upper deck, thinking they might be saved.

As the situation became more desperate they appealed to the stewards to assist them, and continued their work to the last. Every one of them was lost. – Reuter.

£400 BOOK LOST IN WRECK

The copy of Fitzgerald's translation of "Omar Khayyam" with Elihu Vedder's beautiful illustrations, famous as "the most remarkable specimen of binding ever produced," has gone down with the Titanic.

Less than a month ago the work realised no less a sum: than £405 at the auction-rooms of Messrs. Sotheby, where it was purchased by Mr. Lionel Isaacs.

The binding of the book took two years to execute. In the exterior execution of the design the decoration embodies no fewer than 1,500 precious stones, each separately set in gold.

23 April 1912

GOVERNMENT INQUIRY AT ONCE INTO TITANIC DISASTER
Lord Mersey to Preside Over Special Court.

FULL LEGAL POWERS
Mystery of Suppressed News in New York Last Monday.

WHITE STAR WITNESS
Mr. Franklin Says He First Learnt Truth at 6.27 p.m.

MR. ISMAY SPEAKS OUT
The British Government is taking immediate action to lock the

The Daily Mirror
THE MORNING JOURNAL WITH THE SECOND LARGEST NET SALE.

No. 2,651.   Registered at the G.P.O. as a Newspaper.   TUESDAY, APRIL 23, 1912   One Halfpenny.

THE SCANDAL OF THE LIFEBOATS: PUTTING MANY MORE ON THE OLYMPIC AFTER THE LESSON OF DISASTER TO HER SISTER SHIP.

Busy scenes were enacted on board the Olympic at Southampton yesterday. The lessons of the terrible disaster to her sister ship, the Titanic, are already being learned, and when she sails again to-morrow she will have on board no fewer than forty new lifeboats and collapsible boats and about a dozen rafts, which are in addition to the sixteen lifeboats she has hitherto carried. This means that there will be enough boats for everyone on board. (1) A lifeboat being hoisted on the giant liner. (2) Collapsible boats lying on the upper deck.—(Daily Mirror photographs.)

stable door after the horse is gone. There is to be drastic inquiry into the safety of passengers at sea.

Lord Mersey has been appointed to preside over a Court of Inquiry into the loss of the Titanic.

Having been stagnant for seventeen years, the Board of Trade was informed last July by an expert committee of the insufficiency of lifeboat accommodation provided by its rules.

Attempts to take action to remedy its own negligence were strangled by the red-tape methods of the department.

Yesterday the President of the Board of Trade assured the House of Commons "That the whole question will be submitted to searching investigation by the strongest possible Court of Inquiry. I shall not hesitate, if need be, to ask for legislation."

In other words, it has needed the loss of 1,500 or 1,800 lives with the sinking of the largest, best appointed, most up-to-date, and most luxurious liner in history to rouse the Board of Trade from the

somnolence which overpowered it after its great effort in 1894 to keep abreast of the progress in the shipbuilding world.

Mr. Will Crooks in the afternoon secured the right to move the adjournment of the House to call attention to the necessity of the Board of Trade taking immediate steps so that the evidence of officers and crew of the Titanic now on their way to this country might be available for the Court of Inquiry.

At 8.15 in the evening accordingly the member for Woolwich brought forward his motion, which elicited some interesting information from the President of the Board of Trade.

SENATOR SMITH OF MICHIGAN

Mr. W. A. Smith, the senator representing Michigan, who is presiding over the Court of Inquiry instituted by the United States Senate, is not an expert in shipping matters or in law.

Those Englishmen who appear before it are, presumably, appearing voluntarily in a whole-hearted endeavour to lend what help their evidence can afford in clearing up the mystery of the wreck.

The Titanic was a British-owned ship, sailing under the British flag under the Board of Trade regulations. Its captain, most of the officers and crew and the managing director were all British. Senator Smith's capacity for the task of presiding over a commission of inquiry may be judged from the following dialogue reported by *The Times* correspondent. Senator Smith is the questioner and Second Officer Lightoller replies:–

Were there any watertight compartments on that ship? – Certainly, forty or fifty.

Do you know whether any of the crew or passengers took to the watertight compartments as a last resort? – It is quite impossible for me to say, Sir. I should think it very unlikely.

Are the watertight compartments intended as a refuge for passengers? – Oh dear no, Sir, not at any time.

MR. ISMAY'S STATEMENT

New York, April 22 – Mr. Ismay says that when he appeared before the Senate Committee he supposed it was the purpose of the inquiry to ascertain the cause of the sinking of the Titanic and to determine: whether legislation was required to prevent similar disasters in future.

He appeared voluntarily, and he did not suppose that his personal conduct was the subject of inquiry.

During the voyage he was simply a passenger, and was not consulted by the commander about the ship's speed, her navigation or her conduct at sea. He saw Captain Smith only casually.

It was unqualifiedly false to say that he wished the Titanic to make a record or to increase her speed in order to get out of the ice zone.

The only information that ice had been sighted was a message from the Baltic, which Captain Smith handed to him without comment on the deck on Sunday afternoon. He read it casually, and put it in his pocket.

"If," adds Mr. Ismay, "the information had aroused any apprehension in my mind, which it did not, I should not have ventured to make any suggestion to a commander of Captain Smith's experience. The navigation of the ship rested solely with him."

Mr. Ismay says he was asleep when the crash came. He immediately went on deck, and asked about the damage, and then returned to his state-room, dressed, returned to the boat deck and helped to clear the boats.

When all the wooden boats to starboard had been lowered he assisted in getting out the collapsible boats to starboard, and all the women were helped into them.

"As they were going over the side Mr. Carter, a passenger, and myself got in.

"At that time there wasn't a woman on the boat deck nor any passenger of any class so far as I could see or hear.

"The boat contained between thirty-five and forty persons, I should think, mostly women, with perhaps four or five men, and afterwards we discovered four Chinamen concealed at the bottom.

"When we reached the water I helped to row, pushing my oar from me as I sat. This is the explanation as to why my back was towards the sinking steamer."

EVIDENCE BEFORE THE AMERICAN COURT AT WASHINGTON. "A GREY ICEBERG."

Two Lifeboats Tested by the Board of Trade.

When the inquiry into the Titanic disaster was resumed yesterday at Washington the White Star Line, as represented by Mr. P. A. S. Franklin, practically took the public into its confidence with regard to the doubts and hopes they entertained throughout last Monday.

Mr. Franklin, in his evidence, told the committee of all the developments of the fatal Monday. The burden of his testimony turned upon the hour at which the first dread news was received by the company.

It did not reach him until about half-past six, and throughout the day his faith in the unsinkable qualities of the Titanic had caused him to communicate his optimism in interviews in the Press and in statements to the friends of passengers.

He was unable, however, to clear up the mastery of certain telegrams sent out apparently from the White Star offices to the effect that the passengers were safe, and that the Titanic was in tow.

He denied absolutely in his evidence that he had any communication with those in touch with the Carpathia, except what had already been published.

The impression made by Mr. Franklin (says a Reuter's special message) was excellent. It became apparent as the examination went on that many of the committee were altering their attitude of suspicion to a sincere desire to unravel the facts connected with the disaster.

Mr. Boxhall, the fourth officer of the Titanic, stated that in the presence of inspectors of the Board of Trade "just two" lifeboats were lowered both on the same side of the ship before she sailed.

BRITISH GOVERNMENT INQUIRY INTO LOSS OF THE TITANIC

Lord Mersey to sit as Chief Wreck Commissioner, with assessors as a public Court of Inquiry. Titanic survivors arrive next Monday, and taking of evidence will begin at once.

White Star Line undertake to ensure attendance of all required as witnesses.

Every essential witness to be subpoenaed, poorer witnesses to be maintained.

All parties allowed to be represented by counsel. Evidence might be volunteered.

The British Consul-General in New York has been requested to take evidence on affidavit from those who cannot return.

Questions of inaccurate telegrams and insurance to be investigated.

If powers of court proved insufficient Parliament would be asked for further powers.

WHEN MR. FRANKLIN KNEW

Washington, April 22 – Hours before the hearing of the evidence regarding the Titanic disaster was resumed here great crowds swarmed round the building.

Senator Smith, the Chairman of the Committee, was early on the scene.

Mr. P. A. S. Franklin, vice-president of the International Mercantile Marine Corporation, was the first witness called. Asked as to when he first knew that the Titanic had sunk, Mr. Franklin replied:–

"At 6.27 p.m. on Monday. About 2.20 on Monday morning I was awakened by the telephone bell, and some newspaper reporter informed me that the Titanic was sinking. He told me that his information came by wireless from the Virginian."

Mr. Franklin then called up the White Star office, who had received no information, and the Associated Press, who read him a dispatch from Cape Race giving news of the accident.

TELEGRAM TO THE OLYMPIC

"This message," said Mr. Franklin, "was sent at 3.00 a.m.:–

Haddock, Olympic. – Make every endeavour communicate Titanic. Advise position, time. Reply within hour.

Other messages followed rapidly. At 10.27 on Monday morning we got word from the Olympic that at nine o'clock she had been unable to get communication with the Titanic.

She was 310 miles to the south of her, and would maintain the effort to get into communication with her.

Between noon and one o'clock we received this message from the Olympic:–

Parisian reports Carpathia attendance. Picked up twenty boats with passengers.

Baltic returning. Position not given. – Haddock."

Regarding the reassuring statements given out to inquiries at the White Star offices, Mr. Franklin said: "We based them on reports and rumours received from Cape Race by individuals and newspapers. We could not place our fingers on anything authentic."

Mr. Smith showed Mr. Franklin the telegram received by Congressman Hughes, of West Virginia, from the White Star saying:–

Titanic proceeding Halifax. Passengers probably land Wednesday. All safe.

"I ask you," he said, "whether you know anything about the sending of the telegram, by whom it was authorised, and from whom it was sent?"

"I don't, sir. We have had the entire passenger staff examined, and we cannot find out. We appreciate the fact that on the Monday there were many junior clerks in the office and that the work was in great confusion. It is possible that someone who had no absolute information may have sent it."

Mr. Franklin carried a great sheaf of telegrams which had been received on Monday. None of them contained definite information. He said they were all the data upon which the White Star Line had issued its reassuring statements.

When the ill news came he sent immediately for the reporters and began to read them the Marconigram from the Carpathia.

"I read aloud," he said, "'Titanic went down 2.20 a.m.' I was going on with the rest of the message, but, looking up, I discovered there was no reporter in the room. They had all raced for telephones to get the news to the world.

"The first definite news arrived on Monday evening.

"It was from Captain Haddock, and said that the Carpathia had reached the scene of the disaster and found nothing but boats and wreckage, that the Titanic had foundered at 2.20 a.m., that the Carpathia had picked up boats, and, had on board 675 survivors, passengers and crew.

"It was such a terrible shock to me that it took me several moments to think what to do.

"I telephoned to two of our directors. Mr. Steele and Mr. J. P. Morgan, jun., and then went down to tell the reporters."

BOARD OF TRADE GUARANTEE

Questioned with regard to the life-saving equipment, Mr. Franklin said: "It was in excess of the law. It carried a certificate from the British Board of Trade.

"I might say that no vessel can leave a British port without a certificate that it is equipped for the care of human lives on board in case of accident. It is the law."

"Last Friday," he added later, "Mr. Ismay authorised that all our vessels should be equipped with boats and rafts sufficient to take off every passenger and every member of the crew in case of accident."

Do you know anyone – any officer, man or official – whom you deem could be held responsible for the accident and attendant loss of life? – Positively not. Such an accident was not dreamed of. It would be absurd to try to hold some individual responsible. Every precaution was taken. That precautions were of no avail is a source of the deepest sorrow, but the accident was unavoidable.

With reference to the criticisms passed upon the White Star for attempting to return the crew of the Titanic to Europe immediately, Mr. Franklin volunteered the following statement:–

"I think there has been an awful mistake made about the matter. I would like to clear it up. Criticisms have been made that we were trying to keep those men from testifying. This is not so. That was not the reason at all.

"So far as the crew were concerned, it was our duty to return them to their homes. If they had been permitted to roam around here men would besiege them for news; give them presents, and take them away."

"THERE WERE NOT ENOUGH BOATS."

"Many of them would have got lost. We assured you that we would hold any of the officers and men you wanted for the committee. We made a promise to you, Senator Smith, as soon as the boat was docked. There was no attempt on our part to spirit away any member of the crew, to the best of my knowledge and belief.

"What possible harm could those men do us in investigation? They could not tell any more than the passengers. Many of them probably could not tell as much. The worst they could say could not help matters."

You were quoted in Press dispatches on Friday as saying that the Titanic had sufficient boats aboard to care for the entire ship's company. Did you say that? – I don't think I did. There were not enough boats, on board to care for the entire ship's complement at one time.

Further questioned, Mr. Franklin said that at the time of the accident the speed of the Titanic was about four miles an hour below that of the Mauretania and Lusitania.

He denied that any of the company's captains had been given to understand that they were expected to break records.

IMMEDIATELY AFTER
THE CRASH

After Mr. Franklin's evidence had been completed, Mr. Boxhall, the fourth officer of the Titanic, was called.

Questioned with regard to his previous services, he said that as fifth, sixth and then as third officer his duties had always consisted in assisting the senior officers in charge.

Were there any drills or any inspections before the Titanic sailed, asked Senator Smith. – Both. The men were mustered and lifeboats were lowered in the presence of inspectors of the Board of Trade.

How many boats were lowered? – Just two, sir.

One on each side of the ship? – No, sir. Both on the same side. We were lying in dock. He did not know if the lowering tackle ran free or not on that occasion.

In lowering the lifeboats at the least did the gear work satisfactorily? – So far as I knew.

Are they supposed to be loaded from the boat deck? – That's a matter of opinion, but boats are always lowered to the level deck.

But under ordinary circumstances the boat deck is really the loading deck of the lifeboat – Yes.

Witness said that at the time of the tests all the officers of the Titanic were present.

Were all the lifeboats on the Titanic sufficiently fastened and in a position to be lowered? – All of them. There were fourteen lifeboats, two seaboats and four collapsible boats. Under the weather conditions experienced at the time of the collision the lifeboats were supposed to carry sixty-five persons.

"Under the regulations of the British Board of Trade," explained the officer, "in addition to oars, there were in the boats water-dippers, bread, balers, a mast, sail, lights and a supply of oil in the boats. All these supplies were in the boats when the Titanic left Belfast.

ICEBERGS AT HAND

"I could not say whether they were in the vessel when she left Southampton."

Questioned by the Chairman, Mr. Boxhall said he was relieved at ten o'clock by Mr. Murdoch, who remained on the bridge until the accident occurred. The sixth officer, Mr. Moody, was also on the bridge. The quartermaster was in the crow's nest.

Captain Smith had told him the positions of certain icebergs which he had marked on the chart.

You knew you were in the vicinity of the Great Banks? – Yes, sir.

Did you see Captain Smith frequently on Sunday night? – Yes, sir; sometimes on the upper deck, sometimes in the chart-room, sometimes on the bridge and sometimes in the wheelhouse.

Was the captain on the bridge or in any of those other places when you went on watch at eight o'clock? No, sir. I first saw the captain about nine o'clock.

Did you see Mr. Ismay with the captain on the bridge or in the wheelhouse? – No, sir, not until after the accident.

Do you know when he dined that night, where he dined or with whom? – No, sir.

Witness did not believe that Captain Smith had been away from the vicinity of the bridge at any time during his watch.

When did you see the captain last? – When he ordered me to go away in a boat.

ON THE BRIDGE AFTER COLLISION

The witness said he was just approaching the bridge when the collision occurred, but he couldn't see what had happened. The senior officer said, "We've struck an iceberg." There was just a little ice on the lower deck.

It was a glancing blow with only a slight impact, so slight that he didn't think it serious.

Going immediately on the bridge, he found Mr. Murdoch, Moody and Captain Smith. The captain asked what was the trouble.

Mr. Murdoch informed him that the vessel had struck an iceberg, adding that he had borne to starboard and reversed the engines to full astern, after ordering the watertight doors to be closed.

"We all walked to the end of the bridge," he continued, "to look at the iceberg, which we could see only dimly. It was lying low in the water, and was about as high as the lower rail, or about thirty feet out of the water.

"I had great difficulty in seeing it, as it was dark grey in colour. Then I went down to the steerage quarters, and inspected all the decks near the spot where the ship had struck."

What did you find? – I found no traces of any damage. I went

directly to the bridge and reported accordingly.

MAIL SACKS FLOATING ABOUT

What did the captain do? – He ordered me to send the carpenter to sound the ship, but I found the carpenter coming up with the announcement that the ship was taking water. Then I went below to the mailroom, where I found the mail sacks floating about while the clerks were at work. I went to the bridge and reported.

What next occurred? – The captain ordered the lifeboats to be made ready.

Mr. Boxhall assisted to clear the lifeboats, and after that went to the chart-room to get the vessel's position, which he gave to the captain. This he took to the wireless operator.

Until the ship went down he was employed in sending up rocket signals.

"I was trying to attract the attention of a ship which was directly ahead of us. I had seen her lights. She seemed to be meeting us.

"She was not far away. She got close enough, it seems to me, to read our electric Morse signals.

"I told the captain. He stood with me for a considerable time trying to signal her. He told me to tell her in Morse and rocket signals: 'Come at once. We sinking.'"

Did any answer come? – I didn't see them, but two men say that they saw signals from the ship.

How far away do you think that the ship was? – Approximately five miles.

Asked if he knew what ship it was, the witness said he did not. He had learned nothing about it since. He declared that several of the stewards and captain all said that they had seen signals.

"First," he said, "we saw her headlights, and a few minutes later her red sidelights. She was standing closer."

The ship – in his opinion – was about five miles away. By order of the captain he sent her Morse rocket signals to come at once, but he saw no answer.

The passengers did not seem to be very anxious to get into the boats.

The witness was still under examination when the Committee adjourned at 6.20. – Reuter's General and Special Services.

AT THEIR POSTS BELOW
(FROM OUR OWN CORRESPONDENT)

Southampton, April 22 – At last the list of survivors from the Titanic is approximately complete and corrected, and it is possible to proceed with some certainty in enumerating the terrible toll of dead.

One fact that stands out in glowing brilliance is the established heroism of the thirty-four engineers who stayed at their posts to the end, and not one of whom has survived.

The duties which kept the heroic engineers of the Titanic at their posts till death were threefold.

They had to keep the ship afloat if possible, to maintain pumping operations, and to keep the dynamo at work generating the electric light.

Their plight in the stokehold after it was flooded and the boilers burst or were flooded, causing clouds of scalding steam, is terrible to think of, and this applies also, of course, to the firemen and coal trimmers.

The majority were Southampton men, and because their splendid heroism has hitherto been scarcely mentioned I give the full list of the thirty-four names, with their addresses.

"The bravery of the captain and other officers on deck deserves the highest respect, of course," said one of the officers of the Olympic to me to-day, "but it must not be forgotten that the engineers showed equal heroism, and their chance of ever seeing the sky again was almost nothing.

"WORSE FATE THAN DROWNING."

"They must have realised the hopeless condition of the vessel long before any passengers, but they stuck to their posts in imminent danger of explosions, and it is probable that many were killed by even more dreadful means than drowning."

As Lord Charles Beresford writes in *The Times* to-day: "Many comments have been justly made regarding the heroism on deck but nothing has been said of the heroism below."

He points out, too, that "a man will face death with greater equanimity on deck than working below," and says:–

It is stated that the lights were burning until a few minutes before the ship took her final plunge.

This proves that the officers and men below remained at their posts when they must have known that death – the most terrible and painful that it is possible to conceive – awaited them at any minute, either by the bursting of a steam pipe or water rising in a compartment.

Those below must have heard the muffled sound of the ice tearing through the ship's side.

Within ten minutes or a little more they knew that the pumps would not check the rising water, yet for over two hours they remained at their posts, as was evinced by the lights burning and the few of them who were saved being picked up after the ship went down.

That so many people were saved was due to the fact that those working below remained at their posts working the dynamos and the lights burning, and never came on deck to state what had really happened.

Again and again the indomitable pluck and discipline of those who work below in the engine and boiler rooms is illustrated when some terrible disaster of the sea occurs, but on no occasion have these trails been more brilliantly shown.

"All honour and respect to those men," concludes Lord Charles Beresford, "whose names will be recorded on the roll of fame for gallantry in a sudden and unlooked-for disaster."

WHOSE BABIES ARE THEY?

Paris, April 22 – A pathetic interest attaches to the mystery of the identity of two little children – a boy and a girl – who were saved from the Titanic.

I learn from Monte Carlo that a Mr. Hoffmann called at Cook's offices there on March 25 and booked berths for himself and his two children – a boy and a girl, aged four and six.

Mr. Hoffmann paid several visits to the office with his children, and appeared to be an antiquarian, specially interested in old prints.

The employees believe that he came from Bavaria and that he was making a tour round the world. He had been staying at Nice, at the Hotel des Voyageurs.

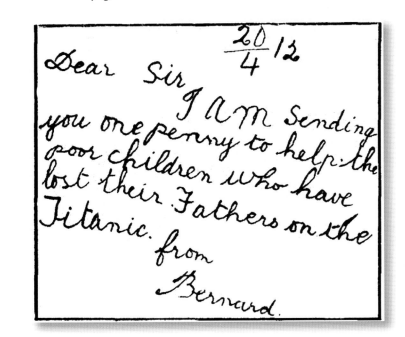

A letter sent to *The Daily Mail* from a small boy, who sent a penny to the relief fund.

He first asked for a through ticket for Australia, but he returned to the offices and said he was afraid that the journey was too long for his children, and that he would continue his tour by going to New York.

24 April 1912

NO GLASSES FOR LOOK-OUT MEN FINAL CAUSE OF CRASH(?)

"Could Have Seen Iceberg Soon Enough to Avoid It."

BOAT THAT WAS NOT FULL
Officer Admits That He Did Not Return to Pick Up Drowning.

SIGNAL TO RETURN
Passenger Says It Was Ignored in Spite of Women's Protests.

WARNED OF ICEBERGS
More remarkable evidence was given yesterday when the Senatorial inquiry into the loss of the Titanic was resumed at Washington.

Mr. Pittman, third officer, said that when the great liner crashed into the iceberg she was going at 21½ knots – the greatest speed attained during the trip.

After the Titanic had plunged under and there were drowning people in his neighbourhood, he was prevailed upon by passengers not to take his lifeboat to their rescue, though it could have held twenty more.

The look-out man, Fleet, stated that he had asked for glasses, but had been refused them. With them he could have seen the iceberg in time to get out of its way.

Major Penchen, a passenger, said that the man in charge of the boat he was in gave orders to row away from the ship, after they heard a whistle, the signal for them to go back. This order was given in spite of the protests of the married women, the reason given being that it was "our lives against theirs."

UNKNOWN SHIP AND ICE WARNING
Washington, April 23 – Owing to the confusion caused by the crowded condition of the room yesterday the public were excluded from the Senatorial inquiry into the loss of the Titanic to-day, but the Press was admitted.

This step disappointed hundreds of persons, mostly women, who crowded about the corridors.

Mr. Boxhall, the fourth officer, who was under examination yesterday, was not able to appear owing to indisposition and his place was taken by Mr. Pittman, the third officer.

Boat drills, he said, were always held at Southampton and Queenstown. The drill carried out on the Titanic at Southampton consisted in lowering and lifting two boats.

Was anything else done? – No, sir. The drill was to satisfy the British Board of Trade. We lowered the boat and sailed around the harbour. We then returned to the ship. It is customary aboard ship to have boat and fire drill every Sunday. In the Southampton drill about eight men went with each boat.

Then only sixteen men participated in this drill? – Yes, sir.

ONLY ONE WAY TO FIND ICEBERG
Was there any fire drill on the Titanic after she left Southampton? – No, sir, none.

Did you hear anything about ice on Saturday? – No, sir.

Did you hear anything about a wireless message mentioning ice? – Yes, I did. It was either on Saturday night or Sunday morning, when Mr. Boxhall put it on the chart.

Did you see any ice on Sunday? – No, I didn't. The fact that the temperature was lower would not indicate the presence of ice. In this country and in our country the temperature changes are such that one wants an overcoat one day and cool clothes the next, but that is not due to ice. In all my navigation of the sea I have seen only one iceberg.

Senator Smith suggested that the proximity of ice was indicated in a number of ways, such as the effect on the sky, change of temperature, the glint of the sun or moonlight on it.

The witness replied: Virtually the only way to discover the proximity of icebergs is to see them.

You say that the fourth officer reported ice on Saturday night, and marked it on the chart with a cross. Was this mark on or near the ship's course? – As near as I recollect, it was north of our course.

SIX ICEBERGS 150 FEET HIGH
Did you see any ice on Monday? – Yes, when I was in the lifeboat going to the Carpathia I saw several icebergs, maybe half a dozen of them, about 150ft. above the water.

Senator Smith questioned the witness as to his whereabouts on the night of the collision – "From six to eight on that evening," he replied, "I was on the bridge, after which I went to my berth."

Did you hear anything about a warning by the Californian that ice was in the vicinity? – No.

You heard nothing whatever from the second officer, Mr. Lightoller, or the captain when you were on the bridge that night? – No. The Titanic had been keeping a special look-out for ice on Sunday. This was done because the captain had been warned that ice was near.

Who warned him? – I don't know.

Asked again about the iceberg warnings, Mr. Pittman said: I did hear about Mr. Lightoller's warning to Mr. Murdoch about ice. While on the ship we talked about it ourselves. On Sunday night Mr. Lightoller remarked that we would be in the vicinity of ice about the time of his watch.

Continuing his evidence, the officer said: "I left my cabin at about 11.50 on Sunday night, just after the collision. There was the smallest impact.

"To satisfy myself I went forward. I saw the ice, and then walked back. I saw a flock of firemen coming up. I asked them what was the matter, and they said, 'There's water in the hatch.' I looked down and saw water flowing over the hatch.

"Then I went up on the deck. I met a man in a dressing-gown, who said, 'Hurry. There's no time for fooling.' Then I went to the boats."

Did you know who that man was? – Not then. I do now.

Who was it? – Mr. Ismay.

"Later this man told me to get the women and children into the boats. I lowered one, and then Mr. Ismay came to the boat and helped me.

"I put in quite a number of women and a few men, and then I called for more women, but there were none to be seen. Then I stepped back on the ship again.

"The officer Murdoch told me to get into the boat and row around to the after gangway. I thought that was the thing to do, because I expected to bring all the passengers back to the ship again."

Were the passengers reluctant to get into the boats? – Well, no, sir.

"Just before the boat pulled away, Murdoch leaned over and shook hands with me and said 'Good-bye. Good luck, old man.' I pulled away, intending to remain near the ship in case a wind should spring up."

There were five members of the crew in the lifeboat commanded by him, and he carried forty passengers. His boat did not have lights, as required by the Board of Trade.

The women behaved splendidly. All of them wanted to help in the rowing to keep themselves warm. The boats were some distance from the Titanic when she went down. She suddenly got on end and dived right straight down.

Did you hear any explosions? – Yes, sir, four. They sounded like big guns in the distance.

LET THE BOAT DRIFT

When you shook hands with Murdoch, did you expect to see him again? – Certainly. I expected fully to be back on the ship in a few hours.

Did you hear any cries of distress? – Oh, yes.

"I heard no cries of distress before the ship went down," he explained. "The cries were probably several hundred yards away.

"Then I told my men to get out the oars and pull towards the wreck so that we might be able to save a few more."

They demurred, he continued, saying that it would be a mad idea, but he corrected himself at once by saying that it was not the crew who demurred, but the passengers. Even the women did not urge him to go back. He yielded to the importunities of the passengers and let the boat drift aimlessly.

Describe the scenes. – Don't, sir, I would rather not.

Senator Smith pressed him on this point, and Mr. Pittman gave harrowing details of the last scene, the relating of which evidently caused him great pain.

He was asked if the screams were intermittent or spasmodic. – It was one long, continuous moan. The moans and cries continued for an hour.

He appeared acutely sensitive with regard to Senator Smith's question as to why he drifted while people were drowning in the neighbourhood.

He admitted that his load of forty persons did not tax the capacity of his boat, which, he said, would have carried sixty at a tight fit. He had transferred women and children from his boat to boat No. 7.

Both these boats could have held more people, then? – Yes.

Why were not more taken? – There were no more women about when my boat was lowered. I can't say about No. 7. I think that some boats had as many as sixty in them when they reached the Carpathia.

"When I saw the light of the Carpathia, I slipped the rope that held our two boats together, and pulled for it. This was about four o'clock. All moans and cries had ceased.

WHITE LIGHT ON THE HORIZON

While you were lying on your oars, did you see any lights of any kind apart from those of the Carpathia and the other lifeboats?

Yes, sir. We saw a light on the horizon. A white light.

Was it on the track of the Titanic? – Yes, sir, but we did not follow it. It might have been one of our own boats.

The witness did not see any Morse signals on the Titanic, but twelve or more rockets were fired.

He saw Mr. Ismay on the Titanic when the lifeboat left. He did not see him again until the two of them were leaving the Carpathia at New York.

He believed it was true that with regard to the boats not more than 1,200 out of more than 2,000 passengers and crew could have been saved, even under favourable circumstances.

Mr. Burton interrogated him about the white light he had seen from the lifeboat. The witness said that it appeared to him like a fixed light. It might have been a star. He did not see any red side light.

He could only say that what he saw was an apparently fixed white light, which might have been a star.

He had never heard anything of a steamer called the Hellig Olav, but there might be a boat of that name.

TRAVELLING AT GREATEST SPEED

The Hellig Olav docked in New York on April 17, and is reported to have encountered an iceberg near the spot where the Titanic sank.

It has been suggested that it was the Hellig Olav's lights that Mr. Boxhall saw.

By a series of searching questions, Mr. Fletcher brought out the fact that when the collision occurred the Titanic was going at the greatest speed attained during the trip.

"You say," he asked, "that you were going at twenty-one and a half knots at the time of the accident?" – Yes, sir. We left Southampton under about twenty and a half knots, which was increased to twenty-one, and later to twenty-one and a half.

Then, when the Titanic crashed into the iceberg, you were going at top speed? – I suppose so, sir.

The Hellig Olav, a steel twin screw steamer of 10,091 tons, is a Danish vessel, fitted with wireless telegraphy apparatus.

LOOK-OUT MAN'S ASSERTION

Frederick Fleet, who was in the crow's nest of the Titanic when the collision occurred, was the next witness.

He said that on Sunday evening some time after ten o'clock he reported a black mass of ice ahead to the officers on the bridge. He could not say how long that was before the collision.

What did you do when you saw the iceberg? – I sounded three bells and then telephoned to the bridge, I got prompt response to my ring, and the report was not delayed.

How large was the berg when you first saw it? – About the size of two large tables, but it got larger as we went along, and when we struck it was about 50ft. or 60ft. high above the water.

After you gave the telephone signal, was the ship stopped? – No, she didn't stop until after she struck the iceberg, but she started to go to port after I telephoned.

How did you know? – My mate noticed it.

Where did the iceberg strike the ship? – On the starboard bow, about 20ft. from the stem. There was little impact, just a sharp grinding noise.

Did you have glasses? – No.

Isn't it customary for look-outs to use glasses in their work? – Yes, but they did not give us any on the Titanic. We asked for them at Southampton, but they said there were none for us.

Whom did you ask? – Mr. Lightoller.

They had glasses from Belfast to Southampton, but had none from Southampton.

If you had had glasses, could you have seen the iceberg a bit sooner? – Yes.

How much sooner? – Enough to get out of the way.

Were you and Leigh disappointed that you had no glasses? – Yes.

WILL-O'-THE-WISP LIGHT

Did the officers on the bridge have glasses? – Yes.

Were there other lights ahead when you were in the crow's nest? – No, sir. We didn't see the light off the port bow until after we were in the lifeboat.

What was the colour of the light you were pulling for? – White.

The Committee then adjourned.

FIRST PASSENGER'S EVIDENCE

When the inquiry was resumed at 3.53, Major Arthur Penchen, of Toronto, who was ordered by Mr. Lightoller to man one of the lifeboats, was the first passenger to give evidence.

When the crash came, he said, he thought that it was merely a large wave that had struck the ship, and went out.

"I met a friend, who said, 'We've struck an iceberg.' So we went on the deck and saw the iceberg.

"Fifteen minutes later I met Mr. Charles M. Hays, of the Grand Trunk Railway. I asked him, 'Have you seen the ice?' He said, 'No.' I then took him up and showed him it."

THIS BOAT CANNOT SINK

"Then I noticed that the boat was listing, and I said to Mr. Hays, 'She's listing. She should not do that.' He said, 'Oh, I don't know. This boat can't sink.'

"I went back to the cabin deck, where I met men and women coming up. They were looking most serious. I met my friend Beattie, and asked him what was the matter. Beattie said, 'The order is for the lifeboats; it's serious.'

"I couldn't believe it at first, but I went to my cabin and changed

to some heavy clothes. When I got on deck again the boats were being prepared for lowering on the port side.

"Women came forward one by one, accompanied by their husbands. They would only allow women to pass, and the men had to stand back. The second officer stood there, and that was the order enforced. No men passengers got into the boat."

25 April 1912

An extraordinary incident occurred at Southampton yesterday. The Olympic – the sister ship of the ill-starred Titanic – was due to leave for New York at noon, and everything was in readiness for the vessel to depart, when, to the amazement of everyone, a large number of the crew began to file down the only remaining gangway. The men included 150 firemen, seventy-two trimmers, thirty-four greasers and twenty-nine others, and they alleged that there was insufficient lifeboat accommodation, although the number, it is understood, had been increased to an extent equal to the full number of the people aboard.

▶ (1, 3 and 5) A dramatic incident: A young fireman who, finding he could not leave the vessel aft, slid from ship to shore down a cable 70ft. long. All his money dropped into the water. (2) Bringing his kit ashore. (4) A scuffle with the police. A number of the men had to be forcibly removed.

OLYMPIC FIREMEN REFUSE TO SAIL
Liner Held Up at Southampton at Last Minute.

285 SUDDENLY LAND
Last Man Slides Down Mooring Ropes as Ship Is Starting.

ANCHORED OFF RYDE
Seamen Said to Have Struck, but Afterwards Agreed to Sail.

A remarkable and unexpected sequel to the Titanic disaster was reported from Southampton yesterday.

The great liner Olympic was to have sailed from that port at noon for New York. Her boat accommodation had been increased to an extent which, it was understood, was equal to the full number of souls on board.

At the last moment – five minutes before sailing time, in fact, however, nearly 300 firemen, greasers, trimmers and others refused to sail.

Throwing their kits on the quay or carrying them on their shoulders, they marched ashore by the sole remaining gangway. A noisy meeting was held, the result of which was that the men decided to remain on shore.

The Daily Mirror

THE MORNING JOURNAL WITH THE SECOND LARGEST NET SALE.

No. 2,653. THURSDAY, APRIL 25, 1912 One Halfpenny.

285 MEMBERS OF THE OLYMPIC'S CREW REFUSE TO SAIL ON THE GROUND THAT THERE WERE NOT ENOUGH LIFEBOATS.

As reason for their action they alleged that
(1) There are not sufficient seamen on board to man the lifeboats.
(2) Collapsible boats are unseaworthy.

After a considerable delay, the Olympic was towed down Southampton Water to await a relay of firemen off Ryde, where she anchored. At 8.30 a tug went out to her with about fifty firemen, but at eleven o'clock one out-of-work fireman was the only fresh recruit waiting in the White Star office.

The crew was still nearly 200 short, and the White Star office at the dock gates was still picketed.

There was no prospect of the Olympic getting away even to

Cherbourg till the morning.

There are 1,400 passengers booked for the journey, including those who will embark at Cherbourg and Queenstown. The Duke of Sutherland is among them.

Last night it was reported that some passengers on the liner were expressing anxiety about travelling with either a short-handed crew or a scratch crew.

DRAMATIC JOURNEY ON A ROPE
(FROM OUR OWN CORRESPONDENT)

Southampton, April 21 – A sensational incident prevented the sailing of the Olympic at noon to-day.

At five minutes to twelve, when all the passenger gangways had been removed, and after the last visitors had returned to the quay, kits began to be thrown overboard upon the quayside.

A moment or two later several hundred firemen and trimmers began to file to shore back across the crew's gangway aft, carrying their bundles and bags, and assembled in a noisy, threatening crowd upon the quay and in the landing shed.

A sort of mass meeting was at once held in a corner of the vast shed, and an official of the men's union, standing on an empty truck, put the question to the men whether they should return to the ship or keep off her.

He said he had been assured by Mr. Philip Curry, the White Star manager, that there were enough boats for everybody, and that the Board of Trade had approved them, but it was for the men to say whether they would take the risk or not.

A show of hands displaying a large majority for staying ashore, the meeting broke up in less than five minutes, the men sitting themselves on their bags or sprawling on the ground. Several, however, seemed to wish to go back to the ship.

DEPUTATION FROM FIREMEN

Mr. Curry and other officials of the company were joined in a few minutes by Captain Haddock, commander of the Olympic.

They conferred in a little group apart from noisy strikers, and Mr. Curry gave brisk orders to subordinates at intervals, such as "Telephone to town police for help to clear this shed."

"They are mutineers," he said, "for not only did they sign on last Monday, but they mustered this morning, and therefore the voyage, as far as they are concerned, has actually begun."

According to one account after the men left the liner a deputation of five firemen and five greasers waited upon Mr. Curry, and in the presence of Commander Clark, the Board of Trade Inspector and Chief Emigration Officer, said they were not satisfied with the collapsible boats.

Commander Clark said he had made an examination of the boats, and was perfectly satisfied.

Mr. Curry then said he would give the men five minutes to decide their course of action. They thereupon held a meeting on the quay, with the result that they unanimously decided not to return to the ship.

While the rebels were shouting and jeering, a squad of some thirty volunteers for the stokehold walked quickly across the remaining gangway on to the ship, and Mr. Curry followed. The captain had preceded them.

The gangway was then taken up, and the ship was cut off from the shore, except for her mooring cables. It was then that the most dramatic incident of the day took place.

A young fireman woke in his bunk to find that the rest had cleared and it was too late to cross the aft gangway to the quayside.

Immediately he made his way to the forepeak of the vessel and boldly slid down a cable seventy feet long, inclined from the liner to the shore.

Three thousand people on the ship and quay held their breath as he became bunched together like a spider in the middle of the rope. His head hung downwards, his pockets emptied, and all his money fell into the sea, but he reached his friends on the quay in safety.

They shouted to another man up above to follow his example or jump into the sea and "swim for it," promising to get him out, but the man delayed too long, for, with a great roaring of steam from the valves at the top of the first and third of her four funnels, the ship began to stir.

SEAMEN'S WIRELESS MESSAGE

Seaman Lewis, A.B., sent a wireless message to Mr. Cannon, secretary of the Seafarers' Union, at 6.15 p.m. from the Olympic inquiring:–

"Shall crew proceed Olympic, await your decision."

This referred to the seamen only. Of course, the answer given was a diplomatic one.

"Sailors must not say 'I shan't' when they are told to work," explained one of the firemen's spokesmen to me, "but if they all sit on their bunks and say, 'I can't,' the only thing that can be done with them is to sign off their articles and put them on a shilling a month pay, discharging them at the first port of call."

At midnight it was stated that all ranks below boatswain's mate struck on the Olympic, but afterwards agreed to sail.

MEN WANT WOODEN BOATS

Mr. Cannon, the secretary of the Seafarers' Union here, tells me that altogether 285 men came ashore at the last moment.

There were 150 firemen, seventy-two trimmers, thirty-four greasers and twenty-nine storekeepers, fan-oilers, storekeepers' assistants and refrigerator attendants.

"The twenty engineers from other ships who went on board to act as firemen," he said, "can't do the work of 285 men. They could only help get her to Ryde.

"A deputation from this union went to the White Star Line last night and complained about the boats and the sailors being too few for the boats on board.

"The company promised four more sailors, making forty-two instead of thirty-eight, but what good are forty-two for forty-four boats and rafts?

"The men say that they must have wooden boats. That is the reason of it all. We reported to them what the owners said last night, and they talked it over this morning among themselves.

"At sailing time they simply came off when they found there were only sixteen wooden boats on board. They say that of the forty collapsibles sent on board sixteen were rejected by the Board of Trade and put back on the quay where anybody can see them now."

INSPECTOR SATISFIED

Captain Clark, the Board of Trade inspector, said to me:–

"I am not only satisfied that the boats on board are sufficient for all the passengers and crew now on board, but I found the crews of the boats this morning efficient, and I have given my sanction for the ship to proceed."

One of the firemen told me that some of the collapsible boats were unsatisfactory, but Captain Clark assured me that certainly none of the boats on the ship were in a faulty condition.

He had one wooden boat and one collapsible lowered to the water, manned and rowed before he would certify the ship.

It was about half-past one when the Olympic began to move, being led by a powerful tug. Simultaneously telegrams were dispatched to Cowes and Portsmouth for firemen and trimmers, and it was understood that the Olympic would anchor between Netley and Cowes till sufficient men were available.

THUMB THROUGH COLLAPSIBLE

"We demanded wooden boats for everybody yesterday," said one of their spokesmen to me to-night. "We did not get them, so we refused to sail.

"Why, some of these collapsibles sent to the Olympic have the date 1902 on them and have never been in the water. Ten years of storage must have perished the collapsible material.

"One of us poked his thumb through it this morning.

"We are not cowards. We are doing a national service in drawing attention to the inadequacy of these makeshift boats."

ARE OLYMPIC FIREMEN DESERTERS?

Have the stokers who left the Olympic committed a punishable offence? Can they be prosecuted as deserters?

The legal position as between shipowners and employees was kindly explained to *The Daily Mirror* yesterday by an experienced official of the Shipping Federation, Ltd.

"Under the Merchant Shipping Act shipowners have the power to prosecute seamen who desert their ship when they have signed on for a voyage," he said.

"The firemen, trimmers and greasers who left the Olympic must have signed articles for the voyage, and unless they can prove a real grievance they are punished in the usual way by the Board of Trade.

"This takes the form of a black mark – 'voyage-not completed' – in the continuous discharge books which does not improve their chance of getting another job.

"Every seaman has his discharge book, which is his most valuable possession, as it records his character on every ship in which he has served."

FOR RELATIVES OF TITANIC HEROES

'Daily Mail' Women's Fund Realises £27,876 in Six Days.

GENEROUS CHILDREN

Day after day the women of England continue to pour in their tributes to the memory of the illustrious dead of the Titanic. And day after day the splendid total swells for the benefit of the wives and children who have been left stricken behind.

By their magnificent efforts British women are raising a national memorial to the heroes who, in that dreadful last hour of death, made the supreme sacrifice with invincible heroism. It is a memorial which is imperishable.

The record, since *The Daily Mail* made its appeal, is:–

Thursday	£1,298	Monday	£13,000
Friday	£4,100	Tuesday	£24,426
Saturday	£7,433		

Yesterday further contributions brought the total up to £27,876.

JEWELLERY ON VIEW

The jewellery which was sent by a lady from Curragh Camp, Co.

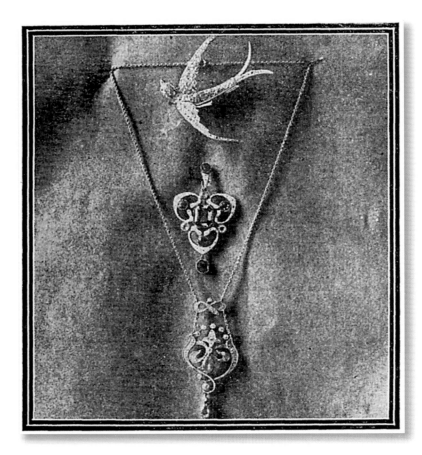

NOVEL ADDITION TO FUND

A novel but very practical and satisfactory addition to the fund arrived in the shape of an amiable-looking plaster-of-Paris dog. It came all the way from the Terminus Hotel, Ryde, and arrived full to the brim with money.

The cast contained exactly £1 3s. 0½ d. in various forms of coinage which had been contributed by those in the hotel. Another dog is also being busily filled to repletion at the present time.

The letters which continue to pour in show how deeply touched the senders of subscriptions are. Many of them thank *The Daily Mail* for having given them the opportunity to contribute. An example of these comes from Bristol:–

As a woman. I feel most grateful to *The Daily Mail* for the special opportunity given us to contribute.

UNEMPLOYED WOMAN WORKER'S GIFT

A splendid letter comes from a girl – a woman chemist – at Erith:–

I enclose you an order for 5s. for the Titanic Fund. I wish it were more, but I am out of work just now, and so have to look ahead. Five shillings seems such a drop in the ocean, but a woman chemist doesn't get a very big screw.

I think that the loss of the Titanic is an appalling disaster, but, as every dark cloud has a silver lining, so it has needed this awful catastrophe to show what stuff our men are made of. Their magnificent courage and self-sacrifice must bring comfort to those who are left behind.

I have drunk deep of the waters of affliction myself, and know in these dark times of doubt and despair what consolation it brings to the crushed heart to know that "they" died doing their duty and giving their lives for another…

Five shillings also comes as "A thankoffering from one whose husband made this perilous voyage in safety only a week before the heartrending and terrible disaster." – H. S. C. Seaford.

And 10s. is sent by "One who might have been a passenger."

SCENES AT THE LOWERING OF TITANIC LIFEBOATS

"No Effort Made to Force Women Into Boats."

SWORE AT MR. ISMAY

Fifth Officer's Astounding Evidence on Titanic's Last Moments.

FIRING FROM LIFEBOAT

Kept Italians From Jumping In by Revolver Shots.

Kildare, to be disposed of for the benefit of the fund was yesterday placed in the centre of the window at *The Daily Mirror* Studios, 63, Strand, London, W.C.

The lady, it will be remembered, wrote quite simply:– "I have no money this quarter, but I wish to send something to help those who have suffered from the loss of the Titanic." And so she sent her jewellery.

She was determined to do something for the fund and to show her practical gratitude, and so she sent something which means more to most women than mere money.

The jewellery reposes on a cushion in the window of *The Daily Mirror* Studios. There are three pieces: a beautiful diamond brooch in the shape of a swallow, a diamond and sapphire pendant and another enamelled and jewelled pendant.

Messrs. J. W. Benson, Limited, the well-known jewellers, who have restored the ornaments, state that the diamond brooch and the diamond pendant are each worth £25, and the enamelled pendant four guineas.

LINER NEAR THE TITANIC

Californian Was Only 20 Miles from the Sinking Liner.

Lord Mersey, the chairman of the Special Inquiry which is to investigate the loss of the Titanic, visited the House of Commons last evening and had a consultation with the President of the Board of Trade.

Some new disclosure is meanwhile added each day to the slowly unfolding story of the disaster as told at the United States Senate inquiry.

The most interesting point in the evidence yesterday was the statement made by Fifth Officer Lowe, of the Titanic, who told the Committee that he peremptorily ordered Mr. Bruce Ismay away from the davits because Mr. Ismay became overexcited in helping to lower the officer's lifeboat. Mr. Ismay obeyed.

No clue is yet forthcoming as to the identity of the mystery ship seen by many persons on the Titanic less than five miles distant after the collision.

The Leyland liner Californian's captain says he was less than twenty miles away, and might have saved every life, but he was held up by the ice field and his wireless was not working.

SENATOR
SMITH'S STATEMENT

Washington, April 24 – Public interest in the Senate Committee's inquiry into the circumstances of the Titanic disaster showed no signs of relaxation this morning.

Frederick Fleet, who was the look-out in the crow's nest at the time of the disaster, and whose evidence yesterday was so sensational, was again called to the witness-stand.

He was unable to give any further information as to the mysterious light.

The boat in which he was contained about thirty passengers. There were no women on deck when it left, and the men who were made no attempt to enter. He heard only the faintest cries for help.

Did you go back to help? – No, sir. Some of the passengers wanted to, but the Quartermaster in command ordered us to keep on rowing.

At this point Mr. Smith, the chairman, interrupted the proceedings to make a statement.

He intimated that all the British subjects summoned to appear before the Committee would be detained in Washington as long as their presence was required.

So far all the witnesses had given their evidence voluntarily and there had been no hitch, but attempts had been made outside to dictate to the Committee the procedure to be followed. That would not be tolerated.

FIFTH OFFICER AND MR. ISMAY

Mr. Harold G. Lowe, the fifth officer of the Titanic was then called.

Mr. Lowe stated that before the Titanic sailed on what was her maiden and her last voyage one drill of the crew was held – at Southampton. He was in charge of one of the two boats lowered. "The entire drill," he said, "consisted in rowing about the harbour for half an hour. There was a fire drill previous to the general drill in Southampton."

Did you ever hear of ice in the vicinity of Newfoundland? – No, sir.

"Never heard of any iceberg?" asked the Senator, surprised. – Yes, sir, off Cape Horn. It was the only one I have ever seen until I saw a number at dawn on the day after the collision.

A TOTAL ABSTAINER

Was the ship on her true course at the time of the collision? – I was in bed, but from the position on the chart I believe she was.

Was the Titanic on the north track or the south track? – I think the north track, sir.

Can you give the position of the ship at eight o'clock that night? – No, sir.

I want you to think hard. If we get the position at that hour we could figure out the speed of the ship by taking the elapsed time between then and the time of the collision. – "The speed of the ship on that day was a fraction below twenty-one knots," replied the witness, reading from notes.

Are you a temperate man, Mr. Lowe? – I am, sir. I say it without fear of contradiction.

I am glad to hear that, because I have just had passed up a note which says that it was reported by a reputable man that you were drinking on the night of the accident.

"Me drinking! It's impossible. That's rubbish, I am a total abstainer," he answered indignantly.

After the accident, which did not awake him, he dressed hurriedly and went on deck where he found people with lifebelts on and the boats being prepared.

"The vessel was tipping about fifteen degrees by the head. When I got on deck, I began working the lifeboats under Mr. Murdoch. Boat No. 5 was the first one we lowered."

Who got into that boat? – I don't know, but there's one man here, and had he not been here I would not have known that I ordered Mr. Ismay away from the boat.

"A steward met me on the Carpathia and said to me, 'What did you say to Mr. Ismay that night on deck?' I said that I did not know Mr. Ismay well. The steward on the Carpathia said that I had used the strongest language to Mr. Ismay.

"Shall I repeat it? If you want me to I will; if not I won't. I happened to talk to Mr. Ismay because he appeared to be getting excited. He was saying excitedly, 'Lower away! Lower away! Lower away!'"

STRONG WORDS TO MR. ISMAY

At this juncture the chairman asked Mr. Ismay about the words used. Mr. Ismay suggested that the objectionable language might be written down. This was done, and after the chairman had read what Mr. Lowe had written, he said, "Why did you say it?"

"Because he was in anxiety to get the boat lowered and was interfering with our work," was the reply. "He was interfering with me.

"I wanted him to get back, so that we could work. He was not trying to get into the boat. Finally, I turned to him and said, 'If you'll get to hell out of here, we can get this boat away?'"

He stepped back without replying.

Mr. Lowe, in reply to further questions, stated that the launching of the lifeboat was altogether successful.

"There was no trouble," he added, "and that is why I spoke to Mr. Ismay as I did."

You think it was properly loaded for lowering? What is the official quota for such lifeboats? – 65.5, floating capacity.

You mean that it can carry sixty-five adults and, say, a boy or a girl.

Mr. Lowe explained that he would not like to put more than fifty in a lifeboat to lower it. The danger was that it might buckle up from the ends.

ENDANGERING OTHERS

Senator Smith: Mr. Pittman said yesterday that there were thirty-five people in lifeboat No. 5. Why could he not have gone to the rescue of the drowning? Would he not have been able to accommodate thirty more with safety in that lifeboat? – No, sir. Had he attempted to rescue those in the water, he would have endangered the lives of those with him.

"I wanted to say a word about that danger," added Mr. Lowe. "I heard Major Penchen say in evidence that the sailors and boatmen could not row. Sailors and boatmen are different. Many sailors may be at sea for years and never go in a rowboat. I was not in a position to order who was to go into the boats.

But you were in a position to tell Mr. Ismay to go to hell? – Yes, because he was interfering with me personally. I wanted him to get away so that I could do something.

He did? – Yes, and I did something.

What was the number of the crew? – So far as I know there were 903 crew.

And with 903 men on board you did not have enough men to man twenty lifeboats properly?

The witness objected to this question, and the Chairman criticised the refusal of the witness to make direct replies.

"You mean enough men present at the boats?" said Mr. Lowe finally. "No, there were not."

Were any men, women or children refused admission to the boats or put out of them after they had got in? – None were refused. The only confusion was created by passengers interfering with the lowering gear. Everything was quiet and orderly.

With everything quiet and orderly, who selected the people for the boats? – There was no such thing as selecting. First we took the women and children, and then the others as they came.

As you passed the women into the boats what did you say? – I simply shouted: "Women and children first. Men stand back."

MAN WHO "SNEAKED IN."

Mr. Smith sought in vain to learn the number of women in lifeboat No. 3. The witness thought that men and women were about equally divided, but he knew none of their names.

Finally he ventured the belief that the boat contained about forty persons.

Why were there not more? – We could not find anyone who wanted to go. They seemed not to care about getting into the boats. They were free to wander wherever they pleased. There was no effort made by the officers or crew either to restrain or to direct the passengers.

Did you see any of the women there? – Certainly, I saw women there, but I didn't have time to go and drag them away. They didn't respond our calls.

"After I lowered three boats," continued Mr. Lowe, "I walked across the deck and met Moody. We filled lifeboats Nos. 14, 15 and 16 on that side. We filled them with women and children.

"There was one man passenger in No. 14, an Italian, who sneaked in. He was dressed rather like a woman. He had a shawl over his head."

Mr. Lowe told the Committee how he tied five lifeboats together and transferred passengers from his boat to other boats.

"I then called for volunteers to row back to the wreck. We picked up four men struggling in the water. Three of them survived, but the fourth – Mr. Hays, of New York – died shortly after we took him out.

You said a moment ago that you waited before returning to the

wreck for things to quiet down. What did you mean by "quieted down"? – Until the cries had ceased.

The cries of the drowning? – Yes, sir. We did not dare go into the struggling mass. It would have sunk us. We remained at the edge of the scene. We would have taken everyone aboard that we could, but it would have been suicide to have gone in.

How long did it require for things to get quiet. I mean for the cries and the screams of the drowning people to cease? – About an hour and a half.

"I OUGHT TO HAVE GONE DOWN."

After a brief adjournment the hearing was resumed at 3.55 p.m., when Mr. Lightoller, the second officer, was recalled.

Mr. Burton asked Mr. Lightoller to relate his conversations with Mr. Ismay on board the Carpathia.

"My fellow-officers and I," he said, "talked over sailing in the Cedric and we agreed that it would be a jolly good idea if we could catch the Cedric. It would result in keeping the men together and get everyone home.

"Mr. Ismay, when the weather thickened, remarked to me that it was hardly possible that we could catch that boat. He asked me if I thought it would be desirable to send a wireless to hold the Cedric. I said, 'Most certainly.' Thereupon a telegram was sent.

"I will say that at that time Mr. Ismay was in no mental condition to transact business. He seemed possessed with the idea that he ought to have gone down with the ship because there were women who went down.

"I tried my best to get the idea out of his head, but could not. The doctor on the Carpathia had trouble with Mr. Ismay on this ground. I am sure that the doctor will verify my statement.

"I was told on the Carpathia that when the chief officer, Wild, who was working forward at a collapsible boat, told Mr. Ismay that there were no more women to go he stood back. Wild, who was a big powerful man, led him to the boat and put him in."

HOW THE COLLISION OCCURRED

Quartermaster Describes Officers' Step When Iceberg Was Struck.

Robert Hitchens, quartermaster of the Titanic, was then called. He said: "I was at the wheel at the time of the collision. I went on watch at eight o'clock.

"Later I heard the second officer order the sixth officer to pass the word along to keep a sharp look-out for small ice. At ten o'clock I went to the wheel.

"All went well until 11.40, when three gongs were sounded from the look-out.

"Then a telephone message came: 'Iceberg right ahead, sir.'

"The first officer rushed to give the order: 'Hard a-starboard.' The second officer reported: 'Helm hard over, sir.'

"By that time we were on to the iceberg. We could hear the grinding of it.

"Captain Smith came out, rushing to inquire what was the matter. He was told we had struck an iceberg.

"He immediately told Mr. Murdoch to close the emergency doors. He was told that that had been done.

"The ship was discovered to have a list of five degrees to starboard within the five minutes.

"I stayed at the wheel until 12.23.

"One of the officers said at that time: 'Well, get out the boats.'

"I was in charge of No. 6, and was ordered to pull away towards a distant light.

"We had on board thirty-eight women, a seaman, myself, an Italian lad, and the Canadian major who testified yesterday.

"I told them that we would have to pull away from the ship, as she was going down by the head. Everybody had to row. I even asked the ladies.

"We started for the light.

"The ladies were getting nervous. One of them, Mrs. Meyer, accused me of using bad language, of wrapping myself in all the wraps, and drinking all the whisky.

"This I deny. I stood all night at the tiller through the cold. I would much rather have been at an oar than at the tiller, but I could find no one to take the tiller."

Did you have any trouble with Major Penchen? – Yes, sir. When he came aboard he tried to take command. I told him he was there to take orders. Fleet did most of the work.

Did the women urge you to go towards the Titanic? – No, sir; not that I remember.

Major Penchen testified that when you were asked to go back to rescue the drowning you said that you weren't going back after "those stiffs." – Yes. I saw that in the newspapers this morning. It is a lie. I never used that word since I was on board.

OFFICER'S REVOLVER SHOTS

The following additional passages from Mr. Lowe's evidence throw light upon the question as to whether rescues might have been attempted by the lifeboats after the Titanic sank.

How many were there on your boat when you came alongside the Carpathia? – About forty-five.

Where did you get them? – Off a collapsible boat. I took off one woman and twenty men. When I took them off the twenty-one were up to their ankles in water, and would have sunk in three minutes.

Did you hear any pistol shots on that Sunday night? – I heard them, and fired them.

When? – As lifeboat No. 15 was going down the ship's side I expected it would double up under our feet as it was. As we were lowering away I saw a lot of Italians at the ship's rail, glaring and ready to spring. I yelled, "look out" to the men, and fired down the ship's side.

How far was your lifeboat from the ship's side? – About three feet from the rail. I know I didn't hurt anyone.

How many shots did you fire? – Three times I fired at the three decks. I fired horizontally along the boat. – Reuter's Special Service.

"SMALL DOTS IN THE SEA."

Liner Passengers See Woman Clasping Babe Among Titanic's Floating Dead.

New York, April 24 – The German steamer Bremen reported upon her arrival here to-day that she had sighted a hundred bodies from the Titanic.

The officers were very reticent with regard to the tragic spectacle, but several of the passengers were more ready to give accounts of what they saw. Mrs. Johanna Stunke, a cabin passenger, gave a vivid picture of the scene from the liner's rail.

"It was between four and five o'clock on Saturday afternoon when we sighted an iceberg. As we drew nearer we could make out small dots floating in the sea, which we knew were bodies of the Titanic's passengers.

"A feeling of awe and sadness crept over everyone. Approaching closer, we passed within a hundred feet of the southernmost of the drifting wreckage.

"We saw one woman in a nightdress with a baby clasped closely to her breast. Several of the women passengers screamed at the sight and left the rail in a fainting condition.

"There was another woman fully dressed with her arms tightly clutching the body of a shaggy dog. We noticed the bodies of three men in a group clinging to a steamer chair, and just beyond were the bodies of a dozen more, all in life preservers and locked together as they died in the struggle for life.

"We could see white life preservers dotting the sea all the way to the iceberg." – Reuter's Special.

CALIFORNIAN 20 MILES OFF

Boston, April 24 – Mr. Lord, captain of the Leyland liner Californian, says that that steamer was less than twenty miles from the Titanic when the latter foundered, and that if he had known of her plight all the passengers might have been saved.

He denies that the Californian was the steamer passing within five miles which disregarded the distress signals, and adds:–

"I calculate that we were from seventeen to nineteen miles distant from the Titanic on the Sunday evening.

"About 10.30 in the evening we steamed into an immense icefield. I immediately shut down the engines and awaited the daylight with engines stopped.

"Our wireless apparatus was not working, so that we did not learn of the Titanic's distress until the morning, through the Virginian, and we then started for the scene of the disaster." – Reuter.

"OF WHAT ARE ICEBERGS COMPOSED?"

Washington, April 24 – Senator Smith asked a number of questions of witnesses which were apparently of an immaterial character. Afterwards he disallowed a number of questions put by some of his colleagues, and several members of the Committee, evidently being dissatisfied with his decision, left the room.

One of the questions put by Senator Smith to Fifth Officer Lowe was: "Of what are icebergs composed?" "Ice!" replied the witness. – Exchange Telegraph.

Washington, April 24 – Much comment is being made on the slowness of the Committee and its lack of nautical knowledge. It has been suggested that it should be assisted by a naval expert.

Senator Smith, for instance, to the amazement of the audience, yesterday asked if the ship had sunk by the bows or by the head. – Reuter's Special.

PROTESTS BY WITNESSES

New York, April 24 – According to information received here it is understood that members of the crew of the Titanic have protested privately to the British Ambassador, Mr. Bryce, against the indignity of their detention in the United States.

It was expected that Mr. Ismay and Mr. Franklin, of the White Star Line, would call at the British Embassy to-night in order to present their grievances, but Senator Smith has ordered an evening session, so that the inquiry may be hastened. – Exchange Telegraph.

QUARTERMASTER IN CUSTODY

Washington, April 24 – Hitchens, a quartermaster of the Titanic, who was subpoenaed on board the Celtic at New York this morning, arrived here this afternoon in custody to give evidence.

Hitchens intended to sail for England to-morrow, and the

chairman of the Committee sent a deputy to prevent him from doing so. – Reuter.

BRITAIN AND THE U.S. INQUIRY

The British official attitude to the American Committee investigating the Titanic disaster was stated in the House of Commons yesterday by Mr. Acland, Under-Secretary for Foreign Affairs. It was to the effect that:–

American law empowered a Committee of either House to summon witnesses and administer oaths.

Any person refusing to answer was guilty of a misdemeanour.

Hitherto there had been no cases of a foreign inquiry into the wreck of a British ship.

With their general good sense the American Senate and people would see that it was not desirable to detain persons wanted for the inquiry in England. No doubt if circumstances arose in which protection was desired for British subjects summoned by the American Committee instructions would be sent to the Ambassador.

Mr. Acland told a questioner that no complaint had been made by persons brought before the Committee that they were not receiving fair and honourable treatment.

NEW REGULATIONS WITHOUT DELAY

Many further questions were addressed to Ministers regarding the disaster, and the following fresh facts were brought to light:–

There will not be a moment's delay in issuing the revised regulations.

Expert advisers are at work.

It will not be necessary to wait for the report of the advisory committee before issuing new regulations.

Distress wireless calls from ships have precedence over all other wireless messages.

26 April 1912

OLYMPIC'S ALL-DAY WAIT FOR FIREMEN

Liner Still Held Up Off Ryde But May Sail To-day.

STRIKERS' DEMANDS

Will Not Sail Unless Eighteen Loyal Men Are Dismissed.

The Olympic was still lying off Ryde and unable to proceed on her voyage to New York at an early hour this morning, the difficulty arising out of the firemen's refusal to sail not yet having been overcome.

At the same time, it is hoped to get the liner away at eight

o'clock this morning. A hundred firemen arrived from Portsmouth late last night and the remainder necessary were expected at 2 a.m. from Liverpool.

Nearly 300 firemen, trimmers, greasers and others, it will be recalled, left the liner on Wednesday, five minutes before she was due to sail, alleging as reason for their action that there were insufficient seamen on board to man the lifeboats, and that the collapsible boats were unseaworthy.

A new difficulty arose yesterday. The Seamen's Union demanded that the eighteen firemen who remained on board on Wednesday should be dismissed. The White Star Company, however, firmly refused to agree to this.

During the day a deputation of firemen proceeded in a tug to the Olympic, and witnessed tests of the liner's collapsible boats, which decided them to advise the men to return to work as soon as a new collapsible boat was put on board in place of one found faulty.

When the delegates returned to Southampton, however, they found that the men, who had gone home, said they would not sail in the ship, no matter what the result of the boat demonstration might be, unless those who had remained on the ship on Wednesday were taken off.

WILL SAIL ON ONE CONDITION
(FROM OUR SPECIAL CORRESPONDENT)

Cowes, April 25 – Mr. Curry, the manager for the White Star Company at Southampton, after his brief visit to Southampton this evening made the following statement to me:–

"The position is briefly as follows," he said.

"The union officials, who came down on the tug together with nine firemen appointed by the other men as delegates, saw the demonstration of the boats.

"Four Berthon boats were lowered into the water, manned, and rowed round entirely to the satisfaction of the union officials and delegates, with the exception of one boat only, which, after it had been in the water for two hours, was leaking a little, presumably having been slightly damaged in the course of being launched.

"Arrangements were made with the union officials and the delegates that they would immediately return to Southampton and urge the men who left the ship yesterday and were standing by for orders from the union immediately to return to the ship, provided we put on board one other boat in the place of the one that had got damaged. This we agreed to do.

"But on the arrival of the tug at Southampton it was found that the men had all gone away, and that before leaving had said that they would not sail in the ship, no matter what the result of the boat demonstration might be, unless the men who had remained on the ship yesterday were taken off."

"This the White Star Line did not see their way to comply with."

Messrs. Lewis and Cannon, the president and the secretary of the Seafarers' Union, told me that they were going to try to persuade the men to go to the ship.

The men had dispersed at 5 p.m., tired out after picketing all night and waiting about all day, and are likely to adhere to their arrangement not to meet outside the White Star office to-morrow morning before seven o'clock.

FEELING AGAINST COLLAPSIBLES

The feeling against collapsible boats here is very strong. All kinds of seamen have told me they are difficult to open, and, indeed, that it is impossible for any but seamen thoroughly practised to get them open at all in bad weather.

"The material sticks," said a harbour look-out man to me, "and I remember a test when thirty of us could not haul the boat apart in half an hour; and had to get tackles to pull it open. And when at last it was got into shape the canvas split all along one side.

"Sharp rock or a piece of ice would cut the canvas like a knife, and they are always liable to overturn till an evenly distributed dead weight of passengers is in them."

DELEGATES TEST THE COLLAPSIBLES

Mr. Lewis, president of the Seafarers' Union, described the visit of the firemen's delegates to the Olympic as follows:–

"The firemen of the Olympic met at seven this morning. About eight o'clock Mr. Blake, the superintendent engineer of the White Star Company, said the company were agreeable to an inspection of the Olympic's lifeboats if the men would appoint a deputation.

"Nine men, together with Mr. Cannon, secretary of the union, and myself, proceeded in a tug to the Olympic. We were not received on board, but Captain Haddock intimated that he was waiting instructions from Liverpool.

"Just after two o'clock the captain sent for myself and Cannon, and agreed to the delegates inspecting any four collapsible boats they cared to select.

"We picked four out and they were lowered into the water. After they had remained in the sea three hours' we again inspected them.

"We found that three of them were seaworthy. The other had a hole in the bottom and was found to be leaking badly."

At this point Mr. Cannon intervened and said the footboards

were awash, and the outer and inner skins had swollen with water.

Mr. Lewis, proceeding, said that the attention of Commander Clarke was drawn to the boat's condition. Some of the sailors and the delegates decided that it was unseaworthy, and he and Mr. Cannon told the captain they were prepared to recommend the men to return to work, subject to the unseaworthy boat being replaced.

ONLY ONE GRUMBLER!
(FROM OUR SPECIAL CORRESPONDENT)

On Board the Olympic, April 25 – The passengers on board are taking the situation very calmly and philosophically. They laugh and joke about it, and appear to be bent on making the best of a bad job.

They spend a lot of time in the gymnasium, riding horses and indulging in physical drill. Elder members are going in for breathing exercises. There are no newspapers on board.

The delay, however, is having serious consequences in many cases.

One American passenger said to me: "If I do not make Minneapolis by Sunday week I shall lose £10,000."

A lady and gentleman who are on their honeymoon trip had made arrangements for a big house reception when they got back to the States, but all their arrangements have been upset, and the reception will have to be cancelled.

The only grumbler on board is a passenger who spends most of his time walking up and down the deck in a state of furious indignation. He keeps trying to speak to the captain, and failing that has to be content with promenading the deck, complaining of the delay and railing at fate.

He has been advised by friendly passengers to address his complaints to the Firemen's Union!

PICKED UP BY WARSHIP

"Short cut" methods are to be adopted by the U.S. Senate Commission inquiring into the Titanic disaster.

Each member of the Commission, it is announced, will separately examine batches of the Titanic crew in private, and decide how many of them it will be necessary to require to give evidence in public before the whole Commission.

The two witnesses yesterday, Mr. Marconi and Mr. Cottam, the wireless operator of the Carpathia, indicated why information as to the disaster was not forthcoming until the Cunarder docked in New York.

SENATOR SMITH OVERRULED

Washington, April 23 – The internal dissension which has been brewing for some time in the Senate's Committee became evident to-day.

From the first several members of the Committee have felt that the chairman, Senator Smith, had been engineering the business of the Committee without consultation with the other members.

Some of the members resented his plan of holding all the forty principal witnesses at Washington until the cross-examination of all had been completed. Trouble has been particularly aroused by the holding of the Titanic's crew.

Mr. Ismay has repeatedly requested to be allowed to conclude his evidence and to depart for England. Mr. Franklin has also asked for permission to return to New York, if only for a few days.

Senator Smith stood out against these requests. Senators Burton and Bourne have indicated their disapproval of the chairman's methods frequently by breaking into his cross-examination.

These members now intend that the hearing of the Titanic's officers and crew shall be taken at the earliest possible moment, so as to permit of their return to England.

This concession followed Senator Smith's defeat on a vote on the question of keeping Quartermaster Hitchens. The Committee overruled Senator Smith, and released the quartermaster.

"SHORT CUT" METHODS

At the end of the session it was formally announced that it had been decided to adopt "short cut" methods to conclude the hearing of evidence.

Just before the adjournment Senator Smith rose and said:–

"Some rumours have reached me that there is friction and lack of harmony among the members of the sub-committee. I have the concurrence of my Associates in saying that that statement is absolutely untrue. Personally, I have never heard of the slightest friction."

After the adjournment of the committee, Senator Newlands, in an interview, explained the committee's decision.

"We have determined," he said, "to hear the members of the crew of the Titanic, and because of the large numbers of these men we will proceed with the hearing without the attendance of the public. Each member of the committee will examine his quota of these men." – Reuter's Special.

MR MARCONI GIVES EVIDENCE

Washington, April 25 – The Senatorial inquiry into the Titanic disaster was resumed to-day. Mr. Marconi was the first witness.

He was questioned (says a Reuter's special telegram) regarding a message sent from New York to the wireless operators on the Carpathia, asking them to hold the news when they reached port for "four figures."

"Yes," said Mr. Marconi, "that message was sent by Mr. Sammis (chief engineer of the Marconi system). I knew nothing about it until afterwards. It wasn't sent until she had passed Sandy Hook and was nearing port.

Senator Smith: How far can the station at Cape Race maintain communication with a vessel? – Between four and five hundred miles in the day and considerably over 1,000 miles at night.

There is no alarm signal on the instruments now to attract attention? – No, but I may possibly devise one.

Unless the operator sat constantly with the receiver on his head he would not get a signal. If wireless was to be of service to others in distress, ships should have operators continuously on duty.

Operators' pay in England averaged from 17s. to 50s. a week, with board and lodging.

Asked if he had any communication with Cape Race on Sunday or any day up to the arrival of the Carpathia Mr. Marconi made the following statement:–

"I had no direct communication. I telephoned my office frequently on both days, and urged that every means should be tried to get information.

"I learned between 7.30 and 8 o'clock on Monday evening that the Titanic had sunk and of the rescues made by the Carpathia, and asked for further information.

"I was told by my operator that it would probably be impossible to get any, as the Carpathia was extremely busy with messages from the captain and the passengers on board."

CONGRATULATED MR. BRIDE

"On boarding the Carpathia after she docked I went directly to the wireless room and congratulated Mr. Bride on what he had done.

"Mr. Cottam, the Carpathia's operator, was not there. He telephoned me later, and asked whether he might give out a report of the wreck. I told him he might under the circumstances.

"There is an ironclad rule of the company prohibiting operators from acting as reporters.

"This is probably why no reports of the disaster were forthcoming from the Carpathia on her way to New York."

Mr. Marconi denied sending a message asking Mr. Cottam to meet him and Mr. Sammis at an hotel and telling him to keep his mouth shut. Senator Smith then proceeded to read the following wireless messages picked up by the United States battleship Florida:–

8.12 p.m. – Operator Carpathia. Say, old man Marconi Company taking good care you keep mouth shut. It's fixed you get good money do best clear.

8.30 p.m. – Operators Carpathia, Titanic arranged your exclusive story dollars four figures, Marconi agreeing say nothing until see me. Where are you now? – J. M. Sammis.

9 p.m. – From Sea Gate to Carpathia. Go Strand Hotel West 14th-street see Marconi "C".

9.30 p.m. – Sea Gate to Carpathia. Personal to operator Carpathia. Meet Marconi and Sammis 502, West 14th-street keep month shut. – Signed Marconi.

"I never authorised those messages," said Mr. Marconi, "but I consented to the operators receiving money."

Mr. Marconi did not think that the privilege he gave Mr. Cottam had anything to do with his failure to get information, depriving the public of details.

Mr. Marconi repeatedly insisted that he did not suppress details of the disaster. The Carpathia's operator had told him that no message was ever received from the warship Chester asking for information for Mr. Taft. If it had been he would certainly have answered it.

"When I told the operator to take something for the story I meant that the newspaper reporters would be so interested in what he had to say that without his holding back any general information, they would be willing to pay him for his personal experiences."

TITANIC'S WIRELESS CALL

Mr. Cottam, the operator on the Carpathia, repeated the statements made by him in New York regarding the Titanic's signals.

The first message from the Titanic was "Come at once, have struck a berg. This C.Q.D." He assisted the Titanic to communicate with other ships, the Titanic operator saying that escaping steam on board was interfering with his instruments. He told how he got into touch with the Olympic, Californian, Hellig Olav, Baltic, Mount Temple, and others.

Did you know that the message was from the President? – No. It was only signed by the commander of the Chester. He asked once about Major Butt.

Is there any rivalry or enmity between Marconi operators and those of other systems? – There is some feeling.

Did any feeling exist between the operators on the Titanic and the one on the Frankfurt, who did not reply promptly to the Titanic's C. Q. D.? – No, sir, I would have answered the operator of the Frankfurt in the same way that the Titanic did, "Keep out, you fool," if it had been my place to when the Frankfurt answered the Titanic's C.Q.D. call. When there are only two hours between life and death twenty minutes is a long time. I don't know what else but a fool to call a man who is so foolish as to interfere with other communication in answer to the C.Q.D. and ask "What's the matter?" twenty minutes later.

The committee adjourned shortly after four o'clock until to-morrow. – Reuter.

MOTHER IDENTIFIES TWO WAIFS
(FROM OUR OWN CORRESPONDENT)

Paris, April 25 – The mystery of the identity of the two little French boys, Louis and Lolo, who were rescued from the Titanic, appears to have been solved by the mother's identification of marks on the younger child.

These marks, which were noticed by Miss Hays, who now has custody of the children in America, have been described, says the *New York Herald*, by Mme. Navratil, of Nice, who claims the children.

One mark is behind the child's right ear and the other on the body. Mme. Navratil's description fits the children exactly. Miss Hays says: "There is no longer any doubt that Mme. Navratil is the mother. We kept the marks secret, knowing that the real mother would be able to describe them."

The children are named Lolo (for Michel) and Momon (for Edmond), and were, it now appears, travelling with their father, who used a friend's name.

VISIBILITY OF ICE

Most Easily Detected at Night from Deck Line, Says Sir E. Shackleton.

What may prove a most important point in the forthcoming British inquiry into the Titanic disaster was touched upon by Sir Ernest Shackleton at Falmouth yesterday.

Sir Ernest was referring to the disaster, and in this connection he expressed a hope that the British inquiry would be composed of experts in their own particular branch of knowledge. For instance, he continued, the question as to the visibility of ice at night time was most important.

Many sailors knew, and especially those who were accustomed to navigating in ice-laden seas, that the higher above the deck the less was it competent to judge of the approach of ice.

He had his men as close to the water-line as possible in misty weather and at night time.

When travelling near ice, if viewed from a high angle, an iceberg would blend with the sea, whereas from the deck line it would loom up almost on the darkest night.

SAFETY ON BIG SHIPS

On the other hand, a marine engineer attached to a world-famous shipbuilding firm yesterday expressed to *The Daily Mirror* the opinion that the Titanic's height would have enabled her more quickly to sight ice.

"The bigger the ship the safer she is. The Titanic's size would

not have made her unmanageable if the berg she hit had been seen in time, nor would she have been less liable to run into it if she had been going slower than she was."

This, generally, was the opinion of the expert consulted. He said:–

"In an emergency a boat of the Titanic's size answers her helm perfectly at any speed above three or four knots, and the fact that she is provided with almost three times as many bulkheads as a much smaller vessel makes her chances much greater in the event of collision.

"I admit that, going full speed, a ship like the Titanic could not be stopped in less than a mile or so if her engines were put hard astern. But in that her full speed is not so great as that of smaller ships, this disadvantage is not peculiar to her type.

"In other respects, too, the bigger the ship the better off is she in a case such as the Titanic's.

"She could pick up ice quicker because she is higher out of the water and her horizon, therefore, greater. And she is steadier in rough weather, which means that her horizon is steadier, especially through glasses."

QUEEN ALEXANDRA AND MR. STEAD

A striking tribute to the memory of Mr. W. T. Stead was paid at a memorial service in Westminster Chapel last evening.

Not only was the spacious building filled with a congregation representing practically every interest with which the veteran journalist identified himself, but the preacher, Dr. Clifford, read messages expressive of sympathy and sense of loss from home and from lands far distant.

Among these messages was one from Queen Alexandra, who telegraphed to Mrs. Stead:–

"Do in my name let family know how much I grieve for them all." Her Majesty was represented at the service by Major-General Brocklehurst.

THE BODY OF MR. STEAD

New York, April 25 – *The New York Times* suggests that the name W. Year, which appears in the list of bodies recovered by the Mackay Bennett, transmitted by wireless telegraphy, is probably W. Stead, the American Morse signals for the two names being almost identical.

Note. – In the American and International Morse codes the signals S (. . .) and T (–) are, if written together, identical with the signal for V (. . . –).

As regards the final letter, operators using the American Code

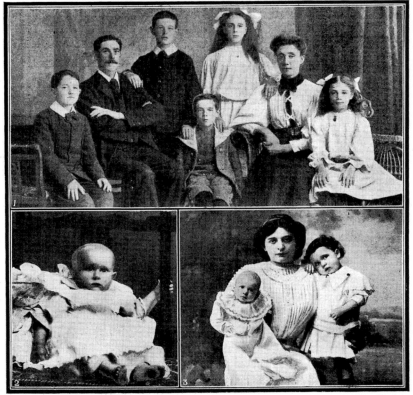

The Daily Mirror
THE MORNING JOURNAL WITH THE SECOND LARGEST NET SALE.

No. 2,654.   Registered at the G.P.O. as a Newspaper   FRIDAY, APRIL 26, 1912   One Halfpenny.

FAMILY OF EIGHT, WHO WERE ON THE TITANIC BY CHANCE, ALL DROWNED IN THE DISASTER BECAUSE THERE WERE NOT ENOUGH LIFEBOATS.

Of the many sad cases of the Titanic disaster, few are more tragic than that of the Goodwins, of Kensington, all of whom were drowned. The family consisted of father, mother and six children, and it was only by chance that they were on the Titanic. They originally intended to sail during Easter week, but waited for the New York on account of the coal strike. At the last minute, however, they were transferred to the ill-starred liner. They were on their way to join Mr. Goodwin's brother at Niagara, where they intended to settle. (1) Mr. and Mrs. Goodwin and five of their children. (2) Sidney, the baby, aged eighteen months. (3) Mme. Navratil, of Nice, with her two children, who are believed to be Louis and Lolo, the French boys who were rescued. Mme. Navratil is certain they are hers, because of a number of coincidences she has noted. She is divorced from her husband, who took the children away.

might possibly read the signal D (– . .), which is the same in both codes as R (. . .) – Reuter.

FAMILY OF EIGHT VICTIMS OF CHANCE
Last Minute Change of Liner to Join Titanic.

"ALL GONE."
Among all the tragic stories of the Titanic disaster few – if any – are more distressing than that related yesterday to *The Daily Mirror* by Mrs. Berry, of Brook Green, Hammersmith.

123

Through a change of liners at the last moment, a whole family of eight emigrating to Canada has perished.

The victims were Mrs. Berry's sister, with her husband and six children, named Goodwin.

It is, indeed, one of the most saddening features of the calamity, as shown by the official figures of the Board of Trade, that of the 105 children on board the Titanic, it was only possible to save fifty-two. Of five children in the first class and twenty-four in the second class all were brought safely to land on the Carpathia, but of the seventy-six children in the steerage, but twenty-three survive, the remaining fifty-three having gone down with the great liner.

For a week Mrs. Berry was in complete ignorance of the fate which had overtaken the family. She did not even know they were in any danger, for she thought they were on board the liner New York. But, suddenly, two words cabled from America brought the dreadful, stunning news of her bereavement.

Mrs. Berry said that the family – Mr. and Mrs. Goodwin and their children, of Melksham, Somersetshire – had originally intended emigrating to America during Easter week.

FATAL DELAY

"But owing to the upset of things caused by the coal strike," she said, "they had to postpone their journey.

"They made new arrangements, and had booked passages on the liner New York. Not hearing to the contrary, we at home fully thought they had sailed on that boat.

"But it now seems that they were transferred to the Titanic almost at the last moment, and the next thing we heard was that they were all drowned.

"When I read the awful tidings last Sunday night – seven days after the disaster – the shock was terrible. It was so sudden and utterly unexpected that no words can express my feelings.

"My brother-in-law's mother, an old lady of seventy, brought the dreadful news. I was going to the evening memorial service for the Titanic victims at St. Barnabas Church, Addison-road, when I met her. The sight of her surprised me greatly, for she does not get about much nowadays.

TRAGEDY IN TWO WORDS

"'I've come to tell you about Gussie' – Augusta was my sister's name – she said. I did not understand what she meant at first. She did not say any more then, but handed me a cablegram from relatives at Niagara Falls, to whom the family were going.

"'All gone!' was the message. Nothing more than that.

"I do not quite know what I said or did when I realised what the words meant. I had lost eight of my nearest and dearest relatives."

205 BODIES FOUND

New York, April 25 – The following message has been received by wireless from the cable steamer Mackay Bennett:–

"Bodies are numerous in latitude 41.35 north, longitude 48.37 west, extending many miles, both east and west. Mailships should give this region a wide berth.

"The medical opinion is that death has been instantaneous in all the cases, owing to the pressure when the bodies were drawn down in the vortex.

"We have been drifting in a dense fog since noon yesterday, and the total number of bodies picked up is 205." – Exchange Telegraph.

PASSENGERS INSPECT LIFEBOATS

New York, April 25 – Almost every passenger on the three transatlantic liners leaving New York to-day became personally an inspector of the vessel's lifeboats.

During the hour preceding the sailing of the liners the decks were thronged with hundreds of passengers, who regarded with critical eyes the boats and rafts stored on them. – Reuter.

FOOTBALL FOR TITANIC FUND

In accordance with the proposal made by the council at their meeting last Friday, it has now been definitely arranged that the match for the F.A. Charity Shield shall be played on the ground of the Tottenham Hotspur Club on Saturday, May 4; kick-off, 3.30. The whole gate receipts will be given to the Lord Mayor of London's fund in aid of the sufferers from the Titanic disaster.

27 April 1912

VOYAGE OF THE OLYMPIC TO NEW YORK ABANDONED

Fifty-Three Men Arrested After Leaving Their Ship.

EXTRAORDINARY SCENE

Seamen Advised by Naval Officer That Their Conduct Is Mutinous.

The White Star liner Olympic yesterday gave up her voyage to New York, and returned to Southampton.

Most of her 102 first-class passengers travelled up to London last night. Her 330 second and 500 third-class passengers are to

be kept on board, if they desire it, at the company's expense till arrangements have been made for their transfer to other boats.

The Olympic had been held up off Ryde since Wednesday afternoon owing to the refusal of nearly 300 firemen, greasers and other members of her crew to sail owing, at first, to alleged ineffective lifeboat accommodation.

Why the voyage was abandoned is best explained in the following message sent by the White Star Line to the Postmaster-General yesterday:–

Regret to inform you that after shipping satisfactory engine-room crew, the deck and hitherto loyal men in engine-room refused duty, asserting they would not sail with substitute men.

Under these circumstances we have been compelled to order Olympic back to Southampton and abandon the voyage.

"Earnestly hope you will secure for us official support in efforts we intend making to secure proper punishment of crews for mutinous behaviour, as unless firmness is shown now we despair of restoring discipline and maintain sailing."

The arrival of the substitute men on the Olympic late on Thursday night was the signal for an amazing midnight scene, vividly described by our special correspondent on board the Olympic.

Fifty-three of the fifty-six seamen on the liner hoisted their kits on their shoulders and marched down the gangway to a tug that lay alongside.

They could not be persuaded to return on board, and were handed over to the police. In the afternoon they appeared before the magistrates charged with disobeying lawful commands and were remanded.

WHAT WAS SEEN FROM THE CALIFORNIAN
Steamer That Sent Up Rockets, but Would Not Answer Wireless Call.

CAPTAIN'S EVIDENCE
Member of Crew Declares He Saw Titanic on Night of Disaster.

Conflicting evidence was given at Washington yesterday before the United States Senate Commission Inquiry into the Titanic disaster, at which Senator Smith is presiding.

It has already been stated that the Titanic before going down sent up electric Morse signals to try and attract the attention of a ship, which Mr. Boxhall, the fourth officer of the Titanic, computed to be approximately five miles away.

Captain Smith told him, said Mr. Boxhall, to signal to the ship, telling her in Morse and rocket signals: "Come at once. We sinking."

Witnesses from the Californian told the Commission yesterday that they had seen rockets sent up by a steamer on the night of the disaster.

A donkey-engineman of the Californian declared that he saw the Titanic plainly before midnight.

Captain Lord said he saw a steamer, which he was sure was not the Titanic, send up rocket signals about one o'clock in the morning, and told the wireless operator to call the ship, which was four or five miles away. They could get no answer and the ship afterwards steamed away.

The Californian was nineteen miles away from the Titanic, and it would have been impossible to see either Morse or distress signals.

"ROCKETS TEN MILES AWAY."
The first of the witnesses from the Californian before the Senate Commission at Washington yesterday, says a Reuter special telegram, was Ernest Gill, of Liverpool, a donkey-engineman.

Senator Smith first read an affidavit made by Gill on Wednesday, in which he declared that he was actuated by the desire that no captain who refuses or neglects to give aid to a vessel in distress should be able to hush up the matter.

Gill in his affidavit stated that several members of the crew, whom he had urged to join in protesting against the conduct of the Californian's captain in disregarding the Titanic's rockets, refused because they were afraid that they would "lose their jobs."

He said that he saw the Titanic most plainly. He came on deck on the Californian at 11.56 p.m. as the vessel's engines stopped. They were drifting in floe ice.

From the starboard rail he saw the broadside lights of a very large steamer. At midnight he went to his cabin.

He could not sleep and went back to the deck to smoke a cigarette. Ten minutes later he saw a white rocket ten miles away to starboard.

A second rocket went up at the same place seven or eight minutes later.

He did not notify the bridge, because it was not his business. They could not have helped seeing the rockets.

Gill swore that he then turned in. At 6.40 he was awakened by orders to turn out to render assistance as the Titanic had gone down.

He heard the second officer, Evans, telling the fourth officer, Wooten, that the third officer had reported rockets during his watch. Gill said that he knew then that it must be the Titanic he had seen.

Mr. Evans said that the captain had been notified of the rockets by an apprentice officer, whose name he thought was Gibson. The skipper ordered Morse signals to be sent to the distressed vessel. Mr. Gibson again reported rockets to the captain, who told him to continue the Morse to the distressed vessel until he got a reply. No reply was received.

Gill said that the next remark he heard Evans make was, "Why the devil don't they wake the wireless man."

The entire crew, according to Gill, talked among themselves about the disregard of the rockets.

PREPARED TO REBUT
STATEMENTS

Captain Lord, of the Californian, who said that he was prepared to rebut the last witnesses' statements, then gave evidence.

The only communication he had with the Titanic was about 10.15 (ship's time) on the night of Sunday, April 14, when he told her that he was surrounded by ice and had stopped.

Did the Titanic acknowledge the message? – Yes, sir. He told us to shut up and keep out – something like that.

"We got the C.Q.D. call," he continued, "from the Virginian about six o'clock in the morning of April 15."

Do you know anything regarding the Titanic disaster of your own knowledge? – Nothing.

Did you see any of her signals or anything of the ship herself? – No.

Was the Titanic beyond your range of vision? – Yes; 19½ or 20 miles away.

If you had received the distress call on Sunday evening how long would it have taken you to reach her? – At the very least two hours under the ice conditions.

When you got to the scene did you see any wreckage? – Yes, a little; but considering the size of the disaster there was very little. It looked more as if a fishing smack had been wrecked.

Did you see any icebergs? – We were surrounded by them.

I don't want to seem impertinent, captain, but there was a report that there had been some attempt to prevent you coming here to testify. Do you know anything about any attempt? – I don't think there was anything of the kind. When I was served with the subpoena I asked the assistant general manager for permission and I was permitted to come.

Do you know whether your wireless operator was on duty on Sunday night after he sent the warning message? – I think not. I went by his room about 11.45. There was no light and that would indicate that he had gone to bed.

SHIP THAT SENT UP ROCKETS

Captain Lord then went on to make the following statement:–

"I did not see any distress signals. When I came on to the bridge at 10.30 on Sunday night the officer said he thought he saw a light.

"It was a peculiar night. We had been having trouble with the stars, mistaking them for lights.

"Then a ship came up. I asked the operator if he had heard anything. He replied that he had the Titanic, to which he had given the ice message.

"Then this ship came up and lay within four or five miles of us. She lay there all night, but we couldn't hear from her.

"It was not the Titanic. I am sure of that.

"About one o'clock I told the operator to call this ship again. She sent up several rockets, but would not answer.

"I told him to ask her who she was. I heard him calling her when I went to bed, but she did not answer.

"I have a faint recollection of hearing the cabin boy, about four o'clock, saying something about the ship still standing by. Soon after she steamed away.

"This boat sent up several white rockets, but they were not distress signals.

"In the position in which the Californian lay, nineteen miles away from the Titanic, it would have been impossible to see either Morse or distress signals.

"The first news of the disaster reached me shortly after five o'clock on Monday morning, when the Frankfurt reported that the Titanic had sunk after hitting an iceberg. The ice conditions that night were very deceiving."

WIRELESS OPERATOR
AND TITANIC

Cyril Evans, the wireless operator on the Californian, was then called.

"I turned in at 11.25," he said, "I never heard any distress signals from the Titanic. In the evening the Titanic called me and exchanged signals.

"I said, 'Here's a message for you about ice.' He said he had heard me send it to other ships. He then gave the wireless signal for 'Enough'."

"What time was the ice message sent to the Titanic?" asked Senator Smith.

In reply, Evans read:–

April 15, 5.35 p.m., New York time. – Californian to captain Titanic, 43.3 N., 49.9 W. – Passed three large bergs, three miles to southward us.

When did you communicate with the Titanic? – 9.5, New York time.

"I went outside five minutes before that, when we stopped," went on Evans. "The captain said we stopped because of ice. He

told me to advise the Titanic.

"I called the Titanic and said: 'Say, old man, we surrounded ice.' He replied: 'Shut up. I'm working with Cape Race,' and said I had jammed him.

"I did not hear him again direct, but he knew he was sending messages to Cape Race. I didn't take them down. I don't know what they were, I'm sure they didn't relate to ice, or I would have taken them down, I went to bed at 11.30.

"I was awakened at 3.40 by the chief officer, who said he had seen rockets and wanted to get some information.

"I called, and the Frankfurt answered with news of the sinking of the Titanic. The Virginian called before I left the key and furnished more information."

Did anyone tell you about Captain Lord being informed three times that night about a ship sending up rockets? – I think Gibson, the apprentice, told me that the captain was called and told about the rockets.

The rockets were talked about in the ship generally by the crew. While the Californian was on the way to the scene he heard the men say that five rockets had been sent up and that the captain had been roused. The apprentice got out Morse signals and tried to get into communication with the distressed vessel. No effort was made to use rockets on the Californian.

At a quarter to six the Committee adjourned until the morning.

It is expected that Mr. Thomas H. Moore, captain of the Mount Temple, will be examined in the course of the morning.

LINERS IN PAIRS SUGGESTED

Mr. Franklin, the vice-president of the International Maritime Company, was the first witness called yesterday.

He was closely questioned regarding the messages received and sent out by the White Star Company during the day of the disaster before the fact that the Titanic had sunk became known, and he denied that there had been undue delay in communicating the information at the company's disposal.

Mr. Franklin floated the suggestion that ships should cross the Atlantic in pairs.

BRITISH INQUIRY BEGINS

The British inquiry into the Titanic disaster has already begun.

Evidence from survivors is being taken by the English Consul-General in New York, Mr. Walter Courtenay Bennett, and when completed will be sent to London for use at the Court of Inquiry here.

The first sitting of the Wrecks Commission will be held next Thursday at the Scottish Hall, Buckingham Gate. The members of

the Commission, as announced last night, are as follows:–

Loud Mersey.
Rear-Admiral Hon. S. A. Gough-Calthorpe.
Prof J. H. Biles, M.I.C.E.
Captain A. W. Clarke.
Commander F. C. Lyon.
Captain Hon. C. Bigham (sec).

A fifth assessor has yet to be appointed by the Home Secretary. Lord Mersey is officially styled Wreck Commissioner, and he sits with five assessors, constituting a Court of Inquiry.

ON THE BRIDGE WITH A CIGARETTE
(FROM OUR OWN CORRESPONDENT)

New York, April 20 – The English Consul. General, Walter Courtenay Bennett, began an investigation here into the Titanic disaster yesterday, examining the survivors at the Consulate.

The evidence will be collected and sent in a complete form to the Wrecks Commission in London.

Mr. Courtenay Bennett told me that several survivors have important evidence bearing on the case.

Quartermaster Hitchens sailed for Liverpool in the Celtic yesterday, accompanied by the look-out man, Reginald Lee, who, with Fleet, was in the crow's nest when the Titanic struck the iceberg.

Lee, who was not examined at Washington, told the Consul-General that the night was clear overhead, but that a haze on the horizon prevented a sight of the berg until it was close to the liner.

It is his belief that had the helm been ported but a few seconds before the Titanic might have been saved.

Lee is a fine type of sailor. He was twelve years in the Navy, and bears a high character from his officers.

Chief Officer H. W. Wilde, who was last seen on the bridge smoking a cigarette, waved good-bye to Second Officer Lightoller as the Titanic's bows went under in the final plunge.

12 MEN FROZEN ON ICEBERG
(FROM OUR OWN CORRESPONDENT)

New York, April 26 – Captain Petersen, of the North German Lloyd liner Prinzess Irene, which arrived here last night from Genoa with 400 cabin and 1,540 steerage passengers, stated that at 5 p.m. on Wednesday last their wireless operator intercepted a message transmitted by an unknown ship, which read as follows:–

"Passed iceberg this morning bearing twelve bodies of men frozen stiff. All were fully dressed, wearing caps and life jackets."

Captain Petersen said that he believed the message referred to an iceberg which must have been near to the Titanic when she sank, and that the twelve men swam to the berg in a desperate effort to save themselves.

The S.S. Minia, which has reached the cable ship Mackay Bennett, states that the bodies of Mr. Charles M. Hays, Colonel Astor and Mr. Isidor Straus have been picked up.

29 April 1912

Scarcely had the Carpathia with her survivors of the Titanic catastrophe reached New York, than the Senate Investigating Committee held their first meeting at the Waldorf-Astoria Hotel. The first witness called was Mr. J. Bruce Ismay, the chairman of the White Star Line, who has been so much blamed in New York in connection with the disaster. Giving evidence on the first day, Mr. Ismay said that at the time he got into a lifeboat "there wasn't a woman on the boat deck nor any passenger of any class so far as I could see or hear." Mr. Ismay, who is seen in the centre of the photograph with his hand to his chin, is shown giving his evidence before the committee. He is also seen in the portrait.

TITANIC CREW NOT TO BE "PRISONERS"
Survivors Refuse To Remain at Plymouth.

THE HOMECOMING
Woman's Despair Turned to Joy at the Eleventh Hour.

Remarkable incidents marked the arrival at Plymouth yesterday of the Red Star liner Lapland with 167 survivors of the Titanic's crew – 147 men and twenty stewardesses.

Elaborate precautions had been taken by the Board of Trade and White Star Company to detain the survivors until their depositions had been received; but the men refused to stay, and ultimately a special train was provided to take the majority to Southampton.

There, late at night, mothers, wives and sweethearts met them with tears of joy.

MEN REFUSE TO REMAIN
(FROM OUR OWN CORRESPONDENT)
Plymouth, April 28 – The elaborate schemes of the Board of Trade and the White Star Company with regard to the treatment of the survivors of the crew of the Titanic went all awry to-day.

Directly the crew, on arriving at the docks, saw the beds on the floor and the dinner of ham, boiled eggs and coffee awaiting them, they became quite unmanageable. They threatened to rush the dock

The Daily Mirror
THE MORNING JOURNAL WITH THE SECOND LARGEST NET SALE.

No. 2,656.   Registered at the G.P.O. as a Newspaper.   MONDAY, APRIL 29, 1912   One Halfpenny.

MR. J. BRUCE ISMAY, CHAIRMAN OF THE WHITE STAR LINE, BEING CROSS-EXAMINED BY SENATOR SMITH BEFORE THE INQUIRY COMMISSION IN NEW YORK.

Scarcely had the Carpathia with her survivors of the Titanic catastrophe reached New York, than the Senate Investigating Committee held their first meeting at the Waldorf-Astoria Hotel. The first witness called was Mr. J. Bruce Ismay, the chairman of the White Star Line, who has been so much blamed in New York in connection with the disaster. Giving evidence on the first day, Mr. Ismay said that at the time he got into a lifeboat "there wasn't a woman on the boat deck nor any passenger of any class so far as I could see or hear." Above, Mr. Ismay, who is seen in the centre of the photograph with his hand to his chin, is shown giving his evidence before the committee. He is also seen in the portrait.—(Ellis and Walery.)

gates, and when asked for their depositions many replied:

"I was asleep in my bunk. Give me a pass to go out."

About twenty men gave depositions. Then the authorities gave it up, and abandoned the plan of keeping the men here till to-morrow.

HOMECOMING OF THE SURVIVORS
(FROM OUR SPECIAL CORRESPONDENT)
Southampton, April 28 – There were very pathetic scenes to-night when the 10.15 special train conveying the Titanic survivors arrived from Plymouth at the West Station and ten minutes later at the Dock Station.

They had come safely home, these survivors and heroes of the greatest sea tragedy in history, and their wives, sweethearts and relatives went to greet them and give them a loving welcome.

As the train steamed slowly into the West Station the survivors thrust their heads out of the carriage windows and cheered and waved handkerchiefs. The men jumped quickly to the platform, and

The cutter containing officials from the Seafarers' Union alongside the tender containing crew members, who refused to be kept as "prisoners".

wives and sweethearts threw their arms round them and kissed them again and again.

Among the crowd at the Dock Station was a woman who had come to greet her brother. As the survivors passed along she shouted: "Where is Frank?"

"Here I am," a voice replied, and the woman threw herself into her brother's arms. So great was her joy that she almost fell fainting to the ground.

Another poor woman who had been waiting at the dock to meet her husband failed to see him.

She went in and out among the crowd calling him in vain. Gradually the crowd dispersed, and still the woman searched in vain.

Then the awful thought struck her that he was drowned.

She lifted up her arms and ran out of the station shrieking hysterically: "Oh, God! God! not here!"

Two women came to her aid, and, holding her arms, prevented her falling fainting to the ground. Her husband, they said, consoling her, must have got out at the West Station.

This assurance partially reassured her, and she went quietly and tearfully to her home, where, to her great joy, she found her husband awaiting her!

Particularly distressing was the case of Mrs. Barrett, a fireman's wife, who gave birth to twins soon after the Titanic left Southampton on her fateful voyage. She received a telegram a few days ago stating that her husband was saved, and she had been eagerly looking forward to meeting him to-night.

She was cruelly disappointed, and on learning this morning that he was among the drowned had a relapse.

Already weak, she collapsed at the terrible news, and is now lying seriously ill in a fatherless house, with her, now, six children.

CLOSELY-GUARDED SURVIVORS
(FROM OUR SPECIAL CORRESPONDENT)

Plymouth, April 28 – This morning at eight o'clock the Red Star liner Lapland arrived and anchored in Cawsand Bay, three miles from Plymouth Dock.

The tender Sir Francis Drake, with officials of the White Star Company and a handful of passengers and friends, who were able to prove overnight that they were not journalists, on board, left the dock at 6.45. Immediately after her went the tender Sir Walter Raleigh to obtain the Lapland's mails.

A third tender, Sir Richard Grenville, was also sent out carrying no passengers, and evidently intended for the conveyance to the sheds on the quay, converted into a temporary "gaol," of the survivors of the Titanic's crew.

Mr. Lewis, the president, and Mr. Cannon, the secretary of the British Seafarers' Union at Southampton, to which all the seamen and firemen survivors of the Titanic's crew belong, went out in a small sailing cutter, The Queen, to meet the liner. I was permitted to accompany them.

When the liner at last appeared it could be seen that her deck forward was covered with Titanic men, all of whom were personally known to Mr. Lewis and Mr. Cannon.

Mr. Lewis made a trumpet of his hands and bellowed: "Don't say a word till they let your union officials come aboard. They would not let us go on either the pier or the tender. They mean to shut you up and hold an inquiry."

Presently the Sir Richard Grenville came round the breakwater and headed straight for us, when a signal was made for Mr. Lewis and Mr. Cannon to go on board. This they at once did.

Apparently – so resolutely had the survivors earned out the suggestion made by their union officials – the Board of Trade officials found it impossible to proceed with their work of examining the crew until this had been done.

The Sir Richard Grenville cruised about for two hours and finally docked at noon, and from the closed gates there came a burst of cheers as the stewardesses came ashore. But no one was allowed within.

Two large bags of gold arrived in a cab for the payment of the crew, and were carried in through the grills and the police cordon. A few of the survivors clustered at the window of their improvised dining-room, looking out on the street from the first floor, and flung open the sash to converse with friends in the crowd.

One survivor leaned out and said sadly to a man he recognised:–

"Joe's gone. The boat wouldn't come back to him when he was swimming."

And there was a depth of tragedy in that simple statement that created a sudden silence.

"DON'T MIND ME, SAVE YOUR OWN LIVES"
Titanic Survivors Tell of Captain Smith's Unselfish Heroism.

36 WHO WERE "BRITISH."
(FROM OUR SPECIAL CORRESPONDENT)

Plymouth, April 28 – The following graphic stories of the Titanic disaster were given to me by surviving members of the crew who arrived here to-day. Each further reveals the heroism of those who remained to die.

Thomas Threlfall, leading fireman, of 128, St. Mark's-cottages, Liverpool, said:–

"I was in my bunk when the crash came. Jimmy put his head in at the door and said:–

"'For God's sake! Get up here! She's run into something!'

"There were not three of us in the crew that believed for an hour afterwards that the ship would sink. We thought that when the water had found its level she would still float.

"If ever there were thirty-six Britishers, they were the engineers of that ship.

"The Yankee saloon passengers were brave men. They put their wives on the boat. I saw one woman jump out of a boat to try to get back to her husband on the ship.

"Many women could have been saved, and their husbands, too, if the women had got in the boats when they were told, and had not clung round their husbands' necks."

"KNEW SHE MUST GO DOWN."

"When the boilers broke out of the ship it was dreadful. Mr. Lowe, the fifth officer, was in command of my boat, and I heard him say:

"'Thank God! Perhaps she will float now with all that weight out of her.'

"Then she broke again, and we knew she must go down.

"I was in boat No. 14. We had forty-five women in it. Mr. Murdoch, the first officer, sent the boat away, and he said – they were the last words I heard him utter:

"'Pull away fifty or one hundred yards, and wait for orders. You must look out for wreckage.'

"Before I went up to the boats the second engineer, Mr. Hesketh, said: 'We have done all we can. You must get out now.'

"Boat No. 14, into which I got, was the last boat but one on the port side and the last but one to go.

"Mr. Lowe had a revolver in his pocket, and I heard him say before the boat was launched:

"'Bear in mind. I will have no dirty work here. I will kill two at a time.'"

"DIED A HERO'S DEATH."
Paddy McGough, leading fireman, said:–

"People fancied in my boat that they could see lights, and said over and over again, crazy like: 'There's a light! There's a ship!'

"We were told when we put off to throw out our painters, so as to keep close together, as Mr. Murdoch thought we would have a better chance if we kept in a cluster. All the crew wish to deny the statement that one of the firemen tried to cut the lifebelt off Phillips, the first Marconi operator.

"Captain Smith said, as we pulled off: 'Don't mind me, men. Save your own lives. God bless you!'"

"It was the suction of the Titanic when she sank that the officers told us to be most afraid of," another fireman said.

"Me and my mate, William Small, of Russell-street, Southampton, had been together for years. I saw him lower his own boat and refuse to go in it. He died a hero's death."

"The last I saw of Jimmy Keating," said a greaser, "was on the No. 2 fore hatch changing his clothes ready to go down below at twelve o'clock to take his watch.

"That shows you what the discipline was. The ship had struck more than ten minutes then, and he was going down below, cool and calm. He never came up again."

SWAM WITH BABY TO BOAT

A stoker told of his escape by means of a raft consisting of a cabin door and a few other wooden objects which had been hastily collected.

I do not know (he said) how many of us took refuge on that raft, but I do know that from the fearful cold six of them died before we were taken off. We were there, I believe, about three hours.

A fireman said that he believed that when the watertight doors were closed one of the engineers, who had been injured in the collision, was shut up in a small pump-room below. It was impossible to get him up, and he had to be left to his death.

The terrible cries from the Titanic were described by a leading fireman:–

We heard them from the boats, he said, and to drown them I asked one of the women to sing. She started, "Eternal Father, strong to save" and we all took it up.

Speaking of Captain Smith's heroism at the last, Harry Senior, a fireman, said:–

As I was swimming to the boat I saw the captain in the water. He was swimming with a baby in his arms, raising it out of the water as he swam on his back. He swam to a boat, put the baby in, and then swam back.

So confident were some of the stokers in the security of the ship, said a stoker, that some of them, whilst the boats were being lowered, when the band was playing a waltz tune, were dancing and smoking.

MR. ISMAY PLEASED

Washington, April 28 – Mr. Bruce Ismay left here yesterday for the purpose of taking a rest. His destination has not been made public, but he said he would return on Monday.

Mr. Ismay expressed great satisfaction at the evidence given yesterday before the Senatorial Commission of Inquiry. He was greatly cheered by the stories related by the stewards and seamen, which showed his conduct in an excellent light.

To relieve the penniless condition of those sailors who have been summoned as witnesses by the Commission the fees of four dollars a day to which they become entitled at the conclusion of the investigation were advanced to them yesterday evening at Mr. Ismay's request. – Reuter.

HELD UP BY ICE ON WAY TO TITANIC

Further attempts to fix the identity of the "mystery ship" whose lights were seen from the sinking Titanic were made at Saturday's sitting of United States Senator Smith's Committee of Inquiry.

According to the report of the proceedings transmitted by Reuter's general and special services, Captain Moore, of the C.P.R. liner Mount Temple, was called, and said that at 12.30 a.m. on April 15 he was informed that the Titanic, which he reckoned was about forty-nine miles distant, was sending out C.Q.D. messages.

He at once ordered full steam to be put on, and called up all the spare firemen, directing that they should be given an allowance of rum to encourage them. In the dash towards the scene of the disaster the Mount Temple, about 3 a.m., had to put her engines full speed astern to avoid a small schooner lying ahead of her.

The schooner was coming from the direction of the Titanic. The Mount Temple also had to slow down on account of ice, and she was finally obliged to stop for a few minutes at 3.25 (ship's time), when she was about fourteen miles from the Titanic.

Asked if the schooner's light might have been that seen by Mr. Boxhall and others on the liner when the Titanic was firing distress rockets, Captain Moore said it might have been the light of a tramp steamer, about 6,000 tons, and apparently a foreigner, which passed to starboard of the Mount Temple, and did not answer to wireless, she had a black funnel with some device on the band near the top.

The Titanic undoubtedly had not fixed her position properly. She must have been eight miles further east than the spot reported.

Creeping slowly through the ice, the Mount Temple reached a point very near the Titanic's reported position at 4.30 on Monday morning. There he counted between forty and fifty icebergs and saw nothing else but the strange steamer.

The witness then read the messages that passed between him and the Titanic, one of them asking the Mount Temple to get all boats ready as she was sinking fast.

LIFEBELT FOR MR. STEAD

Andrew Cunningham, a stateroom steward on the Titanic, said that the order to call all the passengers was not given until fifty minutes after the collision. Mr. Stead was the last of the passengers under his charge to put on a lifebelt. After that he saw him no more. He said:–

Mr. W. T. Stead asked me to show him how to put on his lifebelt. I put the lifebelt on him. It was the last I put on.

Did you ever see Mr. Stead again? – No, sir.

The following are extracts from the evidence of Frederick Ray, another steward:–

I helped to load several boats. Just as we were about to lower one of the boats a large woman was helped in. She kept sobbing and cried out: "Let me get out of here. I have never been in an open boat in my life." Then a baby wrapped up in a blanket was thrown. When my boat left there were three or four men on the deck.

I put a lifebelt on Mr. Guggenheim. I then went on deck and assisted in launching lifeboat No. 7. Mr. Pittman and Mr. Ismay helped in keeping the falls clear. This was on the boat deck. Mr. Ismay called out for men to form a line so as to let the ladies through, Mr. Murdoch also kept calling for ladies, saying: "Are there any other ladies here?"

Before this boat was lowered I assisted in loading boat No. 5. A woman came along before it was got off and Mr. Ismay called to her to get in. "I am only a stewardess sir," she said. Mr. Ismay said: "That makes no difference. You are a woman. Take your place," and she came away with us. Mr. Murdoch ordered me into boat No. 5.

A man and a woman were standing beside the boat. She had her arms around his neck and was crying. I heard her say: "I can't leave without you. I can't leave you." I turned my head away, and the next moment I saw the woman with the man sitting behind her in the boat. Just then a voice said: "Throw out that man," but we were already being lowered away, and the man remained.

When she went down I saw a crowd of people on her after deck, Mr. Pittman wanted to go back to help those in the water and gave orders to do so. The women pleaded with him not to, asking why they should risk their lives in a hopeless effort. Alfred Crawford, another steward, in his evidence stated that when the Titanic struck the iceberg he went below and told his passengers to dress warmly.

Mrs. Straus placed her maid in boat No. 8 and passed a rug to her, and was about to get in herself, when suddenly she turned and flung her arms around her husband's neck, saying: "We've been all these years together. Where you go I go," and refused to get in.

This evidence was followed by an impressive pause, the story arousing profound emotion, one or two women being moved to tears.

HALIFAX AWAITS TITANIC'S DEAD
Sad Preparations for Arrival To-day of Funeral Ship
(FROM OUR OWN CORRESPONDENT)
New York, April 28 – Preparations are now practically completed at Halifax for the reception of the bodies of the Titanic victims which arrive by the Mackay Bennett to-morrow.

Undertakers are arriving with quantities of embalming fluid, and rows of coffins are piled high on the pier of the navy yard. Undertakers' wagons are to be seen driving through the streets in all directions.

The most recent message received at Halifax from the Mackay Bennett is:

"Confirm report that the bodies of Colonel Astor and Mr. I. Straus are on board. Due Monday with bodies."

It is known that the ship has picked up 219 bodies, and now great anxiety prevails among relatives as to which have been buried at sea owing to the lack of embalming fluid on the funeral ship.

Private cars, which will be waiting at the station, will carry away the bodies of Colonel Astor, Mr. Widener and Mr. C. M. Hays, president of the Grand Trunk Railway.

190 IDENTIFIED
The White Star Company, says a Reuter's message from New York, has received a wireless message from the Mackay Bennett stating that eighty-two additional bodies of those who perished in the Titanic disaster have been recovered and identified.

Up to Saturday the number of dead identified was stated to be 171. Yesterday the total reached 190. Among the bodies identified is that of Mr. Wallace H. Hartley, the gallant leader of the ship's band, who went heroically playing to their doom.

Another victim identified is Mr. Frank D. Millet, the American painter and journalist. Mr. Millet had resided in London for a considerable time, and was in his sixty-seventh year.

AUTOMATIC DISTRESS SIGNALS
A new type of wireless recorder is wanted for ships at sea.

Messages were received in the early days of wireless telegraphy by means of a "printer," which inked the Morse signals on a travelling paper ribbon, a wireless engineer told *The Daily Mirror* yesterday.

These inkers, or printing telegraphs, were abandoned because they could not be made sufficiently sensitive for long-distance work.

The telephone was found to be a far more delicate recorder, as even the faintest signals could be heard in the form of buzzes which a trained operator could detect.

But for the purposes of general safety, and of recording the distress signals from a ship near enough to be reached in time to render help, it would be a simple matter to have an auxiliary receiver, of low sensitiveness, which would record the messages from, perhaps, twenty-five miles round on a paper ribbon.

It very often happens that on cargo boats there is only one operator, who is not on duty during the greater part of the night.

In such cases as these the moderate distance recorder would prove of great value. When the long-distance receiving apparatus was put out of use for the night, the range of the inker might be increased.

1 May 1912

FUNERAL BOAT ARRIVES AT HALIFAX
Mackay Bennett Brings 190 Bodies Into Port.

EVIDENCE OF EXPLOSION
The cable ship Mackay Bennett reached Halifax yesterday morning with her terrible freight of victims of the Titanic catastrophe. She reported that she had recovered over 300 bodies, of which more than 100 were so mutilated that their injuries must have been caused by an explosion.

One group, of thirty, among which were the bodies of several women, were found beside an upturned lifeboat.

In her tragic cruise the ship sighted the iceberg that drove the Titanic to her doom. From its side extended a "large wedge-shaped blade, grim memorial of the deadly triumph of natural forces over man's puny handiwork."

FUNERAL SHIP'S ARRIVAL
New York, April 30 – The cable steamer Mackay Bennett, with bodies picked up near the scene of the Titanic disaster, passed into Halifax Harbour at eight o'clock (American time).

The vessel steamed directly into the Government Dock, where the bodies were landed and guarded by bluejackets.

All shipping was kept outside the channel, and no persons were allowed at the dock except Government officials. Mourners, undertakers and Pressmen gathered outside, waiting.

The bodies will be transferred to undertakers following the embalming. Only one woman was present at the dock, a woman undertaker from St. John's.

The Mackay Bennett recovered 306 bodies from the wreckage, of which 190 were aboard.

The bodies are remarkably well preserved, but most of them had very little clothing on when found and several women were in night attire.

FORTY MILES AREA SEARCHED

The body of a baby boy two years old was recovered.

Canon Hind, the chaplain on board the Mackay Bennett, specially commends the captain, officers and crew, who did their work in a splendid manner. The first bodies recovered were found at eight o'clock on Saturday. The same night the burial service was solemnised amid the icebergs. Canon Hind expresses regret at the fact that a representative of the White Star Line did not accompany the mission.

The officers report that the work of recovering the bodies was terribly difficult. Two boats' crews were continually employed whilst daylight lasted. The bodies which were found extended over an area of forty miles surrounding the position of the sunken vessel.

One group of thirty, including several women, was found alongside an upturned lifeboat. A woman's red skirt was attached to an oar, and had apparently been used as a distress signal.

Various indications showed that the boat was afloat some time after the Titanic foundered.

KILLED BY EXPLOSION?

Amongst the dead were 116 mutilated beyond recognition. Arms and legs were fractured, and the features in many cases so terribly cut and bruised that it is declared the injuries could not have been caused by the sea or wreckage, but must have been the effects of a terrific explosion.

Many of the dead were identified by papers, letters and cards, and most of the watches found had stopped between 2.10 and 2.15.

The bodies of the first-class passengers found were in groups.

The question of the disposition of the valuables found on the recovered bodies will be settled by arrangement between the American Consul and the Hon. G. H. Murray, the Premier of Nova Scotia.

In the absence of any treaty between Great Britain and America the

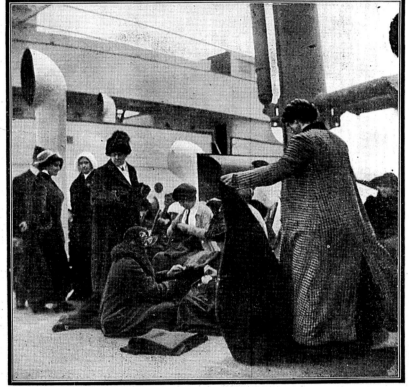

The Daily Mirror

THE MORNING JOURNAL WITH THE SECOND LARGEST NET SALE.

No. 2,658.   Registered at the G.P.O. as a Newspaper   WEDNESDAY, MAY 1, 1912   One Halfpenny.

WOMEN PASSENGERS ON THE CARPATHIA CLOTHE AND TEND THE SURVIVORS OF THE TITANIC TRAGEDY.

When rescued from the Titanic lifeboats by the Carpathia many of the women were very scantily clad, as they had retired for the night when the giant liner crashed into the iceberg. This fact, of course, added tenfold to their sufferings as they drifted about in the piercing cold awaiting rescue. Once aboard the Cunarder, however, everything possible was done for their comfort, passengers giving up their cabins and ransacking their trunks for clothes. The photograph shows women passengers sewing and distributing clothes. If the garments did not fit these kindly ladies took needle and thread and made the necessary alterations.

Premier has agreed to arrange and facilitate the transfer of personal effects to relatives on the presentation of proper credentials.

Whilst in the neighbourhood of the disaster the Mackay Bennett sighted the iceberg with which, it is supposed, the Titanic collided. Bodies, deck chairs and wreckage were strewn all around, and the berg was cracked in several places, huge rents being visible as the result of the collision.

From the side of the iceberg projected a large wedge-shaped blade, evidently torn from the liner. The berg had evidently been shattered by some great impact. – Exchange Telegraph.

AMERICAN INQUIRY ENDING

Washington, April 30 – Mr. Bruce Ismay was called before the Senate Inquiry Committee to-day and repeated the evidence he gave at New York. – Exchange Telegraph.

The crew of the Titanic, says a Reuter's message from Washington, who were released by the Senatorial Committee on Monday night, are preparing to leave for New York.

Mr. Lightoller, the second officer of the Titanic, is already in New York, and the other officers, Messrs. Pittman, Boxhall and Lowe, are in Washinton superintending the arrangements for the departure of the crew. The Senatorial Committee has not yet decided how many passengers will be called before the inquiry.

It is thought possible that there will be a recess, in which the Committee will formulate plans regarding its future proceedings.

Indications point to an early conclusion of the investigation, and the passage of remedial shipping legislation before the adjournment of Congress.

ONE OF "EIGHT TO TWELVE WATCH."

"I should love to hear or see his name as dead or alive, as my dear loved one was on the eight to twelve watch."

Such is the pathetic communication received by *The Daily Mirror* from Mrs. Barlow, wife of a fireman who was on the Titanic. She also speaks of the engineers:–

"They say they were brave and stuck to their posts, and I have no doubt they were heroes – God bless them for it! – but what about the firemen on watch at the time?

"The eight to twelve watch seems to have suffered the same as the engineers."

She has heard no news about her husband, but still hopes for the best.

MR. ISMAY SUBPOENAED

Washington, April 30 – Under the procedure of the Admiralty Court, Mr. Bruce Ismay was summoned to appear this afternoon before the Commissioner to give evidence to be used in a suit which has been brought by Mrs. Louise Robbins against the White Star Line.

Mrs. Robbins' husband, Mr. George Robbins, is among the Titanic's missing.

Attorneys for Mrs. Robbins made application for the summonses to the Admiralty Court when they learned that Mr. Ismay and the officers of the Titanic were about to be released by the Senate Committee.

Subpoenas have also been issued for the attendance of Mr. Lightoller, Mr. Boxhall, Seaman Fleet and Mr. Bride, the wireless telegraph operator. – Reuter.

JEWELLERY REPORTED SAVED

A two-word cablegram "All saved!" was received at Lloyd's yesterday from Philadelphia, and is believed to refer to Mrs. G. D. Widener's three pearl necklaces; which it was previously thought had been lost with the Titanic.

The necklaces represented a value of £140,000, one being worth £80,000 and two worth £30,000 each. This jewellery was heavily insured at Lloyd's, and the loss would have added considerably to the huge liabilities already incurred.

AID FOR HELPLESS

Public Trustee Suggested as Best Administrator of Titanic Funds.

Who will administer the distribution of the Mansion House Fund to sufferers from the Titanic disaster?

The important work of allocating pensions and endowments to the widows and orphans is the subject of a notable suggestion by Colonel Lockwood, M.P., P.C., in a letter to *The Daily Mirror*. He urges that the best possible person to deal with this matter is Mr. C. J. Stewart, the Public Trustee; whose work as an investor of public moneys is so well known.

Colonel Lockwood writes:–

I have had some knowledge of the benefits of this gentleman's experience in the past both as regards public funds and even such minor details as lower-class marriage settlements.

On every occasion his help has been most willingly given and usefully employed. No trouble has been too much for him – in short, I have found his help invaluable.

I would suggest that his assistance should be sought from the earliest possible moment, both as regards the allocation and distribution of the fund.

As a public official, he is beyond suspicion, and I find that all classes are beginning to understand the advantage of consulting him.

"OUR FAITH IN THE SHIP."

A lucid and succinct account of the loss of the Titanic has reached *The Daily Mirror* from one of the stewards, A. M. Baggott, of Southampton.

It was written by him, on board the Carpathia while all the scenes of the tragic night were fresh in his memory, and shows how utterly those on board failed to realise the terrible imminence of the danger.

I was just falling asleep in No. 5 peak, which accommodated thirty-eight stewards (he begins dispassionately) – the time was 11.40 – when I was thoroughly aroused by a severe vibration of the whole fabric which lasted probably about fifteen seconds.

I and several of the men at once sat up and comments were made

R.M.S. "TITANIC"

April 14, 1912

The First-Class Menu
PRIVATE

First Course
Hors D'Oeuvres
Oysters

Second Course
Consommé Olga   Cream of Barley

Third Course
Poached Salmon with Mousseline Sauce, Cucumbers

Fourth Course
Filet Mignons Lili
Saute of Chicken, Lyonnaise
Vegetable Marrow Farci

Fifth Course
Lamb, Mint Sauce
Roast Duckling, Apple Sauce
Sirloin of Beef, Chateau Potatoes
Green Pea   Creamed Carrots
Boiled Rice
Parmentier & Boiled New Potatoes

Sixth Course
Punch Romaine

Seventh Course
Roast Squab & Cress

Eighth Course
Cold Asparagus Vinaigrette

Ninth Course
Pate de Foie Gras
Celery

Tenth Course
Waldorf Pudding
Peaches in Chartreuse Jelly
Chocolate & Vanilla Eclairs

French Ice Cream

as to what had happened….

All the men but one lay down again and some composed themselves for sleep. That one slipped out, and came back shortly afterwards, saying we had struck a berg.

About fifteen minutes after the vessel struck the steerage passengers who were quartered forward were sent to the after-end of the ship, as their compartments were beginning to fill.

As they filed past the door of No. 5 several of us got out of bed to see the "fun," and remarks were passed, still in a humorous vein.

Incredible as it may seem, such was our faith in the ship that the majority of us turned in once more as it was so bitterly cold.

We were only finally roused out by one of the assistant second stewards, who came in and said, "Come on, boys. Turn out now as you never have before, and put on something warm."

We then dressed. Word was passed for us to don our lifebelts and muster on the boat deck, which was done in a quiet and orderly manner. When I reached my boat I assisted in ripping off the canvas cover.

The boat was swung out by the patent davits (which, by the way, should be in every modern ship).

I was sent to bring up, with a few others, as many ladies as we could find. They were slow in coming.

We then began to lift them into the boats, several of them showing disinclination to help themselves, and even protesting. These were bundled in by sheer force.

We got all the women in this boat who were then visible – between forty and fifty in number, I should estimate.

THE LAST DINNER SERVED ON THE TITANIC

◀ The menu of the last dinner that many of the Titanic's passengers ever partook of. It was served on the last evening the liner was afloat.

WORKING FOR SHIPPING PEACE

An attempt to settle the shipping dispute at Liverpool was made yesterday.

Representatives of the men were given interviews with officials of the companies affected, and it is believed the basis of a settlement may be obtained.

Mrs. Thomas Pears, a first-class passenger survivor from the Titanic, landed at Plymouth yesterday, but declined to make any statement.

GAMBLER ON THE TITANIC GIVES HIS LIFE FOR OTHERS

One of the heroes of the Titanic disaster was Jay Yates, who, before perishing, helped many women into the lifeboats. Yates, who was alleged to be a gambler, a confidence trick man and a fugitive from justice, handed the below note to a passenger he assisted, asking her to see it was delivered. The note was written on a page torn from a diary and signed J. H. Rogers one of his aliases.

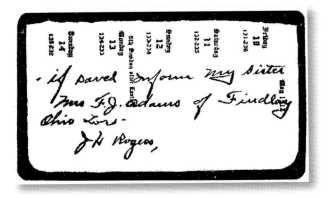

SPECIAL

The London Inquiry

---

2 May **1912** – 18 December **1912**

There were so many questions raised by the sinking of the Titanic and at the London Inquiry it seemed everyone came in for some blame. It all makes it appear like a very modern story. Everything from the ships, to design, to the ethics of who did and who didn't return to pick up survivors, came under scrutiny. In the end apart from the findings of the inquiry it came down to how much it had cost.

◀ Archie Jewell one of the look-outs giving evidence at the British Inquiry, Scottish Drill Hall, Buckingham Gate, London. 4 May 1912.

TITANIC INQUIRY OPENS IN LONDON TO-DAY

Model of the Lost Liner to Assist the Court.

ARRAY OF K.C.s.

Both Crown Law Officers and Other Counsel for Board of Trade.

PHILADELPHIA SAILS

200 of the Olympic's Passengers Leave on American Liner.

Probably the largest array of counsel on record will attend the Board of Trade Inquiry into the loss of the Titanic, which opens to-day under Lord Mersey at the Scottish Hall, Buckingham Gate.

The public will be admitted to the proceedings so far as the limited accommodation of the hall will allow. These are the main questions which the Court will attempt to solve:–

The seaworthiness and safety of the Titanic.

The circumstances leading to the wreck.

Whether there was any contributory default, and, if so, how and by whom.

What can be done to prevent similar disaster in future.

Changed regulations as to the safety of human life on steamers.

Special attention will be directed, too (Mr. Buxton stated yesterday), to the respective numbers of lost and saved in each class.

For the general convenience of the Court a large model of the liner has been prepared.

All the big shipping lines will be represented, as well, of course, as the Board of Trade, among the leading counsel employed being:–

BOARD OF TRADE

Attorney-General (Sir Rufus Isaacs).
Solicitor-General (Sir John Simon).
Mr. Butler Aspinall, K.C.
Mr. S. A. T. Rowlatt.
Mr. Raymond Asquith.

WHITE STAR LINE

Sir Robert Finlay, K.C.
Mr. F. Laing, K.C.
Mr. Maurice Hill, K.C.

CANADIAN-PACIFIC AND ALLAN LINES

Mr. W. Norman Raeburn.

Mr. W. Hamar Greenwood, K.C.

Other parties to the inquiry will be the builders and the owners of the vessel, the surviving officers and the officers of some of the ships in the vicinity of the disaster.

Most of the officers will have their interests represented.

FORM OF PROCEDURE

The procedure will be on the usual lines of a Board of Trade Inquiry.

Sir Rufus Isaacs will make a long opening statement, dealing with the ship, its equipment and the voyage, the progress up to the disaster and the consequences of the disaster, and the safeguards that might be taken for the future.

This statement will be corroborated by witnesses on oath. Witnesses called by the Board of Trade can be cross-examined.

Finally, Lord Mersey will raise any point not elucidated by the previous procedure.

Suggestions made yesterday by M.P.s, which will be among those considered by the inquiry, included the following by Mr. Bottomley:–

That each passenger should be furnished with a ticket showing the number and position of the lifeboat to which he was assigned in the event of accident.

Mr. Buxton thought that there would be practical difficulties in the way of giving each passenger a ticket with a number corresponding to the number of the lifeboat he would enter in the event of a disaster. "What would happen if, in rough weather, some lifeboats, were destroyed?" he asked, But he undertook to consider the suggestion.

LINERS TO PROCEED IN PAIRS

Mr. Buxton promised, too, that he will consider the suggestion, although it appears to him to be hardly feasible, of arranging with the United States Government that during the period of danger from icebergs it should be enacted that the great liners should travel two together, within easy reach.

He also states that lifebelts are tested by the officers of the Board of Trade in regard to their carrying properties, and the officers are instructed not to pass a belt that is not able to float in fresh water for twenty-four hours with 15lb. of iron attached thereto.

Sir Kinloch Cooke asked the Foreign Secretary whether he would consider the advisability of opening negotiations with other countries with the object of calling into being a convention to consider the best means of insuring the most effective service of wireless telegraphy for the purpose of saving life at sea.

Mr. Samuel, the Postmaster-General, who replied, said that a

conference on the subject would be held in London next month, and he was considering the best method of bringing the question of rendering wireless telegraphy more effective for saving life at sea before the representatives.

IN THE CITY OF COFFINS
(FROM OUR OWN CORRESPONDENT)

New York, May 1 – Thirty embalmers worked all night at the improvised morgue at Halifax preparing for the inspection of more of the unidentified dead.

Police guarded the silent building throughout the night, and from time to time wagons rolled away with the claimed dead.

The unidentified list, with the exception of two tentative identifications made last night, viz., Arthur White and Assistant-Purser Clark, stood at sixty when the grim work was resumed to-day.

Mr. George Widener, jun., of Philadelphia, left Halifax, in a private car convinced that the body buried at sea was that of his father's valet, and not that of Mr. Widener.

Others, with their hopes shattered by yesterday's developments, also started for home, but a few are awaiting the arrival of the cable ship Minia with a meagre addition to the list of bodies recovered. The same strict regulations enforced yesterday prevailed at the morgue to-day.

Exhausted by their vigil and not very hopeful of finding their dead among what appear to be mostly, the bodies of seamen, those entitled to make inspections were not early in arriving this morning. The Inter-Colonial Railway funeral procession across the entire Continent started at 8.45 o'clock this morning when the I.C.R. express left for the West.

Weeping relatives and friends of the Titanic victims arrived at the station an hour before the departure, and waited impatiently to begin the sad journey home.

MR. ISMAY IGNORES SUMMONS

Washington, May 1 – Senator Smith is going to New York personally to investigate the statements which were made yesterday by Mr. Edward J. Dunn before the Senate Committee, to the effect that the news of the Titanic disaster was known in New York before it was actually made public.

Mr. Bruce Ismay, Mr. Franklin and the Titanic officers went to New York yesterday evening, acting on the advice of their counsel, and ignored the summonses to attend the Admiralty Court in the suit brought by Mrs. Robbins against the White Star Line on account of the loss of her husband in the Titanic.

In an interview Mr. Ismay is quoted as saying: "I believe that Senator Smith and his colleagues have been fair and impartial in a difficult inquiry." – Reuter.

200 OLYMPIC PASSENGERS SAIL
(FROM OUR OWN CORRESPONDENT)

Southampton, May 1 – No untoward incident marked the departure from Southampton at noon to-day of the American Line steamer Philadelphia for New York.

It was suggested that, owing to the trouble on the Olympic, other ships of the International Mercantile Marine, in which the White Star and American Lines are incorporated, might be affected, but there was no ground for this rumour.

As a matter of fact, the firemen and seamen on the Philadelphia were mostly American and signed on in New York. In any case, the officials of the men's unions do not anticipate that any further trouble will arise at this port. The Philadelphia took out 200 second- and third-class passengers of the Olympic.

The passengers before leaving handed to the local manager of the White Star Line a resolution expressing their gratitude for the generous treatment they had received during their detention in the port owing to defection of the Olympic's crew.

The White Star Line have decided that the Olympic will miss the trip to and from New York commencing last Wednesday, altogether. No other vessel will take her place on the return trip, which should start next Saturday. The Olympic will sail from Southampton on May 15, and passengers are now being booked.

During the season, which commences to-day, the White Star Line's vessels, the Olympic, Majestic and Oceanic, will each maintain a three-weekly service across the Atlantic. The Oceanic (17,300 tons) and the Majestic (10,000 tons) are both twin-screw vessels and considerably smaller than the triple-screw 45,324-ton Olympic.

4 May 1912

GRAPHIC STORIES BY SEAMEN AT TITANIC WRECK INQUIRY

Attorney-General Retells What Is Known of Disaster.

LIFEBOAT SCENES
How Women and Children Were Got Off the Sinking Liner.

SPEED AMONG ICEBERGS
Look-out Man Complimented by Lord Mersey on His Evidence.

Yesterday, at the London Scottish Drill Hall in Buckingham Gate, S.W., the Titanic inquiry began in earnest, and extremely poignant evidence was taken.

After Lord Mersey had rescinded his decision of the day before and granted permission for the British Seafarers' Union, to which 228 of the crew belonged, to be represented at the inquiry by Mr. Lewis, of Southampton, and for the Imperial Merchant Service Guild also to be represented, Sir Rufus Isaacs began his formal opening statement.

The Attorney General spoke for two hours at the very slow rate of about sixty words a minute. He was remarkably unimpassioned but always interesting, and clearly enumerated the various lists of figures which occurred in his speech.

After him two seamen of the Titanic, Archibald Jewell and

Joseph Scarrott, gave lucid and thrilling narratives of the last scenes on the doomed ship and the handling of the lifeboats.

Mr. Lloyd George, Captain Haddock and Lieutenants Alexander and Holles, from the Olympic, and Mr. Harold Sanderson, managing director of the White Star Lines were present.

The Ladies' Gallery, with accommodation for several hundreds, was occupied by only one lady and one policeman.

A sounding-board had been fixed overnight before the platform on which the President and his assessors were seated, making it look rather like a great box lying on its side with the lid open. But it was very little easier to hear than on Thursday, and members of the public at the back of the hall used field-glasses continually, the light being bad and the witnesses and other principals in the dramatic scene being so far off. Every cough and sneeze in the huge

printed cards are displayed in prominent positions.

Workmen were busy unpacking huge cases which conveyed models, plans and maps; while other workmen from Messrs. Harland and Woolf, the Belfast shipbuilders, who constructed the ill-fated vessel, were busily occupied erecting a fine model of the lost vessel.

The dimensions, of the model, which shows the starboard side of the vessel, are such that every plate and its size are clearly marked. The model, which is 9ft. long, or about 100th of actual size, is mounted on a table, and can be turned in any direction required by a wheel.

On the same side of the room is a very large chart of the Atlantic Ocean, giving the courses to be followed at various seasons of the year. In addition, a drawing of the vessel (scale – 1 in 32) hangs from the gallery on the other side of the hall. Here every compartment, boiler, state-room and smoke-room, is clearly marked.

Captain the Hon. C. C. Bigham, the eldest son of Lord Mersey and secretary of the Commission, was anxiously supervising details, and was particular in seeing to the supply of books and copies of Acts of Parliament bearing on the Merchant Shipping Act.

◀ Titanic Disaster. Passenger Sir Cosmo Duff-Gordon giving evidence at the British Inquiry Scottish Drill Hall.

SIR RUFUS ISAACS' STATEMENT

In opening his long and clear statement the Attorney-General said that it would be based on information founded at present on very slight material. He was confining himself to those facts which he could prove by evidence.

In the circumstances there was little in what he said that is not already common knowledge concerning the disaster. After outlining the dimensions of the Titanic, "a British ship built at Belfast," and referring to the number of passengers (1,316) and crew (892) carried on her last voyage, he spoke of the vessel's bulkheads.

The vessel, he said, had fifteen bulkheads. That was what he made it on the plan – fifteen watertight bulkheads and a number of watertight doors. It might be necessary to go more fully into that later in the inquiry.

She was designed on the principle that she would remain afloat in the event of any two adjoining compartments being flooded.

THE USE OF BULKHEADS

Assuming that two of the adjoining compartments were flooded, she was built so that there would still be a free board of some 2ft. 6in. or 3ft. in the bulkhead.

hall reverberated. Lord Mersey's questions to counsel and witnesses sounded like whispers.

At the end of the day's proceedings, however, the Attorney-General-announced to the President that the acoustics were so much improved that there would be no need to consider the question of changing the hall, and Lord Mersey concurred.

NINE-FOOT MODEL OF TITANIC

The Scottish Hall – or, to be more precise, the drill hall of the Queen's Westminster – in Buckingham Gate presented a busy aspect yesterday afternoon. It was in the hands of the Office of Works, being made ready for the Titanic inquiry. The floor space is marked out, for Press, counsel, reserved and witnesses; the gallery is for ladies and the public. Huge

Therefore the result would be, according to the design of this vessel, supposing that she had come into collision, either with another vessel or even with an iceberg or any other obstacle, that so long as not more than two of her adjoining compartments were flooded, she would float in perfect safety, particularly in a calm sea.

Then the Attorney-General described the voyage which started on April 11, up to the hour of the disaster on the following Sunday, April 14. As far as one was able to fix it – it was not possible to fix it with precision, at any rate with the material before him at present – it must have been about 11.30 at night when the casualty happened.

It was a starry night, and the atmosphere was clear – some witnesses said particularly clear. There was no moon. Sir Rufus Isaacs emphasised the fact that the speed of the Titanic on Sunday, April 14, was 21 knots.

"And, so far as I am able to gather, from the evidence, that speed was never reduced during the whole of that day, right up to the time of the collision with the iceberg, and, according to the evidence we shall place before your Lordship, notwithstanding warnings that there were icebergs in the neighbourhood."

At the present moment they were able to bring before the Court evidence of two vessels – one the Coronia and the other the Baltic – having, by means of telegraphy, informed the Titanic during the day that icebergs, growlers and field-ice were reported in the track along which the Titanic was proceeding.

He explained that, so far as he followed it, the distinction between icebergs and growlers is, that the growler is an iceberg with very little protruding above the water. Though the Attorney-General's speech contained no new facts or figures, he emphasised certain points in such a way as to throw new light upon them.

For instance, all except five of the first-class women passengers were saved, and, as it was known that some women refused to leave their husbands, the presumption was that these five might be thus accounted for.

LOOK-OUT'S CLEAR EVIDENCE

The first witness, Archibald Jewell, of Bude, Cornwall, was called at 12.50 p.m. He was a look-out man on the Titanic, and had been in the crow's nest from eight to ten on the fatal night with another seaman named Simon.

He is in very bad health as a result of his exposure after the wreck, and had to consult a doctor at Southampton, but he gave his evidence promptly and clearly, and it was listened to with strained attention from all parts of the hall. His comrades from Southampton came and leaned on the rail of the gallery over his head.

Mr. Scanlan, M.P., representing the National Seamen's and Firemen's Union, questioned him very narrowly about the use of glasses by look-out men, and Lord Mersey's questions on this point were even more searching. Jewell said the only other ship he had made voyages on was the Oceanic, and there he had glasses, but there were none on the Titanic, for him.

MOONLESS, STARRY NIGHT

Sir John Simon, Solicitor-General, undertook his examination, and opened by questions concerning the duties of look-outs. There were six members of the crew, said Jewell, appointed to act as look-outs, and he was in the crow's nest from 8 to 10 p.m. on April 14 – the day of the disaster – with another, look-out named Symons.

The men on that duty took two hours each. As long as the weather was clear, only two men were on the look-out. The weather was clear. There was no moon and the night was starry.

At 9.30 a message was received, on the telephone from the bridge: "Keep a sharp look-out for all ice, big and small." He thought it was the second officer who sent the message. Up to that time they had seen no ice, and when he and Symons were relieved at ten o'clock by Fleet and Leigh he passed the message on to them, having seen no ice at all. After he had turned in, witness was wakened by a crash.

ICE ON WEATHER DECK

Rushing on deck, he saw ice on the weather deck, but went below again, "because we did not think there was any harm. Later the bo'sun cried 'All hands on deck.'"

His boat was No. 7 on the starboard side. He knew that by a boat list in front of their forecastle. When he went to the boat after the collision orders were given to the hands to clear the boats, and he assisted in clearing No. 7.

Then he heard the first officer, Mr. Murdoch, say: "Lower away to the rail," and then: "Women and children in the boats." No seamen had then been put in the boat, but they were standing by.

The President: How many seamen man each of these boats ? – Two sailors, so many firemen and so many stewards. At the time there were not many passengers about. They were afraid to go into the boats, and did not think there was anything wrong. They put into the boat all the women and children they could see. There were some men passengers, there, and three or four Frenchmen got into the boat.

Solicitor-General: Was there any excitement? – No, none at all. It was very quiet. No. 7 was pretty full before she was lowered. There were no lights on the boat. He thought a lifeboat was usually provided with a light.

The President: Whose business is it to look after the light? – The men at Southampton who come aboard the ship.

Continuing, witness said that Hobb was in charge of the boat and that the other seaman was named Weller. All but four of the passengers on board were women and children.

"We came away from the ship and we saw her settling and had to pull away clear."

He added, that he was sure his boat, No. 7, was the first to be lowered on the starboard side. They were all down by the time his boat pulled away from the ship.

You pulled away from the side because you saw that these other boats were pulling away? – Yes.

How far away did you go? – We only went just a little way at first, so that we could hail to them on board of the ship. For some time we remained about twenty yards from the vessel.

Did you see any signs then of her sinking? – Yes, we could see she was going down by the head. That was very slow at first. The other boats by that time were further away from the vessel. When they thought she was sinking by the head they pulled clear a long distance away. That was about half an hour before she disappeared.

What did you see happen to the Titanic before she went down, and as she went down? – I could see her gradually sinking. Then we could see people running about on deck before the lights went out.

"As she went down by the head," he continued, "her lights began to go out. Then we could hear some explosions as she was going down.

"I saw her stern right up in the air. As her stern went up in the air the lights went out. The stern remained in the air only a few moments. It went down pretty fast."

ICEBERGS ALL AROUND

"I heard two or three explosions soon after one another, and not long before the Titanic disappeared – just as the stern went up into the air.

"My boat, picked up no bodies from the sea, but three from Mr. Pitman's boat came aboard as they had more room. I was pulling all the time until we reached the Carpathia, about seven or eight o'clock in the morning.

"Hobb was pulling also, and others tried to row; when it became light we could see many icebergs. There were icebergs all round us. As we had drifted all night, I could not tell how far we were away from the spot where the Titanic sank. There was wreckage, but that would have drifted also."

Mr. Scanlan (for the National Sailors' and Firemen's Union): Were you equipped with glasses on the Titanic? – We never had any glasses.

On other boats on which you have been was it usual to supply glasses? – We had them on the Oceanic. Witness added that he believed his mate on the Titanic asked for glasses.

Did any firemen or stewards assist in the lowering of the boats at the drill? – No, sir, only sailors. The practice, he added, included a row round the harbour.

The President: You were in the boat something like eight hours? – Seven hours, sir.

Had you anything to eat? – No, sir.

Or to drink? – No, sir, nothing. He added that biscuits and water were supposed to be put in the boats in port.

The President: Do they put water on board at the commencement of the voyage? – Yes.

How often is it changed? – I could not say.

Have you known it ever changed? – I have never seen it.

At the conclusion of Jewell's evidence Lord Mersey went out of his way to compliment him on the clear way he had told his story.

SEARCH FOR LIVING AMONG THE DEAD
Sailor's Vivid Narrative of Lifeboat's Terrible Cruise.

HOW THE TITANIC SANK

The second witness examined was Joseph Scarrott, an A.B. on the Titanic, and his long narrative proved even more sensational than Jewell's. He spoke so readily and intelligently that he was allowed to tell his own story, and a wonderful tale it was.

His voice was very clear, and his language was simple but intensely dramatic and sometimes picturesque, as when he likened the fatal iceberg, as he saw it, to the Rock of Gibraltar.

He at first was given charge of No. 14 boat, as the only seaman on board, and had on board fifty-four women, four children, two firemen, three or four stewards, "not more than four"; then Mr. Lowe, the fifth officer, came on to it.

"There was one man who was not a real fireman or steward," said Scarrott, "but I don't know who he was."

Scarrott's vigorous phrases, as when he spoke of "persuading" the men who tried to rush the boat on deck and throwing out three times a man who jumped in again and again, caused a titter in the hall, quickly checked, of course, by the right feeling of all present.

He explained that some of the men who tried to rush the boat were foreigners, and could not understand what was said to them.

A TERRIBLE PICTURE

His account of the subsequent rescue of some of the floating survivors by his boat after the Titanic sank made his audience hold their breath. One could almost see the mass of bodies floating on an ice-cold sea through which it took quite half an hour to row a few yards to rescue a man praying and calling for help from a floating stairway.

A woman sobbed audibly in the hall. Lord Mersey and the assessors were visibly touched and thrilled. He began his evidence from the dramatic moment when at about 11.30 he heard three bells from the crow's nest.

"Then I felt a sort of shock," he went on, answering Mr. Aspinall, K.C., "just as though the engines had been put full astern. It was the same sort of vibration, enough to wake anybody up from their sleep.

"The bo'sun ordered 'All hands on deck; turn out the boats; take the covers off and place them amidships.' At that time the iceberg was not a ship's length ahead. The ship's starboard quarter was coming away from the iceberg. I cannot say if the ship had headway on at the time."

Scarrott went on to state that the iceberg was about as high as the boat deck, sixty feet front the water.

"It resembled the Rock of Gibraltar," he explained, "and was very, much after the same shape."

Lord Mersey: Like a lion couchant.

ATTEMPTS TO RUSH BOAT

Scarrott went on to tell how he assisted with four boats before he joined his own boat, No. 14, on the port side. He put himself in charge of the boat as the only sailorman there. After seeing that the boat was in order he started taking the women and the children into it.

"There were some men who tried to rush the boat, foreigners they were, because they could not understand the order I gave them. And I had to use a little persuasion with the boat's tiller," he added, amid laughter.

"I prevented five getting in," he explained. "One man jumped in twice, and I had to throw him out the third time."

Mr. Aspinall: Did you succeed in getting all the women and children who were about there into the boat? – Yes. There were fifty-four women and four children, two firemen and three or four stewards. Mr. Lowe, the fifth officer, was also in the boat.

The seaman-witness then gave a lucid account of the escape from the ship.

"I told Mr. Lowe I had had a bit of trouble in the rushing business and he said 'All right.' He pulled out his revolver and fired two shots between the ship's and the boat's side and issued a warning to the remainder of the men about there. He told them if any more rushing took place he would use it.

"The officer asked me how many I had got on board and I told him as near as I could.

"No. 14 was then lowered to the water, but hung up. The fore part rested on the water, but the after part was about 10ft. up, the boat being at an angle of about 45deg.

"I called Mr. Lowe's attention to it and asked the man lowering aft to let her right down. Eventually I cut one of the after ropes and let her down with the releasing gear.

"We then rowed clear of the ship – just clear, because we were afraid of the suction, four men were rowing.

"There was one man in the boat who was not a sailor, though at the time, we thought he was. He was a window-cleaner on the boat.

"Mr. Lowe was steering and we pulled about 150 yards away from the ship. Four other boats were there, and, having, ascertained they had no officers on board them, Mr. Lowe told them to keep near him and act under his direction.

"The ship sank after she broke in two, the stern remaining afloat a couple of minutes after that, and then we all rowed to where she went down to see if we could pick up anybody.

"When we left the Titanic she was sinking slowly by the head. As the water seemed to get up to the bridge she seemed to increase her way going down.

"She was right up on end then. The stem was right out of the water, and one could see her propellers and part of her keel."

After remaining on the scene until all hope of further rescue on the spot had to be abandoned, Mr. Lowe ordered all the boats to be tied together, with the object of attracting the notice of passing steamers.

"While that was going on," said Scarrott, "we heard cries coming from another direction, and Mr. Lowe decided to transfer our passengers among the other boats and then make up the full crew of men and go in the direction of the cries.

"Then we went among the wreckage. When we got where these cries were we were amongst hundreds of dead bodies floating in lifebelts.

"It was dark at that time. The wreckage and the bodies seemed to be hanging in one cluster. We got one man – a passenger, he was – but he died shortly after he got into the boat."

WITHIN OAR'S LENGTH

"We got to others then. We pushed our way among the wreckage, and as we got towards the centre we saw a man – I have since found out he was a storekeeper – on the top of a staircase or a large piece of wreckage, as if he was praying and at the same time calling for help.

"When we saw him we were about as near as that wall (fifteen yards) from him, and the wreckage was so thick – and I am sorry to say there were more bodies than there was wreckage – that it took us quite half an hour to get that distance to that man.

"We could not row the boat through the bodies. We had to push them out of the way, to force our way to the man.

"We could not get close enough to get him right off, only within reach of an oar. We pulled him off with that, and he managed to hang on and got into the boat. We got four men into the boat and one died."

The Titanic sank about two and a half hours after she struck the iceberg at 11.40 p.m., the witness told the Court, and it was about one o'clock when boat No. 14 was got into the water. They started to get the women and children in the boats at about 12.30.

NO LAMP IN BOAT

What were you doing in that hour and twenty minutes? – Getting the boats ready for lowering. My boat was in good order, but there was one thing we found was not in her, and that was the boat's lamp. There was an ample supply of water, because we drank some of that. It was good fresh water.

The boats were in a place where the first-class passengers were allowed to go if they were lowered? – Yes; and the second class.

First- and second-class passengers in those circumstances would have a better chance of getting to the boats? – Yes; because they were always allowed to go on the deck where they were lowered.

Mr. Scanlan (Sailors' and Firemen's Union): You state that the first- and second-class passengers had a better chance of getting to the boat deck than the third class? – Yes.

Is it not the case that from the time the collision happened until you were ready to take in passengers there was ample time for the women and children in the steerage to be brought to the boat deck? – Yes; there was ample time.

Do you consider, as a practical seaman, that it is very important that a lifeboat laden as this one was with passengers should be provided on a dark night with a lamp? – Yes.

The President: That is a question for me. You may ask me the question at the proper time. I should probably not answer it. (Laughter.)

ONLY ONE CAPABLE SEAMAN

Witness added, in answer to Mr. Scanlan, that a list of the crew for No. 14 boat was hung in the forecastle. His name was on it, but he did not know how many more.

How many men are necessary for the proper handling of a boat of that size? – Eight, and a man at the tiller in a storm certainly would be necessary to safely navigate a boat. When we left the Titanic there was only one man on board who was a capable seaman.

"That was myself," added witness, apparently as an after-thought.

Mr. Lewis (Seafarers' Union): Can you say whether it was difficult for the third-class passengers to get on the boat deck? – It was difficult.

The President: In what sense? – There was only one ladder leading to it.

Subsequently witness

Thomas Scanlan, National Sailors' and Firemen's Union Counsel.

admitted that there was a ladder on both sides of the ship.

In further reply to Mr. Lewis, Scarrott said that there were forty-two or forty-three seamen on board the Titanic. At least four men were required to lower each boat, so that to lower the boats would require at least sixty-four skilled men.

COMMISSION TO VISIT OLYMPIC

When they had left the Titanic they saw one collapsible boat that was waterlogged and not serviceable, and they took the passengers off it.

The President: It was serviceable enough to keep afloat and preserve the lives of the people on it? – Yes.

Sir Rufus Isaacs: Did you notice any difference in the temperature on Sunday? – Yes; it was cold, very cold indeed after sundown; colder than it had been previously on the voyage.

The Attorney-General said that, as the result of yesterday's experience, he thought it would be as well if the inquiry were to be continued in the Scottish Hall. There had been a considerable improvement in the acoustic properties.

The President agreed, and having said that he and his assessors would travel to Southampton on Monday to view the Olympic, he adjourned the inquiry until Tuesday morning.

6 May 1912

CAPTAIN ROSTRON TELLS HIS STORY

How He Was Wakened at Midnight to Speed on Journey of Rescue.

Captain Rostron, of the Carpathia, who has returned to Europe from New York, has just broken his silence concerning the rescue of the Titanic passengers for the first time.

He has told his story to a *Daily Mirror* staff photographer who went out to Gibraltar to meet the Carpathia. Here are some of the points of the captain's interesting narrative:–

"I had just retired for the night on Sunday, April 14, when I heard someone entering my cabin without knocking. I called out 'Who's that?' and a voice replied:–

"'I have just received a Marconi signal of distress from the Titanic, giving her position, and saying she has struck an iceberg and is sinking.'

"'Are you sure it was the Titanic?' I asked the operator. 'Yes,' he replied.

"'Then keep in touch with them, and say we are coming to their assistance.'

"I sent for the chief officer, giving him the position of the Titanic and instructions to alter our course. Meanwhile the chief engineer

Captain Arthur Rostron of the S.S. Carpathia.

had received instructions to make full speed ahead.

"Our average speed is about thirteen knots, but we were soon doing nineteen knots. I then sent for the doctors and heads of departments, and reading the Marconi report impressed on them the gravity of the situation, and that everything should be got ready at once for the reception of the passengers of the Titanic.

"At this time I quite expected to reach the Titanic before she sank.

"It was splendid to watch the way in which my men went about their different duties. Blankets were warmed, boats were made ready for lowering and in the kitchen hot soup was made. At 2.40 a.m. I saw from the bridge a flare and shortly afterwards sighted the first iceberg. Several times I had to alter the course of the ship to clear the bergs. At this time I had eight men on the look-out at different parts of the ship.

"Never before have I experienced such an anxious time. We picked up the first boat, which contained mostly women and children, at 4.10 a.m., and as the survivors came aboard the Carpathia they were met by stewards, who wrapped them in warm blankets, and escorted them to the saloon, where they were given hot soup. I should like to mention that the passengers gave me every assistance in caring for the survivors, many giving up their berths for the bad cases, others allowing them to share. Also many ladies and gentlemen gave what spare clothes they had."

WHY THE CARPATHIA
WAS SILENT

"Much has been said in the American Press about the silence of the Carpathia while making for New York. I found it necessary to establish a censorship on the messages which were being sent. This action of mine called forth rather severe comment from the passengers. It was said that I had bought the Marconi and was using it to my own advantage in order to make money. A most wicked lie!

"I had instructed the operator that he was to accept nothing but private messages and the names of survivors. I told the passengers that they could send their Press messages after this had been done. When we reached New York the operator had still about 205 messages to send. Another inaccuracy which appeared in the papers was that I had ignored a message from President Taft, asking for news of his friend Major Butt. I understand that a message was sent to the Carpathia, but it never reached us. I have written to the President, laying the facts of the case before him."

OLYMPIC SEAMEN
ALL DISCHARGED

Charges of Disobedience Proved, But, No Punishment.

"SCALLYWAG SHIP."
(FROM OUR SPECIAL CORRESPONDENT)

Southampton, May 5 – After two hours' deliberation the magistrates who have heard the charge against fifty-three members of the crew of the Olympic of wilful disobedience of the captain's orders decided last evening at Portsmouth to dismiss the charge.

It was just seven o'clock yesterday evening when the magistrates returned to the Bench in the Police Court at Portsmouth Town Hall, and Sir Thomas Bramsdon, who is himself a solicitor, thus addressed the accused, who stood at the back of the court in a wide semicircle:–

"We have decided that the plea of justification must fail and we are satisfied that the ship was quite seaworthy and that the captain had never given permission for the men to go ashore. Therefore we are against Mr. Emanuel, for the defence, on all points, but in passing judgment we cannot drive out of our minds the thought of the recent calamity."

"AS HUMAN AS OTHER PEOPLE."

"No doubt that had influenced you to a great extent. You are just as human as other people. I should like to see the feeling of confidence between the members of the crew and the White Star Company completely restored, and hope that the men will be taken back to work.

"I cannot think that the White Star Company wish to see the men punished. We feel that we cannot send these men to a term of imprisonment, nor do we think we should inflict a fine. We have powers under the Probation Act for First Offenders, but we feel that the interests of justice will be met by dismissing the information. This cannot be looked upon as a victory for the men, for we have found you guilty of wilfully disobeying the lawful commands of the captain."

Mr. S. H. Emanuel in his concluding speech for the defence in the afternoon emphasised the admission of Captain M. H. Clark, the Board of Trade surveyor here (who, by the way, is not the Captain Clarke of the Board of Trade appointed an assessor on the Titanic Inquiry Commission), that it was no part of his duty to examine the Berthon collapsible boats on board the Olympic, but only to see that the boat drill was properly carried out.

"SHIP MANNED BY SCALLYWAGS."

"He does not pretend that he made any inspection of them at all," said Mr. Emanuel. The real trouble was due to temper and want of tact on the part of the White Star officials. I submit to you that the men had a perfect right to do what they did, because they had reason to believe the ship was going to sea with an incompetent crew.

"They did not see their way to risk their lives in a ship manned by all the scallywags of Portsmouth, known to the police throughout this borough, men whom no one cares to associate with, and men who never ought to have been taken on board that ship without some sort of inquiry.

"This is not a case of mutiny. It was not until these guttersnipes of Portsmouth went on board that these respectable men said: 'We refuse to sail with incompetent and incapable men.' The men wrote to Captain Haddock before leaving the ship, and told him how sorry they were to have to leave, and these are now deeply sorry that they had to leave the Olympic, but they still repeat that nothing will induce them to sail in one of this line's ships unless with a competent crew."

The fifty-three accused left the court and returned later in the evening to Southampton, where each man received 10s. at the offices of the British Seafarers' Union. It would have been 20s. apiece, but as it was long after banking hours there was only a limited amount of cash available.

I am informed that thirty-one firemen from among the large number who left the Olympic at sailing time last Wednesday week have signed on for the White Star liner Oceanic, leaving next Wednesday.

7 May 1912

COMMISSION VISITS THE OLYMPIC

Lord Mersey and the Assessors Inspect Titanic's Sister Ship.

CARPATHIA'S SPOONS
(FROM OUR SPECIAL CORRESPONDENT)

Southampton, May 6 – Lord Mersey, the Special Wreck Commissioner, presiding over the Titanic inquiry, together with his assessors, to-day visited the Olympic in the great new dock here.

The party of six were driven in two closed motor-cars to the quay alongside the Olympic, which had a barrier of hurdles to keep out everyone else, and was guarded by a strong force of police.

Captain Haddock and his officers were on board, and so was Mr. Philip Curry, the Southampton manager of the White Star Line.

Luncheon was served in the first-class saloon, and the commissioners before returning to London thoroughly examined the ship.

NEW SEARCH FOR BODIES

Ottawa, May 6 – At the request of the White Star Company and the relatives of victims of the Titanic, the Canadian Government has commissioned the steamer Mont Magny to make further search for bodies. She will cruise through part of the Gulf Stream, which was not searched by the Mackay Bennett and the Minia. The Mont Magny leaves Halifax to-day. She is equipped with a wireless installation. – Reuter.

SPOON SOUVENIRS OF DISASTER

When the Carpathia arrived at New York with the survivors on board, writes our special correspondent, who met the boat at Gibraltar, a sudden famine in spoons occurred. The stewards looked into the matter, and found that over 200 were missing! It was subsequently discovered that they had been taken as souvenirs of the disaster by some of those on board the Carpathia. A large number of forks vanished in the same way.

8 May 1912

HELMSMAN'S STORY OF THE TITANIC

What Happened on the Bridge When the Liner Struck.

More members of the crew described the circumstances of the Titanic catastrophe when Lord Mersey's court sat for the third time yesterday at the Scottish Hall, Buckingham Gate.

Then George William Beauchamp, a fireman, was examined by Mr. Raymond Asquith. Clean-shaven and of sallow complexion, he wore a blue handkerchief round his neck, and his coat collar was turned up. These are the main points of his story:–

"I was below when the ship struck. There was a slight shock and a sound as of a roll of thunder. 'Stand by' and then 'Stop' were the orders telegraphed from the engine-room. Immediately the order was given to stand by the watertight doors dropped. A few minutes afterwards an order was given to draw fires. Water was coming in on the plates where the stokers stand. I went to the starboard side of the vessel and helped the ladies and children into boat 13. There was an officer superintending the loading of the boat."

LADIES WOULD NOT ENTER BOATS

"There were some ladies who would not go into the boat. I heard two or three say that they would not go away in the boat. The ship struck about 11.35 p.m., and, according to a gentleman in my boat,

who had a watch, she sank two hours and ten minutes later. I did not look at the time to see if there was a compass in the boat, but I do not believe there was. There was no lantern or lamp in the boat and no water or provisions."

Robert Hitchens, the quartermaster who was at the wheel when the Titanic struck, began by describing the intense cold felt on the evening of the disaster.

It was bitter cold when he went on watch at eight o'clock.

Do you remember the vessel striking? – Yes.

Did you notice the time? – Yes, twenty minutes, to twelve. Just as she struck I had the order, "Hard a starboard," given by the first officer, who relieved the second at 10 o'clock. The ship was swinging to starboard and had just swung two points when she struck.

Was Captain Smith on the bridge? – No, he was in his room.

NO CHANGE IN SPEED

According to the log the speed was 45 knots in two hours? – Yes, sir.

What I want to know is, up to the time of hearing the three bells struck was there any change in the speed at which the vessel had been proceeding? – No, sir; none whatever.

Sir Rufus Isaacs: Can you tell us how long it was after the collision that the ship had stopped? – Immediately.

You remained at your post? – Yes, sir.

What did you hear? – Just about a minute after the collision Captain Smith rushed out of his room and asked Mr. Murdoch, "What was that?" He said, "An iceberg, sir." The captain said, "Close the watertight doors." Mr. Murdoch said, "They are already closed."

"I heard the captain say, 'Get all the boats out and serve out the belts.' That was after twelve. The captain then saw from the instrument that the ship was carrying a list to starboard."

He was relieved at 12.25 by Quartermaster Perkins, and was then ordered to get the cover of the port side collapsible boats. He did not, so far as he knew, have any station on a boat.

Did you know which boat your station might have been? – No, we never had any boat drill whilst we were there.

NO STATIONS FOR LIFEBOATS

Did you see the lists of the stations for the boats on board? – No, sir, I never saw any lists put up anywhere.

Were there any other passengers on the deck as far as you could see when you got the order to lower away? – Yes.

Women? – I think there were one or two women. They did not care to get into the small boat.

William Lucas, a sturdy A.B., who said the shock of the collision, which occurred while he was playing nap, nearly knocked him off his feet, stated that he had noticed the cold begin to increase.

Mr. Rowlatt: Did you look at the thermometer? – No. I only put on an extra jersey. (Laughter.)

The passengers on the boat deck, as far as he knew, were all of the first class. The boats lowered from that deck were not full by a long way.

Why was that? – Because there were no women knocking about.

The last boat to get away on the port side was the collapsible boat. A lady called out that there were no sailors or plugs in it, so he got in. The water was then up to the bridge of the Titanic, and the boat floated off.

"I transferred the women from my boat to No. 8 boat and got in myself, as they wanted a seaman."

They went, continued witness, to another collapsible boat which was overturned; thirty-six people were clinging on top of that, and they took them on board.

No. 8 boat had forty people on board when she left the ship, and after taking on the people from the collapsible boat she had about eighty on board.

The collapsible boat had a false bottom, explained witness, and he could not tell if there was a plug. He did not think there was.

There was water in the boat, and, he added, "the passengers wanted to leave the collapsible boat, so I left them.

"Before I left," said witness, "I heard shouts of 'Any more women and children?' and shouted, myself."

Could those shouts have been heard in the third-class quarters? – No, certainly not.

9 May 1912

OLYMPIC FIREMEN ON OCEANIC

The White Star liner Olympic left Southampton yesterday afternoon for New York, among her crew being some of the firemen who left the Olympic fortnight ago.

Mme. Navritill, the mother of the French children saved from the Titanic, will join the vessel at Cherbourg. She intends to visit New York, and will bring the children back with her.

A new patent for safely launching lifeboats from the largest liners in the roughest weather, brought out by Sir Bryan Leighton (Bart.), was examined at the Hotel Cecil yesterday, when the ingenious device was explained by the inventor himself.

THE MAN WHO SIGHTED THE ICEBERG
Dramatic Narrative by Titanic's Look-out Man.

SEEN THROUGH A HAZE
Stoker Recalls Fire That Broke Out in Coal Bunker.

WHY BOAT WAS NOT FULL
Lord Mersey's Commission heard further graphic accounts of the circumstances of the Titanic disaster yesterday. Before Leading Stoker Barratt resumed his evidence, Sir John Simon outlined to the Court the effect of his previous evidence. Barratt, recalled, said that water was coming in behind the watertight door in No. 5 coal bunker, and was pouring into No. 6 bunker as well. He ran up to the promenade deck, and saw that No. 13 boat was full. Apart from third-class men passengers he did not see any others on this deck.

"The women were coming up from aft. I do not know where they were coming from. There were only two boats left."

Barratt said he went to boat No. 13, which was just on getting full. Five-sixths of the people in it were women. There was no officer in the boat. He got in, and about three people after him, and then the order was given by someone on deck: "Let no more people get in that boat. The falls are breaking."

ONE BOAT UNDER ANOTHER
"No. 13 boat was lowered thirty seconds after us," he went on. "It was coming on top of us. The oars were tied up, and, after I had cut them adrift, I shoved the oars against the ship's side and told them to lower away. When we got into the water the current drifted us under No. 15. They did not understand the order to clear the falls, and I had to cut them. As I did so I felt No. 15 touch my shoulder."

You were in charge of the boat until the Carpathia picked her up? – No, sir. I gave the tiller to somebody else. I was so cold I could not feel my limbs. I had only thin gear on. Some woman put a cloak over me, and I don't know what happened then.

While the women were being put in the boat the men stood in a line, as though at "Attention," waiting for the order to get into the boat.

Answering Mr. Harbinson, Barratt said that No. 13 boat was not lowered until all the women had been taken off the deck.

◀ Look-out on the Titanic Mr Reginald Robinson Lee leaving the Celtic at Docks on 6 May 1912.

FIRE IN A BUNKER
Mr. Lewis elicited from him the information that when the ship left

Southampton a fire was discovered in the coal bunker between Sections 5 and 6. The bunker had to be cleared right out on the Saturday.

"After we had cleared the bunker the builders' men wanted to inspect the bulkhead. It was damaged, and I attributed that to the fire."

The President: Do you think the fire had anything to do with the disaster? – That would be hard to say.

Another typical seaman, short, clean-shaven, wrinkle-lined, stepped into the box when Reginald Robinson Lee was called.

He was one of the look-out men when the iceberg was sighted.

There were no glasses provided for the look-out men on the Titanic, though night glasses were certainly, better than eyesight. One of the other look-out men asked for glasses, but was told there were none.

"I came on duty at ten o'clock. It was a starlight night, but at the time of the accident there was a haze right ahead. In fact, it was extending more or less all round the horizon. It was very cold, freezing, and colder than it had been before on this voyage. Soon we had all our work cut out to pierce through the haze."

"ICEBERG RIGHT AHEAD, SIR."

"The first thing reported was after seven bells (11.30) struck. Nine or ten minutes afterwards three bells were struck by Fleet, meaning 'Something right ahead.' Then immediately he rang the telephone up to the bridge, and said: 'Iceberg right ahead, sir.' The reply came back from the bridge: 'Thank you.' As soon as the reply came, the helm must have been put hard a starboard, because she sheered over to port and it seemed as though she might clear it.

"Then she struck and a certain amount of ice came aboard the ship on the fore well deck. It seemed as if she struck before the foremast. The berg was higher than the forecastle. (About 55ft. out of the water.) This berg was just a vast dark mass that came through the haze. As the boat moved away from it there was just a fringe of white on top.

"When we first saw the iceberg it might have been half a mile off or less. When I came down from the crow's nest at midnight water, was coming into No. 1 hatch just outside the seamen's mess."

After leaving the Titanic did you see the lights of any other steamer before the Carpathia? – There was a ship apparently, ahead of the Titanic as she was then. It disappeared afterwards.

Lee said the crow's nest men talked among themselves about the absence of glasses for the look-outs. They asked each other what had become of the binoculars which were in the crow's nest on the trip from Belfast to Southampton.

Mr. Harbinson: Did you know there was ice about? – Yes, we could smell it.

The President: What do you mean by "smell it"? – The sudden change in the temperature, my Lord.

The first witness in the afternoon, John Poingdextre, an A.B. on the Titanic, said that the weather at the time of the accident was terribly cold, but fine and clear. He went to get his boots, and as he was searching for them the wooden bulkhead which separated the forecastle from the third-class cabin broke, and he had to fight waist-deep through the water to escape.

Mr. Aspinall: On your way to the boat deck would you go near where the third-class passengers could get out of their quarters up to the deck? – Yes; they were already up.

"I saw them with their baggage on the deck. There was a large number of them – fifty or 100. They consisted all of men, foreigners. I saw no women. The women were berthed aft, away from the men altogether."

ATTEMPT TO RUSH BOATS

Mr. Lightoller, the second officer, and himself were the only seamen to deal with the hundreds of passengers who had gathered round waiting for a place in the three boats – Nos. 12, 14 and 16.

They put about forty women and children each into No. 12 and No. 14, the full carrying capacity being sixty-five.

Do you know how it comes that there were not more put in these boats? – The reason is that the falls would not carry any more.

Did the passengers behave well? – They did not where I was. They were trying to rush boats Nos. 12 and 14. They could not lower the boats as they ought to have done because the second- and third-class men passengers were on the boat falls crowding round, and they could not get them clear.

They heard cries, and were looking for survivors for fifteen minutes, but saw nothing except 200 deck chairs. What is the nearest you think you got to the cries? – About 100 yards, sir.

"I can account for not getting to where the cries were coming from," said witness, in answer to another question: "There were not enough sailors in my boat to row there in time."

MIGHT HAVE BEEN A STAR

Describing his adventures after the Titanic foundered, Poingdextre said that he saw an "imaginary light." There is such a thing at sea as seeing an imaginary light. "You see it, and then it is gone again."

It was a white light, and might have been a star. To reassure the women in his boat he told them, that they would soon be rescued, as a ship was coming.

An important fact that has not previously been brought out was referred to by Poingdextre, who said that when his boat was lowered it appeared to him to be full. "A person with a lifebelt on," he added, "takes up twice as much room as one without."

James Johnson, who served as night watchman in the first saloon, stated that he was standing in the saloon when the ship jolted, and he was nearly knocked over a table.

He took the precaution twice to go and ascertain which boat he was allocated to in case it was going to be launched.

Why did you take that precaution? – I did it on a principle of my own because I am a Scotchman, I suppose. (Laughter.)

"AT A LEFT ANGLE."

No one who wanted to get into his boat, said Johnson, was kept back. The boat was lowered to the bottom deck, but no one got in there.

He told of borrowing a razor from a man named McCulloch, who said if they ever met in Southampton he could return it. It came in handy for cutting the lifeboat adrift.

They saw the "mystery light" for quite twenty minutes on the port bow.

"Was it at a right angle on the port bow?" queried counsel. "A left angle, I should think," came the unexpected reply that evoked the laughter of the Court.

One of the witnesses said it was two points off? – I don't know a point, sir, unless it's in billiards. (Laughter.)

How many oars were there in your boat? – Four; two were rowing and two were dipping – doing their best.

Were you rowing or dipping? – I was rowing, I think.

MISSING SON'S RETURN

Messrs. Quilliam, of Liverpool, solicitors, acting on behalf of the relatives of Thomas Hart, fireman, of Liverpool, supposed to have been lost in the Titanic, have received a remarkable statement from his mother.

She says that her son has turned up, and informs her that he had had his discharge book stolen from him. Someone evidently signed on the Titanic with Hart's name and credentials, and it was he and not Hart who was drowned.

"While the women were being put in the boat the men stood in a line as though at attention waiting for the order to get into the boat." – Leading Stoker Frederick Barratt at the Titanic Inquiry yesterday.

That was how they waited, and waiting met death, those heroes of the Titanic, for whose dependents the appeal is made to the Women of England.

"Women and children first." They knew – and, knowing, kept – the White Man's Law of the Sea. And now women, and children too, are hastening to pay what tribute they can to the men who sacrificed themselves, who gave their all.

The splendid example which some little girls and boys set of giving their Saturday money, and their savings to *The Daily Mail* Fund for the sufferers is being rapidly followed by other little girls and boys all over the country. Their small subscriptions – and it does not matter the least how small they are – are beginning to total up into quite a considerable amount.

They have the proud knowledge of knowing, and it is something to be proud of, that they have helped to make the magnificent total of £49,101, which was reached yesterday.

10 May 1912

SUCKED DOWN WHEN THE TITANIC SANK

Trimmer Tells of Being "Lifted Up" Two Fathoms.

HOUR'S WAIT FOR DEATH
Fireman's Story of Lady Passengers' Fear of Being Swamped.

WHY BOAT DID NOT TURN

James Johnson, the Scottish saloon steward of the Titanic, was again put in the witness-box yesterday morning, when Lord Mersey's Commission resumed its inquiry at the London Scottish Drill Hall, Buckingham Gate.

He told of being in one of the first boats away, and was three-quarters of a mile off when the liner sank, rowing in pursuit of the mysterious light.

"Did you try and row on towards the wreck?" asked Mr. Rowlatt.

"No, we stayed off nearly three-quarters of a mile," he replied. "The officer asked if we were to go back, but we were just nearing an iceberg, and a lady said, 'No, it was dangerous.'"

May I take it that the boat could have gone back towards the wreck if it had been decided to do so? – Yes.

ASKED THE LADY PASSENGERS

Mr. Scanlan (for the Seamen and Firemen's Union): Is it your evidence, that the fourth officer, who was in charge of your boat, decided for himself as to whether it was possible for him to go and rescue the people from whom he heard shrieks, or that he consulted the lady passengers on the boat? – He asked the lady passengers.

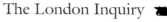

Is it fair to assume that if the officer had given instructions on his own responsibility instead of consulting the frightened passengers you could have got in a very short time to the people struggling in the water? – I don't think they were frightened.

Mr. Harbinson (for the passengers): Have you any idea of what class the people came from in your boat? – Mostly third class. The ladies, he repeated, showed disinclination to go in the boat.

Mr. Cotter (for the Stewards' Union): Were any orders given to the stewards after the collision? – The bedroom stewards were told to go to every room and put life preservers on every lady and get them out of their cabins.

MR. BRUCE ISMAY'S EFFORTS

Could not the stewards have got the women on to the boat deck from each class? – You could not drive the women. I tried but could not do it.

Your contention is that they were told and the women would not go on deck? – I am certain of it. I saw Mr. Ismay trying to drive a few into a boat. He had bedroom slippers on and a dust coat, but they would not go in for him.

The Attorney-General (to witness): You told us about Mr. Ismay. Was Mr. Ismay still on the Titanic when your boat left? – Yes. He was doing as much as any individual man could do. He was trying to entice the women into the boat.

The next witness, Thomas Patrick Dillon, a trimmer, replying to Mr. Raymond Asquith in the fewest possible words, told of his escape from the engine-room after the Titanic struck.

Immediately after the collision, he said, the watertight doors closed, and as soon as the engine had been reversed the chief engineer ordered the men to reopen the door.

SUCKED DOWN TWO FATHOMS

"We could open it just far enough to get underneath." From the engine-room, he said, he made his way into two adjoining stokeholds and opened the watertight doors on the way.

Dillon said he saw the last boat leave the port side of the ship. "I heard the order, 'The last boat will leave the ship; any more women there?' There were two women on the well deck, and we chased them up the ladder to the boat deck."

Did you wait on the poop until the ship actually sank? – Yes.

How did you get off the ship? – I left her in the water, sir.

The President: Am I to understand that you were actually on board the Titanic when she went down? – Yes, my Lord.

Were you sucked down by it? – About two fathoms.

Did you then come up to the surface? – I seemed to get lifted up. I swam for twenty minutes, and was picked up by one of the boats. When I got in I was unconscious.

◀ Trimmer Thomas Patrick Dillon told of his escape from the engine room and how he was sucked down two fathoms.

SIXTY MINUTES WAITING FOR DEATH

Did you see any other passengers in the water? – Yes.

How many? – About 1,000 – no women.

Mr. Lewis (for the Seafarers' Union) put some questions which brought out more sketches of vivid tragedy in the last hours.

"How long," he asked, "were you waiting on the poop for the boat to go down?"

"About sixty minutes," said Dillon, and an expression something, like terror seemed to rest on his face, which was drawn and working with emotion.

You could see the passengers. Was there any commotion? – No, none at all.

They were simply waiting for death? – Yes.

You were picked up unconscious. When you came to what did you find? – A sailor, and a passenger lying on top of me in the boat dead.

How he and another greaser slid down the falls of a lifeboat was told by Thomas Ranger.

It was the last boat, which was full of women and children, but came back to the liner because there were only two men in her. Scott, his mate, fell in the water, but was picked up by the boat, and they got away just in time. Afterwards they went back and picked up several more people. As they left the Titanic they heard a band playing.

Alfred Shiers, fireman, said that there were about forty people in the boat he was in. The passengers they took away were all women. After the Titanic sank they were rowing back to pick up people when the female passengers in the boat told the officer, Mr. Pitman, who was steering, not to go back.

FEAR OF SWAMPING

Mr. Harbinson: And the officer did not go back because of what these female passengers ordered him? – The female passengers said that if the boat went back it would be swamped, and the officer then gave its instructions to lay on our oars.

If you yourself had been in charge would you have gone back if you believed there was a large number of people in the water? – No.

Charles Henrickson, a leading fireman, was next called, and a tall man in a white sweater and grey suit came forward.

After describing the scene on board, he was asked whether he saw the Titanic sink, and replied in the affirmative.

Did you go back to pick up anybody? – No.

Why not? – I proposed going back, but the others objected. They would not listen to me – none of the passengers or anybody else.

The President: Am I to understand that when you were picked up by the Carpathia there were only twelve people on board? – Yes. There were two women and three men passengers, two seamen and four others of the crew.

"LADY DUFF-GORDON OBJECTED."

Mr. Rowlatt: Who was it that objected? – The women.

What were the names of the passengers? – I heard the name of one of the passengers – Duff-Gordon.

Did you hear the names of the others? – I think his wife was there, Lady Duff-Gordon.

Did his wife object? – Yes, she was scared to go back in case of being swamped.

The President: Was there so far as you know any danger of the boat being swamped if you had gone back? – It would certainly be dangerous.

Do you know the names of the other members of the crew on board this boat of yours? – Some of them. They included, I believe, Simmons, the cox; Collins, a fireman; Sheath, a trimmer; and Tailor, a fireman.

When Lady Duff-Gordon objected, did her husband reprove her? – He upheld her.

Witness told Mr. Scanlan that one reason why it would be dangerous to go back would be because, they had no lamp.

The President: Were you the only person to propose going back? – I never heard any others. Duff-Gordon and his wife said it was dangerous, and that we should be swamped.

Am I to understand that because two of the passengers said it would be dangerous, you all kept your mouths shut and made no attempt to rescue anyone? – That is right, sir.

A PRESENT OF MONEY

Was any money given to you by any of the passengers when you got on the Carpathia? – Yes.

What did you receive? – An order for £5.

Who from? – Duff-Gordon.

What did the other members of the crew get? – The same.

The President: Did you know at the time you would receive the £5? – No.

Are you sure? – Yes.

It came as a pleasant surprise? – Oh, yes, of course.

In reply to Mr. Potter, Henrickson again repeated his assertion that he heard no mention of any promise of money until they sighted the Carpathia.

11 May 1912

SUCCESSFUL SALE OF GIFTS AND RELICS

£300 Realised for Women's Fund in Few Hours.

TOTAL NOW £51,703

To-day's Great Empire Concert on Behalf of Titanic Sufferers.

CHILDREN'S EFFORTS

Boys and Girls Continue Their Contributions and Collections.

The splendid total of £51,703 has now been contributed by the women of England towards the fund which *The Daily Mail* opened for the benefit of the sufferers who were left destitute by the loss of the Titanic. Part of the fine sum which came in yesterday was due to the sale at Selfridge's of the jewellery and other articles which sympathisers had sent in in lieu of money. Many of these were personal sacrifices

How successful was the sale may be judged from the fact that within a few hours of its opening as much as £300 had been realised by the disposal of some of these gifts. Much of the success was undoubtedly due to Miss Marie Tempest, who took the part of auctioneer-in-chief, helped by a representative of Messrs. Hampton, Pall Mall.

Miss Tempest, who looked very charming in a lace-covered gown of green satin, drove each bid home with a sharp tap of the ivory hammer, which had been presented to her by *The Evening News* as a souvenir of the occasion.

In a sympathetic little speech, the first actress-auctioneer declared that anything bought at the sale might always be regarded as a priceless treasure, since it commemorated "one of the greatest deeds of heroism in history."

CHIEF BAKER'S 2½ HOURS IN ICY WATER
Thrilling Story of Escape After Titanic Broke Up.

CLUNG TO COLLAPSIBLE
How His Recognition by a Cook Saved His Life.

SWIM TO LIFEBOAT
Pending the arrival of the Adriatic with officers of the Titanic, the cross-examination was yesterday adjourned of leading fireman Henrickson, whose allegations concerning the passengers in lifeboat No. 1 caused such a sensation on Thursday.

Lord Mersey, before the first witness was called, asked that a list of the boats, their crews, the number and sex of passengers on each should be prepared by the Attorney-General.

Then Frank Morris, a first-class bathroom steward, related his experiences when he was aroused after the collision. His boat. No. 14, was in charge of Mr. Lowe, the fifth officer. It contained at first about fifty-three women and children, who were transferred to another boat, the men pulling back after the ship had gone down.

They picked up only three persons, but later took about eighteen persons out of a collapsible boat. In all they carried about twenty-eight souls when picked up by the Carpathia. Answering Mr. Scanlan, Morris said they saw hundreds of people in the water, but they were not all crying for help; they might have been unconscious or they might have been dead.

John Joughin, chief baker on the Titanic, had a thrilling story to unfold.

His boat was No. 10. Mr. Wild, chief officer, and a good many passengers were there, and Mr. Wild shouted to the stewards to keep the men back, but there was no need for the order. They made a line and passed the ladies and children through. The discipline was splendid. No. 10 was swung out and the stewards, firemen and sailors all got in a line to pass the ladies and children down.

BROUGHT WOMEN FORCIBLY
After we had got it about half full there was a difficulty in finding ladies for it. They ran away from the boat and said they were safer where they were.

As far as you know, was any distinction made between the classes? – Not at all. The emergency door from the third-class quarters to the boat deck was open.

"As we could not find sufficient women to fill the boat two or three others went with me and forcibly brought the women to the boats."

Did not they want to come? – No, sir. They were squatting down on the deck.

Did you put them in the boats? – We threw them in. We could not put them in; we could either hand them in or just drop them in.

He said he was supposed to be captain of the boat, but as there was not sufficient room, he remained on the ship when the boat was lowered.

"Then I went to my room again," he proceeded, "and had a drop of liqueur I had down there. I saw the old doctor and spoke to him and then went upstairs again.

"By this time all the boats seemed to have gone, and I threw about fifty deck-chairs overboard – for something to cling to.

"I went into the pantry for some water, and while there I heard a crash and a noise as though people were rushing along the deck. I looked out on deck and saw people rushing aft to the poop."

TITANIC'S LAST GASP
What was the sound like? – Buckling and crackling. It was like as if the iron had parted.

"I kept out of the crush of people as long as I could. I went down to the well-deck, and just as I got there she gave a great list to port, and threw everybody in a bunch. It was not that one side of the vessel rose, but one side fell."

Can you give us some idea of how many people there were in this crush? – I have no idea. They were piled up, many hundreds of them.

What happened to you? – I eventually got to the starboard side of the poop. I hung on to the poop-rail. I was outside of it on the side of the ship.

"Just as I was wondering what next to do she went," said the witness simply.

Did you find yourself in the water ? – Yes.

Did you feel you were dragged under? – I do not believe my head went under the water at all. It might have wetted it, but no more.

He was a good swimmer, and did not attempt to get anything to hold on to. It was calm as a pond, and he was just paddling, treading water. His lifebelt was an excellent support.

"Just as it was breaking daylight I saw what I thought was some wreckage, and started to swim towards it slowly.

"I then found it was a collapsible not properly afloat, but on its side, with an officer and, I think, about twenty-five men standing on the top or rather the side of it. The officer was Mr. Lightoller."

Did you get on this? – I swam towards it.

They could not take you in? – Well, you see, there was no room for any more. They were standing on it then.

Did you stay near it? – I tried to get on it, but I was pushed off, and I, what you would call, hung around. I eventually got round to the opposite side, and a cook on the collapsible recognised me and held out his hand. He just held me, and I got the edge of my lifebelt hitched on to the side of the boat.

Was the water very cold? – I felt colder when I got into the lifeboat. I was hanging on to this collapsible, and eventually a lifeboat came in sight.

"They got within fifty yards of us," he continued, "and then they sung out that they could only take ten people on board.

"Then I said to this cook who was holding me: 'Let go my hand, and I will swim to the boat. I am going to be one of the ten.' I was taken into the lifeboat.

"I was hanging on to the collapsible boat about one and a half hours, so that I was in the water about two and a half hours altogether."

Answering Mr. Cotter, Joughin said that there was a difficulty in getting the women to go into the boat. He threw a couple of children in and a steward caught the mother to put her in.

Then she seemed inclined to step in, but slipped, and, being head downwards, the steward held her by the foot for a moment and then she was dragged in on the deck below.

Why did you not get into the boat when she was swung off? – It would have set a bad example if I had jumped in.

"LIFE SAVED BY LIQUEUR."

I suggest that the liqueur helped you to save your life. How much did you have? – Oh, about half a tumblerful.

Samuel James Rule, another bathroom steward, a short, stoutish man, with a close-cropped red beard and moustache, was next called.

He was awakened by the stopping of the engines, and getting up went to various parts of the ship, but found quietness and calmness everywhere.

He then returned to his cabin, and shortly after the chief steward came and gave the orders:–

All hands to the boat decks with the lifebelts. The bedroom stewards to see that the passengers had their lifebelts and were out of their rooms. The rooms to be locked up after they left them.

Mr. Ismay, he said, was helping to put people into No. 3 boat, and an officer – he thought it was Mr. Lowe – was giving directions.

BOAT WITH ONLY TWELVE

Boat No. 1 was already launched and the order was given to those in it, "Stand off from the ship's side and return when we call you."

"That, your Lordship will remember," said-the Attorney-General, who was examining witness, "is the boat with five passengers and seven of the crew."

Rule afterwards went round and distributed bread and biscuits to every boat on the starboard side except Nos. 1 and 3/8, which had then been launched. He did not go on the port side. Eventually, he was ordered into No. 15, the last boat on the starboard side to leave.

"We could find no more women and children to go," he said. "We sent scouts round the decks but could find none. There were sixty-eight people in this boat, of whom four or five were women, three children, and the rest men.

The President: That is contrary to previous evidence.

The Attorney-General: Yes, I know.

The Court was then adjourned till Tuesday morning. On Monday all the counsel engaged will visit the Olympic at Southampton and an expert will be provided by the White Star Line to explain points on the ship.

MR. ISMAY'S RETURN

The Adriatic arrived at the lightship, Queenstown, yesterday, and was joined immediately after by Mrs. Bruce Ismay and Mr. C. Bower Ismay, who were soon in conference with Mr. J. Bruce Ismay.

Mr. Ismay, though not wholly recovered from the awful ordeal he has passed through, has benefited materially by the rest on the passage across. He will be examined before the Commissioners at the inquiry now sitting in London, and courts the fullest inquiry in every direction.

13 May 1912

MR. BRUCE ISMAY'S HOMECOMING

Baby Survivor of Titanic Idolised on Returning Liner.

FRENCHWOMAN'S TRIBUTE
(FROM OUR SPECIAL CORRESPONDENT)

Liverpool, May 12 – A sympathetic sense that Mr. Bruce Ismay has not been given fair play caused a large crowd to assemble on the landing-stage yesterday morning, when the Adriatic landed her passengers from New York, and give the White Star chairman a welcome home. He was accompanied by Mrs. Ismay, Colonel Concanon of the White Star Line; Mr. Bower Ismay and Captain

Bartlett, marine superintendent of the White Star Line, all of whom had joined the Adriatic at Queenstown.

A large number of telegrams had been sent to Mr. Ismay on board the Adriatic expressing sympathy. Among them were messages asking whether he would see representatives of the Press. In reply to these requests, Mr. Ismay issued the following statement:–

Mr. Ismay asks the gentlemen of the Press to extend their courtesy to him by not pressing for any statement from him.

First, because he is still suffering from the very great strain of the Titanic disaster and subsequent events.

Again, because he gave before the American Commission a plain, and unvarnished statement of facts which have been fully reported.

And also because his evidence before the British Court of Inquiry should not be anticipated in any way.

He concluded with a message of thanks, for all the sympathetic communications sent to him.

PARISIENNE'S IMPRESSIONS
(FROM OUR SPECIAL CORRESPONDENT)

Liverpool, May 12 – Mme. Aubart, the last woman to leave the Titanic before it sank, reached Liverpool on the Adriatic yesterday on her way back to Paris, and gave me some of her impressions of the catastrophe that has left upon her its indelible mark.

"I had in my cabin," she told me, "jewels worth £4,000, as well as many trunks of dresses and hats. One does not come from Paris and buy one's clothes in America. That is understood, is it not? Nothing could I take with me; nothing at all. Just as we were, in our night-clothes, Marie and I went on deck, where the lifebelts were put round us.

"On the deck there was no commotion; none at all. Oh, these English! How brave, how calm, how beautiful! I, who am a patriotic Frenchwoman, say that never can I forget that group of Englishmen – every one of them a perfect gentleman – calmly puffing cigarettes and cigars and watching the women and children being placed in the boats."

THE PHLEGMATIC ENGLISHMAN

"So I have seen them in Monte Carlo. It was the phlegmatic Englishman in his most sublime form. Marie got into the lifeboat and then I. We were the last women to leave the ship. My last sight of the upper decks was still a group of those Englishmen, still with cigarettes in mouth, facing death so bravely that it was all the more terrible.

"I am tired," she said in conclusion. "I go to Paris at once. There will I sleep so that I may forget. But never will I forget the bravery of those wonderful Englishmen who acted as no other men would do. Those officers and men were every one of them a glory to humanity."

BABY SURVIVOR'S HOMECOMING
(FROM OUR SPECIAL CORRESPONDENT)

Liverpool, May 12 – Baby Dean, the youngest of the Titanic survivors, arrived here yesterday morning in the Adriatic, with her mother, widowed by the disaster, and her little brother.

Mr. Dean was a tobacconist, who thought that there would be a more prosperous future for his two-year-old son and three-weeks-old girl if he went overseas. So, with £50 in gold sewed up in a belt, he embarked on the Titanic with his wife and children.

Baby – just a warm little bundle of lovable humanity – was wrapped in blankets and thrown into the lifeboat, where she was caught by a big sailorman, who kissed her and wrapped an oilskin round her. Not once did she cry. Baby's mother was cold and frantic with grief, but everyone in the boat made it a duty to see that baby should be kept warm and comfortable.

COLLECTED £50 FOR BABY

Then Mrs. Dean was enabled to return to her home near Southampton, and baby, although only six weeks' old, began her second crossing of the Atlantic. All the passengers in the Adriatic knew of baby's history, and there began a great rivalry among the women passengers of the first and second class. Every woman in the liner felt that she had a prescriptive right to hold baby in her arms.

They meant well, but baby began to get worried at the class jealousies of women who were prepared to tear her to pieces for the privilege of dandling her for a few minutes. A kindly officer, however, came on the scene. With the wisdom of a Solomon he ruled that, subject to Mrs. Dean's consent, baby might be held by first- and second-class passengers in turn for not more than ten minutes each.

So deeply did the passengers fall in love with baby that they made a little collection for her, raising more than £50. This will help Mrs. Dean along for a while, and will, serve to remind her how her daughter turned the heads of a whole ship.

WOMEN'S FUND AMOUNTS TO £53,168
No More Money Is Now Required – The Lord Mayor's Letter of Thanks.

The Women's Fund to-day amounts to £53,168, of which £50,000 has already been handed over to the Lord Mayor's Fund by *The Daily Mail*. No more money is required. The Lord Mayor states that he does not think it necessary to appeal any further to the generosity of our readers. All those who are still making collections are therefore requested to return their subscription lists with the amounts collected as quickly as possible to the Chief Clerk, Titanic Fund, *The Daily Mail*, Carmelite House. The following is the Lord Mayor's letter:–

Please accept my heartfelt thanks for your cheque for £10,000, which brings the total received by me from *The Daily Mail* Women's Fund for the relief of the sufferers by the loss of the Titanic to the splendid amount of £50,000. A very large sum of money is now available for the relief of the widows and children of the Titanic heroes, and, although detailed figures are not yet available as to the exact amount that will be required, I do not think it necessary to appeal further to the generosity of your readers.

The women of England have done nobly, and on behalf of the sufferers, I tender them my heartfelt thanks. At the same time, allow me to express to the proprietors of *The Daily*

Mail my gratitude for the masterly manner in which the Women's Fund has been organised. It is a glowing example of the powerful influence for good possessed by your, great newspaper.

(Signed) THOS. BOOR CROSBY, Lord Mayor.

CONTRIBUTIONS STILL TO BE ADDED
Yesterday £508 was received. This does not include the profits of a magnificent concert on Saturday at "Shakespeare's England," when a crowded audience of 8,000 people assembled in the Empress Hall at Earl's Court to celebrate the inauguration of the exhibition. As several thousands of the tickets were sold through members of the different choirs, which took part, it is impossible to give, the amount which will accrue to the fund from the concert.

Amongst the other contributions still to be added to the fund are the proceeds of the concert which is being organised at the Kensington Town Hall to-night, by Miss Marta Cunningham, under the patronage of the Princess Louise. The Mayor and Mayoress of the Royal Borough and the chief members of the council have promised to be present, and they, with the Lord Chief Justice, Lord Alverstone, Sir Charles and Lady Stanford, Sir Aston and Lady Webb, are all bringing parties.

The concert promises to be a great social success. Eight of the prettiest debutantes of the season have promised to sell programmes, and the majority of the more expensive seats have been sold. The hall will be beautifully decorated with flowers, which have been given by Sir John Barker, and the artists who have given their services include Mme. Janotha, Miss Evangeline Florence, Miss Marta Cunningham, Mrs. Adrian Ross, Miss Palgrave Turner, and Mr. Acton Bond.

THE ICEBERG WHICH MIGHT HAVE SUNK THE TITANIC DRIFTING IN THE ATLANTIC.

SEVEN WEEKS OLD BABY SAVED FROM THE TITANIC: CHEERS FOR MR. ISMAY
The youngest survivor of the

Titanic disaster arrived at Liverpool on Saturday on board the Adriatic. Baby Dean, who is only seven weeks old, was the pet of the liner during the voyage, and so keen was the rivalry among the women to nurse this lovable mite of humanity that one of the officers decreed that first- and second-class passengers might hold her in turn for not more than ten minutes. Mr. Dean was among those drowned, but Mrs. Dean and her two children were saved.

Mr. Bruce Ismay, the chairman of the White Star Line, who has been so baited by the American Press, was among the Titanic survivors who arrived on the Adriatic. Mr. Ismay is highly esteemed in Liverpool, and was so loudly cheered on landing.

14 May 1912

WIDOW'S OCEAN QUEST

Atlantic Journey to Scatter Flowers on Spot Where Titanic Sank.

A touching ceremony was witnessed on board the Carmania, which has just arrived at New York, when the liner was in the vicinity of the spot where the Titanic was lost. Among the passengers on board (says Reuter) was a Mrs. J. L. Loring, whose husband was one of the victims of the Titanic disaster, and when informed that the Carmania had reached the neighbourhood of the wreck she scattered an armful of flowers into the sea in memory of her husband.

The 500 cabin passengers on board stood on deck with heads bowed, the men being uncovered, and many of the women wept with emotion. Mrs. Loring made the trip especially to be able to pay this tribute to her late husband Both the Carmania and La Savoie report having sighted big icebergs, the former in latitude 39deg. 9min. N. and 42deg. 24min, W., and the latter in 39deg. 15min. N. and 47deg. 40min. W.

It is stated that those seen by the Carmania were farther south than any before reported.

The steamer Montgomery reports by wireless telegraphy that she has picked up the bodies of four victims of the Titanic disaster.

15 May 1912

DRAMATIC MOMENTS AT TITANIC DISASTER INQUIRY

Ship with List to Starboard Seen from Californian.

WAS IT THE LINER?

Apprentice's Vivid Story of Rockets from Ship 5 Miles Off.

CAPTAIN'S EVIDENCE

Vessel Believed To Be Tramp That Answered No Signals.

There was a dramatic moment at the Scottish Hall, Buckingham Gate, yesterday afternoon, during the evidence before Lord Mersey's Titanic Wreck Commission. Only three witnesses appeared during the whole day – the master of the Californian, the Leyland liner that was within twenty miles of the Titanic when she sank, and an apprentice and the second officer on the same vessel.

One main point it was sought to establish, but at the end of the day the battle for the truth was still undecided. This was the question – was the Californian the ship of the mystery lights which so many on board the Titanic say they saw a few miles distant when the liner had struck the iceberg.

All, the morning the interplay of question, and answer between counsel and witness or Lord Mersey and witness had proceeded inaudible to most of the public, who had assembled in large numbers hoping to hear what was going on. The shuffling of feet, the impatient creaking of chairs, the constant walking to and fro behind the crowded ranks of those who stood, indicated the strain of listening to the duel of lawyers and seafarers.

"THE LIGHTS LOOK QUEER."

But there came a moment when Sir John Simon was examining the apprentice, James Gibson, in the gentle, understanding way that coaxes so much out of witnesses, when the creaking and the shuffling ceased, and all leaned forward expectantly, hands behind ears, to catch what fell from the lips of the boy who stood facing the Court, striving to reveal the truth as he knew it.

It seemed that he was describing the going down of the Titanic as viewed from a vessel only five miles away, that he had unconsciously been a witness of the dread catastrophe that has wrung the emotions of a world of men and women

His language was technical, but understandable enough. The second officer and he were on the bridge of the Californian observing a vessel believed to be a tramp steamer. They had seen rockets fired into the air from her direction, they had sent up Morse signals by lamp to which no answer came, they had wondered what the rockets meant.

At 1.20 the officer said to him, "Look at her now. She looks very queer out of the water. The lights look queer."

"A HEAVY LIST TO STARBOARD."

Slowly, by dint of question upon question, which the audience strained every ear to catch, the Solicitor-General extracted from the boy witness – he is a youth of twenty – what he had seen.

"She seemed as if she had a heavy list to starboard." He was certain of this. Her port light, her red light, was higher in the water than it had been when he had first looked at the ship. Moreover, the white glaring lights after seemed different somehow, he could not explain how.

The luncheon interval brought a welcome relief to the strain of examination to which the youth had been subjected, and the laymen in the audience went out convinced that they had heard the story of one who had seen from a distance the last hours of the Titanic.

Yet further examination could not shake Gibson's conviction that the ship he had seen could not have been the Titanic but a tramp steamer, and the second officer, who followed, was rooted in the belief that they could not have been gazing upon distress signals from the mammoth liner.

LADY DUFF-GORDON'S RETURN

A largely-increased gathering filled the seats set apart for the public long before 10.30, and the ladies gallery was well occupied before Lord Mersey and his assessors took their seats. As the morning wore on the public were attracted to the court in ever-increasing numbers until they stood five or six deep across the hall behind the rows of chairs.

Sir Robert Finlay (for the White Star Line) obtained leave to further postpone till Friday his cross-examination of the witness Henrickson, who, giving evidence concerning the boat in which Sir Cosmo and Lady Duff-Gordon left the ship, alleged that they urged him not to attempt rescues of the drowning. Sir Cosmo and Lady Duff-Gordon were on their way to this country on board the Lusitania.

"They will arrive to-night," said Sir Robert, "and, under these circumstances, subject to your Lordship's approval, I think it would be highly desirable that the cross-examination should be postponed in order that Sir Cosmo and Lady Duff-Gordon may be here and may have the opportunity of making their statement and of taking any steps they think proper."

Sir Cosmo and Lady Duff-Gordon were among the passengers of the Lusitania who landed at Liverpool yesterday. They journeyed to London in the company of their son-in-law, Lord Tiverton.

♦ Stanley Lord, master of the Californian.

CAPTAIN LORD'S EVIDENCE

Sir Rufus Isaacs said he proposed to call evidence from the Leyland liner Californian. The liner was said to have seen, distress rockets fired from a vessel, which, according to a donkey-man, was the Titanic, and to have taken no notice of the signals.

There was no doubt, as he understood the evidence, that rockets were seen, and that the Californian was not at any great distance from the Titanic. But whether it was the Titanic she saw or not was a matter, which could only be determined after the evidence.

(The Titanic, it should be noted in view of the times mentioned in the evidence, struck at about 11.40 p.m. and sank at about 2.20 a.m.)

Lord Mersey having stated that he could not accede at present to an application of the Californian's owners and officers for legal representation, Mr. Stanley Lord, master of the vessel, was called, and described how he arrived in the same ice field as the Titanic. From 10.21 p.m. onwards till daylight the Californian stopped in field-ice with her head pointing at first north-east, but subsequently veering round a point or two.

"KEEP OUT," REPLIED TITANIC

Close upon eleven o'clock on the Sunday night he saw a steamer's light, but did not think it was the Titanic, and remarked so at the time. It was then six or seven miles away. About eleven o'clock he said to his Marconi operator, "Let the Titanic know that we are stopped – surrounded by ice."

His operator then reported to him that the Titanic's operator told, him to "keep out," as he was busy with Cape Race. The witness continued to watch the approaching vessel until 11.30, when it stopped. It seemed to be a medium-sized ship, like his own.

The third officer attempted to communicate with it by Morse lamp, but got no reply. Captain Lord went to the chart-room shortly after midnight. At twenty minutes to one he was told the steamer was in just the same position, and at a quarter past one the second officer reported that he had seen a white rocket.

After evidence as to the position of the Californian, Lord Mersey said that apparently the Titanic would be at that time fourteen or fifteen miles away. Sir R. Finlay suggested nineteen miles. The witness, further examined, said the third officer had stated that the vessel had two masthead lights.

TWO MASTHEAD LIGHTS

Lord Mersey: That is important. The Titanic had two masthead lights.

Captain Lord pointed out that he and the second officer saw only one light. There were "any amount" of vessels with two masthead lights.

The Attorney-General: At a quarter to twelve did the third officer say that the deck lights appeared to go out? – No.

Lord Mersey: Was anything said to you about the deck lights? – Not to me. I have heard since of a remark of the kind.

The witness explained that the second officer made the remark to the third officer – he did not know when, and he never asked.

He did not hear at the time that the ship fired more than one rocket. He had since heard she did, and that the second officer sent a boy to call him. He remembered the boy coming to the chart-room, where he was lying down, but the lad said nothing. Not until seven o'clock did he hear that several rockets had been fired.

The Attorney-General: Did you remain in the chart-room when you were told the vessel had fired a rocket? – Yes.

He was under the impression that the rocket was not a distress signal, because, if it had been, the report would have been heard, the ship being only four or five miles away.

When he received a wireless message from the Virginian at six o'clock (the next morning) stating that the Titanic had struck a berg and sunk he proceeded to the scene.

The Attorney-General: Were you quite comfortable in your own mind when you heard that the Titanic had sunk? – I thought we ought to have seen her signals if she was nineteen miles away as indicated.

[The witness subsequently said the position given him by wireless was incorrect, and that she was thirty-two miles away.]

Have you ever heard what the steamer was that sent up the rockets if she was not the Titanic? – I have heard nothing about it.

Does it not strike you it must have been the Titanic? – No; I am positive it was not. It would be utterly impossible for anybody to mistake the Titanic.

That would depend on the distance? – You could not mistake it at four or five miles.

The witness told Lord Mersey that the last seen of the ship sighted from the Californian was when she steamed away about two o'clock, going west and south-west. This was the second officer's report.

WHAT THE APPRENTICE SAW

James Gibson, a twenty-year-old apprentice on board the Californian, followed his captain. When he came on duty at midnight, he said, he saw on the starboard beam, from four to seven miles away, a white masthead light and a red side-light. There was also a glare of white light on the after deck.

The Solicitor-General: Did you see any second white light? – No, not distinctly.

A light was flickering and he thought that they were trying to call them up by means of the Morse light. He went to the Morse keyboard and signalled to them, but came to the conclusion that the light was not a Morse light.

At five minutes to one, after he had been off the bridge for twenty minutes, Mr. Stone, the second officer, told him that the ship had fired five rockets.

The Solicitor-General: What else did Mr. Stone say? – That he had reported it to the captain.

What else? – And that the captain had instructed him to call her on the Morse light.

Did he tell you whether he had tried to call her up on the Morse light? – Yes.

What had been the result? – She had not answered him, but fired more rockets.

Did you see her fire these further rockets? – I saw three – white ones.

What did you notice between one o'clock and 1.20, looking at her through your glasses? – The second officer remarked to me: "Look at her now. She looks very queer out of the water. The lights look queer."

Did he say what he meant? – I looked at her through the glasses, and the lights did not seem to be natural. When a vessel rolls at sea her lights do not look the same.

NOT EXACTLY IN DISTRESS

The Solicitor-General: What did you see through the glasses? – She seemed as if she had a heavy list to starboard.

What was it you could see that made you think that? Do you mean the masthead light was not immediately over the other lights? – The lights did not seem to look as they did when I first saw them.

Did you think yourself when you looked at her through the glasses that something was wrong? – We had been talking about it altogether.

The President: What did you say to each other? You had

been watching this ship, what were you saying? – He remarked to me that the ship was not going to send up the rockets at sea for nothing.

The President: As I understand it you and the second officer came to the conclusion that it was a ship in distress? – Not exactly.

What then? – That everything was not all right.

Subsequently, he said, he was ordered by the second officer to report to the captain that the vessel had disappeared towards the south-west and that she had fired eight rockets.

Harking back after lunch to the altered appearance of the ship, the Solicitor-General asked:–

What do you mean when you say that later on when you looked at her, you thought she had got a list, or that her lighting looked queer? – The red side-light seemed to be higher out of the water.

After the Second Officer Stone had given evidence the Court adjourned.

MR. BRUCE ISMAY'S £10,000 GIFT

With the object of starting a permanent fund to assist the widows of those who lost their lives while on active duty in the mercantile ships of the United Kingdom, Mr. Bruce Ismay has written to Lord Derby, Lord Mayor of Liverpool, offering to contribute £10,000 and his wife £1,000.

WIDOW'S PICTURE FILM

Pathetic Record of Wedding Owned by Bride Bereaved in Titanic Disaster.

One of the many young widows who are mourning husbands drowned in the wreck of the Titanic, Mrs. Daniel Warner Marvin, of New York, has a pathetic record of her marriage in a moving picture film of her wedding ceremony, which took place at the beginning of March.

There were twelve honeymoon couples on board the Titanic returning from Europe, and eleven of the brides are widows, among them Mrs. Marvin. Hers was the first wedding known to have been recorded by means of moving pictures, and it was at her own suggestion, on her wedding eve, that this was done. Mr. Daniel Marvin's father is the head of one of the largest American moving picture firms.

The bride's maiden name was Mary Farquharson, and the parents of both bride and bridegroom reside in the fashionable Riverside Drive. The wedding ceremony was performed at Harlem Presbyterian Church, and afterwards bride, bridegroom and guests went through the ceremony again for pictorial purposes in front of an operator.

The Daily Mirror

THE MORNING JOURNAL WITH THE SECOND LARGEST NET SALE.

No. 2,670.   WEDNESDAY, MAY 15, 1912   One Halfpenny.

TRAGIC SEQUEL TO THE FIRST WEDDING TO BE CINEMATOGRAPHED: AMERICAN BRIDE WIDOWED BY THE TITANIC DISASTER.

The latest craze in America is to have your wedding cinematographed. It was the idea of Miss Mary Farquharson, a pretty American girl, to have moving pictures of her wedding, and when she was married to Daniel Marvin, whose father is the head of a large cinematograph firm, the ceremony was performed twice, the second occasion in the presence of an operator, whose duty it was to record every incident on his instrument. Little did the happy couple dream that their married life would be cut short before the end of the honeymoon. After their marriage they toured Europe, and were returning on the Titanic, Mr. Marvin (in the circle) being one of the victims. Mrs. Marvin, who is seen above in her wedding-dress, was saved. The other photographs are from the film of the ceremony.

Mrs. Marvin thus possesses a record of her husband's features and personality, which is an inestimable comfort to her, and *The Daily Mirror* is able to-day to reproduce pictures enlarged from single sections of the film, which have a pathetic public interest, in view of the calamity which brought such terrible sorrow upon the bride.

17 May 1912

THE FIGHT FOR THE TITANIC'S LAST LIFEBOAT

Ex-Navy Man in Charge Tells "Daily Mirror" His Story.

68 IN LEAKING BOAT
Steward's Evidence at the Inquiry About Third-Class Passengers.

REFUSALS TO LEAVE SHIP
(FROM OUR SPECIAL CORRESPONDENT)

Southampton, May, 16 – One of the most thrilling narratives of the Titanic disaster is that of Frank Dymond, an ex-Navy man, who was placed in charge of boat No. 15, the last to leave the ship on the starboard side.

"Our boat had been damaged by striking the ship's gunwale when we were first lowered," he said. "The men on the second deck had to step across, about two feet from the rail to the side of the boat. There was a rush. Men clambered across anyhow. I saw we were full up, and I called out loudly, 'Lower, away!' Three men fell into the sea, and one foreigner I had to hit as he jumped, and he, too, fell.

"Fred Barrett called up from boat 13 below us, 'Stop lowering, or you will swamp us.' I shouted this to the men above, and we stopped six feet above the water. No. 13 got clear, and we dropped with a splash. We all got wet, and some water came into the boat. The current drifted us under the propellers of the Titanic, which were sticking up in the air. She drew 33ft. of water, and her keel at the stem was 12ft. above our heads.

"It had taken us an hour to get the boat away, and was then about half-past one. We drifted about 300 yards away."

WITH HIS CHILD IN HIS ARMS

"There had been a lot of trouble keeping men out of the boat before she left the boat-deck. A foreigner came up with a child in his arms and we tried to get the child from him to put in the boat, but he would not give it up. At last we took him in too. We did not know till afterwards that it was his own child.

"I had a tussle with a man who had two lifebelts on the ship's deck. I had to stretch him out and take one away from him to give to a little Irishman who had none at all. There were sixty-eight people in the boat, including six other men from the stokehold and me. I was the only Navy man, and so I took command. It was fortunate I was there, for I found the plug and put it in, and made them all sit still.

"We had, to move very carefully, for the gunwales were never more than 6in. above the water, and she was leaking on one side just about the water level, where she had been bumped on the ship's gunwale. We were only able to get at five of the eight oars, and the men only rowed to keep warm.

"I had my left hand on the tiller, and could not move to use my right instead. Noss sometimes relieved me with his left hand. Even now my left hand goes numb sometimes. I could not feel with it on the Carpathia. I had nothing on at all but a flannel sweater and dungaree pants. A spare sweater I had tucked in my belt I gave to a little trimmer named Fredericks beside me to put round his neck. Fred Barrett, in 13, was the same.

THE EXPLOSIONS AND AFTER

"It was bitter cold. The water was one degree below freezing point, and the air was colder. We had been in the water about fifteen minutes when the first explosion occurred. That was what finished her. If she had broken in two the after part would have floated, for she was not ripped all the way along by the collision.

"The stern came down after the first explosion, and fifteen minutes later came another explosion, which must have been her aft boilers, for the stern went right up, and all the lights went out. Then we heard the most awful noise one could possibly hear. Her machinery shifted with a grinding roar, and there were dreadful shrieks and cries on board and around her in the sea.

"And then, about fifteen minutes later, and forty-five minutes from the time we entered the water, she plunged. There, was one 'Dago' in the boat who kept crying out, 'We are lost! We shall all be drowned!'

"And if I could have reached him I would have brained him with the tiller, for he was scaring the women. The rest of the men were quiet. I made the women sit as low in the boat as possible to shelter them.

"Even when 15 was in the water I did not believe the ship would sink altogether. One of the pleasantest things I remember is what a little Irish girl said to me in the boat. 'It's like this, sir,' she said – she called, me 'sir' because I was in command – 'we know we are along with Englishmen, and we know we will get saved if there is any chance.'

"We burnt shirts, handkerchiefs, rags and bits of flannel raised up on the boathook. There were plenty of matches in the men's pockets, but the rags only smouldered after the first blaze. A few men smoked cigarettes they had in their pockets."

FREAKS OF MEMORY

After the sensational evidence from the members of the Californian's crew, Lord Mersey's Court came back again yesterday to witnesses from the Titanic.

Durrant, the wireless operator on the Mount Temple, having been recalled for a brief spell in the witness-box, one of the Titanic's bathroom stewards named Rule, who was not cross-examined last week, was again called and questioned about a discrepancy between his evidence and that of a previous witness as to the passengers in the boat.

Another member of the crew had stated that the boat was filled with women, while Rule said nearly all the passengers were men, a number of "scouts" having failed to find any more women. Rule now said he was mistaken on the last occasion regarding the proportions, but he still thought the majority were men.

Lord Mersey: People were dressed in all sorts of garb. Do you mean that you had difficulty in distinguishing between them? – Yes; it was night.

Not when you got to the Carpathia? – It was daybreak then.

There were sixty-eight persons in boat No. 15, including seven of the crew.

Mr. Cotter re-examined the witness, who said his memory had been affected by the disaster.

RETURNED TO THEIR CABINS

John Hart, a third-class steward, said he did not think the collision was very serious, and went to sleep again. Later he received orders to assist in getting the passengers out. Altogether he had fifty-eight persons to look after.

The lifebelts he had left he placed at the disposal of third-class passengers from other parts of the vessel. After a little while the order was given to pass the women and children to the boat deck. Those who were willing to go were shown the way, but some were not willing, and stayed behind.

When they got to the boat deck they found it rather cold, and, thinking themselves more secure on the ship than in the boats, returned to their cabins.

Sir John Simon: Did you hear anyone say they were more secure on the Titanic? – The Witness: Yes. I heard two or three say they preferred to remain on the ship than to be tossed about on the water like a cockleshell.

WOULD NOT BE PERSUADED

He took about thirty women and children on the first visit to the boat deck, and had some difficulty in getting back to his people on account of the number of male passengers, who were trying to get to the boat deck. He succeeded in getting twenty-five more women and children, and took them to the only boat on the starboard side, No. 15. There was room in it, and the people were placed in it.

He himself got in from the boat deck. There were about seventy people in the boat, including thirteen or fourteen of the crew. All the passengers in his boat were third class. When he last left the

third-class quarters there were still passengers there.

Mr. Harbinson: On whose authority did you assure these people that the vessel was not hurt? – I did not do it on my own authority.

Mr. Harbinson: I put it to you that it was in consequence of this assurance of yours that some of the people refused to leave their berths? – It was not so. If you pay a little attention you will find that some people were taken to the boat deck.

Don't be impertinent. – I do not want to be impertinent.

Lord Mersey (to the witness): Did you see anyone keeping back the third-class passengers? – No, my lord.

WITNESS BREAKS DOWN

Robert Victor Pearcey, a third-class pantry hand, said that in response to an order by the chief third-class steward, "Assist all passengers to the boat deck," he helped to fasten on lifebelts, and pass the passengers along the alley way to the companion leading to the boat deck. When no more passengers came along, and he and other stewards who had been showing the way went themselves to the boat deck, he picked up two babies and was ordered by Mr. Murdoch, the chief officer, to get into a collapsible boat and take charge of the children.

"I saw the vessel go down," Pearcey continued, passing his handkerchief nervously over his forehead. "Her lights were burning to the last."

Here witness paused – apparently overcome by the recollection – and when pressed by Sir John Simon to describe fully the sinking of the steamer he made an attempt to illustrate his words by gestures with his hands.

"She went down this way," he said, and then added brokenly, "I'm a bit rough myself, and I cannot describe it."

Sit John came to his assistance, and Pearcey tried again: "She went down by the head – plunging forward – I saw her stern out of the water – the stern was upstanding – the keel was visible."

The pause between the sentences became more painful. Finally he broke down altogether with the words: "It upset me – I cannot describe it."

Edward Brown, a first-class steward, said he assisted in the lowering of several boats, including the portside collapsible, at which Mr. Ismay was helping.

Three or four women were waiting to get in another collapsible. By this time the bridge was under water.

Brown got into the collapsible, but was washed out. When he last saw the women they were struggling in the water. He could not swim, but was kept afloat by his lifebelt.

After being in the water a long time – "it seemed a lifetime" –

he encountered a black object, and found it was a half-submerged collapsible, in which were a number of men, crew and passengers.

He was taken on, and a man and a woman were picked up afterwards.

CAPTAIN'S LAST ORDER

Going back to the last incidents on the ship, the witness said Captain Smith passed with a megaphone while they were dealing with the collapsible, and said: "Well, boys, do the best for the women and children, and then look out for yourselves." He went on the bridge, and the ship sank a few minutes later.

The Solicitor-General then referred to the witnesses from No. 1 boat, with regard to which there was a special matter (the allegations concerning Sir Cosmo and Lady Duff-Gordon) to be cleared up. That would be dealt with separately and taken to-day.

Before the Court adjourned at 3.55 Sir Rufus Isaacs said that at the conclusion of Wheat's evidence this morning he would recall Henrickson, the man who was in charge of No. 1 boat.

COLLAPSIBLE'S TRAGIC FREIGHT

New York, May 16 – The reports brought by the Oceanic, which arrived here this morning, concerning the discovery of one of the Titanic's collapsible boats, containing three bodies, have excited some uneasy feelings regarding the fate of some of those who perished.

The three bodies found in the boat were those of men. One, a fireman, was chained by the leg to a thwart at one end of the boat. The two others were huddled together at the far end of the boat.

In their mouths were small pieces of cork, which Dr. R. S. French, of the Oceanic, believes they chewed in their delirium to ease the cravings of hunger and thirst. In the boat, besides the bodies, which were buried at sea, were found a fur coat, a man's hat and two wedding rings welded together. One body was apparently that of Thomas Beattie. The bodies were picked up in latitude 39.56, longitude 47.01. – Reuter.

FOR 'WIRELESS' FAME
Young England's Rush to Qualify as Ships' Operators.

ROMANCE IN SPARKS

Since the Titanic disaster and the heroic conduct of her two wireless operators there has been an unprecedented rush of young men anxious to become wireless telegraphy operators. Instead of wishing, in the old-fashioned way, to become sea-roving pirates, half the youth of the country now wants to learn the dot and dash of the Morse code.

DEMAND FOR OPERATORS
"We are receiving applications and inquiries from would-be students at the rate of about thirty a day."

This was the estimate of an official of the British School of Telegraphy, Limited, 179, Clapham-road, given to *The Daily Mirror* when discussing the effect of the loss of the Titanic on wireless telegraphy.

"At present there is ample room in the profession. It is one of the few callings not overcrowded, and we should be willing to enter about seventy fresh students at once. We can do with 150 before the year is out. We do not guarantee appointments, but there is no lack of work for qualified operators. In ten days recently we sent fifty-two students into the employ of the Marconi Company. Generally we have placed a hundred students a year, but already this year, owing to the Titanic lesson, we have over 100 appointments to our credit. All who have qualified for Government certificates from this school are in work.

"Harold Bride, of the Titanic, was one of our students, and so was Harold Cottam, of the Carpathia; Llewellyn Jones, of the Montrose, who sent the: 'It is Crippen without a doubt' message from that ship, and S. Coles, the wireless man of the Slavonia, were also former students. It takes forty-six weeks to turn out a capable operator. All we ask in students is intelligence; a previous knowledge of electricity is not essential. The full day course for a year costs thirty-five guineas; but for fifteen guineas a young man can, without interfering with his present work, take an evening course, three nights a week for forty-six weeks, and qualify as an operator."

£400 SALARY
"The starting wage of a junior operator on a liner is £1 a week and all found. An experienced senior operator can command £2 15s. a week and all found on a liner. There are plenty of good jobs to be picked up on land, too. We have one ex-student in an appointment worth £400 a year, and another making £26 a month.

"Students work for five hours a day. They have to learn the Morse code, how to form letters on the Morse key, to read Morse by sound, and to attend lectures. As soon as a student can 'send' at sixteen to eighteen words a minute he starts to 'talk' between this school and our new station at Norwood.

"Other stations are sometimes 'heard' and code messages sometimes picked up, but it is not likely that we should ever pick up an S.O.S. message. To receive that call a receiving station must be adjusted to take messages from the transmitting station."

STORY OF No. 1 LIFEBOAT TOLD BY THOSE WHO ESCAPED IN IT

Day of Dramatic Evidence Before Titanic Commission.

HELMSMAN'S STORY
Henrickson's Alleged Suggestion to Put Back Investigated.

LADY DUFF-GORDON ILL
Sir Cosmo Duff-Gordon Relates History of the £5 Notes.

From a public point of view yesterday's proceedings in the Titanic inquiry were the most dramatic since Lord Mersey's Commission opened.

The allegation of Henrickson, a fireman in the boat that carried Sir Cosmo and Lady Duff-Gordon from the ship, that the passengers discouraged a proposal to attempt to rescue the drowning, formed the basis of the inquiry.

There was an unprecedented crush, some hundreds of fashionably-dressed ladies attending in the hope of seeing Sir Cosmo and Lady Duff-Gordon in the witness-box. On the floor of the hall every seat was filled, and hundreds stood massed behind the chairs.

Henrickson, in his cross-examination, adhered to his story, though he admitted that Lady Duff-Gordon was ill on the boat.

Sir Cosmo Duff-Gordon related the story of his own and his wife's escape from the Titanic on No. 1 boat, and explained the circumstances of the £5 note presents to the members of the crew. He explained that he thought they were quite 1,000 yards from the liner when she sank, but, having only one eye, he might not be considered an expert judge of distance. He was still in the box at the adjournment.

HENRICKSON'S STORY
After the preliminaries had been disposed of Henrickson, the fireman, who was in No. 1 lifeboat, and whose allegations have provided one of the many sensations of the dramatic inquiry, stepped up again to the witness-table, and was cross-examined by Mr. H. E. Duke, K.C., who appeared for Sir Cosmo and Lady Duff-Gordon (Lucile):

As No. 1 lifeboat was being lowered Henrickson told him an officer, whom in the dark he did not recognise, asked him how many seamen there were in the ship:

Henrickson replied: "Two," and the officer then ordered some firemen to jump in. Five did so, and he was one of them.

Mr. Duke: Did you hear what he said about the ladies or passengers? – Yes, he said, "Is there any more ladies about?"

Henrickson said, he knew nothing of the circumstances in which Lady Duff-Gordon got in the boat, and the first time he saw her was when they were lowered.

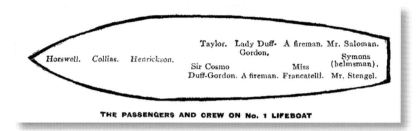

THE PASSENGERS AND CREW ON No. 1 LIFEBOAT

"The officer," he told Mr. Duke, "called out, 'Stand by and come back at call.' He called but the names of the crew in the boat, and said to Symons, the look-out, 'Now, you take command of this boat. These men are under your orders, and see that they obey.'"

"OUGHT TO HAVE GONE BACK."
They pulled around at a distance of 150 to 200 yards from the Titanic, and kept on pulling and resting a minute. They were just pulling about in the direction, of the other boats. Symons was in the stem of the boat, steering and doing his duty, in a very seamanlike way, throughout the night.

I understand you to say you have come to the conclusion that that boat ought to have gone back? – Yes.

When did you come to that conclusion? – When she sank, when we heard the cries, I said we ought to go back.

I understand your present impression is that the boat was prevented from going back by the action of Lady Duff-Gordon? – Yes, they protested against going back.

When did you first make that statement to anybody? – Last Thursday.

Did anybody take a statement in writing as to what you were able to say – a proof of your evidence? – Yes, but I never said anything about the Duff-Gordons until I got here.

When you were in the boat, you told the Court, you said, "It is up to us to go back." To whom did you say that? – To the men who were in the boat. I never said it to anyone personally – I called out.

Have you been a good deal badgered about this business first and last? – Everyone has been asking about the turn and that sort of thing.

Before you made that deposition on Thursday had you said to anybody that Sir Cosmo and Lady Duff-Gordon prevented that boat being put back? – No.

The man who should decide whether the boat should go back was Symons, was it not? – Yes.

Do you know whether Symons heard you? – I do not.

Was this a momentary impulse of yours? – I had heard the cries.

Did anyone reply? – I did not get any replies at all from the crew.

Do you consider they were right or wrong in not following the course which you suggested ought to be taken? – They were right one way and wrong another, I thought they were wrong.

Were you on the best possible terms with Sir Cosmo Duff-Gordon on the Carpathia? – Yes.

Had Sir Cosmo ever spoken to you before that? – Yes, he asked me if I wanted to smoke, and gave me a cigar.

What else did he say to you on the boat? – He said he would get our names and send wires to our friends if he could.

Did Sir Cosmo Duff-Gordon on the Carpathia say: "I am going to make a present of £5 each to the men who were in the boat to make up the loss of their kits"? – No.

These cheques were written and you got yours? – Yes.

Before you left the Carpathia did you and the other members of the boat crew – the small boat crew – write your names on Lady Duff-Gordon's lifebelt as a memento? – Yes.

And you parted with them on terms of respect? – Yes, we were asked to put our names on the belt.

Now, was not Lady Duff-Gordon all the time she was in the boat violently seasick and lying on one side of the boat? – She was.

Was not that her condition when the Titanic went down? – It may have been. I suggest that your statement that she took part in any conversation about the boat going back was a complete error? – I am speaking the truth. Lady Duff-Gordon lifted her head up and spoke now and again.

Mr. Duke put it that all that was said related to her physical condition and her husband's efforts to comfort her.

THE MAN AT THE HELM

A. B. George Symons, a sturdy, clean-shaven man, who wore mourning clothes, was then examined by the Attorney-General. He described the lowering of the boat under Mr. Murdoch's orders.

"Why," asked Lord Mersey, "was the boat lowered away when it was more than half empty?" – He gave me the order to lower away. I am not supposed to criticise an order.

I am not asking you to criticise anybody. I am asking to find out, if I can, why this boat should be lowered when it was more than half empty. – That I could not tell you. That was his own discretion, I suppose.

Symons said he saw rockets sent up, and he also saw, about five or ten miles off, a steamer having Morse lights.

The Attorney-General: You heard cries of persons in distress? – Yes. A decent few.

There was plenty of room in your boat, and if you could have reached any one of them you would have saved a life? – Yes; but I did not think at the time it was safe to go back.

You had ample room? – We could have taken about eight.

The boat's complement is forty? – If we had forty in the boat and the sea rose, it would sink.

But the sea was quite calm. You quite understood you were to go back if called? – Yes.

Did you determine you would not go back without consultation with anybody? – I used my own discretion; I was master of the situation. At the time I thought it was not safe to go back.

Lord Mersey: I want to know why. What was it you were afraid of? – I was not altogether afraid of anything. I was only afraid of endangering the lives of the people I had.

What was the danger; the ship had gone to the bottom at that time? – She had only just disappeared.

Never mind; it had disappeared and gone two miles down. What were you afraid of? – Of the swamping of the boat.

The Attorney-General: Was the question raised about your going back to the people who were shrieking? – None whatever.

"WAS IT NOT COWARDICE – ?"

Answering Lord Mersey, the witness said he was rather surprised that someone did not suggest going back. It seemed a reasonable thing for someone to suggest.

"Was it not cowardice that prevented the passengers and you going back?" asked Mr. Scanlan, M.P. (Seamen's and Firemen's Union), bluntly.

"No!" said Symons.

In reply to Mr. Clem. Edwards, he said he received the £5 in the shape of an order on a piece of paper, and had not changed it.

"Have you paid any money into a bank quite recently?" asked Mr. Edwards.

"That is not for me to answer."

Where is the order? – At home.

How much is the order for? – Five pounds.

You will swear that? – Yes, by Heaven above.

Have you received money from anybody else? – No, no one whatever.

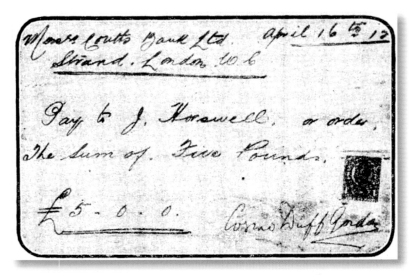

Symons told at length of an unknown gentleman who came to him at his home at Weymouth and interviewed him on the happenings in the boat, and some mystery, attached to the question until Mr. Duke, after the luncheon interval, explained that the gentleman was a solicitor acting on the instructions of a connection of the Duff-Gordons before the latter had arrived from America.

Symons was then examined by Mr. Duke, and asserted that from first to last no one had tried in any way to interfere with his judgment.

It is suggested by gentlemen who were not there that you were afraid to go back? – I was not afraid at all. I knew it was not safe to go back at the time.

Did Sir Cosmo Duff-Gordon or anybody in the boat interfere at all with your making up your mind about that? – None.

Mr. Duke: With regard to the money. When was the first time you heard any suggestion that anybody would get anything from Sir Cosmo Duff-Gordon? – The second day before we got to New York.

While you were in New York were newspapers full of scandalous stories of people who had been on board this boat and whose lives were saved? – Yes, and scandalous reports about myself.

Was there any truth in them? – None whatever.

Is this the only story of this kind set on foot? – About cowardice and money, that was the only story in the papers.

Were you aware of any inducement held out to anyone to take any particular person in that boat? – None whatever. I simply obeyed my orders.

WAS WILLING TO GO BACK

Fireman Taylor, the next witness from No. 1 boat, said he heard a suggestion that they should go back. One of the ladies in the boat, however, according to this witness, said it would be dangerous, and two of the men passengers in the boat agreed with her. Replying to the Solicitor-General, he said Sir Cosmo Duff-Gordon, who was sitting on the same thwart with him, took no part in this conversation.

What was done at this time? – The order was given to row away on our oars. Symons, the cox, gave that order.

Did you or did you not follow the suggestion to return to the place where the ship had sunk? – I was willing if anyone else was.

Witness said everybody in the boat could hear the cries of the drowning when the Titanic sank.

Did your boat ever get within reach of any one of the drowning people? – No.

How much room was there in this boat? How many people could you have taken in? – Twenty-five to thirty in addition to those who were in it already.

Since he had been in this country he had been interviewed by somebody, who said he came on behalf of Sir Duff-Gordon.

Mr. Cotter (for the Stewards' Union): Was any statement made to you at the time you received the £5 present on the Carpathia? – No; he just said: "This is a little present from me." That is all I heard. That was three or four days after.

When they left the Titanic it was a calm sea, and the boat did not rock. The lady whom, he since understood to be Lady Duff-Gordon was seasick.

Was that the lady who objected to going back? The lady who spoke of the boat being swamped? – Yes.

Mr. Duke: Did you have any conversation with Lady Duff-Gordon? – No.

What makes you say she was the lady who spoke? – I did not say so. I was given to understand afterwards that she was the lady.

Are you sure it was a lady in front of you who spoke about the boat being swamped? – Yes.

Was not the lady in front of you seasick for most of the time when the sailors were on their oars? – Yes.

"AN INHUMAN THING."

J. Horswell, the second seaman ordered into boat No. 1 by Mr. Murdoch, said he heard no suggestion either that they should go back or that it would be dangerous to do so.

Mr. Scanlan: Would it have been quite a safe thing to go back and take some of the people in? – Yes, sir.

Would it not have been a proper thing to do? – It would have been the proper thing to do, but I had to obey the order of the coxswain of the boat.

You must have been greatly touched when you heard the cry of those poor creatures. Did you suppress your feelings and say nothing? – Yes.

Don't you think it was an inhuman thing to leave them to perish? – It was an inhuman thing.

Why did you not say so to the passengers? – I had to obey the order of the coxswain.

The President: You won't get away from that, Mr. Scanlan.

SIR C. DUFF-GORDON'S EVIDENCE
Sir Cosmo Duff-Gordon Recounts Dialogue with Sailor.

"ONE CONFUSED WAIL."
Thought All Women Were Off Titanic Before They Left.

Sir Cosmo Duff-Gordon was the last witness of the day, and was still giving evidence when the Court adjourned at 4.10 until Monday. He was the first civilian to appear before the Court, and his well-groomed appearance, as he leant his hands on the table and replied to the Attorney-General, presented a noticeable contrast with the seafaring mien of the witnesses who had preceded. At the time of the collision he was asleep, later he got up and went on the boat deck, there was a dreadful noise of steam escaping.

"A man I spoke to," he went on, "told me there was no danger. It was Colonel Astor. He went down with the ship.

"I went down to tell my wife to dress, and began to dress myself. Miss Francatelli, my wife's secretary, joined us in the cabin, and we went up to the boat deck on the starboard side.

"While three of the lifeboats were being lowered my wife and Miss Francatelli were standing on the deck. They refused to go. My wife refused to leave me and to go in the boat. They stood by while the boats were going.

Your wife and Miss Francatelli were asked to go in the boats? – They were asked two or three times.

Did anyone attempt to place your wife into one of the lifeboats? – Yes. I think it was No. 3. Some men got hold of her and tried to pull her away, but she would not go.

Was the part of the deck where you were standing at this time when you saw the first lifeboat go down clear or full of passengers? – When the first boat had been launched I think everyone had disappeared.

He heard orders given with reference to No. 1 boat, and after a time spoke to the officer and said, "May we get in that boat?" and he said, "Yes, I wish you would," or "Very glad if you would," or some expression like that. There were no other passengers at all.

THOUGHT ALL WOMEN WERE OFF
When the boat was lowered did you think the Titanic was in danger? – I thought it was in a very grave condition.

You noticed there was room for more passengers in that boat? – There would have been more if the oars and masts had been thrown away.

Can you give us any explanation of why it was that this boat was lowered away with so few people in it when there were so many people left on the ship who were in danger? – There were no people visible, I am quite sure of that.

I should like to understand, if I can, what your view was about this. Did you think there was anybody left on the ship at this time? – No, but I thought, certainly, that all the women had got off. I had seen all the women in my particular part of the ship get off. I knew that in all other parts of the ship they were lowering boats.

How far do you think your boat had gone before the Titanic went down? – I have always said 1,000 yards when I told anybody. It is true I have only one eye, and am, therefore, presumed not to be a judge of distance.

Did you hear a cry? – I heard the explosion first and then I heard, I could not say a cry, a wail – one confused sound.

HEARD NO SUGGESTION TO RETURN
They were the cries of persons drowning. There is no doubt about that? – Yes, I think so.

Did it occur to you that there was room in the boat, and that if you could get to the people you could save some? – It is difficult to say what occurred, I was minding my wife, and the conditions were abnormal, as you know, and there were many things to think about. It might well have occurred to one that they could have been saved by a boat.

And that there was room in your boat? – I do think it was possible.

Did you hear a suggestion made that the boat should go back to where the cries came from? – No, I did not.

You never heard that at all? – I heard no suggestion at all.

Did not you think about whether or not your boat would be able to save people in the water? – I do not know. It might have been possible, but it would be very difficult to get back the distance we were away in that darkness.

Do you mean you did not think about whether or not the boat could save some of the people? – I was not thinking about it at that time. I was attending to my wife. Of course, it was rather serious for her.

Did you hear one of the ladies say anything about the danger of being swamped? – No, I did not.

No thought entered your mind at the time that you ought to go back and try to save some of those people? – No, I suppose not.

The President: A witness said it would have been quite safe to have gone back. What do you say? – I do not know, my lord, whether it would have been safe. I think it would have been hardly possible.

Were not the men rowing when you heard the cries? – At the moment the Titanic sank of course everything stopped.

And you heard the cries until the men resumed rowing? – Yes, which was very soon.

We have heard from two witnesses that the suggestion was made that your boat should go back and try to save some of the people. You have been in court when at least one of those witnesses was giving evidence. What do you say about it? – I did not hear any suggestion. That is all I can say.

It is further said that one of the ladies identified by the last witness as your wife was afraid to go back because she thought the boat would be swamped? – I know.

That was heard by a witness on the same thwart as you were? – Yes.

Did you hear your wife say that? – No.

Or any person? – No.

Do you mean it might have happened, but that you do not remember anything about it, or do you mean it did not take place? – In my opinion it did not take place.

And did you hear either of the other men say that if they did go back there was a danger that the boat would be swamped? – I did not hear it, I do not think there was any conversation of the sort.

As far as you are concerned, as I understand your statement, nothing was done at all? – No.

You know now, don't you, that you might have saved a good many people? – I do not know that.

Did you make a promise of a present to the men in the boat? – I did.

CONVERSATION WITH SEAMAN

When? – There was a man sitting next to me in the boat. I could not see him, and I do not know yet who he is. I suppose it would be some time when they were resting their oars, twenty minutes or half an hour after the Titanic had gone down. This dialogue occurred:–

Man: I suppose you have lost everything.

Myself: Of course.

Man: You can get some more?

Myself: Yes.

Man: We have lost all our kit and they won't give us any more, and what is more our pay will be stopped from to-night, and all they will do will be to send us back to London.

Myself: You need not worry about that. I will give a fiver to start a new kit.

That is all there was said about the £5. I said that to one of them, and I don't know who yet.

And when you got on the Carpathia? – There was a little hitch in getting one of the men up the ladders, and Henrickson took up my coat, which I had thrown in the bottom of the boat, and I asked him to give me the men's names. This I believe is his writing.

Lord Mersey (looking at slip of paper): It is merely a list of names? – Yes.

Did you say anything to the captain of the Carpathia about your intention? – I went to see him one afternoon and told him I had promised the crew of my boat a £5 note each. He said it was quite unnecessary, but I said I had promised and had got to give it.

"LUCILE" – DRESS ARTIST

⇒ There was a largely increased attendance of the public at the Titanic inquiry yesterday.

Lady Duff-Gordon, who writes her Christian name Lucie, is a daughter of the late Mr. Douglas Sutherland, of Toronto. Before her

marriage with Sir Cosmo in 1900 she was Mrs. Wallace, and she is a sister of the successful novelist, Mrs. Elinor Clayton Glyn.

She is a pretty, smart woman, quite Parisian in appearance, and is one of the society women who have made decided successes in business. Under the now familiar, name of "Lucile," and with little but her own cleverness to go upon, Lady Duff-Gordon (she was then Mrs. Wallace) founded one of the most celebrated dressmaking businesses in London.

But the business was not always the great success it is to-day. There was a time when there was a stern fight. For Lady Duff-Gordon had to do something of necessity when she thought of turning dressmaking to account.

HOW SHE STARTED BUSINESS

"One morning," she said, in telling the story last year, "I found myself without a shilling, and with a little daughter dependent on me. It then became of urgent necessity that I should do something for myself and for my little daughter. I knew that if I had a talent it was for designing dresses, so, encouraged by a few friends, I started business as 'Madame Lucile.'

"That was fifteen years ago. I was quite alone in a little room in Davies-street, and there I cut out on the floor for want of a proper table, and did all the sewing and everything myself, often working from five in the morning until midnight. Ladies who came to see me often found me cutting out patterns on the floor. Now I have my London house, with 300 girls; my New York one with as many; and I am about to start a place on a similar scale in Paris for the making of my models." (This has since been opened.)

To Lady Duff-Gordon is ascribed the invention of the "emotional" gown. She designs and creates, and she gives to many of them designations to accord with their colouring and design.

"Herb Moon" for example, was a wonderful evening dress, of which the under-dress of bronze satin shimmered through floating draperies of purple chiffon, with gorgeous silver and gold embroideries. "Beacon Fires," "Cornfield," "Apple Orchard," "Dawn of a Happier Day," and "Vain Regret" were also descriptive names given to artistic toilettes.

DOLLS' DRESSMAKER AS CHILD

In explanation of these names Lady Duff-Gordon has said: "My ideas come on the inspiration of the moment. I may think of a word or a phrase, or a line of poetry, and instantly I see the word or phrase take form and colour before my eyes. That is why we give our gowns names."

The art of dressmaking was apparently born with Lady Duff-Gordon, for she says that even when she was a little child her greatest joy was to design and make beautiful gowns for dolls.

"In our games I was always the dolls' dressmaker, receiving as payment rose-drops and monkey-nuts. It was more than a mere childish hobby; it was for me a passion for creating beautiful effects in form and beautiful combinations of colour."

21 May 1912

HOW LADY DUFF-GORDON WAS PITCHED INTO LIFEBOAT No. 1

Further Dramatic Evidence Before Titanic Commission.

SIR COSMO'S STORY
Public Applaud Lord Mersey's Rebuke of Counsel.

"UNFAIR QUESTIONS."
Conversation with Henrickson on Carpathia About £5 Cheques. So pointed were the unsupported imputations made against Sir Cosmo and Lady Duff-Gordon at the Titanic inquiry yesterday that Lord Mersey had more than once to reprove cross-examining counsel.

Both "Lucile" and her husband appeared in the witness-box – Mr. Duke, K.C., their counsel, insisted on calling Lady Duff-Gordon, despite the President's expressed hope that it would not be necessary. Her position, he said, had been made intolerable by the insinuations made against her.

The sum of the allegations against Sir Cosmo and Lady Duff-Gordon is that:

(1) They interposed to prevent No. 1 lifeboat from putting back to the rescue of the drowning;

(2) Sir Cosmo offered members of the crew a £5 note each if they would pull away from the Titanic.

No. 1 lifeboat contained twelve persons in all, namely:–

Crew	Passengers
Symons (in charge)	Lady Duff-Gordon
Taylor	Miss Francatelli
Horswell	Sir Cosmo Duff-Gordon
Collins	Mr. Salomon
Henrickson	Mr. Stengel
Pusey and another.	

It was the story told by Henrickson that formed the basis of the allegations against the Duff-Gordons. He said that he suggested that they should row back to pick up the drowning but that Lady Duff-Gordon, supported by her husband, protested against such a course.

There was a very large gathering of spectators – ladies predominating – when Lord Mersey and his assessors took their seats yesterday morning.

Prince Albert of Schleswig-Holstein and Prince Leopold of Battenberg were among the well-known members of the audience.

SIR COSMO'S EVIDENCE

Sir Cosmo Duff-Gordon immediately took his place as a witness on the inquiry being resumed yesterday morning, and was cross-examined by the Attorney-General. Bending his head forward and resting his hand on the little table, with its carafe of water, and glass in front of him, he listened closely to every word that fell from the lips of his questioner.

"I notice," began Sir Rufus, "that you said in your evidence that there was this conversation between you and the men or one of the men – that you would give them a present of £5 each. Was that made quite early in the history of this boat? Was it before or after the boats had gone back to try to pick up people?"

"I did not know about the boat going back," replied Sir Cosmo.

According to you, then, the boat never went back? – No; I did not know where we were rowing.

Was there no attempt made, so far as you were concerned, to go back and pick up the people? – I did not know that the idea had arisen.

Mr. Scanlan (for the Seamen's and Firemen's Union): Did you hear the order given when other boats were being lowered on the starboard side that women and children were to be first? – I did not know whether I heard the order, but I knew it was the order.

And that the women and children were getting in in large numbers? – In large numbers, yes.

That rule with regard to women and children was observed with regard to all boats launched on the starboard side with the exception of the boat you were in? – No, the boat launched before that one had a few women and was filled up with men.

REQUEST OF THE OFFICER

The boat you were in was clearly an exception to the rule? – No, no exception at all. The women present had all gone into the three lifeboats.

Could you see if there were any women on the port side? – No, I could not see on the port side.

The officer in charge of the boat allowed you to enter? – I said to him, "Can we go there?"

That was a request, of course? The ladies were invited? – The ladies were not invited. They had been invited to go in two or three lifeboats, but they refused to go absolutely. Then, when all the women visible had disembarked, this boat was being manned by some stokers, and I spoke to the officer.

That request of yours applied to yourself? – I did not consider it a request at all. I merely saw the empty boat, and I was with two ladies, and I said: "Can we go there?" Could you see from that position close to one boat whether there were passengers along the boat deck at the other end? – No, my impression was there were no passengers so far as I could see.

You stated, in giving your evidence on Friday, that all the women from your part of the ship, had gone. Did you mean the women who were first-class passengers? – I do not know what class passengers they were.

You do not know whether there were other women on the boat-deck on the opposite side, fore or aft, who were waiting to be taken off? – No.

Under those circumstances, you asked permission for yourself to go?

The President: That is not quite correct. He asked if he might go. You are drawing a wrong distinction.

Mr. Scanlan: Very well. (To witness): Do you recollect who was the officer who was in charge of the launch of No. 1 lifeboat? – I did not know until a few days ago.

EMERGENCY BOAT, NOT LIFEBOAT

Mr. Duke: This was an emergency boat, not a lifeboat. If he will persist in calling it, for his own purposes, a lifeboat, I must protest.

The President: I do not think Mr. Scanlan has been unfair so far.

Mr. Scanlan asked the witness if he knew the name of the officer in charge of the launch, and he said he believed, from what he had since learnt, that he was the fifth officer, Mr. Lowe.

Mr. Lowe was requested to rise in court, but Sir Cosmo could not identify him, saying it was dark and he could not see his face clearly.

Mr. Scanlan: Did you hear that officer say: "Are you ready, Lady Duff-Gordon?" – No.

Did you have any conversation with the officer? – No.

Mr. Scanlan then proceeded to ask Sir Cosmo questions relating to certain statements contained in an article which appeared above the signature of Lady Duff-Gordon.

Mr. Duke said he proposed to call Lady Duff-Gordon.

The President: I was in hopes, Mr. Duke, that we should not have to call her.

Mr. Duke: I think your Lordship must.

DID NOT THINK ANYTHING

The President: If the lady desires to go into the witness-box she must go.

Mr. Duke: The position in which she is put by some of the insinuations that have been made is intolerable to a woman who believes that she has done what she ought to have done.

Mr. Scanlan proceeded to put questions about the cries of the drowning to the witness, when the President asked him not to depart from the point he had raised.

Mr. Scanlan: Is this your evidence, Sir Cosmo – that while the cries of the drowning people were heard there was no conversation whatever between you and your fellow-passengers or between you and the members of the crew? – I said that after the Titanic sank there was a dead silence.

When the people were crying out for help, were you all mute in the boat? – The men began to row at once. I did not know which way.

You made the suggestion in your evidence as a reason for not taking any more people into the boat that there would have been more room if the oars and sails had been put away? – Yes.

As a practical man, you knew it would be very easy to put the oars and sails out of the boat? – As a practical man I must say I did not think anything about it.

Questions were then put to witness by Mr. Harbinson, representing third-class passengers, who asked Sir Cosmo if the conversation in reference to the present took place about twenty minutes after the Titanic sank.

The President told Mr. Harbinson that he was not assisting the Court at getting at the truth. By trying to make out a case against one person or another he did not help him a bit.

Mr. Harbinson: Did you hear cries after the Titanic sank? – I cannot say.

Mr. Harbinson: Did you tell them to row to drown the cries?

LORD MERSEY AND FAIRPLAY

Mr. Duke: I appeal to your Lordship with regard to that class of question. The learned gentleman asks, Did you appeal to them to drown the cries? According to the practice of the Bar, unless you have evidence which will support a gross imputation, you do not make it by a question.

The President: Yes, Mr. Duke, but the ordinary rules of practice do not always apply. Perhaps they ought to, but they don't.

Mr. Duke: I am aware that your Lordship has not the same control over the thing as a Judge in Court.

The President: Never mind. I will do my best to see that the thing is fair.

Mr. Harbinson (to witness): Would it not have been more in harmony with the traditions of seamanship that that should have been the time to suggest to the sailors to have gone to try if they could have rescued anyone? – The possibility of being able to help anybody never occurred to me at all.

That is to say you considered when you were safe yourself all the others might perish? – No; that is not the way to put it.

The President: Do you think a question of that kind fair to the witness? The witness' position is bad enough. Do you think it is fair to put a question of that kind to him? I do not.

Mr. Harbinson: If your Lordship says so, I won't pursue that any further. (Considerable applause from the gallery greeted this decision.)

Proceeding, Mr. Harbinson said: Did you hear a lady in the boat make any protest against the boat going back? – No.

Was a suggestion actually made as to the direction the boat should go? – No; I cannot say there was a suggestion. Someone said: "There was a light there, or there is a light there. Let us go to that."

Was this a man in the bow? – No.

Where was he sitting? – He was sitting two seats in front of me in the seat next to the stern, sitting with his back to the stern. [Henrickson, Taylor, Collins and Horswell were none of them in front of Sir Cosmo Duff-Gordon.]

Was any reply made to that man when he suggested to go in any particular direction? – No.

You made no answer to him? – It was going on all night. It was not that it was said once.

Was it in answer, to this suggestion of his as to the direction in which the boat should go that you said: "I will give you a fiver"? – I really do not understand your question. You must put it plainer.

My question is this – that you heard this observation as to the direction the emergency boat should go. Was it then, twenty minutes after the Titanic sank, that you suggested you should give them a fiver? – No, I see your meaning now. The men calling out had no effect whatever.

The President: If you put your question plainer it would be understood, better. Your question really is this – "Did you promise £5 in order to induce the men in the boat to row away from the drowning people?" That is what you meant to ask.

Mr. Harbinson: That is the effect of it.

The President: Why did you not put it in plainer words?

At this rebuke there was more applause in court, during which Mr. Harbinson sat down.

SYMONS' STATEMENT DENIED

Mr. Clem Edwards, M.P. (for the Dockers' Union): Can you explain why Symons, the captain of your boat, states that just before the boat was lowered the two ladies rushed from the saloon deck by themselves and asked if they could get into the boat, and that then you and two other male passengers rushed up and also asked if you could get in? – No, that is quite incorrect, the whole thing.

When the Titanic had gone down, you were so absorbed in paying attention to your wife that you could not think whether you should go back to the drowning people or not? – Well, if you put it like that.

Do you still think it was natural not to think about going back and saving some of those people? – I think it was natural, but I concede it would have been a splendid thing if it could have been done.

Mr. Duke then questioned Sir Cosmo.

"There were many stories," he remarked, "published in the American newspapers. Did they report interviews with Lady Duff-Gordon?" – Yes.

Do you know whether those interviews had taken place or not? – They had not.

It is suggested that there was some arrangement between the captain and Mr. Ismay and you by which a boat was put at your service. Is there a scrap of foundation for that? – No.

Was there a distinct locality from which you could judge the cries were coming or not? – I think not.

Up to the time when you had a conversation with the man who was beside you about his kit, had there been any suggestion from anybody as to what should be done with the boat? – No.

CHEQUES AND A PHOTOGRAPH

Or where she should row? – No suggestion at all.

At the suggestion of Lord Mersey, Mr. Duke then questioned Sir Cosmo about the giving of the £5 cheques on board the Carpathia and elicited the following account of the incident:–

When Henrickson and I were on the Carpathia I said: "I will see that you will get some money in a few days or give you a cheque shortly." The next day he brought himself to my notice. He had given me the list of names earlier.

Before we reached New York Miss Francatelli wrote out a form of cheque for each person on the list. I went on to the boat deck and saw Henrickson, and told him to get the men together. When they were all together I handed them the cheques, asking each what his name was.

After the cheques were given a man we had met before came up and photographed the crew, and one or two of the passengers snapshotted them. Henrickson put on his lifebelt for the purpose of being photographed.

That photograph was reproduced, and underneath was written: "The group includes Mrs. Astor." That was quite a mistake.

Mr. Duke then questioned Sir Cosmo concerning one of the American passengers in the boat who was constantly calling out, "Boat ahoy!" and "We ought to go (this way or that)."

Nobody, said witness, took any notice of these exclamations, and they had not the least effect on the course of the boat, nor did anything else that was said by anyone.

"REFUSED TO GO."

Her Mind Quite Made Up That She Was Going To Be Drowned.

Lady Duff-Gordon, as the creator of London fashion, was the cynosure of every feminine eye when she followed her husband on the witness stand and even at such a moment as that the minutest details of her dress did not escape the observation of the fashionably-dressed women in the hall.

Eager eyes absorbed the fact that she was wearing a costume of navy blue set off by a low lace collar, a jabot and white lace frills at the wrists. Her black hat was covered by a black veil, and the glove that she removed when she took the Testament in her right hand was white. In a clear, emphatic voice, in contrast with the customary gabble in an undertone, she took the oath to speak the truth and nothing but the truth.

"I only want you to tell me one thing before we get to the boat," said Sir Rufus Isaacs to his first woman-witness since the inquiry opened. "Had there been offers to you to go into any of the lifeboats?"

"Oh, yes," was the reply; "they rather tried to bring me away – the sailors. I was holding my husband's arm and they were very anxious that I should go."

And you refused to go? – Absolutely.

"After three boats had gone down," she went on in reply to Sir Rufus, "my husband and myself and Miss Francatelli were left standing on the deck. There were no other people on the deck, at all visible, and I quite made up my mind that I was going to be drowned.

"PITCHED INTO THE BOAT."

"Then suddenly we saw this little boat in front of us – this little thing" – pointing to its model on the Titanic model at her elbow – and we

saw some sailors and an officer apparently giving them orders.

"I said to my husband: 'Ought we not to be doing something?' He said: 'Oh, we must wait for orders.' We stood there quite some time while the men were fixing up things.

"Then my husband went forward and said: 'Might we get into this boat?' and the officer said, in a very polite way: 'Oh, certainly, do; I will be very pleased.'

"Somebody hitched me up from the back and pitched me into the boat, and I think Miss Francatelli was pitched in, and then my husband was pitched in.

"It was not a case of getting in at all, it was too high. They pitched us in this way into the boat. (Lady Gordon illustrated the method used to get her into the boat by placing her hand under her shoulders.)

"Then two American gentlemen got pitched in; one of the American gentlemen got pitched in while the boat was being lowered down."

"I WAS TERRIBLY SICK."

"The moment we touched the water the men began rowing. I heard orders given, as far as I can remember, 'You will row away from the boat about 200 yards.'"

As far as you know, all they had to do was to row out 200 yards? – Yes.

Did the men start doing that? – At once.

And did you hear any conversation at all in the boat before the Titanic sank? – No.

Let me ask you again. I am speaking now of before the Titanic sank. You understand me? What I am asking you is, before she sank did you hear men saying anything in the boat? – No.

Did you hear anything said about suction? – Perhaps I may have heard it, but I was terribly sick and I could not swear to it.

I am asking you something that I only know from the statement you made to your solicitor. Did you hear voices saying: "Let us get away"? – Yes, that is so.

HEARD TERRIBLE CRIES

Did you hear it said: "Such an enormous boat – none of us know what the suction may be if she is a goner?" – I remember something about the enormous boat and the word "suction." That was, I am sure, long before the Titanic sank.

After the Titanic sank you still continued to be seasick? – Yes, terribly.

Can you recollect very well what happened when you were in the boat? – No.

Your mind was hazy? – Yes, very.

Did you hear after the Titanic sank the cries of people who were drowning? – No, after the Titanic sank I never heard a cry. Before she sank – terrible cries.

Were your men rowing? – They began to row as soon as the boat went down.

Did you hear a proposal made that you could go back to where the Titanic had sunk? – No.

Did you hear anybody shout out in the boat that you ought to go back with the object of saving people who were on the Titanic? – No.

You knew there were people in the Titanic, didn't you? – No, I was thinking nothing about it. Did you say it might be dangerous to go back – you might get swamped? – No.

Sir Rufus Isaacs now sat down, and Mr. Clem Edwards questioned Lucile concerning an article that appeared over her signature in the *Daily News* on April 20.

She denied having written it, and explained that a man wrote it from what he thought he heard her say. Quantities of people came to interview her, she told Lord Mersey.

"QUITE UNTRUE."

This particular man, the *Daily News* man? – No, he did not. He was a friend who was having supper with us the night he arrived.

Are you looking at it now, Lady Duff-Gordon for the first time? – The first time. The last little bit here is also absolutely a story.

Mr. Edwards: Then if your signature appears there, it is a forgery, is it? – Absolutely. You say that a friend came and had supper with you. You suggest that he is responsible for what appears here? – I know he is.

Some of it may be true and some of it may be false? – Would you like me to tell the story?

I should like you to answer my question, Lady Duff-Gordon. Is this true that you watched women and children and some men climbing into a lifeboat and heard an officer say, "Lady Gordon, are you ready?" – It is not true that the officer spoke to me, but I did see women and children carried into the lifeboats.

Mr. Edwards read a number of passages from the article, on which Lady Duff-Gordon's comments were "quite untrue," "an absolute invention," "not true," "I never said that," and similar phrases.

The President: Tell me, Lady Duff-Gordon, who was the gentleman? – He was the editor of the *Sunday American*.

Mr. Lewis: Do you ever write in American papers at all? – Yes, the *Sunday American*.

And the *Los Angeles Evening Herald*? – No.

PUT INTO WORDS BY REPORTER

Mr. Duke: When you were at New York; you went to an hotel, and that evening you dined with your husband? – And several people – six ladies.

Did Mr. Merritt come there? Was he the gentleman you had known? – A great many times.

Had you any idea of any publication of anything of that kind. What did he say to you? – After he had left us half an hour he telephoned to me and said: "Mr. Hearst has just rung me up, and must have your story of the Titanic for to-morrow morning's newspaper. May I tell your story as I have heard it?"

What did you say? – I said yes; and he told me afterwards that he telephoned to their head office all he knew about it, and then a clever reporter put all that into words and it appeared next morning in the *New York American*.

Your friend told a clever American reporter to put it into words, and you were advertised as having written and signed this false article. Was that published in various papers? – All over everywhere.

You had not seen this in the *Daily News* until when? – Just now.

This concluded Lady Duff-Gordon's examination.

LOST HER NIGHTDRESS

Samuel Collins, a fireman, stated that nothing was said in the boat about going back in the direction of the cries in the water. After the liner had sunk the coxswain brought the boat round, and it must have been pulled towards the spot where the Titanic had disappeared.

Did you hear any cries in the water? – Yes.

Did Henrickson propose going back in the direction of these cries? – No one proposed it at all.

Did Henrickson say anything? – Not so far as I know of. He was sitting close to me. I should have heard him. Somebody – one of the crew – passed the word to pull away from the boat to keep away from the suction.

"When we saw the boat sinking," said Collins, "that is a thing I do not wish to explain to you or give you any idea of it. We pulled away a little way, and the coxswain steered the boat round, and we must have pulled in the direction of where the ship sank."

Where the cries had been? – Oh, yes. They continued for about ten minutes.

"THE BOAT WENT BACK"

Your evidence is that the boat went back with the object of trying to save lives? – We did our level best. That is quite right.

Collins stated emphatically that he heard nothing in the boat about money, nothing till they were on board the Carpathia.

Frederick Shee, a trimmer, who helped to man the emergency boat, said that after the ship had gone down the boat rowed back to the other boats.

"The boat went back," questioned Sir John Simon. "Do you mean to where the Titanic sank?" – I cannot say. I am not a navigator.

Robert William Pusey, a fireman, said he did not think anybody suggested they should row in the direction of the cries or that they did row back.

He remembered a conversation about money.

"I will tell you," he said, "how it came about.

"I heard Lady Duff-Gordon say: 'There is my beautiful nightdress gone,' and I said: 'Never mind about your nightdress as long as you have got your life.'

"Then a man said: 'We have lost our kit and our pay will be stopped'; and then it was that the promise was made to give £5 each for a new kit."

This was at about 3 a.m. when everything was quiet. Everybody, he pointed out to Lord Mersey, had been in a dazed state of mind.

SECOND OFFICER AND ICE

The evidence concerning lifeboat No. 1 having concluded and Sir Cosmo and Lady Duff-Gordon having left the court, more evidence was taken from Titanic stewards and stewardesses.

Then came Mr. Lightoller, the tall, clean-shaven second officer, who told of the warnings of ice and the speed of the Titanic – 21½ knots – just before the disaster.

He gave some interesting particulars concerning the sighting of bergs. A slight swell or breeze always make visible a phosphorescent line round a berg. All ice more or less has a crystallised side, which reflects light – what is termed "ice blink."

On this night for the first time in twenty-four hours at sea he saw an absolutely flat sea – neither breeze nor swell.

Speaking of the fall in the temperature recorded on the night of the disaster, he suggested that it did not indicate anything.

The President: Is it not a fact that when you are approaching large bodies of ice the temperature falls? – Never in my experience, my Lord.

Mr. Lightoller said that Captain Smith came on the bridge shortly before nine o'clock and he had a conversation, with him, the incidents of which, as far as he could remember, were as follow:–

He said it was cold. I said, "Yes, very cold, sir: in fact, it is only one degree above freezing. I have sent word down to the carpenter and along to the engine-room and told them it is freezing, or will be

during the night." We then commenced to speak about the weather. He said, "There is not much wind." I said, "No, it is flat calm, as a matter of fact."

We went on to discuss the weather. He said: "It is perfectly clear," and I said: "Oh, yes." At that time you could see the stars setting with perfect distinctness on the horizon.

We then discussed the indications of ice. I remember saying there would probably be in any case a certain amount of reflected light from the berg. He said: "Oh, yes; there will be a certain amount of reflected light."

Replying to further questions, he admitted that he sent a message to the crow's nest shortly after the captain had left him, telling the men to keep a sharp look-out for ice, especially growlers.

TURNED IN AGAIN

When a liner is known to be approaching ice is it, or is it not, in your experience usual to reduce speed? – I have never known speed to be reduced in any ship I have ever been in in the North Atlantic in clear weather on account of ice. After handing the ship over to Mr. Murdoch, he looked around the deck to see that all was right and then turned in. At the time of the impact with the iceberg he felt a jar and a grinding sound.

"I lay there for a few minutes; then, feeling that the engines had stopped, I got up. I went out on to the boat deck, on the port side, where my room is.

"I then crossed over to the starboard side and looked out of the door. Everything seemed to be all right there.

"I could see the commander standing on the bridge. It was pretty quiet, so I went back to my bunk and turned in again. I remained there for about half an hour, but did not go to sleep.

"I wrapped myself up in my rug and waited for someone to call me if they wanted me.

"By and by Mr. Boxall came in and said quietly: 'Do you know we have struck an iceberg?' I said: 'Yes, I know we have struck something.' He then said: 'The water is up to F deck in the mail-room."

The inquiry was adjourned until to-day.

PHOTOGRAPH OF TITANIC SURVIVORS CLEARS UP A MYSTERY

The right photograph was produced by Mr. Duke, K.C., at the Titanic inquiry yesterday to prove that Mrs. Astor was not in the boat in which Sir Cosmo

Duff-Gordon and Lady Gordon left the Titanic. This picture of survivors was taken on board, the Carpathia, and it was erroneously stated that the lady wearing a fur coat was Mrs. Astor. As a matter of fact, she is Lady Duff-Gordon, and the other lady is her secretary, Miss Francatelli. Sir Cosmo had already stated that Mrs. Astor was not in the boat.

TITANIC BAND HEROES

Massed Orchestra of 500 Musicians at Albert Hall Memorial Concert.

One of the most interesting events of the week is the impressive memorial concert at the Albert Hall next Friday afternoon in honour of the Titanic Band, who went down with the ship, playing, to the last.

A massed orchestra, the biggest combination of instrumentalists which has ever appeared in public, consisting of the seven chief London orchestras combined, is uniting to do honour to their fellows.

During the singing of the hymn "Nearer, My God, to Thee," specially orchestrated by Sir Henry Wood, who will conduct, Sir Henry will turn his back on the 500 musicians after the first four bars, and will lead the vast audience through the now historic verses of the hymn.

Tickets, from 1s. 6d. to 12s. 6d., may be obtained from Mr. R. F. McConnell, 10, Newman-street, Oxford-street, and the usual agents.

THE ADVENTURE OF MR. LIGHTOLLER

Second Officer's Plain Story of Titanic's Sinking.

CAPSIZED ICEBERG

No Moon, No Breeze and an Absolutely Calm Sea.

UNIQUE CONDITIONS

More valuable perhaps than any evidence that preceded it was that of Second Officer Lightoller, of the Titanic, before Lord Mersey's Commission yesterday.

It was the plain, concise, harmonious story of an experienced navigator that the officer unfolded, and though in many places it was at variance with the story told by many survivors, as one listened to the practised mariner one could see through his eyes all that befell. His story came first, unfolded with the skilful aid of the Solicitor-General's facile questionings before an audience greatly thinned since the previous day.

Mr. Lightoller was assisting in the launching of the boats on the port side. He said that No. 4 had gone, and he was at No. 6 before he noticed any list.

It was suggested to Mr. Lightoller that the period that elapsed was an hour and a quarter, but he declined to commit himself definitely. "All I can say," he said, "was that I first noticed the list when I was at No. 6."

When No. 6 was lowered he called attention to a light he could see on the port side, and remarked that it was probably a sailing ship, and that if a breeze sprang up she might pick them up.

"I was generally reassuring the passengers," added Mr. Lightoller.

▶ Mr. Lightoller centre, Mrs. Lightoller right.

DID NOT THINK SHIP WOULD SINK

This boat was lowered with forty-two people in it, but he ordered the gangways below to be opened with a view to sending boats to the gangways later to fill them up if necessary.

Lord Mersey remarked later "It has been suggested to me that you would not have the gangway door opened on the port side because it would be dangerous."

"I had not time, to take all those things into consideration," was the reply. At this time, he added, he did not think the ship was going down, though he knew the position was serious. The general order "women and children first" was well observed.

Sir John Simon: Was the discipline good? – Excellent.

The male passengers behaved themselves well? – Splendidly.

In regard to No. 4 boat, Sir John Simon pointed out that, though it was a full-sized lifeboat, it only held forty people.

MEN WHO GOT OUT OF THE BOAT

In your judgment did you fill it as full as you safely could? – Yes.

Would the men on the boat know they could take more when they became water-borne? – Yes.

In reply to further questions from the President, Mr. Lightoller said he gave no order to the boats to remain near the gangway doors, but if the doors were open those in the boats must have seen them open by the light, and they would have been within call of the boatswain.

He told the story of the port collapsible boat which they got swung out, a matter of no great difficulty, but occupying some time.

"We had great difficulty in filling her with women," said Mr. Lightoller. "We had to call out several times for more women. On one occasion someone standing, close to the boat said : 'Oh, there are no more women!' and then, I think, several men managed to climb in.

"Just then or a moment afterwards someone sung out at the back: 'Here are a couple more!' Naturally, I thought they were women, and the men got out of the boat again and put the women in. If I remember right I think this happened on two occasions."

Do you mean the men gave up their places in the boat? – Yes.

ROOM FOR MORE MEN

When the boat left did she contain men and women? – No men there that I knew of. I believe it was on that boat that a couple of Chinese or somebody like that got on. I heard later. They hid underneath the thwarts or something.

Were there any more women thereabouts at that time? – None whatever. I am under the impression that I could have put some more women in if there were any more, and I could have put some men in, but I did not feel justified in giving the order for the men to get in because, as fair as I knew, it was the last boat to leave the ship, and I wanted her to get away well and safely.

Was good order maintained? – Splendid.

Was there any attempt to rush that boat? – None whatever.

"Tell me what your own experiences were," said Sir John Simon, and the answer was a thrilling story of a hairbreadth escape, interrupted or helped on here and there by questions directed to elucidate some point.

I was swimming out towards the head of the ship. I could see the crow's nest distinctly, and I suppose as the water was so bitterly cold, it was a natural instinct to get out of it. I soon realised it was rather foolish, and I tamed to swim clear. The next thing I knew I was up against that blower on the fore part of the funnel (pointing to the model, behind him).

The water rushing down the blow-hole held me there a little time against the grating. Then after a while there seemed to be a rush of air from down below up the blow-hole, and I was blown away from it.

I had been dragged below the surface – it seemed a long way; still, I don't suppose it was many moments I was down. Then I came to the surface. I had a lifebelt on.

I found myself alongside the collapsible boat that had been fastened on the deck. It was still shut up and bottom upwards.

I just clung on to a bit of rope or something and stayed there for a little while, and then the forward funnel fell down. It fell within three or four inches of the boat. It lifted the boat bodily, and the boat fell about twenty feet clear of the ship.

Did you notice when you came up to the surface near this collapsible boat whether the whole of the ship had disappeared? – Oh, no, all the funnels were above the water.

Can you describe to us what it was happened to the ship? – Are, you referring to the reports of her breaking two?'

Yes. – That is utterly untrue. The ship could not have broken in two.

He continued with a lucid picture of the last moments of the monster ship.

The next thing I remember I was alongside this collapsible boat again, and there were half a dozen people standing on it. I climbed on to it, and then turned my attention to the ship.

The third, if not the second, funnel was still visible – certainly, the third was, but I am not quite sure about the second. The stern of the ship was then clear of the water.

She was gradually raising her stern out of the water. Even at that time I think the propellers were clear of the water, but of that I will not be certain.

I am rather under the impression that the whole of the third funnel was visible.

The President: It seems to me that the ship would almost be perpendicular.

The Witness: It did eventually become quite perpendicular.

The Solicitor-General: Did you continue watching the after-part of the ship? Did it settle on the water again? – It did not settle again.

ABSOLUTELY PERPENDICULAR

You are confident it did not? – Perfectly certain. Mr. Lightoller was emphatic on this point. He continued:–

After she had reached an angle of about 50 or 60 degrees, there was a rumbling sound, which I attribute to the boilers leaving their beds and crashing down on or through the bulkheads. The ship all the time was coming more and more perpendicular, until finally she attained the absolute perpendicular, and then went down very slowly. The only thing which might have been attributed to an explosion was when, in the first place, I stuck to the blower, and, in the second place, immediately before the forward funnel felt there was an uprush of certainly warm water.

You were under water at the time and not in a very good position to hear it? – No.

Then he described the scene on the collapsible which he reached, and the transfer to the lifeboat which contained about seventy-five persons, including Bride and Phillips.

Perfectly distinctly, at a distance of not more than five miles, he saw a light. As far as he could see, there was nothing to prevent the vessel from coming to the Titanic.

Distress signals, he said, burst at a great height and threw out a large number of white stars. These signals could not be mistaken, and they were not the least like company signals.

A NIGHT IN 100 YEARS

Of remarkable interest, were Second Officer Lightoller's observations and theories concerning the weather conditions that prevailed at the time of the disaster.

"It is very difficult I think," he replied to Sir John Simon, "to come to any conclusion as to why this iceberg should not have been seen with greater distinctness.

"Of course, we know now that the extraordinary combination of circumstances that existed at that time, you would not meet again once in a hundred years, as they existed on that particular night. Of course, everything was against us, everything.

"In the first place, there was no moon. Then there was no

wind, not the slightest breath of air. Most particularly of all, in my opinion, is the fact, the most extraordinary circumstance, that there was no swell on the water. Had there been the slightest degree of swell I have no doubt that they would have seen the iceberg in plenty of time to clear it."

SEA LIKE A TABLECLOTH

"The sea was like a tablecloth, like a floor. I guarantee that ninety-nine men out of 100, going across the Atlantic regularly, could not recollect anything like an absolutely calm sea."

After a question from the President he went on:–

The berg into which we ran must, I think, have broken off shortly before. It must have capsized. That would leave most of it above the water practically black ice. Or it might have been a berg broken from a glacier, with the blue side towards us, but even in that case there would still have been the white outline that Captain Smith spoke about, and a white outline should be distinctly visible in sufficient time to clear it, provided it is not cloudy weather and there is starlight. In such a case there was bound to be a certain amount of reflected light.

Again, had we been approaching a field of ice of more or less extent, looking down on it, it would have been clearly visible. The only thing I can account for is that probably it was a berg overturned, as they most frequently do. A berg will split in pieces, and when it splits there are noises that are often spoken of as explosions.

When a berg splits it will turn over, and that brings most of the part that had been in the water above the water. Questioned by Mr. Scanlan, the officer said he could suggest no means beyond those in use whereby ice could be detected earlier by the look-out men.

He totally disagreed that nine men were necessary to man a lifeboat. Four were sufficient. The Titanic had a great number of crew to man the boats. The President stated the ship was manned far in excess of legal requirements.

Counsel for the Sailors' Union contended that such requirements were insufficient. After eight hours' evidence Mr. Lightoller stood down, and the inquiry was adjourned for the day.

BOARD OF TRADE CRITICISED

The loss of the Titanic was the cause of strong comment last evening in the Commons when the House went into Committee of Supply on the Board of Trade Estimates.

Major Archer Shee moved the reduction of the salary of the President of the Board of Trade by £100. The present inquiry, he said, could not take the place of the House of Commons in dealing with the President of the Board of Trade. The inquiry was called by the Board of Trade, and had to report to it. The regulations, Major Archer Shee said, were redrafted fourteen years ago and again in 1902.

The damning fact which convicted the President of the Board of Trade was, said Major Archer Shee, the fact that he had neglected to carry out the recommendation of his own Committee which made important recommendations ten months ago. The Board of Trade had been dilatory in enforcing a proper complement of wireless operators, which, if insisted upon, might have meant the saving of lives on board the Titanic.

Mr. G. Terrell contended that the Board of Trade had, shown absolute neglect and unconcern in matters relating to shipping. The regulations were quite out of date.

Lord Charles Beresford urged that they must not do anything which would affect our commercial and shipping interests to the advantage of other countries. Mr. Holt said the shipowners of the country would welcome a full inquiry into the safety of life at sea.

PHILANTHROPY IN MEMORIAM

Philadelphia, May 21 – Mr. Peter A. B. Widener has endowed a home for crippled children with an additional sum of £800,000 in memory of his son George D. Widener who perished in the Titanic disaster. – Reuter.

23 May 1912

LIGHTS OF THE MYSTERY SHIP

Titanic Fourth Officer Tells of Sending Up Distress Signals.

DID SHE ANSWER?

Three more officers of the Titanic were examined before Lord Mersey's Commission at the London Scottish Drill Hall yesterday, but little new light was shed on the circumstances of the disaster.

Mr. Pitman the third officer, who was questioned by Mr. Aspinall (for the Board of Trade), was saved in lifeboat No. 5, of which he was placed in charge by Mr. Murdoch, the first officer.

He was aroused by a noise that suggested the ship was going to anchor, and going on deck was told by Mr. Lightoller that they had struck something. When he went forward to see what damage had been done he met firemen running up, and they said water was coming into their quarters. He heard the order, "Get the boats filled with women and children," and went to No. 5 boat.

He saw Mr. Ismay close to the boat, though he did not then know who it was. Mr. Ismay remarked to him: "We are uncovering the boat. There is no time to lose. Get them filled with women and children." I then went to the bridge, and saw Captain Smith and I told him what Mr. Ismay said. He said, "Carry on."

When he got back to the boat he put a number of ladies in it. Mr. Ismay helped, and between thirty and forty ladies and two children were put into the boat.

Mr. Aspinall: Why did you let the male passengers in? – Because there were no more women around. At least, there were two there, but they would not come.

HOW SHE WENT DOWN
Asked by Mr. Aspinall to describe how the Titanic sank, Mr. Pitman took a model of the steamer in his hands, and, gradually depressing the bow until the stern was almost perpendicular above the bow, he said: "That is the position I saw her in. She gradually disappeared like this; went on end and went down that way."

He agreed with Mr. Lightoller's evidence that the liner did not break in two, nor did the after deck right itself.

When the Titanic sank he heard screams, but did not go in their direction as he thought there was such a mass of people in the water that they would have been swamped.

Mr. Pitman told too, of seeing the mysterious light about five miles away – the stern light of a ship.

During the afternoon before the disaster the course of the Titanic was altered to southward, presumably to avoid reported ice.

MYSTERY SHIP'S LIGHTS
After the third officer, the fourth officer, Mr. Joseph Grove Boxhall, a youthful-looking young man, who has been unwell for some time since the disaster. After he had gone down below, and been told by the carpenter that the ship was making water fast, he went on the bridge, where "there were quite a lot of men."

He saw two masthead lights of a steamer approaching. When he looked again, after working out the ship's bearings in the chart-room and taking them to the wireless operator, the vessel was too far off for her port light to be visible. Meanwhile he sent for distress signal rockets, and from six to a dozen were sent off at five minutes' intervals. He saw no sort of answer, nor did Captain Smith, but some people said she showed a light – probably a Morse lamp.

"I judged her to be a four-masted steamer between five and six miles away. Then she turned round, very slowly, until at last I saw only her stern light.

Another dark, clean-shaven man of seamanlike appearance took his stand at the witness table when Harold Godfrey Lowe, fifth officer, was called and gave his account of the collision.

Mr. Rowlatt: What was the boat to which you belonged? – I don't know.
Lord Mersey: Why didn't you know? – I don't know why I didn't, but I didn't.
Was it your business to find out? – I suppose it was.
And you did not do it? – No, sir.

"BUNDLED HER IN."
Did you use a revolver at all? – I did. While I was on the boat deck, just as they started to lower two men jumped into my boat. I chased one out, and, to avoid another occurrence of that sort I fired my revolver as I was going down each deck. There were about sixty-four people in the boat and in his opinion his boat was more than full enough to lower with safety.

Mr. Scanlan asked why boat No. 1 was allowed to leave the ship with only five passengers on board? – I did not know who was there. I cleared the deck.

Lord Mersey: When you put the people in it there were no other people left on deck? – There were no people left on the starboard deck. I did not search the port side, as I wanted to get the boats away. I had no time to waste.

Mr. Holmes: Did you say, "Lady Duff-Gordon come along"? – I said nothing to her. I simply bundled her into the boat.

You were some time rescuing one man? – Yes; it was rather awkward to get at it. You could not row, because of the bodies. You had to push your way through them.

Mr. Cotter: Did you see Mr. Bruce Ismay? – Yes.

Did you see him go into a boat? – No. I told him – what I said – and I told the men to go ahead preparing No. 3 boat, and Mr. Ismay went there and helped them. He did everything in his power.

TO-MORROW'S GREAT CONCERT
How the General Post Office Bestirred Itself In Memory of Titanic Band.

The public has awakened to the true significance of the unique concert which is being given at the Albert Hall to-morrow (Friday) in honour of the heroic Titanic band. It is now certain that the greatest orchestral combination which has ever appeared before the public will have an audience inferior to none that has gathered on any of the historic occasions in which the Albert Hall has participated.

Yesterday there were queues of people in Newman-street waiting to buy tickets. The cheaper seats are already sold out. Far more offers of help are being received than can possibly be accepted. For example, yesterday a little ten-year-old Hungarian girl came up to the offices in Newman-street with her violin to ask if she might play in the orchestra, but had to go away disappointed.

Even the General Post Office has bestirred itself in the interests of the musicians' concert. Three days ago so great was the volume of work on the telephone at the Newman-street Office that the G.P.O. were asked to put in another instrument. They promised it in six weeks.

"But the concert is on Friday," they were informed. "What concert?" said the Post Office. "The Titanic band concert." "Oh! Titanic band concert," said the Post Office, and the instrument was installed in three days.

Immediate application should be made for tickets to Mr. R. F. McDonnell, 10, Newman-street, Oxford-street, or the Albert Hall, or the usual agents.

24 May **1912**

DID CAPTAIN SMITH KNOW OF THE ICE?

New Wireless Warnings That Reached Titanic Operator.

NOT SEEN BY OFFICERS

Did Captain Smith knowingly run the Titanic into an oblong region of icebergs?

Did wireless warnings reporting ice, transmitted from passing ships on the fateful Sunday, ever reach him?

These were the two questions which Lord Mersey, his assessors and the array of eminent counsel thrashed out at the inquiry yesterday with the help of a highly-placed Marconi Company official and the assistant operator of the Titanic, Harold Bride.

Six vessels were stated by the Solicitor-General to have indicated the position of ice in messages to the Titanic. Their reports showed an oblong area of ice bounded on the south by lat. 41.25. The liner went down in lat. 41.46.

The message placing ice as far south as 41.25 was sent two hours before the crash, from the steamer Mesaba. Earlier the Amerika had sent a report of ice at lat. 41.27, long. 50.8.

Sir Robert Finlay, early in yesterday's proceedings, said he thought he could satisfy the President that the Mesaba and Amerika messages never reached the commander or any officers of the Titanic.

Mr. Turnbull, the deputy manager of the Marconi Company, produced copies or messages sent to and from and via the Titanic, and explained that it was a common practice to relay messages to land via another ship.

ICE REPORT VIA TITANIC

The operator on the Amerika, he said, wished to send the following message to the Hydrographic Office in Washington for distribution thence to ships:–

S.S. Amerika, via Titanic. Amerika passed two large icebergs in 41.27 N., 50.8 W., on April 14.

Mr. Turnbull said that the Cape Race station had assured him that this message was received direct from the Titanic, and Lord Mersey said he was satisfied that it reached the Marconi operator (Phillips, who lost his life) on board the Titanic.

In general practice, witness emphatically told Sir John Simon, such a message for retransmission would be treated as a private message, but the operator, seeing its contents and knowing how important it was, would without any doubt whatever communicate its contents to the commander. A new message acknowledged by the Titanic was then read. It was received from the Baltic just before noon on the Sunday, and reported icebergs in lat. 41.51. (N.B. – All the ice reported was between 49deg. and 51deg. west of Greenwich.)

The message sent from the Mesaba bore on the form a note by the operator, S. H. Adams, that the Titanic operator had received it with thanks. Lord Mersey pointed out here that it would be very extraordinary if a man in the Marconi room did not communicate a telegram of this kind to the captain.

BUSY AT HIS ACCOUNTS

Harold Bride, a curly-haired, self-possessed young man of twenty-two, but looking a mere boy, then stepped on the witness-stand. The only ice message that he personally received, he said, was from the Californian to the Baltic between 5 and 5.30 on the Sunday afternoon. He overheard it.

Previously the Californian had stated that she had an ice report for the Titanic, but he did not acknowledge it at the time, as he was busy, making up his accounts. After the collision Phillips, at Captain Smith's direction, sent out "C.Q.D." signal, which was answered by several ships, including the Frankfort, Carpathia and Olympic.

Captain Smith later ordered them to clear out of the room as the ship was sinking. Phillips persisted in maintaining communication with the Carpathia for some time. Young Bride retold the story of the fight with the stoker who tried to rob Phillips of his lifebelt, and detailed the manner of his escape after he was washed from the deck with the last collapsible.

Mr. Lightoller, the second officer, recalled and examined by Sir R. Finlay, said he heard nothing of the telegrams containing ice warnings said to have been sent by the Amerika and the Mesaba.

◗ Captain Smith.

KNEW NOTHING OF MESSAGES

It was customary for messages to be sent direct to the bridge, and if the captain was not there or in his quarters they were opened by the senior officer on watch. Had such a message as that of the Mesaba referring to pack ice been received by the officers, he had no doubt the Mesaba would have been communicated with immediately.

Solicitor-General: How many messages about ice have you any knowledge of on the 14th? – I have a distinct recollection of the message brought and read out by the commander.

Were not other messages received? – To the best of my belief, some other messages might have been received, but I cannot recollect having seen them.

Mr. Boxhall, the fourth officer, also said he knew nothing about the Amerika and Mesaba messages.

The strength of the Gulf Stream was too strong, and there was a set-back before they reached this latitude.

He saw several reports about ice and gathered that the Titanic would soon be in the region of the ice, although he could only remember one message being posted up on the noticeboard.

Mr. Pitman, the third officer, and Mr. Lowe, the fifth, also said, they knew nothing about the Amerika and Mesaba messages.

The inquiry then adjourned till to-day.

THIS MORNING'S GOSSIP

It is said that the young widow of the late Colonel Astor, who was a victim of the Titanic disaster, is wearing only white as mourning for him. Her mother strongly objects to black for so young a woman, and her indoor dresses will therefore be of white crêpe.

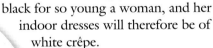

Undoubtedly the fashion of black, mourning, is less common than it was, and, one may think, rightly. For the colour of mourning, as the practice of different races shows, is merely a fashion, and a tribute of respect to the dead need not, one thinks, be also a means of depressing the living. Cases of widows who wear white mourning, especially during the summer months, are by no means uncommon. Lily Duchess of Marlborough wore white in the house after the death of her husband, Lord Marcus Beresford, and Princess Henry of Battenberg, it is remembered, appeared in white on more than one occasion during her time of mourning.

25 May 1912

TITANIC'S LAST WIRELESS CALL

Evidence by the Man Who Heard Her Appeal for Help.

LOOK-OUT AND GLASSES

Lord Mersey's Titanic Commission adjourned yesterday until after the Whitsuntide holidays – next Tuesday week – and the Attorney-General announced that the evidence of all the officers and crew was concluded.

There was some little discussion as to the actual scope of the inquiry, and the President made it clear that their main object was to ascertain the cause of the disaster, fix the blame, and find out whether the life-saving devices were deficient.

He did not propose, therefore, to call scientific and expert evidence to report upon all the means that should be taken in future in regard to lifeboats, bulkheads, etc., with a view to averting similar calamities. It would be sufficient to confine their attention to general recommendations and make their report as soon as possible.

LAST WIRELESS MESSAGE

Harold Cottam, the wireless operator of the Carpathia, who got the call for help from the Titanic, was examined by Sir John Simon, and told a dramatic story of how he received it. He was preparing to go to bed, but had to wait for a confirmation message from the Parisian. At last he wrote out a previous communication and reported it to the bridge.

"Then I sat down and asked the Titanic if he was there," he went on, "because there was a batch of messages from Cape Cod. His only answer was:–

"Struck a berg. Come at once. (He sent his position). It is a C.Q.D."

Cottam then reported the message to the officer of the watch and the Carpathia was immediately headed for the Titanic's position. He kept in touch with the Titanic all the time. Could you overhear what the Titanic was trying to say to other ships? – I was helping the Titanic to communicate.

Cottam went on to explain how he got the Olympic and Titanic into communication, and how at 1.27 a.m. (ship's time) he heard:–

Come quick as possible, old man; the engine-room filling up to the boilers.

The last message he heard was at 1.50 (ship's time). The signals were good right up to the end.

Cottam said that a great many messages were sent after the people were taken on board from the Titanic's boats. One of the messages was to the Olympic, and ran as follows:–

Mr. Ismay's orders Olympic not to be seen by Carpathia; no transfer to take place. – Rostron, captain (of the Carpathia).

Sir John Simon: I suggest it means Mr. Ismay was giving his direction as to the respective courses to be taken by the two ships.

Sir Robert Finlay (for the White Star Line): If the survivors on the Carpathia could have seen the Olympic they might have supposed that there was the Titanic – not lost after all. There was some idea of that sort, about not stirring the feelings of the people on board.

IF HE HAD HAD GLASSES

Frederick Fleet, one of the look-out men in the Titanic's crow's nest at the time of the collision, was next called. He said instructions were given to him when he went on watch to keep a sharp look-out for small ice and growlers. During the first part of the watch the horizon could be seen clearly, but afterwards a slight haze came on. It was nothing much. It did not affect their sight ahead, and they did not report it to the bridge.

The Attorney-General read extracts from the evidence of Lee, Fleet's mate in the crow's nest, who said: "We had all our work cut out to pierce through it."

Lord Mersey: I am not at all disposed to give credit to Lee's evidence on that point. It is quite inconsistent with the other evidence.

Fleet, further questioned, said he gave the signal, striking three bells immediately, and then, going to the crow's nest, saw a black object high above the water right ahead.

Mr. Scanlan: Do you think if you had had glasses you could have seen the iceberg sooner? – Certainly.

How much sooner, do you think? – In time for the ship to get out of the way.

So it is your view that if you had had glasses it would have made all the difference between safety and disaster? – Yes.

Would not that depend whether you had the glasses to your eyes or not? – When I had had an order from the bridge to keep a sharp look-out I should have had the glasses in my hand.

MEMORIAL TO JACK PHILLIPS

The proposed memorial to the late Jack Phillips, the Marconi operator of the Titanic, it was decided last night at a public meeting in Godalming, his native town, is to take the form of a drinking fountain in the main Portsmouth Road, in the centre of the town.

NEW YORK'S SOCIAL HERO
Round of Entertainments for Captain Rostron, of the Carpathia.
(FROM OUR OWN CORRESPONDENT)

New York, May 31 – After the eulogistic references to him in Senator Smith's extraordinary speech and the honour paid to him by the Senate, Captain Rostron, of the Carpathia, who did his duty so promptly and manfully at the Titanic disaster, is the popular hero of New York. He has been overwhelmed with invitations to luncheons, dinners and theatres until the Carpathia sails on Tuesday.

To-day he was the guest of honour at an informal luncheon at the residence of Mrs. John Jacob Astor in Fifth Avenue, when Mrs. J. B. Cummings and Mrs. J. B. Thayer, both Titanic widows, were also among the guests. On Sunday the captain and his officers will occupy a box at a concert of massed naval and military bands for the benefit of the families of the Titanic musicians.

With his officers Captain Rostron occupied a flag-adorned box last night at the Winter Garden, a variety theatre like the London Empire, and they received a tremendous ovation from an audience of 2,000, who stood cheering and waving hats and handkerchiefs.

After a comedian on the stage had indicated the box where Captain Rostron sat the performance was suspended for fifteen minutes while the band played the "Star Spangled Banner" and Miss Josie Collins sang "God Save the King." On leaving the theatre the captain passed through a long line of men and women waiting to shake hands with him.

MAN WHO WAS SAVED

Impostor Who Said He Was a Titanic Survivor Sent to Prison.

A strange fraud was described yesterday at Lowestoft, where George Ladbrooke Evans was sentenced to three months' imprisonment for obtaining money by false pretences. Evans went to a house in Lowestoft, it was stated, representing himself to be the third petty officer of the Titanic. He said he was business agent for Lady Duff-Gordon, who was coming to Lowestoft under doctor's orders for sixteen weeks, and wanted apartments for her.

He asked change of a £5 note, but was only given a small sum, with which he decamped. He said his wife was drowned in the Titanic disaster, but he was saved in the same boat as Lady Duff-Gordon. Convictions for previous frauds were proved against Evans.

5 June 1912

MR. BRUCE ISMAY TELLS HIS STORY

Keen Examination at Titanic Inquiry of White Star Chairman.

WHO OWNS THE LINE?
Attorney-General Exhorts Mr. Ismay To "Be Frank."

LEAVING THE SHIP
Mr. Bruce Ismay was the witness of the day when the Titanic inquiry was resumed by Lord Mersey yesterday. He was called shortly after twelve, and was still giving evidence when, four hours later, the hearing was adjourned till this morning.

Sir Rufus Isaacs conducted his examination, and questioned him first concerning the nationality of the White Star Line. He proceeded to questions concerning the building of the Titanic and the Olympic.

Have you (he asked) any financial interest in the way of shareholding in Messrs. Harland and Wolff? – Absolutely none. Lord Pirrie, who is on the Oceanic Steam Company, is also on Messrs. Harland and Wolff.

Mr. Ismay said the Titanic had cost approximately £1,500,000. He sailed on her from Southampton on her maiden voyage.

You went because you wanted to travel on the maiden voyage? – That is right.

Because in your capacity as managing director you desired to see how the vessel behaved, I suppose? – That is it.

DID NOT PAY HIS FARE
You weren't there as an ordinary passenger? – As far as the navigation of the ship was concerned – yes.

What I am suggesting is, it would not be right to describe you as an ordinary passenger, because of the interest you took in the Titanic and because of your natural watchfulness of the behaviour of the Titanic on her first voyage? – I looked upon myself simply as an ordinary passenger.

Lord Mersey: Did you pay your fare? – No, sir, I did not. (Laughter.)

Sir Rufus Isaacs: That rather disposes of the ordinary passenger theory. – Mr. Ismay did not agree and Sir Rufus Isaacs said he would not press the point.

On the 14th did you get information from the captain as to ice reports? – The captain handed to me ice message which he had received from the Baltic on the Sunday (reporting icebergs and field-ice and giving bearings).

That message was handed to you by the captain? – By the captain.

NO SPECIAL IMPORTANCE
Because you were managing director of the company? – I don't know. It was simply a matter of information.

Have you read it? – Yes; but I glanced at it very casually.

When he handed it to you as managing director it was for you to read? – Yes.

Mr. Ismay said he did not read the message then. In the afternoon he spoke about it to two passengers – Mrs. Thayer and Mrs. Ryerson – but he did not recollect what he said.

He attributed no special importance to the ice report. It conveyed to him that they were approaching within the region of ice, but not that the ice lay in the track of the Titanic.

Sir Rufus Isaacs then tried to discover from Mr. Ismay his exact attitude towards the speed of the Titanic.

The revolutions had increased from sixty-eight up to seventy-five. Her full speed was seventy-eight, said the White Star chairman.

The Attorney-General: If you will search your recollection a little – this question of speed interested you very materially. You as managing director of the company were interested in the speed of the vessel? – Yes.

NO SLOWING DOWN
Your intention was to get to the maximum speed before you reached New York? – The intention was if the weather was suitable on Monday or Tuesday to drive her for a few hours at full speed.

He had discussed this question with Mr. Bell, the chief engineer, at Queenstown on the Thursday, and he therefore knew on Sunday morning that, with beautiful weather on the Monday, the ship would go at full speed for a few hours. This presumably would have necessitated lighting more boilers.

The Attorney-General said the evidence was that the additional boilers were lit up at 8 a.m. on the Sunday, and might have been connected on the same night.

There was no slowing down of the vessel after that ice report was read? – Not that I know of.

You knew, of course, that the proximity of icebergs was a danger? – There is always more or less danger with ice.

Had you no curiosity to know whether or not you would be travelling in the region in which ice was reported? – I had not. I knew we were in the region of the ice through this Marconi message.

You were managing director. The captain thought this of sufficient importance to bring the marconigram to you. He gave it to you and you put it in your pocket. You knew you would be approaching that night? – I expected so.

And therefore that it behoved those responsible for the navigation of the ship to be very careful? – Naturally.

And, more particularly, if you were approaching ice in the night, it would be desirable, would it not, to slow down? – Witness hesitated.

The President: Answer the question. – I say no.

The Attorney-General: Mr. Ismay, be frank with us.

Sir Robert Finlay: He is frank.

The Attorney-General: I don't think he is if you ask me.

Sir Robert Finlay: There is not the slightest justification for that statement.

Proceeding, Mr. Ismay said: If a man can see far enough to clear the ice he is perfectly justified in going full speed.

The Attorney-General: Then apparently you did not expect your captain to slow down when he had the ice report? – No; certainly not.

It seems to have been rather in accordance with your views that the faster you could get out of the ice region the better? – Assuming the weather is perfectly fine, I say the captain is quite justified in getting through it.

NEVER ON THE BRIDGE

The President: If you have a perfectly good look-out and can see ice at a sufficient distance to enable you to steer clear, that would be sufficient?

The Attorney-General: Assuming the "ifs" which your Lordship has put, yes. (Laughter.)

The Attorney-General: Assuming you can see far enough to get out of the way at whatever speed you are going, you can go at any speed you like. That is what it comes to.

He gave the marconigram back to Captain Smith at about 7.15. That was the only time he spoke to him that evening. The captain said he wished to put the message up in the officers' chart-room.

You had not been on the bridge? – I had never been on the bridge during the whole trip.

Mr. Ismay then told the story of the collision. He was told both by Captain Smith and by the chief engineer that the damage was serious, and he helped to get the boats out and put some of the women and children in. All the women he saw on the boat deck got away in boats.

NO ORDER TO GET IN

The Attorney-General: Did you realise that they were not all the women and children on board the ship? – I did not.

How long did you remain on the Titanic after? – I think an hour and a half or longer.

Did you think it was in a serious condition? – As time got on I did.

Did you tell anybody? – I did not.

So far as you are aware, were any of the passengers told the vessel was sinking? – Not so far as I know.

Will you tell us what happened when you had got the women and children in? – After all the people who were on the deck had got in, I got in as she was being lowered away.

There was no order to get in? – No.

Did any other passenger get in? – Yes, Mr. Carter.

Did you think when you left the vessel that she was rapidly going down? – I did.

With regard to supplying binoculars to look-out men, Mr. Ismay said he believed the company formerly supplied binoculars, but afterwards it was left to the discretion of the captain. The company had never considered the use of searchlights.

The captains had no special instructions with regard to ice, but they had a general instruction that the safety of lives and of the ship was to be the first consideration.

Mr. Scanlan, recalling the witness' conversation with the chief engineer, asked: What right had you, as an ordinary passenger, to decide the speed at which the ship was to go, without consultation with the captain?

Lord Mersey: I can answer that – none. It is no good asking him that. He has no right to dictate as to speed.

Mr. Scanlan: As a super-captain?

Lord Mersey: What sort of person is a super-captain?

Mr. Scanlan: As I conceive it a man like Mr. Ismay, who can say to the chief engineer what speed the ship was to go.

Lord Mersey: The captain, is the man to say that.

MR. ISMAY AND THE LAST BOAT

In examination by Mr. C. Edwards, for the Dockers' Union, Mr. Ismay said, "We thought the Titanic was unsinkable."

Mr. Edwards: What was the ground upon which you based that belief? – Because we thought she would float with two of the largest compartments full of water, and that the only way she was at all likely to be damaged was in case of collision with another ship running into her and hitting her in the bulkheads.

Answering further questions, Mr. Ismay said he put the marconigram warning the Titanic of the proximity of ice into his pocket in a fit of absent-mindedness, and kept it there for five hours.

Asked whether he got into a boat when the Titanic was sinking, Mr. Ismay answered simply: "I did."

Did you know there were some hundreds of people on that ship? – Yes.

Do you agree that, apart from the captain, you, as the responsible managing director, owed your life to every other person on that ship?

The President said he did not think that was a question which should be put to the witness.

Mr. Ismay said he helped to place women and children in the boats. "I was standing by the last boat," he added, "watching everybody in, and as the boat was being lowered away I got in."

LADY ROTHES AT THE HELM

Alfred Crawford, a bedroom steward, was the first witness called after the Whitsuntide recess. He got away in boat No. 8, which was steered by the Countess of Rothes. It was at this boat that Mrs. Isidor Straus refused to leave her husband and both were left behind together.

There were four members of the crew in the boat and about thirty-five passengers – all women. Captain Smith pointed to two masthead lights on the port side of the Titanic, and told him to row towards them and afterwards return. The four men were at the oars, said Crawford, and a lady was steering.

Mr. Aspinall: Did she steer well? – Yes, sir. Very well, indeed.

Do you know her name? – The Countess of Rothes. The Countess at the helm reported to me from time to time about the position of the lights. A short time before daybreak we came to the

CAPTAIN ROSTRON TELLS HIS STORY.

How He Was Wakened at Midnight to Speed on Journey of Rescue.

Captain Roston, of the Carpathia, who has returned to Europe from New York, has just broken his silence concerning the rescue of the Titanic passengers for the first time.

He has told his story to a *Daily Mirror* staff photographer who went out to Gibraltar to meet the Carpathia. Here are some of the points of the captain's interesting narrative :—

"I had just retired for the night on Sunday, April 14, when I heard someone entering my cabin without knocking. I called out 'Who's that?' and a voice replied :—

"'I have just received a Marconi signal of distress from the Titanic, giving her position, and saying she has struck an iceberg and is sinking.'

"'Are you sure it was the Titanic?' I asked the operator. 'Yes,' he replied.

"'Then keep in touch with them, and say we are coming to their assistance.'

"I sent for the chief officer, giving him the position of the Titanic and instructions to alter our course. Meanwhile the chief engineer had received instructions to make full speed ahead.

"Our average speed is about thirteen knots, but we were soon doing nineteen knots. I then sent for the doctors and heads of departments, and reading the Marconi report impressed on them the gravity of the situation, and that everything should be got ready at once for the reception of the passengers of the Titanic.

"At this time I quite expected to reach the Titanic before she sank.

"It was splendid to watch the way in which my men went about their different duties. Blankets were warmed, boats were made ready for lowering and in the kitchen hot soup was made.

"At 2.40 a.m. I saw from the bridge a flare and shortly afterwards sighted the first iceberg. Several times I had to alter the course of the ship to clear the bergs. At this time I had eight men on the look-out at different parts of the ship.

"Never before have I experienced such an anxious time. We picked up the first boat, which contained mostly women and children, at 4.10 a.m., and as the survivors came aboard the Carpathia they were met by stewards, who wrapped them in warm blankets and escorted them to the saloon, where they were given hot soup.

"I should like to mention that the passengers gave me every assistance in caring for the survivors, many giving up their berths for the bad cases, others allowing them to share. Also many ladies and gentlemen gave what spare clothes they had.

WHY THE CARPATHIA WAS SILENT.

"Much has been said in the American Press about the silence of the Carpathia while making for New York. I found it necessary to establish a censorship on the messages which were being sent.

"This action of mine called forth rather severe comment from the passengers. It was said that I had bought the Marconi and was using it to my own advantage in order to make money. A most wicked lie!

"I had instructed the operator that he was to accept nothing but private messages and the names of survivors. I told the passengers that they could send their Press messages after this had been done. When we reached New York the operator had still about 205 messages to send.

"Another inaccuracy which appeared in the papers was that I had ignored a message from President Taft, asking for news of his friend Major Butt. I understand that a message was sent to the Carpathia, but it never reached us. I have written to the President, laying the facts of the case before him."

conclusion that the vessel whose lights we saw was turning round and leaving us.

Replying to Mr. Scanlan (for the Sailors' and Firemen's Union), Crawford said that in the boat there was room for twenty more people. The crew consisted of two sailors, one kitchen maid and himself. He thought that was sufficient.

Mr. Scanlan: But you had to get the assistance of the passengers? – It was not necessary. They helped to keep themselves warm. They did not assist in the lowering. The Countess of Rothes volunteered to steer.

Mr. Lewis (for the Seafarers' Union) asked witness if it was suggested on board the boat that they should return to the Titanic? – Yes; but the ladies said: "No, no. Obey the captain's orders."

Mr. Lewis: Did the men agree with the suggestion? – Yes, I think so.

MOST OF THE LADIES OBJECTED

Mr. Lewis suggested that it was because the ladies objected that the boat did not return, but Lord Mersey demurred, and the question was thrashed out at some length, the President asking questions from written instructions handed over to him by Mr. Lewis.

He elicited the fact that a seaman named Jones suggested going back to the Titanic, but that the ladies – most of the ladies – objected.

The Attorney-General corrected the President when he said "the ladies," because that term would include Lady Rothes.

"I know from her statement," said Sir Rufus Isaacs, "that it was not her view. She is rather concerned about it."

WHAT THE DONKEYMAN SAW

After brief evidence had been taken from two able seamen who went off respectively in boats 10 and 16, Ernest Gill, the donkeyman of the Californian, was called, Sir Rufus Isaacs introducing him in a little speech, of explanation.

It was at one time suggested, he said, that this witness had made in America statements which were not true about distress signals having been sent up. But the story told by Gill in America had been very much confirmed by the evidence that had been put before the

English Court, and witness was fully justified in what he said in America.

Gill then told his story in a clear, unhesitating way, describing how he saw over the starboard rail a large passenger steamer with two rows of lights and several groups of lights, apparently saloon deck lights – probably less than ten miles away.

"After I had talked over the matter with my mate and had gone off watch," said Gill, "I went on deck to smoke a cigarette. I could not see the lights of the steamer at all. Apparently she had steamed away. That was after one bell – between half-past twelve and one.

"Looking round I saw what appeared, to be a falling star. It descended and then disappeared. I did not pay any attention to that.

"Probably about five minutes later I looked over and could see at the water's edge on the horizon what was unmistakably a rocket. There was no mistake about it."

The positions of the falling star and the rocket were the same. Shortly afterwards he went below, and was awakened at 6.30 next morning and told by the chief engineer to hurry up and get the boats ready.

6 June 1912

WHY THE TITANIC WAS THOUGHT SAFE

White Star Manager Explains Line's Point of View.

MANY IMPROVEMENTS

Remote Contingency of Getting Everybody Off in Lifeboats.

Mr. Bruce Ismay's ordeal was not finished when Lord Mersey's Titanic Commission resumed yesterday morning.

He again took his stand at the witness table to reply to the questions of Sir Robert Finlay, who is acting on behalf of the White Star Line. Within a minute or two he was replying to the 18,900th question asked since the inquiry began.

"Have you ever on any occasion," asked the ex-Attorney-General, "attempted to interfere with the captain, on your voyages across the Atlantic with regard to the navigation of the ship?" "Never," was the emphatic reply.

If I rightly follow the gist of some of the questions put to you yesterday, it was suggested that you ought to have done or said something to Captain Smith in regard to what precautions should be taken. Would that be in accordance with the practice you always follow? – It would be absolutely outside of our province.

Asked why the captain handed him the marconigram,

Mr. Ismay said he thought it was handed to him simply as a matter of information – as a matter of interest. No other messages except the message from the Baltic were handed to him.

TURNED THE CORNER

Sir Robert Finlay: You have told the Court that when you were getting near the ice region something was said at dinner? – Yes; it was said we had turned the corner.

Do you know whether you had run further south when the corner was turned? – No; I knew nothing at all about it.

Mr. Ismay was questioned again as to how he actually left the ship. Sir Robert Finlay read an extract from the evidence of the witness Brown, who said that Mr. Ismay was standing in the boat, assisting women and children from the Titanic's deck.

You say that is not correct. You helped the women and children in? – I did.

But not from inside the boat, and you did not get into it? – Until she was leaving the vessel.

The light they rowed for was a dull white light on the starboard side, not, in his opinion, the light of the Californian, which was on the port side.

A discussion between Lord Mersey and various counsel as to the boat accommodation and a certain design for forty boats for the Olympic and Titanic elicited from the Attorney-General the statement that Mr. Carlisle, the designer of the Titanic, would be called.

Asked how the number of boats on the Titanic compared with the Board of Trade regulations, Mr. Ismay said that the Board of Trade would have asked for 7,500 cubic feet boat space with regard to the Olympic and Titanic, and they had 11,300 or 11,400.

CONVERSATION WITH ENGINEER

Questioned about a conversation held at Queenstown with Mr. Bell, the chief engineer, Mr. Ismay said:–

"Bell came to my room, and I spoke to him in regard to the coal on board the ship.

"I also said there was no chance of the ship arriving in New York on Tuesday, and that we had very much better make up our minds to arrive on Wednesday morning at five o'clock, and that, if the weather was fine and bright in every respect on Monday or Tuesday, we could then take a run out of the ship.

"This could not, of course, have been done without communication with the captain."

"So far as you were concerned," asked Sir Rufus Isaacs, after a discussion about ice in the Atlantic course, "did it strike you as a serious thing that you would encounter field-ice? – No, I don't think it did.

I can't understand why it did not. – The natural thing for the commander to do would be to take steps to avoid it. Therefore, it did not concern me.

You knew, I presume, that you had not boats sufficient on the Titanic to accommodate all the passengers and crew? – Yes.

NOT THINKING ABOUT IT

So that, when the last boat left the Titanic you must have known that a number of passengers and crew were still on board the vessel? – I did.

And you have told us you did not see any on the deck? – I did not. There were no passengers on the deck.

Where were the passengers? – I can only assume the passengers had gone to the after end of the ship.

The President intimated that he would very, much like to know:–

Whether any other liners were following the Titanic's track in the direction of America on April 14.

What those steamers were.

Whether they received the messages about the ice.

And what speed they used. Whether, in fact, upon receipt of warning as to the ice German liners or French liners slowed down.

Sir Robert Finlay remarked that the Board of Trade would doubtless be able to obtain all the information his Lordship required.

Mr. Ismay then left the witness-box.

MANAGER'S STATEMENT

Mr. Harold Sanderson, manager of the White Star Line, made an interesting statement as to his company's view of the safety of the Olympic and Titanic.

Asked to indicate the special features of the Titanic to which he attached importance Mr. Sanderson said:–

"The vessel had a special wireless installation for long-distance messages. She was built with an unusual number of watertight bulkheads, fifteen in all, which were specially constructed, as far as possible in one fair line.

"They were built in excess of the requirements at Lloyd's, and the plating was also specially strong and in excess of what Lloyd's stipulated.

"The Titanic had a double bottom, which was carried nine-tenths of her length, and was divided for the amidship section into four tanks.

"The power for the wireless installation came from three different sources.

"The pumping arrangements were also exceptional, each boiler compartment having its own equipment."

Questioned by the Solicitor-General as to the manning of the Titanic, he said that it had an efficient staff of officers and crew.

Captain Smith was their senior commander and had been in the service of the company since 1880.

He had been a commander since 1887. He was a man of special merit, otherwise he would not have been in that position. The three senior officers were also men of excellent ability.

After the luncheon interval the Solicitor-General asked Mr. Sanderson: What is the view of your company as to the expediency of providing more boats than there were on that ship?

"I think to answer that question," replied Mr. Sanderson, "I should have to divide the subject into two, and to tell you what was in our minds before the accident happened."

A REMOTE CONTINGENCY

"I do not think it had ever been in our minds, nor do I think it had been in the minds of any of the experts who had been responsible for the framing of the regulations, that the whole ship's company of a ship like the Titanic could in any conceivable circumstances be put afloat in the boats.

"Nor do I think if provision were made for it that, in fact, you would in ninety-nine cases out of a hundred succeed in utilising those boats by filling and launching them. The weather conditions would have to be such that I should look upon it as a very remote contingency, and one to be avoided at all costs.

"Therefore, in my judgment, I would rather devote myself to accomplishing, in fact, what we thought we had done with the Titanic – to make her so safe that we should not have to consider the possibility of putting these people afloat. And, having regard to the extraordinary nature of the accident which happened to the Titanic, I still do not feel that it would be a wise or necessary provision to make; that is to say, to provide boats for everybody on board ship.

"I do think, further, that we might advantageously increase the boat accommodation somewhat, and I am looking forward to the recommendation which will be given by this Court for our guidance, and I am certain the public will accept it gratefully. In the meantime, in order to satisfy the public, on whom we are dependent for our living, we are putting on the ships more boats than I think it is wise to do."

DIFFICULTY OF MORE BOATS

"I think if we were to carry enough boats on the boat deck to be equal to the number of people on board, we should have the boat deck so crowded that it would interfere with the efficiency of the working of a great many of them.

The Solicitor-General: What would be the difficulty in increasing the boats on the boat deck? – There is no real difficulty in increasing the boats on the davits. The difficulty I have in mind applies to the boats we cannot put on the davits and which will have to be put across the ships.

But davits might be provided and then slung along the length of the boat deck? – Speaking generally, I think they might, but before you take that as definite I should like to have a word with the nautical adviser as to whether there is any part of the vessel where it is not wise to have a boat.

The President: Have you considered the advisability of using double davits? – I have never heard of double davits.

Look at this plan. Tell me whether the additional boats suggested there could be or would be conveniently placed on board the Titanic. It is an addition of fourteen boats, seven on each side? – I should say, my lord, I think they might be. They would accommodate about 910.

Answering other questions, he said that he could suggest no improvement upon the construction of the Titanic. She was as simple as a vessel of her size could possibly be made.

8 June **1912**

WAY TO DECK BARRED
Sensational New Story by Titanic Chef's Secretary.

NAVAL EXPERT'S "IF."

Some sensational evidence was interposed yesterday morning when the Titanic inquiry was resumed by Lord Mersey at the Scottish Hall.

Before Mr. Wilding, the naval architect, continued his testimony the Attorney-General called Paul Mauge, secretary to the chef of the à la carte restaurant on the Titanic. When he was awakened after the collision by an alarm bell, he said, he went on deck and found Captain Smith encouraging women to enter the boats "because no lady and no gentleman liked to go. Everybody thought they would be safe."

Mauge ran downstairs and wakened the chef, who "had lost consciousness of himself."

Sir Rufus Isaacs: Do you mean he was agitated and lost his head? – Yes. I make him dress as quickly as I can.

"WAY BARRED BY STEWARDS."

A remarkable statement followed. On his way to the boat deck, said the witness, he was met by several stewards who barred his way. He told them who he was, and they allowed him to pass. But a crowd of cooks and their assistants were not allowed to get to the second-class deck, which was the route to safety.

"They could not get up," he added. "That is where they died."

Why could they not get up to the boat deck? – Because some stewards were there, and would not let them pass.

You were allowed to pass? – Me and the chef because I was dressed like a passenger. I think that is why they let me pass. I can't say.

The President: Am I to understand that two or three stewards

were keeping back sixty men? – I can't say if they tried to pass. They could not have done, because I stood on the second-class passenger deck for half an hour, and I did not see them.

CHEF TOO STOUT TO JUMP

From this deck, said Mauge, he made his way to the boat deck and jumped into a boat as it was being lowered.

Asked if the chef went too, witness replied: The chef was too fat, I may say. (Laughter.)

Attorney-General: He was too stout, and he would not jump? – He would not jump. When I was in the lifeboat I shouted to him in French: "Saute!"

He said something, but I could not hear what it was because at the same time a man said to me: "Shut up, foreigner!" and another man on the Titanic tried to pull me off and take my seat.

Mr. Edward Wilding then continued his expert evidence as to the construction of the Titanic, comparing her double bottom to those of the Mauretania and Lusitania. If the ship had driven on to the iceberg stem on, he was sure she would have been saved. She would have killed every fireman in the firemen's quarters, but the ship would have come in.

The President: Do you think if the helm had not been starboarded there would have been a chance of this ship being saved? – I believe the ship would have been saved, and I am strengthened in that belief by a case which your Lordship will remember, where the Arizona, one of the large North Atlantic steamers, thirty-four years ago went stem on into an iceberg and came into port.

Mr. Rowlatt: You said it would have killed all the firemen? – I am afraid she would have crumpled up in stopping herself. The momentum of the ship in stopping would have crushed in her bows for eighty or one hundred feet. She would have telescoped against the iceberg.

11 June 1912

WHITE STAR GIFTS TO THE CARPATHIA

Rewards for Captain and Every Member of the Crew.

◀ Captain Rostron (seated centre) and officers of the S.S. Carpathia.

CUNARD LINE HONOURED

Mr. Alexander Carlisle and the Titanic's Lifeboats.

ADVICE UNACCEPTED

The White Star Line announced last night that the Cunard Company had acceded to their request to be permitted to make the following presentations in recognition of the Carpathia's work after the Titanic disaster:–

Captain Rostron £105 0s. 0d.
Surgeon McGee, Purser Brown, and Chief Steward Hughes (each) £52 10s. 0d.
Every other member of the crew 1 month's pay.

A further offer by the White Star to reimburse the Cunard for the outlay involved in the Carpathia putting back to New York with the survivors was not accepted.

The Cunard Company intimated that they consider it a privilege that the Carpathia and her crew were the means of picking up the Titanic's survivors, and that it was not their intention to make any claim in respect of salvage or life-saving or expenses.

MR. CARLISLE'S EVIDENCE

Further expert evidence, largely of a technical nature, yesterday occupied Lord Mersey's court of inquiry into the wreck of the Titanic.

Mr. Alexander Carlisle, formerly general manager of Messrs. Harland and Wolff's, testified to the accuracy of an interview with him reported in *The Daily Mail* on April 18.

Mr. Aspinall, K.C., called his attention to the following statement:–

When working out the designs of the Olympic and the Titanic I put my ideas before the davit constructors, and got them to design me davits which would allow me to place, if necessary, four lifeboats on each pair of davits, which would have meant a total of over forty boats.

Mr. Carlisle, who produced the designs, explained that he pointed out to Lord Pirrie and other people connected with Harland and Wolff's that the Board of Trade would probably require much larger boat accommodation on the large ships.

"I was then," he said, "authorised to go ahead and get out full plans and designs, so that if the Board of Trade did call upon us to fit anything more we should have no extra trouble or extra expense."

INTERVIEW WITH DIRECTORS

These plans, said Mr. Carlisle, were submitted to Mr. Ismay and his co-director, Mr. Sanderson. Mr. Ismay was the only one who spoke.

"I came especially from Belfast in October, 1909, with those plans, which were worked out, and also the decorations, and Mr. Ismay and Mr. Sanderson, Lord Pirrie and myself spent about four hours together.

You mean to say Sanderson was discussing these plans? – Mr. Sanderson, I think, never spoke.

Did he stay for four hours without speaking? (Laughter.) – No; that was over the whole of the decorations. We took up that day the entire decorations of the ship.

Never mind the decorations. We are dealing with the lifeboats. – The lifeboat affair took five or ten minutes.

It was your view, was it; that it was desirable to have these davits on board the ship, so that if the Board of Trade required you to increase the boat accommodation you could easily comply? – That's it.

LORD MERSEY'S QUESTIONS

Then for ten minutes Lord Mersey cross-questioned him as to who was responsible for the lifeboat accommodation of the Titanic.

"Were you?" asked the President. – If I had been there – No, no. Were you? – No.

That seems to be a grudging "no." – Not in the least.

Well, and who was? – The owners in the first place. The White Star Company gave Harland and Wolff a very free hand in the building of the ships, but they could not build a ship any bigger than the order.

"We have a very free hand, and always have had, but I don't think we could possibly have supplied them with any more boats for the ship without getting the sanction and the order of the White Star Line."

Did you try? – You must remember I retired on June 30, 1910, before the ship was launched.

Do you suggest, according to the views which were entertained at that time, that there were enough boats or not? – Personally I consider there were not enough boats.

Did you ever say so? – I have said so over and over again in the works.

To whom? – I said it at the Advisory Committee of the Board of Trade on May 19 and 26, 1911, before either of the ships went to sea.

Will you tell me to which of the representatives of the White Star Line you ever said: "The Olympic and the Titanic are going away with an insufficient supply of boats"? – To no person, as I was not there.

Witness explained that he had nothing to do with the finishing, and knew nothing about the boats.

Then whose business is it to know about the boats? – It is the owners.

Then I do not understand these arrangements. The owners left all these questions to the wisdom of Harland and Wolff? – If they made certain changes in these ships they would have to make them in the Adriatic and other boats.

Are you suggesting now that they would be influenced by the fact that if they supplied more they would have to put more into their other steamers? – I don't know what was their reason.

What do you think was their reason? – I can't tell.

Mr. Scanlan questioned Mr. Carlisle as to the proceeding of the advisory committee.

"The main thing is this," replied witness, "the committee was practically at the end when I was asked to join it. I was only at the last two meetings and the majority of the points had

been well considered.

"It was understood that if an Act of Parliament was brought in by the Board of Trade it would not only affect a ship like the Titanic, but go back on to the old ships, and it would be unfair to go in for fitting too many boats when they possibly could not get room on the old ships.

"At that time and on that occasion the two plans which I have there were submitted. I left them in the room. I did not take them away."

The President: It stands in this way. You made the plans in 1909; you left Harland and Wolff in 1910; you went to the Board of Trade in 1911, and took these plans with you? – I did.

Mr. Scanlan: I want to make this clear. At the time you submitted your plans to the White Star Line directors Mr. Ismay was present? – Yes.

And there was no reason why, if the White Star people wanted more boats, they should not go ahead and instal sixty-four? – Certainly.

ADVISED THREE TIMES
AS MANY

The President: Am I to understand you advised them to instal sixty-four? – I merely put my ideas before them.

Did you say there should be sixty-four? – I thought there ought to be three on each set of decks. That would mean forty-eight.

Whereas, in point of fact, how many were there? – Sixteen.

Mr. Edwards: Do you know why no definite decision, had been arrived at up to June, 1910, as to the number of boats? – I should say they were entirely waiting to see what the Board of Trade would require.

The President: Quite so. They were living in hopes that the Board of Trade would not ask for any more. In answer to the Board of Trade counsel, Mr. Laing, Mr. Carlisle said that he was asked to join the committee two days before it finished, and they had come to certain conclusions on certain points.

"The chairman drew my attention to the fact that if I pushed my ideas for all ships, the Bill would have to go back, and it would not be fair.

"And he said they had no doubt that ships would have more boats than were required by the Board of Trade. I did not consider it satisfactory, and I told them so, but I signed it."

The President: Why on earth did you sign it? – I don't know why I did. I am not generally soft, but I must say I was very soft the day I signed that.

The inquiry was once more adjourned.

STOCKS AND SHARES
MARCONI PROFITS

Referring to the Titanic disaster, the directors remark: "The recent terrible catastrophe upon the Atlantic Ocean has again brought prominently before the notice of peoples of all nationalities the immense value of Mr. Marconi's invention and the necessity of its more general use by ships at sea. There can be little doubt that this terrible catastrophe brings us nearer to the day when ships of every nation will be compelled to carry this greatest life-saving apparatus."

12 June 1912

SIR RUFUS ISAACS AND MR. ISMAY

White Star Chairman Not Regarded as Ordinary Passenger.

SKIPPER AND ICE

What was Mr. Bruce Ismay's precise position on board the Titanic?

In the course of yesterday's inquiry before Lord Mersey a significant statement on this point was made by the Attorney-General.

Evidence was being given by Captain Hayes, who has been in the service of the White Star Line for twenty-three years, and he told Sir Robert Finlay (counsel for the company) that Mr. Ismay had frequently sailed on boats commanded by him and had never interfered with the navigation of the ship.

Lord Mersey, interposing, quietly observed that, as far as he knew, there was no evidence that he did interfere, and Sir Rufus Isaacs expressed his agreement, but added: "I do not agree that he was an ordinary passenger, or that he was treated as an ordinary passenger."

On Sir Robert Finlay demurring to this, a discussion ensued between the present and the ex-Attorney-General. Sir Rufus Isaacs suggested that the ice report was handed to Mr. Ismay for a specific purpose, and Sir Robert Finlay retorted that there was no evidence of any specific purpose.

Sir Rufus: My impression is that Mr. Ismay admitted very definitely to me that he knew it was given to him, because it was an ice report and a serious one.

Sir Robert: Is it suggested that this was handed to Mr. Ismay by the captain in order that Mr. Ismay might advise him?

Sir Rufus: Oh, no!

Sir Robert: Then I don't know what the suggestion is.

Sir Rufus: Then I have no objection to telling you. The object of giving him the telegram was because he, as chairman of the company, was there; that it was looked upon as a very serious report; that it was given to him because it was a serious report.

"It was given to him to consider and apprise himself of the facts, and it was handed back later on to the captain after a request to do so, and the object of giving it to him, I certainly shall suggest, was that if he had any directions to give with regard to the Titanic that was the time to give them."

DID NOT GIVE DIRECTIONS

The President: The real point of the matter is that he did not give any directions.

Sir Rufus: Except that to my mind an extraordinary thing is that the captain, instead of pinning that thing up in the chart-room, as I should have thought he ought to have done, handed it to Mr. Ismay, or anybody.

"That is a very extraordinary thing I cannot help thinking," concluded the Attorney-General, "that it is very extraordinary that there never was a word exchanged about it."

Sir Robert: There most certainly would be if you were right.

Before this little battle over Mr. Ismay's position between the two eminent counsel, Captain Hayes had told the Court that he never made any alteration in the speed of his ship in clear weather, after receiving ice reports.

He had, he said, steered at full speed between icebergs on a clear night, and had seen an iceberg 60ft. to 80ft. high ten miles off. The conditions on April 14 must have been abnormal.

BOARD OF TRADE WITNESS

After the luncheon interval the inquiry entered upon a new phase, with the beginning of the investigation into the Board of Trade's responsibility.

First witness was Sir Walter J. Howell, who has been forty years at Whitehall-gardens and thirteen years head of the Marine Department. It was elicited that the total loss during a decade on British westbound ships had been eight passengers.

Sir Walter said that, generally speaking, it had been felt that the regulations affecting shipping should not be too hard and fast lest, they should tend to cramp the development of shipbuilding. In 1890 a Committee was appointed which made certain recommendations with a view to reduce the number of lifeboats in view of the new policy of increasing the number of watertight compartments. These recommendations were not acted upon.

MINUTES THAT WERE MISSING

Peremptory Demand to See Board of Trade Records at Titanic Inquiry.

When the Titanic inquiry was resumed yesterday some searching questions were asked Sir Walter Howell, chief of the Marine Department of the Board of Trade, with regard to a letter referring to the alteration of the scale of boat accommodation which was sent to the Advisory Committee of the Board on April 4.

The letter was not actually sent until April 16, the day after news of the Titanic disaster was received. The President demanded to see the minutes of the Board. Sir Walter Howell replied that he had not got them.

The President: You ought to have them here.

Sir Walter: It is not usual to produce minutes.

Ultimately the minutes were produced and the President examined them.

"I wanted the suspicion, if there were any, that the letter was written in consequence of the Titanic disaster, cleared away," he said. "If this evidence is right it is obvious that it was not."

ROUGH SEAS TO ORDER

Titanic Inquiry Suggestions for Boat Tests for Liner Seamen.

Ought sailors to be tested in the handling of liners' lifeboats in a rough sea?

At the resumed proceedings of the Titanic inquiry yesterday Mr. Clem. Edwards suggested that mere testing in a smooth sea was not sufficient.

"How is the test to be applied?" asked the President. "You cannot order a rough sea."

Mr. Edwards: But you can take advantage of one.

The President: But the men might not be there when there is a rough sea. The local officer may say: "It is a pity you did not come here yesterday. We had a wind, and to-day it is smooth and calm. I think it is an outrageous thing to suggest that at Belfast, or Southampton, or elsewhere a local officer is to wait for a rough day in order that the seamen may go out in a boat to show what they can do."

15 June **1912**

SPEEDING UP TITANIC INQUIRY

Attorney-General Will Make No Further Comment on the Duff-Gordons' Conduct.

In the course of the Titanic inquiry yesterday Lord Mersey pleaded for a speedy conclusion and was told by counsel after counsel that they did not wish to call any witnesses. Captain Rostron is to give evidence the week after next.

Sir Rufus Isaacs stated that he did not intend to make any further comment on the conduct of the Duff-Gordons and the President stated that Mr. Ismay's conduct was only material to the extent to which it may have influenced the captain.

Making a statement in the course of his evidence, Captain Young, nautical adviser to the Marine Department of the Board of Trade, explained that if anyone was to blame for the supposed delay between July 4, 1911, and April 16, 1912, when nothing was done, it was himself. It was entirely upon his representations that the boats occupied so much of their time.

18 June **1912**

TITANIC INQUIRY ENDING

Firemen's Curious Objection to Boat Drill on White Star Line.

It is understood that at least two more days will be devoted to evidence before the Titanic inquiry concludes.

At yesterday's sitting there were some curious passages with regard to firemen's objection to boat drill, and the following dialogue passed between the President and Captain Clarke, assistant emigration officer of the Board of Trade at Southampton:–

The President: Is it only in the White Star Line that the firemen object to boat drill? – At Southampton, yes.

Why do they object to it in the White Star and not in any other lines? – I could not tell you.

Have they some dislike for the White Star Line? – I could not tell you.

You cannot tell me why they should dislike the boat drill in the White Star boats and submit to it in the others? – I could not tell you, sir.

It seems peculiar.

Captain Clarke said in his opinion and that of the other men in the service of the Board of Trade the whole staff of the Board ought to be doubled.

18 June **1912**

ICE AND WIRELESS

Valuable Evidence of Mr. Marconi and Sir E. Shackleton at Titanic Inquiry.

Valuable suggestions were made in the course of the Titanic inquiry yesterday when Mr. Marconi and Sir Ernest Shackleton, experts on the two forces that figured so largely in the disaster – ice and wireless – were among those called to give evidence.

Mr. Marconi said he had been giving a great deal of attention to a plan for safeguarding against future disasters, and that was, making the wireless apparatus ring a bell, thereby giving warning that a ship in distress needed assistance.

"Some tests have been made with the apparatus," said Mr. Marconi, "and I have considerable confidence that it can be employed."

Sir Ernest Shackleton said there were many icebergs that appeared to be black, due to the construction of the berg and the earthy matter it contained, with a dead calm sea there was no sign at all to give any indication that such an iceberg was in the way. To detect bergs in thick, hazy weather one man should always be as near the water-line as possible.

22 June **1912**

BLAMED BY COUNSEL

Mr. Scanlan's Comments on Responsibility of Titanic's Chiefs.

When Captain Rostron, of the Carpathia, the last witness to be called before the Titanic inquiry, attended yesterday to give evidence, the Attorney-General, on behalf of the Government, expressed deep gratitude to him for his conduct in the disaster.

Mr. Scanlan (Seamen's and Firemen's Union), first of the counsel to address the Court after the evidence, declared that:–

The disaster was due to a want of seamanship, skill, and proper directions as to navigation.

No extra precautions for safety were adopted. Failure to take these precautions was negligence of a very serious character.

Had there been better discipline among the officers and crew it would have been possible to have launched and lowered lifeboats sufficient to have rescued everybody on the ship.

Even in comparison with other countries the Board of Trade stood condemned for negligence.

Mr. Scanlan further declared that the presence of the managing owner on board, who knew that there was ice ahead and had something to do with the direction of the voyage, clearly made him a responsible party as well as the captain.

MR. ISMAY'S POSITION

Counsel Argue That His Presence on Titanic Was Source of Danger.

Lord Mersey's face burst into one huge smile, which gradually infected the assessors on either side of him, when he took his seat to resume the Titanic inquiry yesterday.

The cause of their amusement was the appearance of the Attorney-General's face, which had evidently been badly scorched and swollen by the sun during the week-end. "You have been qualifying for this place," Lord Mersey remarked to the Attorney-General, who smilingly assented, implying evidently that he had been at sea. "Rufus indeed," murmured a junior counsel.

Mr. Roche, who represents the Marine Engineers' Association, took up the series of counsel's speeches.

"It is one of the noblest traditions of the engineering profession on board ship," he said, "that in case of accident the rule is: 'All hands below.'

"The more closely that tradition is observed the more need is there that they should be given an opportunity, when things are hopeless, of coming on deck and taking their chance with the others of the boat accommodation which one hopes in the future will be available."

Mr. Harbinson, for the third-class passengers, submitted that the handing of the Marconi ice warning by the captain to Mr. Ismay was to invite from the latter some expression of opinion as to the speed of the ship.

"My suggestion is," continued Mr. Harbinson, "that Mr. Ismay's very presence on board had an effect on the navigation of the ship, even though he never said a single word."

Mr. Clem Edwards, M.P., speaking for the dockers, the seafarers, the stewards and the shipwrights, expressed to Lord Mersey their appreciation of the profound patience of the president.

It was certain that in future it was of the highest importance that any person in possession of what might be called "commercial supremacy" should not be allowed under any circumstances to discuss any question of the speed or navigation of the ship.

He was still speaking when the Court adjourned to-day.

BOAT THAT DID NOT GO BACK

Further comments on the positions of Sir Cosmo Duff-Gordon and Mr. Bruce Ismay in regard to the Titanic disaster were made by counsel at the inquiry yesterday.

Resuming his speech, Mr. Clem Edwards (Dockers' Union), referring to the fact that the boat in which the Duff-Gordons were did not go back to the help of the drowning, said:–

We have it on Sir Cosmo Duff-Gordon's own admission that he did say he would give the men £5 apiece to replace their kit. What I am going to say is an unpleasant task. It is this – that a state of mind which, while within hearing of the screams of the drowning, could think of so material a matter as the giving of money to replace kit is a state of mind which must have contemplated the position in which those drowning people were… which must have contemplated the possibility of rescuing some of those drowning.

"I am not going to say that here was a blunt, crude bargain of bribery, but the inference to be drawn from all the circumstances is that the money was offered to give such a sense of importance to Sir Cosmo Duff-Gordon in the boat that the view that they should not go back would weigh the same with the men as if it had been given as a naked piece of advice."

TITANIC INQUIRY ENDED

After thirty-six days the Titanic inquiry came to an end yesterday, when the Attorney-General finished his speech. In his concluding remarks the Attorney-General declared that, speaking generally, the two causes of disaster were the failure to keep a good look-out and the proceeding at too great a rate of speed.

Both at Cook's and the White Star Line it was agreed that there was a considerable falling-off in the number of American visitors to this country this season. Partially the loss of the Titanic and the Presidential struggles might account for the fact.

CLAIMANTS OF ALL NATIONS

Whole of Titanic Relief Fund Required for Bereaved People.

The Mansion House Committee of the Titanic Relief Fund met yesterday when Sir William Soulsby (hon. sec.) stated that, apart from the dependents of the crew, claims had been received in respect of 461 of the 817 passengers lost.

Of these 232 were British, twelve Austro-Hungarians, eighteen Belgians, thirty-three Bulgarians, three Danes, two French, one Italian, sixteen Norwegians, thirty-six Russians, seventy-two Swedes,

The Daily Mirror

THE MORNING JOURNAL WITH THE SECOND LARGEST NET SALE.

No. 2,736.   Registered at the G.P.O. as a Newspaper.   WEDNESDAY, JULY 31, 1912   One Halfpenny.

WHAT WILL BE THE FUTURE OF JAPAN?—NEW EMPEROR FACED WITH THE DIFFICULT TASK OF CARRYING ON THE WORK BEGUN BY HIS FATHER.

Where old Japan survives: Geisha girls in national dress. Portrait, Heir-Apparent.

The new Emperor. He was born in 1879

The Imperial Palace of Chiyoda, at Tokio, where the Emperor died.

Old Tokio. It is from a print by Hiroshige, a Japanese artist, showing the bridge leading into the city before the late Mikado's reign.

New Tokio. The city has been completely Westernised, and the photograph shows the new Stayle Theatre, a very fine building.

A difficult task lies before the new Emperor, namely that of holding for his country the proud position which his father—the maker of modern Japan—won for her among the nations. It is only since the late Emperor came to the throne, nearly forty-five years ago, that Japan has changed her mediævalism for modernity. The picture of the old bridge is taken from a print belonging to Mr. James Tregaskis, of High Holborn.—(Underwood and Underwood and Topical.)

nineteen Swiss and seventeen Syrians.

During the discussion it was apparent from the estimates that although the Mansion House and the other funds exceed £400,000, all of it would be required to maintain the modest allowances now being made for the sustenance of the bereaved people.

31 July 1912

LESSONS OF THE TITANIC WRECK

Disaster Due to Excessive Speed in Ice Region.

◀ Already the Titanic disaster had moved off the front page.

"NO NEGLIGENCE."
Commission Finds Captain Smith Made Grievous Mistake.

RULES FOR SAFETY
Californian Might Have Rescued Many, If Not All.

MR. ISMAY JUSTIFIED

No sensational findings were provided in Lord Mersey's report on the Titanic disaster, which was delivered yesterday at the final meeting of the Commission at the Scottish Drill Hall, Buckingham Gate, S.W.

In cold, unimpassioned phrase, the report, which covers seventy-four foolscap pages, sums up the greatest disaster of the sea, without bias or favour.

Lord Mersey himself read the report in the presence of a small assembly, among whom were several ladies. Mr. Bruce Ismay, the managing director of the White Star Line, which owned the Titanic, was not present.

The main finding of the Court was that:–

The loss of the Titanic was due to collision with an iceberg, brought about by the excessive speed at which the ship was being navigated.

The foundering of the Titanic, it may be recalled, took place on her maiden voyage across the Atlantic at 2.20 a.m. on Monday, April 15.

She was the largest passenger vessel ever built, and left Southampton, bound for New York, on her first voyage on Wednesday, April 10.

It was at 11.40 p.m. on the following Sunday, April 14, that she struck an iceberg. There were 2,201 persons on board, of whom 711 were saved.

Lord Mersey's report says that the root reason why Captain Smith persevered in his course, and maintained his speed, is probably to be found "in competition and in the desire of the public for quick passages rather than in the judgment of navigators. Unfortunately experience appeared to justify it. In these circumstances I am not able to blame Captain Smith."

NO BLAME FOR CAPTAIN

Lord Mersey's finding with regard to Captain Smith clears him of blame. The report says:–

"He had not the experience which his own misfortune has afforded to those whom he has left behind, and he was doing only that which other skilled men would have done in the same position....

"He made a mistake, a very grievous mistake, but one in which negligence cannot be said to have had any part.... It is, in my opinion, impossible to fix Captain Smith with blame.... What was a mistake in the case of the Titanic would, without doubt, be negligence in any similar case in the future."

LORD MERSEY PRESENTS HIS TITANIC REPORT.

UNFOUNDED CHARGE

As to "the moral conduct" of Sir Cosmo Duff-Gordon and Mr. Ismay, Lord Mersey says:–

"The very gross charge against Sir Cosmo Duff-Gordon that, having got into No. 1 boat, he bribed the men in it to row away from drowning people, is unfounded....

"I do not believe that the men were deterred from making the attempt (at rescue) by any act of Sir Cosmo Duff-Gordon's. At the same time I think that if he had encouraged the men to return... they would probably have made an effort to do so, and could have saved some lives."

Subject to the opinion that some of the boats might have attempted to save more lives, Lord Mersey, has nothing but praise for both passengers and crew.

He regretted, however, that some boats failed to attempt to save life when they might have done so. This was particularly the case with No. 1. boat.

The No. 1 boat, it may be recalled, was that in which were Sir Cosmo Duff-Gordon and Lady Duff-Gordon.

Lord Mersey, dealing with the attack on Mr. Ismay says:–

"I do not agree that any moral duty was imposed upon him to wait on board until the vessel foundered.... Had he not jumped into the lifeboat he would merely have added one more life, namely, his own, to the number of those lost."

CALIFORNIAN'S ERROR

Some of the salient features of Lord Mersey's report are as follow:–

The evidence indicates to Lord Mersey that the rockets seen by the Californian came from the Titanic and no other ship.

The Californian could have pushed through the ice to the open water without any serious risk, and so have come to the assistance of the Titanic. Had she done so,

Lord Mersey adds, she might have saved many, if not all, of the lives that were lost. The Californian could have reached the Titanic if she had made the attempt when she saw the first rocket. She made no attempt.

A good and proper look-out for ice was not kept on board. "Without implying that those actually on duty were not keeping a good look-out, in view of the night being moonless – there being no wind and perhaps very little swell – and especially in view of the high speed at which the vessel was running, it is not considered that the look-out was sufficient."

The use of binoculars by look-out men was neither necessary nor usual in such circumstances.

The evidence does not establish that searchlights should have been provided and used, though they may, at times, be of service.

When ice was seen proper and prompt measures were taken.

At least eight boats did not carry their full loads because:–

(1) Many people did not realise the danger or care to leave the ship at first;

(2) Some boats were ordered to be lowered with an idea of their coming round to the gangway doors to complete loading;

(3) The officers were not certain of the strength and capacity of the boats in all cases. The disproportion between the numbers of the passengers saved in the first, second, and third classes is due to various causes, among which the difference in the position of their quarters, and the fact that many of the third-class passengers were foreigners, are perhaps the most important.

The disproportion between the numbers of passengers and crew saved is due to the fact that the crew, for the most part all attended to their duties to the last, and until all the boats were gone.

MISSING WIRELESS MESSAGE

Of the wireless message received at about 1.45 p.m. (Titanic time) on the 14th, the report says the message was sent from the German steamer Amerika to the Hydrographic Office in Washington, stating that the Amerika had passed two large icebergs on the 14th.

That was a position south of the point of the Titanic's disaster. The message did not mention at what hour the bergs had been observed. It was a private message for the Hydrographer at Washington, but it passed to the Titanic because she was nearest to Cape Race, to which station it had to be sent in order to reach Washington.

Being a message affecting navigation, it should, in the ordinary course, have been taken to the bridge. So far as could be ascertained, it was never heard of by anyone on board the Titanic outside the Marconi room.

Lord Mersey was of opinion that when this message reached the Marconi room it was put aside by the operator Phillips to wait until the Titanic would be within call of Cape Race (at about 8 or 8.30 p.m.), and that it was never handed to any officer of the Titanic.

DRASTIC NEW RULES PROPOSED

The following recommendations for foreign-going passenger and emigrant steamships are submitted in Lord Mersey's report:–

WATERTIGHT COMPARTMENTS

The newly-appointed Bulkhead Commission should report upon the advisability of providing ships with a double skin carried above the water-line, and watertight decks.

LIFEBOATS AND RAFTS

These should be based on numbers and not upon tonnage.

Boats should be fitted with a protective continuous fender.

One or more boats should be fitted with some form of mechanical propulsion.

All boats to be fitted with lamps and pyrotechnic lights, compasses and provisions. More searching Board of Trade inspection of boats and life-saving appliances.

MANNING THE BOATS

Enough members of the crew should be drilled to man the boats.

Boat, fire, and watertight drill should be held after leaving port, and at least once a week.

Board of Trade to be satisfied that an efficient scheme has been devised and is known to officers for efficient working of boats, before leaving port.

GENERAL

Continuous day and night service of wireless, with efficient number of trained operators.

PRINCIPAL POINTS OF LORD MERSEY'S REPORT ON TITANIC DISASTER FINDINGS

The Titanic's collision with an iceberg was due to the excessive speed at which she was navigated.

Captain Smith made a grievous mistake but was not negligent.

A good and proper look-out for ice was not kept. An extra look-out should have been placed on the stern head, and a sharp look-out kept from both sides of the bridge.

Practice of full speed at night in ice region was bad, but in the circumstances Captain Smith could not be blamed.

Arrangements for manning and launching the boats in case of emergency were not proper or sufficient.

There had been no proper boat drill, and in the opinion of the Court the Board of Trade should make rules requiring efficient boat drills and boat musters.

The third-class passengers were not unfairly treated.

PRAISE AND BLAME

The gross charge against Sir Cosmo Duff-Gordon of having bribed men to row away from the wreck is unfounded.

The officers did their work very well and without any thought for themselves.

Discipline both among passengers and crew during the lowering of the boats was good, but the organisation should have been better, and more lives would have been saved.

The outstanding circumstance is the omission by the Board of Trade during so many years to revise the rules of 1894.

The lights seen by the Californian were those of the Titanic. The Californian could have pushed through the ice to the open water without serious risk, and so have come to the assistance of the Titanic. Had she done so she might have saved many, if not all, of the lives that were lost.

The conduct of Captain Rostron and the crew of the Carpathia was admirable in every way.

As to the attack on Mr. Bruce Ismay, the Court did not agree that his position of managing director of the company imposed on him a moral duty to wait on board until the vessel sank. If he had not jumped into the boat another life would have been lost.

RECOMMENDATIONS

There should be moderate speed only when steaming at night through ice.

Lifeboat and raft accommodation should be based on the number of persons intended to be carried and not on the tonnage.

That one of the boats should be mechanically propelled, and all should carry lights and lamps.

In all ships a boat drill, a fire drill and a watertight door drill should be held as soon as possible after leaving the port of departure, and at least once a week during the voyage.

An international conference on the working of life-saving devices should be called.

Captains should be reminded that it is a misdemeanour not to go to relief of vessels in distress when possible.

Night and day service of wireless.

WHAT WAS WRONG

Englishmen are often reproached for their habit of never seriously considering any situation until a grave defeat has made it, in a sense, too late for the situation to be considered. It is in matters of administration everywhere that this faculty of not caring, until a kind of desperate eleventh-hour anxiety is forced upon us, is chiefly displayed.

Administration in war – we had to have a desperately "muddled" war before we became aware that we lacked the faculty there; and every day grave voices warn us that one lesson has not sufficed and that even now we are not prepared; or, in the expressive phrase of an Under-Secretary, that "what the Territorials chiefly want is peace." And then administration in shipping – to-day's publication of the Titanic report shows us here again considering anxiously when it's too late. Finally, as to administration in sport – plenty of home truths have been flying about of late concerning our want of that, in reference to the Olympic Games.

1 August 1912

MID-OCEAN MESSAGE

Last Words from Famous Titanic Victim Reported Picked Up in a Bottle.

New York, July 31 – The following message in a bottle has been picked up (says an Exchange telegram) off Block Island and transmitted by wireless:–

April 16 – Mid-ocean on raft. No water. No food.
– MAJOR BUTT.

Major Archibald Butt, President Taft's military aide-de-camp, was returning on the Titanic after a visit to Rome where he went to see the Pope and King Victor Emmanuel. The Titanic went down at about two o'clock on the morning of April 15.

TITANIC PENSIONS FROM £400,000

Over 1,800 Claims for Help from Those Left in Distress.

CHILDREN'S "FATHER"

On October 1 next it is hoped that the widows and relatives of the Titanic victims will receive the first instalments of their pension money – to be awarded out of the combined Titanic funds – about £400,000.

This huge sum of money includes *The Daily Mail*'s, contribution of nearly £60,000 and collections made by other journals and public officials in different parts of the country.

How and to whom the money is to be distributed is the difficult

task which the Public Trustee and its small army of officials are now engaged.

The task of the Public Trustee will be a tremendous one. There are some 1,400 claims to pensions from relatives of the Titanic's lost crew, about 400 claims on behalf of passengers who were drowned, and several hundred children to be looked after.

HELP FOR WIDOWS

The case of every individual claimant has to be carefully investigated – lady commissioners visit the homes of the widows and relatives – and their exact financial needs ascertained.

When every claimant's case has been thoroughly investigated, actuaries will ascertain how the money can be distributed.

At the Public Trustee's Office, *The Daily Mirror* was given particulars of what pensions it is hoped to give to the claimants.

Here is a rough list of the pensions which, it is hoped, will be given to the widows and others in need:–

STEWARDS' RELATIVES	Per Week
Widows	£l00
Children – One	0 3 6
Two	0 5 0
Graduated scale up to (for five)	0 10 6
Father or mother (when dependent)	0 5 0
Other relatives (where dependence can be proved)	0 5 0

FIREMEN AND GREASERS' RELATIVES	
Widows	0 15 0
Children (same as stewards' allowance)	
Father or mother	0 5 0
Brother, sister or nieces (when dependent)	0 2 6

ENGINEERS' RELATIVES

Halt wages. Widows of men who earned from £7 to £20 a month will (it is hoped) receive £3 10s. to £10 a month.

GUARDIAN FOR CHILDREN

"Nothing more intricate and difficult than the allotting of this giant fund can be imagined," said an official. "Here are some of the claimants' forms," he added, producing some closely filled-up papers.

On these forms every detail of the claimant's financial and family position were entered – how much the husband or relative had allowed them, their present means, number of children, etc. An important duty of the Public Trustee will be that of acting as foster father to several hundreds of the bereaved boys and girls, who now have no father to direct them.

"It will be our pleasant duty to keep our eye upon these children when they grow up, to help them to learn trades or professions, and to encourage them to get on in the world," added the official.

"If any of the Titanic widows marry again they forfeit their pension, and the money goes back to the general fund."

2 August 1912

MEMORIAL TO HEROIC BANDSMEN

Permanent Record of Titanic's Musicians To Be Placed in Orchestral Institute.

The heroic band of the Titanic is to have a permanent memorial – in the new Institute of the Orchestral Association.

For this purpose, it was reported yesterday, £225 is to be set aside out of the net profit of £793 7s. derived from the association's concert at the Albert Hall on May 24 last. A sum of £400, earmarked for the families of the dead musicians, has been sent to the Mansion House Fund.

With reference to the article in yesterday's *Daily Mirror* on the distribution of Titanic pensions, the Public Trustee asks us to say that the suggested scale of allowance if adopted would be reduced or affected by the amounts received by the relatives or dependents of the crew from the employers' liability fund and other sources, and, further, before such a scale could be recommended for adoption by the Mansion House Committee the passenger claims will have to be considered.

9 August 1912

MOTHER DIES FROM GRIEF

Grief is believed to have caused the death reported yesterday from Adrian, Georgia, of Mrs. Linnie Futrelle, mother of the novelist, Jacques Futrelle, who went down with the Titanic.

15 August 1912

"SORROW-STREET," SOUTHAMPTON

When a local committee was formed at Southampton yesterday in connection with the distribution of their Titanic Relief Fund, it was stated that the 403 men domiciled in Southampton who perished in the disaster had left 239 widows, 462 children and 213 dependants.

NEW YORK'S TRAGIC BABY
Son Born to Mrs. Astor Who Was Rescued from Titanic.

BRIDE – WIDOW – MOTHER
(FROM OUR OWN CORRESPONDENT)

New York, August 14 – Pathetic interest attaches to the birth in New York to-day of a son to Mrs. Astor, the young widow of Colonel John Jacob Astor, who perished on the Titanic. The baby comes into the world fatherless, and, a tragic little figure, for Mrs. Astor – the beautiful Madeleine Force, as she was – has become bride, widow and mother all within a year of her twenty-first birthday.

Mrs. Astor, who was returning from a honeymoon trip round Europe with her husband, was one of the passengers rescued from the Titanic in the disaster only four months ago. When in the lifeboat in which she was saved, she showed remarkable pluck till picked up by the Carpathia.

Her last two years have been passed in the fierce glare of New York publicity. From the date of her engagement to Colonel Astor – her senior by twenty-eight years – when her intended marriage was fiercely denounced by the American newspapers, to the birth of her child, she has passed through such trouble as, happily, falls to the lot of few women in a lifetime.

Her brief married life – she was married on September 9, 1911, barely a year ago – concluded abruptly with the terrible disaster to the Titanic, the sudden death of her bridegroom, the hardships of hours in an open boat amid the ice, at a time when her health needed every possible care, and, finally, the birth of her heir. So serious was the effect of these accumulated misfortunes that at one time the doctors were in grave doubts whether she would survive her ordeal.

Happily, the young bride-widow has at length, perhaps, found some consolation for all her troubles in the birth of a son, whom Dr. Edward Cragin, her physician, describes as "a vigorous youngster." He weighs 7¾lb., and was born at 8.15 to-day.

John Jacob Astor, his father's name, is to be his.

Even in the hour of her becoming a mother, poor Madeleine Astor could not avoid the attentions of the New York public. For some days past a crowd of women has assembled outside the Astor mansion, 840, Fifth-avenue, expecting news of the birth, and to-day the topic takes precedence of all other news here.

More than once policemen ordered the waiting women away, but

Mrs. Astor sent word "Allow the women to remain in front of the house, if they wish," and the news of the birth of a son was received with keen expression of joy.

16 August 1912

WIRELESS PATROLS OF THE SEAS
Committee's Scheme for Far-reaching Life-Saving.

ETERNAL VIGIL
Tonnage, Not Passengers, as Basis of Rescue Appliances.

TITANIC LESSONS
Lifeboats Under Davits to Hold All On Board Impracticable.

"Prevention is better than cure" may be said to be the keynote to the report, issued yesterday, of the Merchant Shipping Advisory Committee's inquiry into life-saving at sea. Taking into consideration the lessons to be drawn from the loss of the Titanic, the committee emphasise the necessity for taking all possible precautions to provide for the buoyancy of the vessel after an accident.

The committee found that on April 25 last 66 per cent of a total of 521 emigrant ships provided boat accommodation for all persons for whom the vessel was certified. The committee is of the opinion that the standard should continue to be based on the gross tonnage of the vessels.

The committee is of the opinion that it is not practicable to adopt the numbers on board as the standard for the number of boats to be carried under davits. Special provision should be made in regard to vessels of upwards of 640ft. in length. The Titanic, it will be recalled, was 882ft. 9in. length.

The dangers from the use of searchlights and of binoculars by look-out men is also dealt with. A new era in the perpetual patrolling of the sea by wireless is opened in the sub-committee's report.

It is essential, says the report, that it should be impossible for any distress or danger signal to fail to be recorded; that a perpetual watch on the installation be kept, for which purpose the operator on the ship will require an assistant; and that the installation be under the captain's control.

LESSONS OF TITANIC DISASTER
With regard to the lessons to be learnt from the Titanic disaster, the committee say:–

"We fully recognise that the proved impossibility of keeping the Titanic afloat after her collision with the iceberg until the arrival of outside succour has created a new situation, but it is important to bear in mind that the Titanic was a vessel belonging to a special and limited class.

"Therefore, although the circumstances attendant on the loss of the Titanic must be taken into most careful consideration in regard to the life-saving equipment of all passenger ships, they have little, if any, relation to the equipment of the 6,450 cargo vessels engaged in the home and foreign trades, and they have no relation to the equipment to be carried on the remaining 6,351 vessels, of which all but 195 are under 100 tons, of the British mercantile marine.

"Further, the circumstances attendant on the loss of the Titanic have demonstrated the extraordinary difficulty even in calm weather of using to the full on a passenger vessel carrying large numbers the boat accommodation already provided, and thereby emphasised our view as to the necessity for taking all possible precautions to provide for the buoyancy of the vessel after the casualty and efficient means for communicating with the shore or with other vessels. We are satisfied that it is by proceeding on these lines that the safety of the passengers, can be best secured."

TONNAGE, NOT PASSENGERS

Discussing possible amendments of the existing regulations, the committee express the opinion that the gross tonnage of vessels should continue to form the basis for the number of boats to be carried under davits. They add the opinion that it is not practicable to adopt the numbers on board as the standard for the number of boats to be carried under davits.

After suggesting that the existing standard should be maintained, with special provision to be made in the cases of vessels of a greater length than 640ft. the committee formulate their chief recommendations respecting passenger and emigrant ships as follows:–

1. The stability and seaworthy qualities of the vessel itself be regarded as of primary importance and every possible disaster be subordinated to this primary consideration.

2. The existing scale based on the gross tonnage of the vessel be maintained in regard to the number of boats to be carried under davits.

3. The existing scale for additional boat and life-raft accommodation be varied by substituting for a percentage calculated on the tonnage scale, the principal that the carrying capacity of the boats provided under the tonnage scale and of the additional wood, metal, or collapsible boats, and of the approved life-rafts be sufficient to accommodate all persons on board.

4. We recommend that in all vessels of a registered length of more than 640ft. an additional set of davits should be required on each side of the vessel for each length of 80ft. or portion of 80ft. by which the total registered length exceeds 640ft.

DANGER OF SEARCHLIGHTS

With regard to the provision of binoculars for look-out men, the Committee say:–

"Although binoculars are useful in ascertaining the precise nature of an object to which attention has been called, they restrict the field of vision, and that consequently there is a danger that look-out men, if provided with binoculars, might fail to notice an object which would have been picked out with the naked eye.

"We accordingly consider the adoption of this suggestion inadvisable."

Dealing with the use of searchlights in large passenger vessels, the Committee say:

"It is possible that a searchlight would be of value in certain circumstances – for instance, in picking up an unlighted buoy, rock, land, ice or ice field, in passing through a canal, or for salvage purposes. On the other hand, the use of searchlights would be attended by many disadvantages, such as the following:–

"Dazzling the observers on board the ship making use of the lights, especially if the lights are badly placed. General danger to navigation owing to the blinding effect to those on board other vessels and to the possibility of the navigation lights exhibiting the searchlight, being obscured.

"Temptation to make land, buoys, etc., by placing too much reliance on picking of the marks by means of the searchlight. False security when in the vicinity of ice and other dangers."

PERPETUAL WIRELESS WATCH

Dealing with the position of wireless telegraphy in regard to preservation of life at sea, the report of the sub-committee on the subject states:–

Arrangements should be made to ensure that no signal of distress or danger within the range of the instrument be missed.

We have made inquiry whether it would be possible to dispense with constant attendance at the installation by means of some system of call by signal or bell. Although automatic devices of this kind have been invented, none of them have up to the present time been found reliable in practice, and, pending the introduction of a satisfactory device, we consider it essential that a permanent watch on the installation should be kept.

We recommend that all foreign-going vessels compelled to be

equipped with wireless apparatus should be required to carry one fully-qualified operator, and in addition such assistants as will enable a constant watch to be maintained during the absence of the operator.

The wireless operator, adds the report, as well as the transmission and receipt of all messages (other than private messages to or from passengers whilst the installation is being worked under the captain's orders for the sending of such messages), should be under the control of the captain.

5 September **1912**

BOATS FOR ALL

Board of Trade's Revised Rules for Safety of Life at Sea.

Lifeboat accommodation for all on board, the number of boats attached to davits to depend not on tonnage but the length of the ship – that, in brief, is the decision of the Board of Trade after consideration of the report of the Titanic inquiry by Lord Mersey and the recommendations of the Merchant Shipping Advisory Committee.

The revised rules for the safety of life at sea, which were issued last night as a White-paper, affect both foreign-going and home trade ships. In regard to foreign-going ships they state:–

Foreign-going passenger steamers, emigrant ships, and foreign-going sailing ships carrying passengers are in future to provide sufficient lifeboat accommodation for all on board. The number of boats to be attached to davits is no longer to depend on tonnage, but on the length of the ship, and the davits must be placed amidships. This rule is subject to modification.

8 October **1912**

WIRELESS CALLS NOTED ON PAPER

Invention Will Prevent Urgent Messages Being Missed.

A new era in wireless telegraphy has begun. Wireless messages can now be recorded on paper.

This news is of vast importance, for it means that urgent wireless messages for help from ships will never be missed, and that there will be no need for wireless operators to be constantly listening for messages.

If the Titanic had received her fatal blow from the iceberg at 11.50 p.m. instead of 11.40 p.m. not a single soul would have been saved! And it would have been because the wireless operator on board the Carpathia, which received the Titanic distress messages, would have been in bed, and the call for help

would not have been heard.

Now that the messages can be recorded on paper, it will be only necessary for the captain to tear off the messages every few minutes. This means that no urgent message can be missed.

M. Lefeuvre, Professor of Physiology at the Faculté de Médicine of Rennes, is responsible for this important invention, and wireless messages received from a distance of 200 miles have been recorded by his machine.

5 December **1912**

KILLED BY TITANIC SHOCK

New York, Dec 4 – The death occurred in a private hospital here to-day of Mr. Archibald Gracie, one of the survivors of the Titanic disaster. His death was indirectly due to shock caused by his terrible experiences. – Reuter.

Mr. Gracie, who was a colonel in the United States army, was the last man to be saved from the sinking liner, with which he was sucked down. He afterwards managed to reach a raft.

14 December **1912**

CARPATHIAN STOKERS' HEROISM REWARDED

The chief engineer and his assistants serving in the S.S. Carpathia when she made her fast run to save the Titanic's passengers were rewarded yesterday at Liverpool. The Lord Mayor presented a service of plate to Chief Engineer Johnstone, and gold watches to his assistants. The stokers will receive cheques. Photograph shows the Lord Mayor, his wife and Mr. Johnstone.

18 December **1912**

TITANIC INQUIRY COSTS £20,231

The Titanic wreck inquiry cost the country £20,231 5s. 10d.!

This information was given by the President of the Board of Trade in the parliamentary papers last night.

Among the most interesting items of expenditure are the following:–

Wreck Commissioner's salary	£1,050 0 0
Sir Rufus Isaacs	£2,458 2 0
Sir John Simon	£2,425 4 0
Mr. Aspinall	£2,345 12 0
Mr. Rowlatt	£1,249 3 6
Mr. Raymond Asquith	£864 0 0
Detention payments (general witnesses)	£1,908 12 5
Shorthand writing	£622 16 6

The solicitors' bills total over £2,500.

Our Continuing Fascination

For every column inch given over to the disaster, its aftermath and the official inquiries, they have been matched by our continuing fascination with all things Titanic. The stories, rumours, myths and legends that have grown up around the modern world's most defining disasters are themselves worthy of a book.

◀ Captain Edward John Smith died at the helm of the Titanic and his body was never recovered. His daughter, Helen, unveiled this statue of him at Beacon Park in Lichfield, Staffordshire, on 29 July 1914. Lady Kathleen Scott, widow of Captain Robert Falcon Scott, the doomed "Scott of the Antarctic", sculpted the bronze.

16 January 1913

£200,000 FOR LOSS OF HUSBAND

New York, Jan. 16 – Claims for compensation aggregating £l,200,000 have been filed by the survivors of the Titanic disaster.

The largest claim made is that of Mrs. Henry Harris, widow of the theatrical manager, who demands £200,000 for the loss of her husband, £5,500 for the loss of her jewels and about £900 for the loss of her husband's baggage.

Mrs. Futrelle, the wife of the well-known author who went down with the ship, and Mrs. Howard ask £60,000 each, and Mrs. Frank Millet, widow of the artist, £20,000.

16 April 1913

£92,000,000 BUSINESS

What the Public Trustee Has Done in Five Years.

The Titanic Fund of £413,213 was put in the hands of the Public Trustee. Of this £28,627 was expended in single payment lump sum grants chiefly to foreign seamen and passenger dependents and to British persons wishing to go abroad, and widows unencumbered with children who would be able to earn their own living with a lump sum grant. This left the fund (after some other payments) at £383,754, of which £369,622 is invested, and the balance is available in the form of cash for the immediate requirements to continue the periodical payments.

24 April 1913

TITANIC MEMORIAL

▶ The Titanic Memorial Lighthouse on the Church Institute for Seamen, New York, which was dedicated on the anniversary of the disaster. It can be seen for twelve miles out to sea.

STOCKS & SHARES
WHITE STAR DIVIDEND HALVED

Special interest attaches itself to the report, now to hand, of the Oceanic Steam Navigation Company, which owns the White Star Line, in view of the fact that it covers the year of the great Titanic disaster. The sum of £108,158 is written off profits, which were considerably reduced by the disaster, the withdrawal of the Olympic for repairs and by labour disturbances. The net profit amounted to £245,344, of which £225,000 was distributed in March last, being 30

per cent on the share capital. To the balance of £20,344, the amount of £140,171, brought forward, is added, making a total of £160,515. For 1911, the dividend was 60 per cent., or double this year's.

25 September 1913

FORESAW HIS OWN DEATH

Miss Stead Tells of Her Father's Warning of Tragic Fate in Titanic.

There is usually a particularly close affection and sympathy existing between father and daughter, and it is this precious understanding which makes Miss Estelle W. Stead's book, "My Father" – the late Mr. W. T. Stead, who perished in the Titanic disaster – so interesting.

Spiritualism occupies a very big part in the book, which is published by William Heinemann, and Miss Stead tells the story of how the famous Julia's Bureau came to be started. She also points out a curious coincidence in the manner of her father's death and a passage in a book which he published in 1892.

"It is," says Miss Stead, "the description of how one man was saved from an iceberg. The ship on which he was travelling struck an iceberg and went down; all perished save this one man… The incident is purely fictitious, and supposed to take place on the Majestic – and it is a strange coincidence that her captain at that

time was Captain Smith – the Captain Smith who, with the writer of the incident, was to meet his death – through an iceberg – as captain of the ill-fated Titanic."

Miss Stead adds that her father had warning of his approaching death, "During the winter months, he was constantly receiving messages bidding him put his house in order." She ends:–

Three weeks after his passing he came to the Upper Room in the Inner Sanctuary of Julia's Bureau. In that room where he had himself so often spoken of the life to come and conversed with those who had already passed onward, he – the beloved Chief – came and spoke to those who prayed and waited, knowing he would come. Clearly he showed his face that all might see, and as it faded into darkness – his voice ran through the room and he spoke saying, "All I told you is true…"

On the very day that Mr. Stead left England by the Titanic he wrote a letter to *The Daily Mirror* which showed that his daughter's interests were the last thing he thought about before sailing.

Miss Stead also publishes a strange message which came from her brother William on the anniversary of his death to her late father. It tells of the joys of the other existence:–

When I think of the ideas that I had of the life I am now living, when I was in the world in which you are, I marvel at the hopeless inadequacy of my dreams. The reality is so much, so very much greater than ever I imagined.

"I tell you it is better on before always and far better than I dreamed of."

31 March **1914**

MAGNETS TO RAISE THE TITANIC!

The odd plan devised by a very imaginative American engineer for raising the ill-starred Titanic by means of a number of powerful magnets let down from a fleet of vessels.

8 May **1914**

MR. STEAD REAPPEARS

General's Story of How Dead Writer Described Sinking of the Titanic.

That he had seen during a spiritualistic seance the late Mr. W. T. Stead was stated by General Sir Alfred Turner yesterday in London at a meeting under the auspices of the London Spiritualist Alliance.

On the Sunday following the death of Mr. Stead, the general said he (the speaker) was with a palmist who told him that behind him in a picture appeared the head of a man. Afterwards the whole body appeared, and she described it.

It was an accurate description of Mr. Stead, who was holding a little child by the hand.

A few nights after that the voice of Mr. Stead came and spoke at length to him and the Others in the room at the time.

Mr. Stead told them what happened at the last minutes of the wreck of the Titanic, how when the ship sunk they "passed over," but they had not the slightest notion that they had gone, although Mr. Stead knew, well where he was, and that it was no surprise or shock to him except the first short, sharp struggle of drowning.

He (Mr. Stead) set himself to work to try and tell them that they had "passed over," and that there was no more, at any rate, physical suffering for them.

They asked Mr. Stead if he would show himself, and he said, "Not now. If you go to _ _ House on such a day I will show myself to you."

The General said he went, but the seance was not altogether a sympathetic one, and Mr. Stead only came to them twice in short, sharp flashes.

Since then he said he had seen Mr. Stead many times at seances.

"When he has shown himself," continued the speaker, "he has said little, but when he has not shown himself he said a good deal.

"At the last seance he appeared plainer than I have ever seen him before since his death. He said, 'I cannot speak to you to-night but pursue the truth, pursue the truth; it is all truth.'"

10 May **1915**

"THE MAN WHO CANNOT BE DROWNED."

A stoker named Tonner, who says he cannot be drowned. He was saved from the Titanic, the Empress of Ireland, and the Lusitania. In the circle is Joseph Delaney, one of the crew, who was also saved from the Titanic.

MEMORY OF TITANIC DEAD

A memorial service being held on the cutter Modoc at the spot in the Atlantic at which the liner Titanic sank after collision with an iceberg in 1912. A berg still haunts the seas.

Sir Cosmo succeeded to the baronetcy in 1896. He married in 1900 Lucy Wallace, daughter of the late Douglas Sutherland.

Lady Duff-Gordon is Lucille, the famous fashion expert, and a sister of Mrs. Elinor Glyn, the novelist. She also, with her husband escaped from the Titanic disaster. At the inquiry into the loss of the liner the Commission decided that there was no foundation for the

SIR C. DUFF-GORDON

Death of Baronet Who Was Survivor of Titanic Disaster.

Sir Cosmo Duff-Gordon, Bart., who was in the Titanic when the liner sank in the Atlantic on April 14, 1912, with the loss of 1,489 lives, died in London yesterday aged sixty-eight. He had been in failing health for some time.

suggestion that third-class passengers had been unfairly treated. It also exonerated Sir Cosmo Duff-Gordon from charges made against him.

A TITANIC ERROR

Second-Officer Hero Not "Destitute" in U.S.

STRANGE CABLE

Commander C. H. Lightoller, who was second officer of the ill-fated liner Titanic, is a very surprised man.

Yesterday, the twentieth anniversary of the sinking of the ship with the loss of more than 1,500 lives after colliding with an iceberg on her maiden voyage, the following cable was received in London from San Francisco:–

While the anniversary of the sinking of the Titanic is being generally observed, the ill-fated liner's second mate, Charles Herbert Lightoller, whose bravery was one of the features of the disaster, is lying forgotten, helpless and destitute, in Santa Rosa Hospital, near San Francisco.

But Commander Lightoller, who was instrumental in saving 600 lives before the liner foundered, is in the best of health and spirits – at his home at Putney, and the only explanation of the report he can offer is that the man in hospital is suffering from delusions.

"Commander Lightoller has not been to San Francisco for many years," a reporter was informed at his house yesterday. "He certainly was the second officer of the Titanic when she was wrecked and had a wonderful escape.

"Just before the liner went down he jumped into the water and after floating about for some time with a collapsible boat, which there was no time to open, was picked up by a lifeboat, the occupants of which were later rescued by the Carpathia."

25 November 1932

BROADCASTS WHICH WERE NOT

B.B.C. on Its Abandoned Programmes.

TITANIC DISASTER

"Then there was Filson Young's play "Titanic," the protests about which were remarkable, as they referred purely to the subject, the play itself not having been written at the time, and the author having publicly stated that the actual sinking of the ship did not figure in the play.

"This protest was all the more remarkable in that some of the most successful broadcasts of the past have been plays like 'Journey's End' and 'Brigade Exchange' which must have aroused many more sorrowful memories than the sinking of the Titanic.

"In this case the B.B.C. decided to abandon the projected broadcast, as it felt that the play would not obtain a fair hearing and would be prejudiced by the misrepresentation to which it had been subject.

22 April 1935

TITANIC SCANDAL VICTIM DIES

ESCAPED FROM WRECK WITH BARONET HUSBAND

One of the most tragic scandals in sea history is recalled by the death in a Putney nursing home during the week-end of Lucy Lady Duff-Gordon, widow of Sir Cosmo Duff-Gordon, Bart.

Lady Duff-Gordon had been ill with sciatica for several weeks. She married Sir Cosmo in 1900 and had been a widow since April, 1931.

She and her late husband were passengers in the Titanic when the liner struck an iceberg and sank in the Atlantic on April 14, 1912.

The lifeboat in which they left the ship was picked up by the Carpathia. Eventually they returned to England in the Lusitania.

Meanwhile, the rumour had got abroad that Sir Cosmo had bribed the lifeboat's crew to get away from the sinking ship as quickly as possible and so avoid rescuing others.

A seaman declared in New York that the "millionaires' boat" the one containing Sir Cosmo and his wife, was the first away, and that the Duff-Gordons gave £5 to each member of the crew.

When the couple landed in England they saw newspaper placards everywhere branding them as cowards.

One said: "Sir Cosmo Duff-Gordon safe and sound while women go down in the Titanic.".... Newsboys ran by them shouting, "Read about the Titanic cowards!"

"From that time," wrote Lady Duff-Gordon, twenty years later, "my husband became a changed man. His heart was broken. He never lived down the shame."

GIFTS EXPLAINED

Both were completely vindicated of the "moral charge" when the Board of Trade held its inquiry into the loss of the ship.

Lady Duff-Gordon explained the £5 gifts to the lifeboat crew as follows:–

"One of the boat's crew said, 'What about us? We have lost all our kit, and our pay stops from the moment the ship went down.' Sir Cosmo replied, 'Yes, that's hard luck, if you like. At any rate, I will give you £5 each towards new kit.'"

In 1893, when Lady Duff-Gordon was Miss Lucy Sutherland, she was penniless.

But she made herself famous in a few months as Lucile, a dress designer.

Four companies developed from her venture, and at one time she was earning £10,000 a year.

The mannequin parade, as we know it to-day, was her invention.
She was a sister of Mrs. Elinor Glyn, the novelist.

17 February **1940**

RED PAINT OVER TWO STATUES

Southampton police are investigating the disfigurement of two memorials in East Park, Southampton discovered yesterday morning.

Large quantities of vivid red paint were poured over the Titanic memorial and a statue of Lord Palmerston.

The outrages are believed to have been committed by members of an anti-war organisation. In each case the culprits must have climbed nearly fifteen feet to pour the paint over the top of the memorials.

On the Titanic memorial which is surmounted by the figure of an angel, the paint ran down over the inscription: "Greater love hath no man than this…"

The Titanic memorial is to the engineers who died when the liner sank after hitting an iceberg in the North Atlantic.

23 June **1951**

A RELIEF FUND STARTED WHEN A LINER SANK IN 1912

There's still £199,000 in this kitty.

In Room 20 of a second-floor office overlooking Lincoln's Inn Fields, London, Mr. John McCathie is preparing his accounts.

He flicks through the details of the investments.

Because next month this fifty-seven-year-old Civil Servant from Watford, Herts, will present his accounts at the Mansion House.

This grey-haired man with the blue bow tie and the one and a half inches of spotlessly laundered cuff is looking at the shares – because thirty-nine years ago – one Sunday in April – the "unsinkable liner" Titanic hit an iceberg in the North Atlantic.

There were 711 survivors – 1,490 perished. The public subscribed £414,066 3s. for the dependants. Today, £199,040 remains to help 116 dependants who still draw regular pensions from the fund of which Mr. McCathie is secretary on behalf of the Public Trustee.

In Room 20 in Kingsway there is little to remind you of that disastrous night thirty-nine years ago.

Once there was a model of the Titanic on the mantelpiece of the highly black-leaded grate that is never lighted because of the coal shortage. It "vanished" several years ago.

The walls are freshly painted in cream and a thick beige carpet covers the parquet floor. In a mahogany, glass-fronted book-case there are red leather-bound works on finance and administration.

It could be the office of any successful business man, because the Titanic Fund has been run on the best business lines.

By the end of 1850 allowances, pensions and grants to dependants totalled £642,132 12s. 2d.

This was the result of wise investments by the Fund's executive committee. To 1951's dependants, the oldest a widow of ninety-one, the youngest a woman of forty-one, go allowances and pensions from the Fund which bring a dependant's income to £3 1s. a week when State help has been taken into consideration.

Three times a year, at Christmas, Easter and during the summer, the pensioners get a £5 bonus. Grants of up to £25 are available for cases of unexpected hardship.

About twelve people a year put in new claims – few get a grant.

Mr. McCathie and his staff of two women administer other sea disaster funds – including the Lusitania, which was torpedoed by a German submarine in May, 1915. The administration charges for the Titanic Fund are remarkably low. Last year they were £337 7s. 1d.

Occasionally the pensioners think they should get a bigger share of the money.

This cannot be done because the policy of Room 20 is that as long as any of the dependants live there will be an income for them.

Accountants will see that on the day the last pensioner dies, the fund will be exhausted.

Away from the businesslike impartiality of Room 20, lady visitors in Exeter, Liverpool, London and Southampton call in for cups of tea with their customers.

There are ninety-five widows on their books, who lose their pensions if they re-marry. Today the grief of many has given way to practical considerations.

One told a lady visitor recently: "You know, Miss, perhaps it was as well my husband went down. After all, I get more from the fund than we would have got from our Old Age Pensions."

14 April **1962**

THE MAN WHO WOULD NOT BE BLAMED…

At 11.40 to-night it will he fifty years to the minute since the luxury liner Titanic hit an iceberg in the Atlantic.

I have just listened for nearly three hours – the time it took the

cruel sea to claim this 46,000-ton liner and 1,500 lives – to the words of a dead man.

A man who, according to official records, carried the dreadful indictment of having left the people to die.

The voice was that of Captain Stanley Lord. He died three months ago, aged eighty-four, at his home in Wallasey, Cheshire.

But not before he had recorded on 5,000 feet of tape every detail of that historic night – and a complete denial of the charges made against him during the controversial 33-day British Court of Inquiry that followed. – Jack Stonely.

ALLEGATION

The tape, a sworn statement, original radio messages and every detail of the inquiry are in a safe at the offices of the Mercantile Marine Service Association in Liverpool.

It was alleged at the inquiry that Captain Lord failed to answer the Titanic's distress signals when his ship, the Californian, was only a few miles away.

I listened to the words of Captain Lord boom out from a tape recorder:

"They say my ship was eight to ten miles from the Titanic that night. I was at least thirty miles away. We did not see her.

"Officers on the Titanic stated there were no ships in sight when she hit the iceberg. But they claim they saw one at about 1 a.m., steaming towards them and then turn away.

"The inquiry decided it was mine.

"It could not possibly have been. We were stopped by ice at 10.30 p.m. and did not move until six in the morning."

What was Captain Lord's impression of the inquiry – led by the first Lord Mersey?

"Hostile at once. They wanted a scapegoat..."

Mr. Leslie Harrison, general secretary of the Mercantile Marine Service Association, has spent four years collating Captain Lord's evidence.

Attempts to make the Ministry of Transport reopen the inquiry have so far failed.

And the world may never really know all that happened on that dreadful night…

6 March 1968

PLEA FOR TITANIC PROBE – TO CLEAR A FATHER'S NAME

A bid for a new probe into the Titanic disaster was made yesterday almost fifty-six years after the liner sank in the Atlantic with the loss of 1,500 lives.

Heading the campaign is a man who wants to clear his dead father's name.

He is retired bank official Stanley Lord, 59, of Kirkway, Wallasey, Cheshire. His father, Captain Stanley Lord, who died six years ago, was accused of ignoring distress rockets from the sinking ship.

At the inquiry soon after the disaster in 1912, it was said that Captain Lord could have saved many lives if he had taken his own ship, the Californian, to the Titanic's aid.

Yesterday, his Son and the Mercantile Marine Service Association asked the President of the Board of Trade, Mr. Anthony Crosland, to reopen the part of the inquiry which dealt with Captain Lord.

SURVIVOR

The petition is based on an affadavit from a survivor of the Titanic, Mr. Lawrence Beesley of Carew-road, Northwood, Middlesex, who died in 1967.

He gave the time of the last rocket the ship fired.

And if he is correct, the rocket could not have been seen from the Californian.

LETTERS

MUMMY WAS A MYTH!

James B. Archer, Norton Conyers, Ripon, N. Yorks, writes:

Recently you told a reader that he was right in thinking that the liner Titanic was carrying an Egyptian mummy on its ill-fated maiden voyage, I'm afraid this is an old myth. The object in question was a mummy-case of a priestess of Amen presented to the British Museum about 1889.

This case has become the centre of many weird stories – including responsibility for the sinking of the Titanic!

However, in 1934 Sir Wallace Budge, Keeper of Egyptian Antiquities at the Museum, published a detailed refutation of all these tales. He ascribed their origin to the late Mr. Douglas Murray and the late Mr. W. T. Stead, who had said, in print, that the expression on the face of the coffin lid was that of "a living soul in torment" and wished to hold a seance with the purpose of removing the anguish from the face.

The story snowballed and it was rumoured that, because of the "curse" associated with it, Sir Wallace sold the mummy-case to a wealthy American who shipped it on the Titanic

Somehow the American was supposed to have rescued the case but its curse continued so he sold it to a Canadian. The latest owner, experiencing similar evil happenings, decided to send it back to England but it was lost when the Empress of Ireland went down in the St. Lawrence River.

That, roughly, is the legend. The fact is that the mummy-case never left the British Museum. It is still there. But the myth persists, for it is said to give people an odd feeling if they examine it too closely.

In case you wish to experiment, it is exhibit number 22542 in the Second Egyptian Room.

Thanks, James, but we'll take your word for it!

Another point which no doubt contributed to the myth was that W. T. Stead, a prominent journalist and Spiritualist, was himself drowned on the Titanic.

THE TITANIC TO SAIL AGAIN!

An international shipping company is planning to build a new Titanic.

The 75,000-ton luxury liner, Titanic II, will be designed along old-fashioned lines like the original, which was sunk by an iceberg in 1912 with the loss of more than 1,500 lives.

But it will have the latest safety aids, high-speed engines and super-high prices.

Terry Marler, president of the American parent firm behind the project, said yesterday that fares are expected to start at £500 a day. The new ship's maiden voyage, planned for April, 1985, will be between Southampton and New York – like the fateful first trip of her predecessor.

THE WORLD'S COSTLIEST TREASURE HUNT

The race is on for one of the world's great treasure hordes – worth at least £230 million.

The treasure, gold, diamonds, jewellery and one of the world's most precious books, is aboard the wreck of the Titanic.

And yesterday one of the competitors in the race, Jack Grimm from New York, believed his underwater camera teams had located the wreck off the coast of Newfoundland.

The underwater pictures showed a mass of metal in the deep trench where the 46,000-ton liner sank 69 years ago, taking with it 1,513 passengers and crew.

Among those passengers were 57 millionaires all of whom had jewellery and money with them.

In the purser's safe alone, according to the stories, were diamonds worth £125 million and gold bullion worth £80 million.

The book is a jewel-encrusted edition of the Rubaiyat of Omar Khayam.

Items like the ship's bell would fetch a high price as a curio and there would be cinema and television income from the film of the salvage exercise.

Grimm, known as Cadillac Jack, is a 56-year-old former U.S. marine whose larger than life exploits include winning the World Poker Championship in Las Vegas last year.

He spent his honeymoon prospecting for gold in California and now owns 28 oil wells in Texas.

He has spent £1,694,739 of his own money on the treasure hunt so far.

He hopes to use the world's largest submersible, the Aluminaut, to tear into the Titanic's hull and recover the treasure.

His principal rival is brilliant electronics expert Fred Koehler who sold up a thriving electronics business and built his own mini-

➤ Look-out Reginald Robinson Lee (centre wearing flat cap) leaving the Celtic at Liverpool. He was in the Titanic's crow's nest with Frederick Fleet when the iceberg was sighted.

submarine for the treasure hunt.

But there are serious doubts about the chances of either team plundering the wreckage 12,000 feet down.

An expert said: "It is easier to get men on to the moon."

13 December **1982**

MYSTERY

Did this man cause the Titanic disaster?

One man with poor eyesight could have been responsible for the Titanic disaster, in which 1,514 people drowned.

According to a top medical research team there was a deficiency of Vitamin A in the diet of the ill-fated luxury liner's crew which would have caused night-blindness.

The team, sponsored by the Smith Kline Foundation in America, has spent almost ten years examining the theory of a German doctor, Helnrich Wietfield, of Bremen, before he died in 1969.

According to the doctor, who talked to survivors of the disaster and was an expert in night-blindness, the collision of the Titanic with an iceberg on April 14, 1912, took place because the look-out was suffering from a disease known as emphthalmia.

This affects the eyes, especially the retina, and diminishes the ability to see in the dark.

It is caused by a vitamin deficiency in the diet – and the crew of the Titanic is said to have spent the winter of 1911 without work. They had difficulty finding fresh fruit and vegetables rich in Vitamin A.

When the iceberg was spotted it was too late for the liner to turn and avoid the fatal crash.

The German doctor spent part of his career in the German Navy during World War One and found that night-blindness was common when crews had a lack of Vitamin A.

Ironically the look-out on the Titanic – a man called Lee – survived the disaster and went on to give evidence at the subsequent inquiry.

6 September 1985

EXPOSED THE EERIE GRAVE OF A DOOMED LINER
RAISE THE TITANIC! OR SHOULD SHE BE LEFT TO REST IN PEACE

And at last we see her, after all these years. Huge. Ghostly. Still.

Lying where she came to rest after slowly tumbling down through 13,000 feet of freezing water.

All 46,000 tons of her.

Even in the thick night of the Atlantic bottom, eerily slit open by the spotlight, there is no mistaking the massive presence of the Titanic's hull.

There are sights down there that are even more arresting, say the survey team who have located the wreck of the luxury liner 400 miles off Newfoundland.

When she hit her iceberg and sank on April 14, 1912, she was a floating palace of luxury, bedecked with millionaires and lovely ladies, fine crystal and rare wines, delicate china and elegant furniture.

And you can see it, say the team who are probing the wreck with their robot sub. There in the black and the slime.

Unbroken dinner plates. Cases of claret. Bowls, basins and chamber pots.

No doubt, if the little robot submarine probes long and indiscreetly enough, the very instruments of the band who carried on playing while the ship went down.

But one of the few remaining survivors of the sinking says the wreck should be left in peace.

Miss Eva Hart, aged 80, from Chadwell Heath, looked at the picture and for the first time saw her father's grave.

She recalled the agony of watching him prepare to die when she was a seven-year-old being put in a lifeboat with her mother.

Benjamin Hart told his daughter: "Be good. Be nice to Mummy." Then he went down with the "unsinkable" Titanic, he and 1,500 others.

Miss Hart said: "Nobody should ever attempt to raise that ship. It's like robbing a grave.

"We watched that magnificent ship going down. I didn't sleep all night. To hear people drowning is a dreadful sound.

"I think the people died unnecessarily. They wouldn't have if there had been enough lifeboats.

"It was a tragedy of tragedies."

She added: "I have great admiration for the scientists who have found her – but everyone should leave her where she is."

The U.S.-French team who found the ship have no plans to attempt to raise her but other groups have said the operation could be attempted.

It is a measure of just what a hold the Titanic still has on our imaginations.

To the people of 1912, the sinking was more than just a major civil disaster.

They were an optimistic generation and it shook their world rigid. It was like something out of the Bible.

Even seventy-three years later, in our Godless age, we are haunted by the image of the great ship, and the greater-yet floating mountain of ice that sealed its doom.

The wreck is an "incredible sight" says Dr. Robert Ballard, the American marine scientist who helped make the discovery. "It's standing upright on the ocean bed and appears to be in superb condition.

"But one would expect that, given the fact that we are working in extremely deep water that's ice cold and in total darkness.

"Such conditions," he said, "would have preserved the liner."

The Titanic was discovered by a joint U.S.-French expedition, using a robot submarine.

The 12,000 colour pictures of the wreck show eerie relics of the ill-fated cruise.

They include wine bottles, undamaged plates and a small flagpole on the bow.

The water pressure on that part of the ocean floor is 5,800 pounds per square inch.

"The upper part of the bow is in remarkably good condition considering it's the part that struck the iceberg", says Dr. Ballard.

"The under part of the bow is badly damaged but the very small flagpole right on the very tip of the Titanic's bow, is still standing there."

Any attempts to raise the Titanic would be wrong felt Dr. Ballard.

"There are 1,500 souls down there. Attempts to salvage the ship would desecrate their grave."

21 August **1987**
GEMS FIND ON TITANIC

A small leather satchel stuffed with a fortune in jewels and banknotes has been lifted from the wrecked Titanic by salvage operations.

No value could be put on the find which was recovered along with a small safe-box.

There was no identification on the valise so it cannot go to relatives. It will form part of a collection to go on a world tour.

7 April **1992**
TITANIC TUCK-IN

A 95-year-old survivor of the Titanic will sit down next week to finish the meal ruined when disaster struck 80 years ago.

Mrs. Edith Haisman will be at a rerun of the dinner during Titanic Week in Weymouth, Dorset.

She will get the same menu as the night the liner hit an iceberg and sank on April 14,1912.

15 April **1992**
AHOY... TITANIC SALES

A collection of radio signals to and from the doomed liner Titanic fetched a world record £95,700 at a London auction yesterday – the 80th anniversary of the disaster. The previous record for a piece of Titanic memorabilia was £8,250 for a painting sold in 1988. The ship sank with the loss of 1,500 lives after hitting an Atlantic iceberg.

22 January **1997**
TITANIC EDITH DIES AT 100

The oldest British survivor of the Titanic disaster has died.

Last year Edith Haisman, 100, laid a wreath at the spot in the Atlantic where her father went down with the luxury liner in 1912. She was 16 at the time.

Mrs. Haisman, who celebrated her 100th birthday in October, died at a nursing home in Southampton – the port where the Titanic began her fateful voyage.

10 January **1998**

Leviathan: The Titanic, at the Harland & Wolff yard in Belfast, was launched before a crowd of 100,000, sliding down the slipway with the help of 22 tons of soap and tallow spread an inch thick along it.

27 March **1998**
TRAGIC LIFE OF TITANIC LOOK-OUT WHO SHOUTED "ICEBERG AHEAD".

EXCLUSIVE By IAN MILLER

Titanic look-out Frederick Fleet lived a life of torment after blaming himself for failing to avert the disaster.

He believed he was responsible for the deaths of the 1,523 passengers and crew even though he was helpless to prevent the liner smashing into an iceberg on her maiden voyage.

After years weighed down by guilt, the death of his wife pushed him over the edge. Penniless and friendless, he committed suicide and was laid to rest in an unmarked pauper's grave.

But now, more than 30 years after his death, Frederick has been given a fitting memorial.

The British Titanic Society and U.S.-based Titanic Historical Society have paid for a headstone in his native Southampton where he is buried.

Frederick, 25, was in the crow's nest on that fateful night of April 14, 1912.

He was 50ft. above deck when he spotted the chilling outline of an iceberg in the darkness.

He rang a warning bell and lifted a telephone to the bridge, yelling: "Iceberg right ahead!"

"But by then, it was far too late," said Titanic expert Peter Boyd-Smith.

"All he would have seen was this huge black shape. The Titanic was on top of it before anything could be done. There was nothing Fred could have done.

"But he complained bitterly that if he had been

Tragic life of Titanic look-out who shouted 'Iceberg Ahead'

EXCLUSIVE

By IAN MILLER

TITANIC look-out Frederick Fleet lived a life of torment after blaming himself for failing to avert the disaster.

He believed he was responsible for the deaths of the 1,523 passengers and crew even though he was helpless to prevent the liner smashing into an iceberg on her maiden voyage.

After years weighed down by guilt, the death of his wife pushed him over the edge. Penniless and friendless, he committed suicide and was laid to rest in an unmarked pauper's grave.

But now, more than 30 years after his death, Frederick has been given a fitting memorial.

The British Titanic Society and US-based Titanic Historical Society have paid for a headstone in his native Southampton where he is buried.

Frederick, 25, was in the crow's nest on that fateful night of April 14, 1912.

He was 50ft above deck when he spotted the chilling outline of an iceberg in the darkness.

He rang a warning bell and lifted a telephone to the bridge, yelling: "Iceberg right ahead!"

"But by then, it was far too late," said Titanic expert Peter Boyd-Smith.

"All he would have seen was this huge black shape. The Titanic was on top of it before anything could be done. There was nothing Fred could have done.

"But he complained bitterly that if he had been issued with a pair of binoculars he would have

FREDERICK FLEET

1887 - 1965

LOOKOUT

R.M.S. TITANIC

Erected To His Memory

By The

TITANIC HISTORICAL SOCIETY, INC.

Indian Orchard, Mass. U.S.A

AT REST: The tombstone put up 33 years after Frederick's suicide

TORMENT: Frederick was haunted by the disaster

DOOMED: The majestic liner leaves on her fateful maiden voyage

❝ He did no wrong but carried guilt ❞

seen the iceberg sooner." Four years ago divers discovered a pair of binoculars just yards from the bridge of the wrecked Titanic.

Mr Boyd-Smith added: "He carried on blaming himself for what happened for the rest of his life. It must have played on his mind terribly up until his suicide."

The Barnardo's boy, who trained to be a seaman at the age of 12, was rescued in lifeboat number 6 with 40 other survivors.

He was taken aboard the liner Carpathia and spent months in New York giving evidence at the inquiry into the sinking.

He returned to Southampton and to sea, working as a look-out. During the First World War he was a merchant seaman and was later a boilermaker at shipbuilders Thorneycroft and Harland & Wolff, but still went to sea until 1936 to earn extra money.

He married Eva in 1919. They had no children and there are no records of Frederick having any brothers or sisters.

Later he worked on building sites and in the 1960s sold newspapers on the streets of Southampton.

Brian Ticehurst, of the British Titanic Society, said: "Fred was one of life's unlucky people.

"The inquiry never laid any blame on Fred for what happened, but he lived with a burden of guilt for his whole life.

"He tried to live with it, but eventually he felt he had nothing left to live for. It was terribly sad. He would say to people that if he had seen the iceberg earlier all those people wouldn't have died."

During his time as a newspaper seller he would drop into the Southampton Echo social club.

Mr Ticehurst added: "He would choose a table on his own and sit there alone. He was a quiet, lonely man."

Frederick remained convinced that the disaster could have been prevented if he had been issued with binoculars.

National Maritime Museum curator Dr Eric Kentley supports his view: "There's no doubt in my mind that if these glasses had been used, then the tragedy may

❝ Fred was a very unlucky person ❞

have been averted. At the time the Titanic collided with the iceberg the night was clear and bright.

"The crow's nest not having binoculars on any other day would not have made a difference. But on that particular night hundreds of lives could have been saved."

Frederick's despair was obvious in letters to his friend Edward Kamuda shortly before his death.

He and Eva were staying with her brother Philip Legros. He wrote: "I don't know who my parents were. I have been an orphan all my life. My mother left me when I was a baby."

He added that he was "always without money, always in debt".

His final letter read: "My dear friend. Just a few lines to let you know I am in deep trouble. I have lost my wife, also I am leaving my house, the place where I have been living."

Two days later, on January 10, 1965, he killed himself aged 78.

Mr Ticehurst said: "Fred and Mr Legros did not get on and when Eva died it was the last straw for Fred. He felt isolated and was told to get out of the house.

"He packed his suitcases to go but he just went out into the garden and hanged himself from a clothes-line post.

"That was the sight that greeted Mr Legros when he drew the curtains in the morning."

The final insult to his memory is in the multi-Oscar winning film of the disaster starring Leonardo DiCaprio and Kate Winslet where he is shown being distracted by the two lovers.

But Mr Boyd-Smith said: "This is absolute garbage. There's nothing to suggest Fred did not do everything he could have. He was a conscientious look-out."

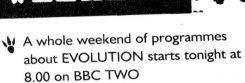

issued with a pair of binoculars he would have seen the iceberg sooner." Four years ago divers discovered a pair of binoculars just yards from the bridge of the wrecked Titanic.

Mr. Boyd-Smith added: "He carried on blaming himself for what happened for the rest of his life. It must have played on his mind terribly up until his suicide."

The Barnardo's boy, who trained to be a seaman at the age of 12, was rescued in lifeboat No. 6 with 40 other survivors.

He was taken aboard the liner Carpathia and spent months in New York giving evidence at the inquiry into the sinking.

He returned to Southampton and to sea, working as a look-out. During the First World War he was a merchant seaman and was later a boilermaker at shipbuilders Thorneycroft and Harland & Wolff, but still went to sea until 1936 to earn extra money.

He married Eva in 1919. They had no children and there are no records of Frederick having any brothers or sisters.

Later he worked on building sites and in the 1960s sold newspapers on the streets of Southampton. Brian Ticehurst, of the British Titanic Society, said: "Fred was one of life's unlucky people.

"The inquiry never laid any blame on Fred for what happened, but he lived with a burden of guilt for his whole life.

"He tried to live with it, but eventually he felt he had nothing left to live for. It was terribly sad. He would say to people that if he had seen the iceberg earlier all those people wouldn't have died."

During his time as a newspaper seller he would drop into the *Southampton Echo* social club. Mr. Ticehurst added: "He would choose a table on his own and sit there alone. He was a quiet, lonely man."

Frederick remained convinced that the disaster could have been prevented if he had been issued with binoculars.

National Maritime Museum curator Dr. Eric Kentley supports his view: "There's no doubt in my mind that if these glasses had been used, then the tragedy may have been averted. At the time the Titanic collided with the iceberg the night was clear and bright.

"The crow's nest not having binoculars on any other day would not have made a difference. But on that particular night hundreds of lives could have been saved."

Frederick's despair was obvious in letters to his friend Edward Kamuda shortly before his death.

He and Eva were staying with her brother Philip Legros. He wrote: "I don't know who my parents were. I have been an orphan all my life. My mother left me when I was a baby."

He added that he was "always without money, always in debt".

His final letter read: "My dear friend. Just a few lines to let you know I am in deep trouble. I have lost my wife, also I am leaving my house, the place where I have been living."

Two days later, on January 10, 1965, he killed himself aged 78.

Mr. Ticehurst said: "Fred and Mr. Legros did not get on and when Eva died it was the last straw for Fred. He felt isolated and was told to get out of the house.

"He packed his suitcases to go but he just went out into the garden and hanged himself from a clothes-line post.

"That was the sight that greeted Mr. Legros when he drew the curtains in the morning."

The final insult to his memory is in the multi-Oscar winning film of the disaster starring Leonardo DiCaprio and Kate Winslet where he is shown being distracted by the two lovers.

But Mr. Boyd-Smith said: "This is absolute garbage. There's nothing to suggest Fred did not do everything he could have. He was a conscientious look-out." Fred was a very unlucky person.

24 June 1999

TYCOON IN TITANIC ROW

A tycoon's plan for a Titanic lookalike casino hotel looks like being sunk.

Bob Stupak's £600million, 280ft. tall creation in Las Vegas would be three times the size of the liner. But city planners blocked it after a storm of protest.

Stupak, who built the 1,149ft. Stratosphere hotel, the city's tallest building, is appealing against the ruling.

He vowed: "It's full steam ahead. Nothing is going to stop me."

2 February 2001

TITANIC MAN DIES

The last male survivor of the Titanic disaster died yesterday in France aged 92.

Prof. Michel Navratil was just three when the liner struck an iceberg near Newfoundland on April 15, 1912.

Prof. Navratil, from Nice, once said: "My father handed me to a woman in the lifeboat. I never saw him again."

Only 706 people survived the tragedy and 1,513 died.

13 June 2001

TITANIC BOY DIES

The last survivor of the Titanic has died. Italian Antonio Martinelli, 89, was just a few months old when the liner sank in 1912.

31 July **2001**

TITANIC WEDDING

A couple who married on the deck of the Titanic were branded "utterly sick" yesterday.

David Leibowitz, 28 and Kimberley Miller, 27, angered the British Titanic Society after they exchanged vows in a tiny submarine resting on the liner, which sank in the Atlantic 89 years ago. But New Yorkers David and Kimberley said the ceremony was "just magical".

29 August **2007**

IS THIS THE KEY THAT SANK THE TITANIC?

MISSING BINOCULARS RIDDLE SOLVED

This ordinary-looking key could have saved the Titanic from disaster.

It unlocks a cabinet holding the ship's crow's nest binoculars and belonged to an officer who was not on board when it left port.

Second officer David Blair was taken off at the last moment in a personnel shuffle and forgot to give the key to his replacement.

Look-out Fred Fleet, who survived the 1912 sinking in which 1,522 died, told an inquiry they would have seen the fatal iceberg sooner with binoculars. When asked how much sooner, he replied: "Enough to get out of the way."

The key explains at last why the look-out had no binoculars.

Mr. Blair, from Forfar, left the key to his daughter, who gave it to a seaman's charity in the 1980s. Next month it is among items expected to raise £70,000 at auction in Devizes, Wilts.

24 September **2007**

SOLD: KEY TO TITANIC

A key that could have saved the Titanic has been sold for £90,000 at auction.

It was for a locker containing the crow's nest binoculars – but an officer going off duty forgot to pass it on. It meant look-outs had to use the naked eye and the liner sank after hitting an iceberg on her maiden voyage in 1912 with the loss of 1,500 lives.

The key was bought at the auction in Devizes, Wilts., on behalf of Tesiro, a diamond house based in Antwerp, Belgium.

An auction spokesman said: "There was a real buzz as the price went up."

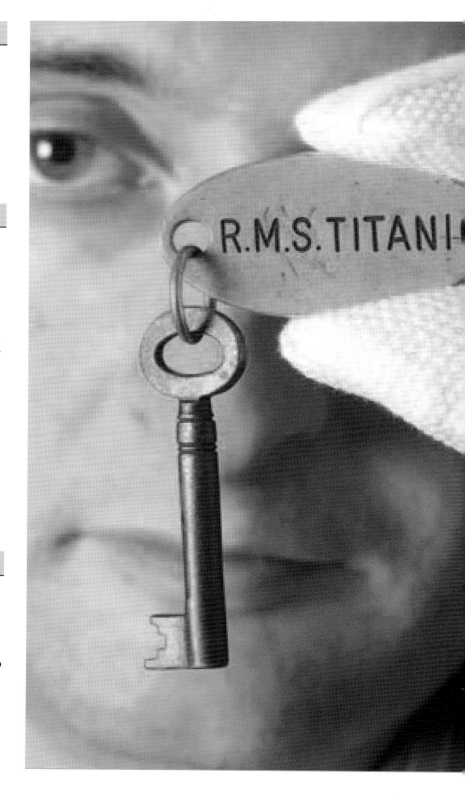

AT 1.45 A.M. ON APRIL 15, 1911 JOHN CHAPMAN'S WATCH STOPPED AS HE AND HIS WIFE WENT DOWN WITH THE TITANIC IT IS FOR EVER... FROZEN IN TIME

This is the pocket watch which shows the moment a couple of newlywed Titanic passengers fell into the sea and died together.

John Chapman, 37, was on honeymoon with new bride Lizzie, 29, when the liner struck an iceberg on April 15, 1912 and sank 35 minutes after they were pitched into the freezing Atlantic water.

Lizzie died after refusing a place on a lifeboat because her beloved husband was not allowed to go with her. She turned to her friend Emily Richards and said: "Goodbye Mrs. Richards, if John can't go, I won't go either."

The couple were travelling to Wisconsin to start a new life, when 1,517 people perished on the liner's maiden voyage.

John's traditional timepiece, now a treasured family heirloom, was recovered with his body and is being displayed for the first time at a Titanic exhibition at the National Maritime Museum in Falmouth, Cornwall. Lizzie's body was never found. Their story was later used as the inspiration for two newly-wed characters in the 1958 Titanic film *A Night To Remember*.

John's great nephew William Sargent said: "The watch was sent back with other personal effects once the body was found and has been passed down the family."

Museum director Jonathan Griffin said: "Titanic is a story with many different levels – perhaps the greatest maritime disaster but one with many touching personal tales."

The couple, who were from St. Neot in Cornwall, had embarked at Southampton with second-class tickets costing £26, purchased from White Star agent George & Co of Liskeard, Cornwall.

John had emigrated to Canada in 1906 before returning to marry sweetheart Sarah Elizabeth Lowry on Boxing Day 1911 at a chapel in the town.

They had been heading to America to be near Lizzie's brother and planned to run a farm and start a family.

Mr. Sargent added: "My father, John Chapman, was named after his uncle who died on the Titanic.

"My dad never liked the sea and always said it was hungry.

"I suppose if you knew your aunt and uncle had perished so famously you would think like that."